———

COUNSELING AND THERAPY
FOR COUPLES

COUNSELING AND THERAPY
FOR COUPLES

MARK E. YOUNG
LYNN L. LONG

Stetson University

Brooks/Cole Publishing Company

I(T)P® *An International Thomson Publishing Company*

Pacific Grove • Albany • Belmont • Bonn • Boston • Cincinnati • Detroit • Johannesburg • London
Madrid • Melbourne • Mexico City • New York • Paris • Singapore • Tokyo • Toronto • Washington

Sponsoring Editor *Eileen Murphy*
Marketing Representative: *Alston Mabry*
Marketing Team: *Christine Davis, Jean Vevers Thompson, and Deanne Brown*
Editorial Assistant: *Susan Carlson*
Production Editor: *Laurel Jackson*
Manuscript Editor: *Barbara Kimmel*
Permissions Editor: *Fiorella Ljunggren*

Indexer: *James Minkin*
Interior and Cover Design: *Katherine Minerva*
Art Editor: *Jennifer Mackres*
Interior Illustration: *Lori Heckelman*
Typesetting: *Joan Mueller Cochrane*
Printing and Binding: *The Courier Co., Inc./ Westford*

For more information, contact:

BROOKS/COLE PUBLISHING COMPANY
511 Forest Lodge Road
Pacific Grove, CA 93950
USA

International Thomson Publishing Europe
Berkshire House 168-173
High Holborn
London WC1V 7AA
England

Thomas Nelson Australia
102 Dodds Street
South Melbourne, 3205
Victoria, Australia

Nelson Canada
1120 Birchmount Road
Scarborough, Ontario
Canada M1K 5G4

International Thomson Editores
Seneca 53
Col. Polanco
11560 México, D. F., México

International Thomson Publishing GmbH
Königswinterer Strasse 418
53227 Bonn
Germany

International Thomson Publishing Asia
221 Henderson Road
#05-10 Henderson Building
Singapore 0315

International Thomson Publishing Japan
Hirakawacho Kyowa Building, 3F
2-2-1 Hirakawacho
Chiyoda-ku, Tokyo 102
Japan

Printed in the United States of America

10   9   8   7   6   5   4   3   2   1

Library of Congress Cataloging-in-Publication Data

Young, Mark E.
    Counseling and therapy for couples / Mark E. Young, Lynn L. Long.
       p.   cm.
    Includes bibliographical references and index.
    ISBN 0-534-34952-8 (alk. paper)
    1. Marital psychotherapy.   2. Marriage counseling.   I. Long, Lynn
L., [date]– . II. Title.
RC488.5.Y56 1997
616.89'156—dc21
                                    97-15913
                                    CIP

To Jora Defalco Young,
earthly companion, friend, co-parent,
and comrade on the spiritual path:
wherever you are is home.
—M. YOUNG

To Stan,
my husband and my heart's inspiration:
whatever path I take leads back to you.
—L. LONG

CONTENTS

PREFACE

Most of us are married. The 1990 Census showed that about 56% of Americans *over age 15* were married and were living with their spouse; another 18% were separated, widowed, or divorced; and only about 24% had never been married (U.S. Bureau of the Census, 1990). These figures do not even take into account the many unmarried couples who live together. Together, the data show tremendous cultural endorsement for the committed relationship (Bubenzer & West, 1993).

Despite the popularity of marriage, however, the divorce rate is high. There are about half as many divorces each year as there are marriages, and odds are only about 50/50 that a marriage will stay intact. As many as 1 in 7 marriages are considered "unhappy," and marital troubles are the precipitating factor in nearly 50% of admissions to mental hospitals. A troubled marriage is a significant factor in many murders and can trigger or exacerbate severe emotional and behavioral problems of children. In fact, marital difficulties may be the most common problem that clients present when they seek any kind of therapy (Bubenzer & West, 1993).

Despite the awareness of the prevalence of marital difficulties and the financial and emotional hardships that divorce causes, the mental health community has not focused strongly on the couple relationship. Until recently, professionals have been affected by our culture's preoccupation with the individual, and training has focused almost entirely on working with a single client. Insurance companies often collude by failing to reimburse clinicians when the diagnosis is a pathological relationship (Kaslow, 1996). And even when finances are not a factor, it has traditionally been much harder to bring both members of a couple to the therapy session. Usually, the wife called with a concern, and the husband, if he attended, participated with reluctance. Thus, a "gender barrier" has existed in couples therapy.

Another set of hurdles is cultural. Therapy of any kind carries a stigma—an implicit admission that you cannot handle your own problems. The intimacies of a couple relationship are some of the last things people want to discuss, and these issues are magnified when it comes to couples from minority cultures. Therapists have not yet found an effective way to get minority couples to consider therapy when they experience problems. Part of the difficulty, of course, comes from language barriers, religious differences, and lack of faith in agencies and institutions. But there is also something else: The way therapy is delivered, and therapists themselves, are geared to the majority culture. As more minority therapists are trained and the American population becomes more diverse, couples therapy must change to become more accessible to those who have traditionally been outside the mainstream.

As we look around, though, we see reason to hope: values are shifting; professionals are flocking to receive training in couples and family therapy, and recent professional literature is focusing on couples therapy as a separate specialty. More programs include multicultural training as part of the curriculum, and more undergraduate and graduate courses address couples issues.

In the community at large, marriage and the couple relationship are still valued institutions—after divorce, more than 80% remarry. The men's movement and other forces seem to be catalyzing a new commitment by men to be good husbands and fathers. More people are attending marriage encounter weekends, and more communication training programs are being offered. The next decade will surely be one of burgeoning growth for this therapy specialty.

An Integrative Model

Research suggests that all mental health professionals are moving toward a more eclectic or integrative view of practice, with less adherence to particular schools (Young, 1992). *Counseling and Therapy for Couples* is one of the first textbooks that proposes a single structure to bring together the major theoretical viewpoints for couples therapy. Because it is a synthesis, the integrative model of couples therapy is nothing new, nor is it intended to be followed slavishly. Rather, it is a structured way of learning couples therapy that will be especially helpful to those who are new to this work, whether they are just beginning as therapists or have been practicing for many years. The model has been extensively tested with graduate students in marriage and family therapy and with practicing clinicians. They tell us that it is easy to apply in actual therapy sessions and gives them a reference point so they can develop plans for the next step. It encourages the therapist to identify workable goals and lead couples to agreement, rather than spending time analyzing the personality of each individual in the couple. The model is a useful starting point or framework for anyone who is struggling or needs direction.

So that the reader will not think this integrative approach is too extreme, let us take a look at the training of group therapists as an example. Although there are still group therapists who call themselves RET or psychodynamic therapists, group work, for the most part, is currently practiced in an integrative, eclectic way, bringing in skills and knowledge from many realms. The theoretical base for group work includes the findings of small-group dynamics and group development. It also involves a recognition of common curative factors (Yalom, 1995). In practice, nearly all group therapists use Rogerian listening skills, help groups break through developmental impasses, and encourage cohesion (a curative factor). These are important foundations regardless of the practitioner's theoretical learnings.

In the same way, this integrative approach recognizes that couples therapy as a therapeutic modality has many different roots. For example, couples therapists who are interested in the specific critical incidents across the life span turn to theory and research from developmental psychology. Couples therapists also deal with crises caused by such stressors as infidelity, chemical dependency, sexual incompatibility, and domestic violence. Research and theory in these areas come from medicine, sociology, linguistics, and even religion. Our viewpoint is that, in the absence of a universally agreed-on paradigm, the integrative position gives therapists the best opportunity to recognize and use contributions from many fields and techniques from various theoretical positions.

Some Notes on Terminology

Use of the terms *counseling* and *therapy* have often been divisive issues in the mental health community. *Counseling* is often perceived as focusing on a relatively "normal" population; therapy, as focusing on more disturbed people. In reality, all counselors and therapists see both people with serious problems and people who are doing well but want to grow.

Therapists and counselors are not very different from each other. Until a few years ago, the American Association for Marriage and Family Therapy (AAMFT) was known as the American Association for Marriage and Family Counseling. Many members of the International Association of Marriage and Family Counselors (IAMFC) are also clinical members of AAMFT. We do not wish to enter into a political debate over these terms or endorse one organization over another. Therefore, we use the term *therapy* throughout this text.

The old standby term, *marriage counseling*, is fast fading from the therapist's lexicon because today, many people who are in couples are not legally married. Commitment and marriage are no longer synonymous; many couples stay together for years and have long, intimate relationships without marriage. And many seek therapy to improve their relationship, even though neither may be contemplating a ceremony. For same-sex couples, marriage is not yet a legal alternative, but these couples can also benefit from therapy. For these reasons, we generally use the term *couple* instead of *marital* or *marriage*.

Goals and Organization of the Book

When we began this book, we had the following goals in mind:

1. To help readers recognize that the couple is a unique and distinct system different from the family, the individual, or the group and requires specific methods of assessment and treatment.
2. To offer readers a simple, practical way of working with couples that does not force them to accept any single theoretical orientation but allows them to choose strategies based on a simple, understandable model.
3. To include wide coverage of topics in couples therapy so that readers are exposed to the key issues and the varieties of couples with which they will be working.
4. To provide active learning opportunities in the text through case examples and role-play scenarios for either reflection or classroom work.
5. To examine the theoretical basis behind various therapy strategies and to make readers aware of the sociological forces affecting couples today.

With these goals, we decided to write a book that would consist of three parts. Part One deals with the knotty problem of how to draw from theoretical bases of practice and develop a treatment plan using our integrative model of couples therapy. Chapter 1 looks at the couple as a unique focus in therapy and the developmental processes that must be considered. Chapters 2 and 3 provide an overview of the foundational schools of thought in marriage and family therapy and illustrate the key systems concepts.

We explain the integrative model in Chapter 4 as one alternative for solving the dilemma of overemphasizing technique versus becoming locked into a single theory's viewpoint. Although the integrative model allows for the use of a range of therapeutic techniques drawn from the various schools of family therapy, we help readers select the methods and techniques that they will find the most effective for working with specific clients. For pedagogical reasons, the model identifies five stages in the therapy process with couples. Although the model is more circular than steplike, students and therapists can use the model to determine where they are in the process with a particular couple and what needs to be done next.

Chapters 5, 6, and 7 are linked. Chapter 5 examines various assessment methods, including paper-and-pencil tests. Chapter 6 shows how the first interview can be conducted and the practical matters associated with helping couples enter the therapy process. Based on the assessment stage, Chapter 7 takes aim at the difficult issue of identifying key goals and planning treatment for couples using the integrative model.

Part Two, "Common Issues in the Life of the Couple," takes a close-up look at the major issues that couples face. In Chapter 8, we address the important issue of couples communication—why it becomes so confused and how it can be fixed. Next, problems in sexuality and intimacy are covered in Chapter 9. In Chapter 10, we examine identifying and healing conflict within the relationship, from arguments to domestic violence. Chapter 11 focuses on the issues associated with divorcing and how couples can learn to navigate this passage. In Chapter 12, "Infidelity in Relationships," we describe various types of affairs and the means for treating them.

Part Three of the book is called "Special Challenges." These four chapters examine particular types of couples who are facing long-term strains and living alternative lifestyles. These include couples with alcohol problems (Chapter 13), couples in blending or stepfamilies (Chapter 14), dual-career couples (Chapter 15), and same-sex couples (Chapter 16).

Acknowledgments

We would like to extend our thanks to our clients, who have been our greatest teachers. Our students in the Marriage and Family Therapy Program at Stetson University provided critical feedback on the model, especially Kim Schoening, Todd Schoening, Jackie Najafian, Jane Updike, Jo Ann Rosenbaum, Joanne Paleolog, Bruce Snipes, and Patricia Collins. Special thanks go to Ximena Mejia for helping to prepare the manuscript. Other students in Marriage and Family Practicum and the Relationship Counseling classes helped us refine our thinking and tested the model with real clients. We also want to thank our colleagues, Candace Crownover and Regina Proskine at the House Next Door, and our consultants, Dr. Judie Wright, Dr. James Framo, Kristi Myers Sutter, J. Melvin Witmer, and Rajinder Singh, for their input. Many experts reviewed this manuscript, including Susan S. Hendrick, Texas Tech University; David M. Kleist, Idaho State University; Daniel Lee, Loyola University; Sarah Moskovitz, California State University–Northridge; and Carol Werlinich, University of Maryland. Their hard work is much appreciated.

Finally, we want to mention our spouses, Jora DeFalco Young and Stan Long, who loved us and supported us through this process.

Mark E. Young
Lynn L. Long

ONE

PRINCIPLES, EVALUATION, AND PLANNING

1

The Couple as a Unique System

KEY CONCEPTS

- The couple is a unique dyad, separate from the individual and family, but the couple influences and is influenced by each.
- Couples must establish boundaries to ensure the integrity of the relationship.
- Couples must address the challenges of individual versus couple needs, family of origin influences, and prevalent myths about marriage throughout their relationship.
- Couples must be able to change, especially when the addition of children alter the family structure.
- Couples need time for intimacy and must deal with issues of competition and power, which can weaken the couple bond.
- Healthy couples are able to see the other person's reality, have a positive philosophy about the relationship, and engage in relationship-promoting activities.
- Healthy couple behaviors include the abilities to communicate, solve problems, avoid blaming, and share tasks equally.
- Societal changes have affected the couple relationship. Among these are increased life span, altered status of women, changes in pregnancy control, and economic changes.
- Couples are also influenced by the partners' similar or different cultural backgrounds and each individual's personality.
- Couples must also adapt to the changes caused by predictable and unpredictable life events, such as the birth of a child, the parenting of adolescents, and the death of family members.
- At the larger systems level, couples are affected by legal and political systems, economic conditions, and so on.
- One element of a couple's development is its ability to confront and master developmental tasks; this chapter presents Wallerstein's seven tasks of marriage.

3

This chapter is designed to orient you to a new world—the world of the couple. It is a world defined by the two people involved, and it is in many ways mysterious to those on the outside looking in. It has its own rules, language, and customs. Therapists who enter this world realize that changing a couple system is one of the most challenging tasks ever contemplated.

For the therapist practiced in individual therapy, the couple presents a tremendous shift in thinking. Many therapists are used to thinking about the therapeutic relationship as a one-to-one relationship; in fact, in individual counseling, the relationship between the client and the therapist is consistently identified as the key to achieving successful outcomes. Certainly, the couple's relationship with the therapist is important in couples therapy as well, but it is definitely less important than is an improved couple relationship. The couples therapist is much more a facilitator than a participant. When couples therapy is successful, the partners often look at each other with gratitude, only nodding to the therapist as an afterthought. In our minds, though, there are very few experiences as exhilarating as watching a deeply troubled couple learn to resolve their conflicts and create a happier home for themselves and their children.

THE CHALLENGES OF BECOMING A COUPLE

The couple is a unique relationship. In a couple, one can find the deepest experience of intimacy in life—of friendship and comfort as well as betrayal and the greatest possible hurt. Being a member of a couple can lead to astounding personal growth and self-awareness, and the failure of such a relationship can cause wounds that take years to heal. Few other relationships have as much power to challenge us and cause such anguish.

What makes the couple relationship different from a friendship or family bond? Bubenzer and West (1992) identified the following six characteristics that set the couple apart. We like to think of these characteristics as "challenges" because each can either support or weaken the relationship.

1. The couple relationship is voluntary, and both parties realize that they do not have to be married. The fact that marriage is a choice can make couples work hard to keep it going. At the same time, the voluntary nature of marriage makes it easy to exit.
2. The couple relationship contains a balance of stability and growth. For the relationship to stay healthy, there must be a sense of predictability and stability but also novelty and flexibility.
3. The couple relationship has a past, a present, and a future. Couples are connected through their past histories and their future plans. Couples cannot rely on their memories alone; they must keep the relationship fresh in the present and develop future goals.
4. Becoming a couple means merging two perspectives and histories, including different values and worldviews. The couple relationship is one in which everything has to be negotiated.

5. Being part of a couple means giving and receiving support. It means thinking of the other person's needs as just as important and valuable as one's own. It also requires that one receive support at times. The relationship must be reciprocal, with both partners giving and both receiving.
6. The couple relationship requires that each person maintain a separate identity and individuality but also have the ability to put that identity aside, at times, for the good of the couple. Conversely, one of the things that binds a couple together is the respect each has for the other's separate identity.

Given these six challenges and the many practical issues involved in being roommates for life, becoming a couple is one of the most difficult and complex tasks of adulthood. Surprisingly, this milestone is frequently portrayed as the easiest and most romantic stage in the life cycle. Rather than viewing marriage or joining as a couple as the solution to one's loneliness and one's personal and family problems, we should acknowledge it as a time of transition to a new life stage, requiring the formation of goals, rules, and a different family structure (Carter & McGoldrick, 1980).

DYNAMICS OF THE COUPLE SYSTEM

A Couple System Has Its Own Boundaries

Minuchin (1974) describes the couple hierarchically as a separate system that must be maintained as such in order to remain healthy. This means that couples must form a boundary or a sort of invisible protective shield around their relationship to ensure protection, privacy, and intimacy in the relationship. If the relationship is to have integrity, then family, children, work, and friends cannot be allowed to interfere with its functioning, no matter how stressful or complicated life becomes. In old wedding vows, the rather severe phrase "forsaking all others" was used to remind couples of the need for such boundaries.

To maintain their distinctiveness as a couple, the partners must create a boundary by letting others know the limits. Couples who do not create a boundary around their relationship are drawn into their families of origin or into previous friendships and then remain part of those systems, sometimes to the detriment of their relationships with their partners. This boundary drawing is particularly hard when there is unfinished business from childhood or when other family members live with the couple. Families normally recognize when an adolescent needs some space to become his or her own person. But they sometimes forget that a couple needs to carve out its own identity too, and they frequently violate the boundaries by trying to influence their offspring to act in the family's interests rather than in the couple's interests.

Boundary Violations Will Occur

A boundary violation can occur when a third party interferes with the couple's functioning, creating the so-called eternal triangle. For a newly married couple, a typical boundary violation might resemble the following scenario: Selena and Marco have been living together for four months, and they are planning a big wedding in the near future. During the weeks leading up to the wedding, Selena spends every Saturday night with her mother, shopping, running errands, and preparing for the big event. The relationship between mother and daughter has always been close, but it appears to have intensified, based on the time they spend together on this important event. Selena now sees her mother every weekend and talks to her on the phone for about an hour every night. Marco is a little annoyed but tells himself that it will all change after the wedding. Marco, on the other hand, spends quite a bit of time deep-sea fishing with his buddies because, according to Marco, Selena is not available. Both express disappointment in the other for not spending enough time together as a couple. Although they have been cohabiting for only a short time, both are worried about the future of the relationship if their allegiances to other relationships are stronger than the couple bond.

The appearance of this kind of pattern does not mean that Selena and Marco will have serious problems. This sort of challenge is a normal part of the couple's development as they begin to decide how their need to relate to others fits with their commitment to each other.

The Couple Relationship Conflicts with Individual Needs

Some people choose marital partners to make up for some flaw they see in themselves. For them, at least initially, the couple relationship provides an avenue to wholeness and security. For others who have been fiercely independent or self-centered, thinking of someone else's needs and negotiating all phases of life is like being imprisoned. Whether or not one is at either of these two extremes, the couple relationship can become a challenge to almost everyone's sense of self. Even the smallest daily activities affect the other person enormously. It is difficult to adjust to having to consider the needs or wishes of another person in every facet of life.

One way that people define themselves is through their friends. When two people become a couple, other relationships normally take second place. When this does not happen, someone is likely to be unhappy. For example, we saw a couple who had been married for 18 months and were expecting their first child. The major problem for the 21-year-old father-to-be was the fact that he had no personal life, since his wife was not interested in continuing their "party" lifestyle. He was on the brink of leaving the marriage when his wife asked him to choose between her and his friends. It is easy to write off this example as one based on simple immaturity. But the tension between one's individuality and being immersed in the couple relationship must be dealt with throughout life.

Consider the following questions:

When it comes to spending free time, how much should be devoted to the couple and how much should each individual be allowed to spend as he or she wishes?

If both members of the couple have job offers in two different cities, whose career takes precedence?

If one person likes action videos and the other likes foreign films, what movie are they going to rent?

At least some of the issues that confront couples have to do with how much of themselves they have to relinquish to become part of the couple. Successful couples do this by making sure that individual time does not interfere with the couple's contract and that time is allotted for the couple as well.

Families of Origin Shape Expectations and Influence the Couple System

Families may attempt to shape the way the newly formed couple thinks and behaves. Other families expect that the couple will set up a household the same way that the parents did. As the couple joins together, both partners also influence their families of origin. Their union can introduce new traditions and new ideas and will definitely bring new people into the mix. It is a transition both for couples and for the families of origin.

It is sometimes difficult for families to adjust to relating to the new couple as a separate unit, rather than to the individual to whom they are tied by genetics or choice. The new couple also faces change because each partner must now relate to his or her parents from the standpoint of being part of a couple, as well as relating as individual adult children. Parents may feel jealous toward the interloper who has more influence than they do; spouses may feel that parents are interfering.

To become a couple, two individuals who have been accustomed to one set of expectations and values in their own families of origin must renegotiate with their partners to accommodate each other and define a new set of expectations. The new expectations provide a blueprint for their lifestyle as a couple.

Let us take a somewhat typical example of a newly married couple, Craig and Stacy, deciding how to celebrate a special occasion. As Craig grew up, he spent most of his birthdays fishing with his friends. It was more or less a family tradition to let the "birthday person" have the day to do with as he or she wished. In Stacy's family, however, birthdays were times for the family to get together—perhaps going out to dinner or having a family party.

During the first year of marriage, the couple had difficulty comprehending these conflicting traditions when each person's birthday arrived. Stacy was hurt that Craig did not plan a party; Craig felt criticized as being selfish when he went golfing with some friends and came home too late for a celebration.

Stacy and Craig's problem may appear to be a minor one, but it illustrates the unanticipated ways in which family backgrounds, traditions, and expectations collide when two people join their lives. Other issues to be defined as two people become a couple include everyday decisions about eating, sleeping, working, and playing, as well as more complex issues such as money management, influences of extended family, gender roles, career choice, conflict resolution, and expressions of love and intimacy.

Myths Challenge the Couple Relationship

Sometimes, couples have unrealistic expectations of themselves, their partners, and the relationship. These myths or unrealistic expectations need to be confronted. Couples begin their relationship with individual sets of expectations they have learned from their own families of origin, from society, and from the media. Often these expectations are unrealistic or are not appropriate for the couple. Once confronted, many such myths are either dispelled or discarded, or else they are adapted to the couple's unique situation.

Many myths are remnants of messages from the family of origin, and sometimes they are replicated by partners without their explicit knowledge of the message. Thus, one partner might ask the other, "Why do we need to spend our vacation this way?" and might receive the reply, "We just do. That's the way we have always done it in my family."

Couples who confront the myths early in their relationship have a better chance of renegotiating the ingrained influences of family and society. As couples explore the unrealistic messages, they are able to create new shared beliefs and traditions for the relationship.

Myths of Couple Relationships

Here are some common myths about couple relationships.

1. If we love each other, we should be happy at all times.
2. We should always be completely honest with each other, regardless of the impact on our partners.
3. We should want to be together all the time and be unselfish with our time.
4. We should agree on every issue in order to support each other.
5. If we have a problem, we must decide who is to blame.
6. We know what the other is thinking, so we do not need to communicate.
7. Good relationships just happen and do not need to be worked on or reevaluated.
8. If we create joint activities, we will be close forever.
9. We do not need friends or family as long as we have each other.

The Couple Must Change and Incorporate Their Children

Another common boundary issue involves the complex shift that couples must negotiate when they become parents. Consider the situation of Jim and Valerie who are in conflict over their needs as a couple and messages from their family of origin.

Jim and Valerie have been married for five years. Their daughter, Emily, is just 2 years old. The spouses have frequent disagreements about how they should spend their time with Emily and about how much time is appropriate. Valerie was raised in a family in which parents did not go out much on their own. Jim grew up in a family of five children, and his parents often went out together to movies, to dinner, and to visit friends. The children made popcorn with their babysitter and had a party of their own on these occasions. Jim is angry with Valerie because she refuses to get a babysitter for Emily; Valerie believes that Jim is not involved enough as a parent and is trying to get her to neglect their daughter as well.

This distinction between roles as spouse and parent may seem simple, but it is very difficult for many couples to achieve. Roles can easily become blurred. Sometimes even therapists confuse the two roles and will talk about the roles of mom/dad and husband/wife as if they are interchangeable. Spouses may even refer to each other as "Mom" and "Dad." The challenge is to keep these two functions separate so that the couple relationship is not erased in the development of a new family. Couples who relate to each other only in their roles as parents (a role filled with anxiety and responsibility) will find that their ability to become intimate is diminished as their role as a separate couple is neglected. Since parenting requires less time as children grow older, couples who relate only as parents may eventually find themselves staring across the breakfast table at someone with whom they have little in common.

The Couple Needs Intimacy

Intimacy is thought to be a hallmark of a couple relationship—a relationship defined by mutual self-disclosure and an understanding of the other person in a partnership of equals. All of these things take time. It is true that the role as part of an extended family requires less of a couple today due to increasing geographical distance between family members. On the other hand, the pressures of work and children now assail both members of the couple much more than when only one partner worked and the other tended the home. Time for each other is now at a premium, and so is intimacy.

Intimacy involves the degree of closeness and caring that each partner feels and expresses. The way the couple expresses closeness is strongly influenced by the needs and expectations that both partners have developed in their respective families of origin. Other factors affecting their expression of intimacy include their individual personality styles, the relationship style they have developed together, and the developmental stage of the relationship (Sperry & Carlson, 1991). In many cases, one partner has grown up in a family with minimal physical contact and little overt communication of love and affection, between parents or toward the children. Expressions of affection may have been in the form of food, money, or other tangible items. Conversely, the other partner may have been raised by parents who spent a significant amount of time communicating with each other and with the children, as well as demonstrating physical affection for family members. Such differences set the stage for varying expectations about intimacy.

The lack of communication about intimacy can lead to relationship stress and can contribute to the termination of the relationship if the partners do not address the issue together and create a positive resolution on which they both agree. Even if they reach an agreement, going against one's training can be uncomfortable at first.

The Couple Must Deal with Competition and Power

Competition and power are key concepts for understanding the couple as a unique entity. Power differentials are determined by identifying whether one partner has the most influence in making decisions or whether the couple shares power in the decision-making process. The degree of competitiveness between the two people determines whether or not solutions that the couple generate are mutual and cooperative or are made by solely one partner (Sperry & Carlson, 1991). Typical issues of competition and power surface when decisions are made about who will primarily handle the money, whose career will take precedence, how the duties at home will be divided, and who will be in charge of planning social activities with family and friends.

Consider the situation of Marti and Eugene, who have been married for five years. They have two children, ages 2 and 4. Marti has given up her career as a social worker to take a part-time position in a day care center so she can spend more time with the children. Eugene has been offered a promotion and a significant raise in salary in his career as a systems analyst. The change will necessitate moving several states away. Marti is unhappy and believes that Eugene should turn down the promotion to stay in their current community. Marti asserts that she has given up her career to assume more child care responsibility and has developed a strong support system of family and friends. She is happy with her work in the day care center and believes Eugene should consider the sacrifices she made early in their relationship. Eugene is angry and claims that he is the primary breadwinner and that the family should go where he has the greatest opportunity to advance his career. In this case, both are competing for their "rights" to either stay in the same location or move to advance Eugene's career. Marti believes she has made changes whereas her husband has not. She wants Eugene to place her desires first. Eugene sees the situation differently. He views increased income potential as a sufficient reason to move. Once again, the issue is not "who is right and who is wrong" but how these two people negotiate the issue in the relationship.

CHARACTERISTICS OF HEALTHY COUPLES

Much has been written about unhealthy and dysfunctional relationships. It is not uncommon to hear people discuss their relationships or families as "dysfunctional"; even therapists are guilty of this. They may speak of the relationship as unhealthy or use the term *interlocking pathologies* to refer to a "sick" couple. We believe it is important that therapists keep the focus on healthy behaviors and strengths in the relationship to facilitate positive change, rather than focus solely on weaknesses and limitations. Following are some of the healthy patterns that Beavers (1985) and Sperry and Carlson (1991) have identified and that we have added to and adapted.

1. *A belief in relative rather than absolute truth.* In any relationship, one's version of the truth must make room for another person's perspective. In a couple relationship, "my taste in furniture is good, yours is bad" is an example of believing

in absolute truth. Healthy couples allow for differences in taste and accept different points of view.

A corollary of this statement is that healthy couples understand that two people can have a different view of the same situation. When couples have this perspective, partners are not always trying to change the other person to take their viewpoint but instead are attempting to listen and understand.

2. *An assumption that the partner has good motives.* Healthy couples respect their partners. They do not assume that the other person is the enemy nor that the other person's annoying habits are directed at them.

3. *A belief that differences will be resolved.* Committed couples understand that a relationship is like a roller coaster. They do not panic when there are moments of anger, disagreement, and estrangement and do not look to third parties to settle minor differences or let off steam. They have faith that the process of their relationship can repair the problems.

4. *A belief in something larger.* Writer Antoine de Saint-Exupéry said that love is not looking into each other's eyes, it is looking in the same direction. Healthy couples often share a belief or mission that is larger than themselves. It may be religious, political, or a family orientation.

5. *The practice of healthy behaviors.* Besides looking at problems and conflicts, the couples therapist should be able to recognize healthy couple behaviors. Such behaviors can be learned, and if they are already established they can be used to support the changes couples wish to make. When these healthy patterns exist, relationship satisfaction is high. Some of these healthy patterns are as follows.

> *Responsibility.* Each partner must acknowledge his or her role in the relationship and refrain from blaming the other for shortcomings. This role includes the maintenance of love and respect and the willingness to choose new behaviors when the old ones no longer work.
>
> *Alignment of Goals.* Each partner must identify personal goals and collaborate on mutual goals for relationship satisfaction.
>
> *Encouragement.* Focusing on positive strengths, support, recognition, acceptance, and confidence are all components of encouragement. These characteristics are essential to creating a healthy relationship (Sperry & Carlson, 1991).
>
> *Open Communication.* Each partner must express feelings openly and honestly. This expression facilitates the development of problem-solving skills, sharing, intimacy, and understanding.
>
> *Empathic Listening.* With this skill, each partner portrays to the other respect and caring as well as acceptance of each other's feelings and beliefs.
>
> *Willingness to Analyze and Discuss the Relationship.* To understand each other, there must be continual communication between both partners to identify strengths and areas of concern in the relationship.
>
> *Demonstration of Acceptance.* Each partner must express verbally and nonverbally his or her belief in the value of the other, particularly when differing opinions are expressed.
>
> *Support of Positive Goals of the Marriage.* Both partners behave in support of the collaborative goals they have set for the relationship. They create

appropriate boundaries for their relationship so that external events do not interfere or deter progress toward their mutual goals.

Joint Conflict Solution. Couples focus on the expression of differences and accommodate each other to find solutions rather than blame and repress feelings.

Commitment to the Equality of the Relationship. Both partners behave in ways to enhance mutual sharing of the workload and continue to pursue new goals and interests.

PSYCHOSOCIAL FACTORS IN COUPLE RELATIONSHIPS

Although couples are likely to follow predictable life stages as they create their own unique relationship, they will also be influenced by societal events and pressures. To understand these stressors, we can examine some different models of marital relationships and the social influences and stressors that affect them.

Models of Marriage

The institution of marriage has changed considerably over the past few generations. The traditional marriage contained culturally defined and prescribed roles and duties to be performed by each partner. Marital rules were once closely associated with sex roles. In the 20th century, men's traditional roles included husband, father, breadwinner, sexual aggressor, financial planner, and household mechanic. Traditional female roles were wife, mother, homemaker, sexual recipient, child care provider, and housemaid (Sperry & Carlson, 1991, p. 2). The agenda for these marriages usually centered on the development of a family and the acquisition of property. Role definition was clear and was based on gender; each partner's contribution to the family goals was based on the traditional male and female role models.

Although divorce was unusual in the United States in past generations, life expectancy for both sexes was shorter than it is today. "'Til death do us part" was not as big a commitment in the early 1900s as it is today. As life expectancy increased and societal expectations shifted, a new model of marriage emerged based on intimacy, companionship, and cooperation, rather than solely on duty and responsibility (Sperry & Carlson, 1991). Equality and choice are central tenets of modern marriage; with the freedom of choice in mate selection, friendship, love, and passion emerged as powerful ingredients in couple formation. This change reflects a basic change in societal values over the century.

Social Influences on Marriage

The women's movement, economic stress, childbearing at a later age, and increased career opportunities have influenced people's choices about when and how to become a couple (Laminna & Riedmann, 1991). These social factors and others have greatly affected the couple. Carter and McGoldrick (1980) describe these influences as potential stressors on the couple (see Figure 1.1) and categorize them as vertical, horizontal, or system level stressors.

Vertical Stressors

Vertical stressors include the internal perceptions that each individual brings to the relationship from the family of origin. *Vertical* refers to the fact that these influences come down to us from the higher branches or earlier generations of our family trees. Memories, behavioral patterns, myths about becoming a couple, family secrets, and legacies from these past generations all shape the new couples, whether or not they are overtly aware of these influences.

Horizontal Stressors

Horizontal stressors are the predictable life cycle transitions, such as the birth of a child, the parenting of adolescent children, and syndromes like "the empty nest" that occur in the normal course of couple development. Horizontal stressors also include unpredictable life events, such as an unexpected death, accident, or chronic illness. These stressors are identified as horizontal, as if a couple's relationship were a time line running left to right on the page. They can be conceived of as marks on a continuum, starting with the couple's first meeting and proceeding until the end

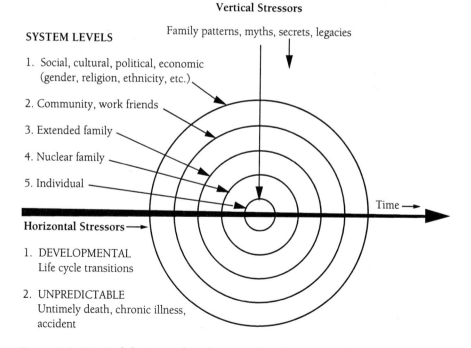

Figure 1.1 Vertical, horizontal, and systems-level stressors

Source: From *The Family Life Cycle: A Framework for Family Therapy,* by E. Carter and M. McGoldrick. Copyright 1980 by Allyn & Bacon. Reprinted by permission.

of the relationship through death or divorce. Predictable and unpredictable events are high and low points on the couple's life line.

Systems-Level Stressors

Systems-level stressors include social, cultural, political, religious, and economic influences. In addition to the impact of extended family members, this group of stressors includes pressures from obligations to the nuclear family, work groups, organizations, and friends with whom the couple interacts during their life together. Some of the more common social stressors for couples include:

- in-laws and extended family members
- religion
- economics
- career
- leisure-time opportunities
- friends
- higher education
- political beliefs
- financial opportunities
- pressure to have children

Let us take a moment to focus on the issue of culture as an influence on the couple. Culture includes family traditions, religion, and ethnicity. Every culture recognizes life cycle transitions based on age, gender, societal role expectations, and traditions (Falicov & Karrer, 1980). For example, reaching age 13 for an American Jewish male provides a benchmark for his entrance into manhood, while the notion of caretaking for older adults in Mexican American extended families is considered typical.

Rituals learned through the acculturation process become a way of life. Dating, courtship, marriage, childrearing, and retirement may be strongly influenced by the early cultural messages each partner received from his or her family of origin. Families can have very strong ideas about retaining old family traditions and cultural practices in the newly formed relationship. The way that a couple celebrates Christmas, Hannukah, or Kwanzaa rituals comes from their individual or combined cultures. It is necessary for couples to be explicit early in their relationship about some of the important beliefs they hold relevant to ethnicity and determine together how they want to incorporate these into their relationship. Sometimes this process requires accommodation and acceptance of each person's differences.

Once the two partners have defined the differences and decided how they want to express cultural values and rites of passage, they must present a united image to both of their families about how they want to celebrate the traditions as a couple. Families may not understand the mutual decision however, and they may try to pressure the couple to reconsider or undermine each other in an effort to carry on the family heritage.

WHAT A COUPLE GOES THROUGH:
TASKS AND DEVELOPMENTAL STAGES

Psychological Tasks of Couples

Wallerstein (1993) extends the concept of "the psychological task" developed by Erikson (1950) as a useful way of describing the life cycle of healthy couples. The model may be more useful today since previous conceptualizations about couple development have been based on the premise that couples marry between the ages of 18 and 22 and remain together forever. Today, divorce and remarriage are as common as the intact marriage. People are marrying later, having children later, or choosing not to have children at all.

Another way of looking at couple development is to examine how couples handle psychological tasks, rather than by observing them from a typical life cycle perspective. These psychological tasks are not bound by time limitations or by traditional notions of the intact couple over the life span. Rather, the tasks Wallerstein (1993) has outlined represent the early and enduring stages of marriage and are applicable regardless of the partners' ages or either one's history of prior relationships. These tasks are as follows.

Task 1: Consolidating psychological separation and establishing new connections with the family of origin. This task is the passport required to travel through life together, separate from one's original family and yet able to maintain healthy contact. For young couples in their twenties, this task is to learn to listen to their parents' advice without rebelliousness and to discover their own solutions without harming the relationship with the older generation. They must learn to spend time with their families of origin but not neglect their own relationship. Although this task is particularly important for young adults, older adults who have been divorced or widowed for a period of time face the same challenges. They must negotiate a new role as part of a couple after being single, and they must maintain contact with adult children. Role confusion is characteristic in this stage, as there are competing loyalties and expectations.

Sometimes these new roles create a change in identity even if the couple has lived together prior to marriage or if either partner has been married before. Expectations may change when the relationship is formalized by a legal commitment. Often, at this stage, the couple matures and yet feels overwhelmed by the dramatic changes. There may have been a sense of fun and freedom living as two separate adults orbiting each other's lives, and the sense of responsibility to each other and competing loyalties after becoming a couple may cast a sobering shadow.

Task 2: Building the marital identity for the couple and for the individuals—togetherness versus autonomy This multifaceted task involves creating a "we-ness." This means a shift from the "I" of self-centeredness to thinking of "I" as a part of "we." When a person in a couple even temporarily abandons self-interest and addresses the concepts of good and fair in the relationship, the capacity for intimacy and friendship blossoms. Closeness requires that each has access to the other and that each confronts and sets aside the narcissistic element to develop the "we" identity. Throughout the cycle of a relationship, there is a push-pull between these two poles of protecting one's individuality and setting it aside for the good of the couple.

Task 3: Establishing the couple's sexual identity Sexual identity refers to the frequency, intensity, and accessibility for the sexual expression of affection between partners. This task promotes a basic connectedness and openness to the "we" part of the relationship, and it means arranging a safe haven (time and place) from the stressors of life. The sexual relationship still requires negotiation after marriage or commitment, even if the couple has engaged in a prior sexual relationship. Partners must find a balance between their differing needs for sex and intimacy.

Task 4: Establishing the marriage as a zone of safety and nurturance The relationship provides a place to address individual and couple failures, struggles, successes, and fears in a supportive, caring atmosphere Each partner should be comfortable enough to turn to the other in times of stress. This task is particularly important because individuals who do not meet their needs for safety and nurturance may be prone to go outside the relationship by engaging in extramarital affairs or by devoting a large amount of time to work, friendships, extended family, or leisure activities that do not include the spouse.

Task 5: Parenthood For couples who choose to have children, the marital relationship must be expanded to include psychological room for a child while safeguarding the relationship of the spouses. There is also a need to examine the flexibility of roles in the relationship, because they will require modification with the addition of children. What expectations about child care and parenting does each partner bring to the relationship? To what extent will children be allowed to subsume time spent as a couple?

For remarrying couples, children may already be a part of the package, which requires immediate negotiation of roles as stepparent, parent, and spouse. This can get complicated when there have been multiple marriages with stepchildren and biological children from prior relationships. The couple's task is to preserve its ability to function and not be compromised and divided by other loyalties.

Task 6: Building a relationship that is fun and interesting A priority of marriage is to keep it alive with new and interesting experiences and with a balance of spontaneity and tradition. A "good marriage" is not a constant but requires continual work to infuse it with excitement and passion. These experiences become part of the couple's shared memories and are part of the maintenance of the relationship in times of acute stress or illness because the couple can reminisce about the "fun" times.

Task 7: Maintaining a dual vision of one's partner that combines early idealization with reality perception Keeping love alive means that each partner stays in touch with the passion initially felt for the other and yet is aware of how that passion has grown into a more realistic friendship over the years. It is also important for both partners to remember the characteristics that drew them to each other and to continue to view them as special and unique qualities. These characteristics should be considered as strengths of the individual and part of the gift that each provides for the long-term maintenance and enhancement of the relationship.

CONCLUSION

The couple is a unique entity in a separate world. It is a world that is affected by the history of the two individuals who comprise it, and it is influenced by present family members, friends, societal influences, and the needs of the two people. Therapists who wish to enter the couple's world need to understand those influences that support healthy functioning and those that create division.

This chapter was designed to help you appreciate the complexities and pressures that affect the couple. In the next two chapters, we take a different perspective, based on the major theoretical positions in counseling and psychotherapy that have contributed to an understanding of couples. These theories are presented to give you historical background, language, and definitions that will be important later on. With couple dynamics and theory under your belt, you will be ready to address the more practical issues of helping the couple deal with its problems and appreciate its strengths.

2

Theories of
Couples Therapy: Part One

KEY CONCEPTS

- Theories of couples therapy have been developed from theories of individual and family therapy.
- Previously, behavior therapy with couples focused mainly on changing reinforcement and improving communication.
- Modern behavior theory applied to couples includes increasing positive reinforcement; learning new skills, including negotiation, communication, and assertiveness; and identifying and modifying cognitive errors.
- Psychodynamic therapy previously treated individuals in the couple separately. The most popular form of psychodynamic work with couples is now object relations therapy, in which the couple is usually seen together.
- Object relations proposes that individuals carry mental images of parents and significant others that affect their relationships with their partners.
- Many psychodynamic theories focus on the "unfinished business" couples bring to their relationship from their families of origin.
- The Bowen theory shares many concepts with psychodynamic theories. Bowen highlighted the importance of *differentiation*, or emotional autonomy, as a goal for each person. People who are more differentiated have better relationships.

Theories are like different human languages. Although most . . . do an equally good job as representational systems, some languages are better than others for solving a specific problem. Street language may be better in a hostage negotiation situation, while proper English would be more useful for a scientific presentation. However, it makes no sense to say one language is closer to the truth or reality than another.
Segal, 1991, p. 184

In the next two chapters we look at five theoretical orientations in couples therapy and their offshoots. Such an overview is helpful for historical purposes but, more important, it helps us identify the common curative factors that theorists have independently identified. For example, in this chapter, you will see that most of the schools of therapy indicate that couples tend to engage in repetitive patterns of unproductive behavior. Nearly all would agree that a primary task of any therapist is to identify these patterns and disrupt them. After looking at theories, we present our integrative model, which draws many of its premises from the five perspectives presented in these chapters.

Although we call Chapters 2 and 3 "Theories of Couples Therapy," it would be more accurate to say that we look at theories of therapy that have been *applied* to couples, because all the theoretical groups we describe originated mainly as individual or family approaches. Couples therapy has been "a technique in search of a theory" because its practice preceded theory development. The need for therapy with couples appeared before it was investigated as an entity separate from individual therapy, and the family therapy "boom" of the 1980s left couples therapy behind. Most of the emphasis has been on working with whole families, including children and other extended family members. Like group therapy, couples therapy has been integrative from its outset, borrowing from the systemic theories of family therapy, psychodynamic therapy, behaviorism, and the study of communication. But perhaps couples therapy is no different than individual therapy at this point in history. This is a time of integration and technique, rather than theory and thought. It is a practical time, and eclecticism and integration hold center stage (Young, 1992; Norcross & Newman, 1992).

In the past, discussions like this tended to compare and contrast different points of view with dimensions on which each theory might be evaluated. But is that really fair to each theory? As the quote at the beginning of this chapter indicates, theories are like different languages, and they lose something in the translation. Although each viewpoint is separate, therapists from different persuasions view many things the same way. Most would agree that thorough assessment is important, as is developing a good working relationship with the couple. Most agree that couples need to work together rather than separately and must find ways to change together. Later, we try to pull together some of these threads that form the basis for our integrative approach.

In keeping with the integrative spirit of the book, we will not be discussing the merits of each therapy as it is presented. We will also not be presenting a lengthy history, detailing the lives of major contributors, nor will we spend much time on minor points of theory. Also, we will not say much about differing ideas about etiology (the causes of problems) unless they relate directly to treatment. You can find this kind of discussion in an introductory family therapy text, such as Horne and Passmore's (1991) *Family Counseling and Therapy*, or in general orientations to counseling theory, such as Gerald Corey's *Theory and Practice of Counseling and Psychotherapy* (1994). What we will do in this chapter is identify key terms, recognize specific couple problem areas described by each theory, and indicate some key therapeutic techniques.

We have selected the theories that are most used by couples therapists today, and we have tried to identify the important techniques. We will not be discussing several influential family therapy methodologies, such as the Milan school, because they have focused very little on couples and have centered their efforts on families with children. Instead, we have included five theories that we believe are contributing most to the understanding and treatment of couples. Specifically, we will study the behavioral, psychodynamic/object relations, and Bowenian schools in Chapter 2, and the structural/strategic and brief therapy approaches in Chapter 3.

The techniques from each approach are merely outlined in these chapters just to give you a feel for the therapies that the theories have spawned. Elsewhere in the text, you will find many methods explained in a way that you can put them directly into practice.

As you read, you may find yourself more attracted to one theory or another, so we have included key references for further reading. Some educators believe that it is important for a counselor or therapist to be trained in a single school of thought so that the student develops a coherent framework in the beginning. This approach has merit because you feel more confident working within one school of thought.

During your study or review of the theories, you might see truth in many or all of them. Integrative theorists try to help students develop a coherent and systematic approach that combines findings from a number of theories. We believe that this is a difficult and arduous task because it requires that you have a great deal of understanding about the full range of theoretical perspectives. It also means you must become proficient with a wider range of techniques. In Chapter 4, "An Integrative Model," we try to combine what is best from a number of theories. Our aim is to help develop a "reflective practitioner" who can, in this information age, provide a systematic therapy while remaining open to new ideas from the ever-expanding field of couples therapy.

BEHAVIOR THERAPY APPLIED TO COUPLES

Behavior therapy is the application of learning principles to the task of changing human behavior. You may like to think that learning is solely an internal, mental process, but try to think of learning as a transaction with the environment—that we are changed by the experiences we have. Behavior therapy is concerned with how people learn and unlearn dysfunctional behavior and how human behavior is maintained by rewards and punishments from the external world and from other people.

Behavior therapy applied to couples has focused mainly on how couples can learn new ways to reward each other more and punish each other less. Behavior therapy is also interested in how couples collaborate in maintaining a problem and how people reward and punish their partners, often unknowingly. Many therapists think that behavior therapy is very mechanical and looks at people as machines. Some of us have a negative attitude about behavior therapy because of its history in the 1960s, when it was associated with delivering electric shock to modify behavior. But modern behavior therapy is not electric shocks or rats in boxes. Modern behaviorists recognize the complexities of human behavior, the cognitive or thinking component, the necessity for a therapeutic relationship, and the need to avoid blame when identifying the causes of couple problems (Bornstein & Bornstein, 1986; Spiegler & Guevremont, 1993).

Modern behavior therapy dealing with couples has three major thrusts: (1) helping couples increase positive reinforcement; (2) teaching new skills, such as communication training or assertiveness; and (3) utilizing cognitive therapy to alter destructive individual thinking patterns. For this reason, some writers have suggested that modern behavior therapy should be renamed social learning family therapy (Horne, 1991) or social learning cognitive therapy (SLC) (Jacobson & Holtzworth-Munroe, 1986). Counselors who reject behavioral methods entirely will be "throwing the baby out with the bath water." Behaviorally oriented therapists are developing many creative formats for working with couples and are reinforcing their findings with good research.

Definitions of Key Terms

Following are some of the important terms used in behavior therapy.

Reinforcer or reinforcement: anything that increases the likelihood that a behavior will be exhibited in the future. Reinforcement is a reward.

Positive reinforcement: presenting something rewarding to a person as a way of strengthening a certain behavior. For example, if one member of the couple has agreed to keep dirty laundry off the bedroom floor, such behavior is positively reinforced when the other member notices when things are cleaned and delivers a compliment or other sign of appreciation.

Negative reinforcement (often confused with *punishment*): anything that, when removed, acts as a reinforcer. For example, if one member of a couple agrees not to play country music when the other is home, the absence of country music operates as a reward (removing a negative).

Punishment: an aversive stimulus; anything that decreases the likelihood that a behavior will be exhibited in the future. For example, if one member of a couple is criticized by the other when he or she expresses an opinion, the criticism (for most people, a moderately strong punishment) decreases the likelihood that the person criticized will express opinions in the future.

Contingency: refers to the withholding of reinforcement until a behavior is exhibited. This makes the reward *contingent* on the behavior.

Contingency contracting: making an agreement regarding the circumstances in which one person will reinforce another's behavior. In couples therapy, contracts are used to increase the amount of positive reinforcers in a relationship. If you do X, then I will do Y is the algorithm of such a contract. In this case, X is something rewarding to one party, and Y is rewarding to the other.

Successive approximation: rewarding each successive step in a new behavior. When a behavior is complex or when it is first being learned, sometimes it is useful to break the behavior into smaller steps and reward each successive step, rather than wait for the full manifestation of the behavior. For example, if one partner is learning to cook for the household, it would be useful to notice the positives during each attempt rather than wait for the perfect meal. Cooking dinner is a complex behavior that takes practice in proper preparation and timing.

Modeling: a therapy procedure based on the discoveries of Bandura, who developed the social learning approach. Bandura, you may remember, found that children who observed violence were more likely to reproduce it in their own interactions. Similarly, positive models can teach positive or prosocial behaviors. In therapy, we try to expose clients to situations where they can observe someone else exhibiting a new behavior. Couples group therapy and relationship enhancement seminars can use this kind of learning because clients can observe other participants. Seeing modeling by a therapist or observing someone in a film can also prompt a new behavior, motivate clients, and reduce anxiety about the novel behavior.

Some Premises of the Theory

Some of the premises of the behaviorist approach that can be applied to couple counseling are as follows:

1. The principles of human learning discovered by Pavlov, Skinner, Thorndike, and Bandura explain how couples have developed maladaptive patterns of interaction. Human beings have histories of past reinforcement patterns, have conditioned reflexes, and can be shaped and changed through modeling and vicarious learning processes.
2. Relationship skills are learned, and treatment normally involves an educational or relearning process.
3. We should strive for precision in identifying a problem and use quantitative measures to validate change. Success should be objectively measurable.
4. The history of the relationship and of one's family is not usually relevant. Covert behavior (not observable), such as thinking about the past, might have an influence on the present, and it might be important to change one's thinking about one's family of origin.
5. When we change rewarding and punishing behaviors of couples, we change their relationship.
6. Modeling positive behaviors is an important way for couples to learn better interaction.
7. Reinforcement is generally a more effective tool in learning new behaviors than is punishment. Punishment tells us what not to do. Modeling and rewarding successful behaviors tell us what to do. Maladaptive behaviors tend to drop off when they are not rewarded.
8. Behavior therapy has contributed significantly to understanding and treating couples communication patterns and in dealing with sexual problems.

Problems That Couples Experience

Maladaptive Communication Patterns

Stuart (1969) was among the first to identify the ways that couples engage in specific types of ineffective and potentially damaging communication exchanges when they experience a conflict. The following are a number of specific patterns in which couples find themselves enmeshed.

Coercive exchanges   In coercive exchanges, one member employs negative reinforcement in return for a positive reinforcement from the other partner. For example, a husband criticizes and argues with his wife until she gives in and lets him win. He is rewarded by getting what he wants (positive reinforcement); she is reinforced by the fact that he stops criticizing and abusing (negative reinforcement). But remember, negative reinforcement increases the likelihood of the behavior's recurring in the future. Therefore, in this cycle the couple is rewarding the husband's abusing behavior (see Figure 2.1).

Withdrawal   This is a cycle of negative reinforcement where arguing over a conflict is so aversive that one or both members of the couple withdraw from the conflict because the negative reinforcement of removing the arguing is so powerful. This action may be a result of the individuals' reinforcement histories. If one grew up in a household where arguing was a constant and destructive pattern and withdrawal was the common coping mechanism, this previous learning may be brought forward into the couple's relationship. In addition, a withdrawing individual has no expectancy that arguing will be rewarded. Such a person needs encouragement because he or she may never have experienced the satisfaction of expressing feelings to another and coming to a joint solution of problems.

Retaliatory exchanges   Research shows that couples who are distressed engage in rapid retaliatory exchanges (Jacobson & Margolin, 1979). Each partner tends to give back negative responses to the other immediately after receiving a negative comment from the partner. Both become so conditioned to respond that often they perceive punishment from the partner when it is not intended. This is what is sometimes called "differential relational currencies" (Villard & Whipple, 1976). Edward Albee's play *Who's Afraid of Virginia Woolf?* demonstrates the retaliatory exchanges of the fictional couple George and Martha, who have spent the evening venomously humiliating each other in front of their cocktail party guests.

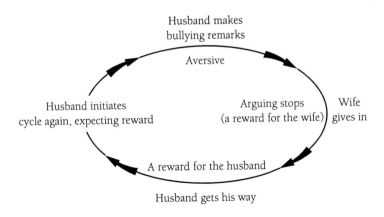

Figure 2.1   Example of a coercive exchange cycle in a married couple

Martha: . . . before I'm through with you you'll wish you'd died in that automobile, you bastard.

George: And you'll wish you'd never mentioned our son!

Martha: You . . .

George: Now, I said I warned you.

Martha: I'm impressed.

George: I warned you not to go too far.

Martha: I'm just beginning.[1]

George and Martha's interaction is sadly quite common. One hallmark of the pattern is the ongoing nature of the fight. It can be picked up just where it left off, seemingly without interruption; as Martha says, "I'm just beginning." This brief dialogue (and the entire play) shows how two intelligent people become engaged in a game of revenge which from which both emerge as losers.

How do people end up in such tragic situations? Punishing remarks to another person can be rewarding temporarily because they put one in a superior position, increasing feelings of self-esteem. Punishing provides a distance from which the initiator can escape from feelings of dependency. Such exchanges may be intellectually stimulating or may be maintained by the fun and sex of making up after the quarrel. All of these motives are at work in Albee's play.

Cross complaining In cross complaining, the partners take turns exchanging different complaints without ever validating the other's concerns. Each complaint is designed to cancel out the other's. The underlying process is one of blaming the partner, and this kind of interaction is typical in couples communication even when it is not severe, as in the following example.

He: Boy, what a day! I am exhausted.

She: Well so am I. I worked hard too.

He: Not like I did. You sit down all day.

She: But then I have to come home and work here all evening.

This kind of interaction does not lead to clear communication because her response to him is based on a hidden agenda. She may be feeling angry that he does not share in the household responsibilities, therefore she is afraid to validate his tiredness. Consider this alternative:

He: Boy, what a day! I am exhausted.

She: You sound tired.

He: I am. What's for dinner?

She: I haven't thought about it. Any ideas?

This interaction does not lead to discussing how they are going to deal with housework, which might be saved for a better time. On the other hand, her response "You sound tired" is a direct answer to his statement. When she acknowledges it, he can move on to the next topic. She then asks a question rather than cross complaining.

[1]Source: From *Who's Afraid of Virginia Woolf? A Play*, by E. Albee. Copyright 1962 by Atheneum.

Summarizing self syndrome (SSS) (Gottman, Notarius, Gonso, & Markman, 1976) Similar to cross complaining, the SSS exchange is something like this:

He: I feel good about this investment plan.

She: That agent has been unreliable in the past.

He: There are a number of good things about the plan that I really like.

She: Did you know that he did some work for Bonnie and she lost money?

He: The plan allows us to take money out of our savings when we need to without interest. Not like our present plan.

Like ships passing in the night, each person's message does not affect the other. He promotes the plan; she is uncertain about the agent's trustworthiness. Neither is hearing the important ideas or feelings the other has to offer. Such patterns lead to win-lose struggles where one person comes out on top—temporarily.

Low Rates of Positive Reinforcement or High Rates of Punishment

Research supports the fact that troubled couples are nicer to other people than to their spouses (Birchler, Weiss, & Vincent, 1975). It is not just that couples punish each other or get involved in communications loops; they also have very few positive exchanges (Wills, Weiss, & Patterson, 1974). Thibaut and Kelley (1959) indicate that people tend to stay in relationships as long as they are satisfying in terms of both rewards and costs. In other words, how much does it cost me to stay in this relationship compared to the rewards that I get out of it? Costs include the amount of time, energy, and money required to sustain the bond. People want highly rewarding relationships but at the lowest personal cost. It may sound cold-blooded, but the decision to remain in a relationship is very much like buying a car; we want the most for the least cost. Sometimes the relationship gives too few rewards, sometimes the cost is too great. Interestingly, it appears that people weigh the rewards and costs in a relationship and compare it with other relationships that they might have. That is how they make the decision to stay or leave a relationship.

It is also interesting to note that research indicates that positive and negative events are thought to be rather independent of each other (Gottman et al., 1976). Increasing the rewards in the relationship will have relatively little effect on the unpleasant aspects of the alliance. Reducing a negative like name-calling will not necessarily make the partner feel that the relationship is very positive.

Often couples come to therapy indicating that they have either too few positives or too many negatives: "We are stuck, in neutral. We don't fight but we don't have much fun together either." This statement exemplifies a couple with few negatives but not enough positives. Over time, many relationships undergo "reinforcement erosion," meaning that things that used to be satisfying in the relationship are not so exciting any more. In behavioral terms, we say we habituate to our partner. On the negative side, a therapist might hear this kind of statement: "We enjoy each other's company and we can really communicate most of the time, but when we get into a fight, we create a lot of damage for weeks to come." Some distressed couples have both low rates of positive reinforcement and high rates of negative or punishing interactions.

Distorted Thinking about the Partner and the Relationship

Cognitive therapy and cognitive behavioral therapy are two names for the branch of therapy that focuses on the role of faulty thinking as the cause of emotional and behavioral problems. Cognitive therapy also proposes that if one's negative or distorted thinking patterns can be corrected, then behavior will change. For example, many of us believe that we are not good at something because of a single attempt to perform the act. We illogically believe that because we once failed, we will always fail.

Cognitive therapy for couples is aimed at attacking distorted thinking about the other person and about the relationship (McKay, Fanning, & Paleg, 1994). Albert Ellis (1977) identified "self-talk," or the irrational sentences that people say to themselves. These thoughts, which can cause emotional disturbance in individuals, are often "nutty" ideas about relationships.

Ellis is known for his A-B-C theory of emotional disturbance. An event at "A" is perceived by the individual, and the individual's beliefs at "B" cause an emotional consequence, "C." If someone brought a black cat into the room (A) and we felt afraid (C), it would be because of the beliefs (B) we have about black cats causing bad luck. So it is not things that disturb us but what we make of these events. In looking at how illogical people are in relationships, Ellis (1985) identified a number of irrational beliefs.

1. I must have love or approval from everyone who is significant to me, especially the one I love.
2. I must be completely competent, adequate, and achieving, and the one I love must know this.
3. When people (including my partner) treat me unfairly or badly, they are to blame and I must see them as bad, wicked, or rotten.
4. When I am rejected or treated unfairly by the person I love, it is the end of the world, a catastrophe.
5. My unhappiness and emotional turmoil is the result of the way people and life treat me, and I have little control to change my feelings.
6. If something appears dangerous (such as the loss of my partner), I should worry about it and make myself anxious.
7. My history of bad relationships caused my present problems and my history cannot be escaped. This has crippled me, and I am unlovable and unable to have a good relationship.
8. Life should turn out better than it often does. People should be kinder and should treat me lovingly at all times. If the people I love treat me badly, it is awful and I will never be able to deal with life's grim realities.

Instead of addressing specific thoughts, several writers have examined general errors in thinking rather than the internal sentences Ellis describes. Aaron Beck (1988) distinguished several *categories* of distorted perceptions, which he identified as the source of depression. Beck found that depression consists of a negative view of the self, of others, and of the future (the cognitive triad). Unfortunately, negative and distorted thinking patterns are "automatic." One does not have to ruminate;

they are immediate reactions. For example, Epstein (1986) gives the example of a spouse who automatically thinks, "He always interrupts me." This automatic thought is not a description of fact, it carries the distortion "always." This is called *overgeneralization* in Beck's terminology of cognitive distortions. If the spouse then concludes "He thinks we have nothing of value to say to each other any more," a new distortion would be detected, *arbitrary inference.* When individuals engage in these distorted thinking patterns, they create anger, depression, and arguments with their partners. By stopping automatic thoughts and introducing more reasonable interpretations of reality, clients rid themselves of negative emotions.

Therapy Methods and Techniques

Listed below are some general guidelines about using behavioral techniques with a couple.

1. Increase positives in the relationship first. Try to bind the couple together by increasing the good feelings about the relationship so that each partner begins to see it as a source of satisfaction.
2. Collect objective evidence about the problem. By focusing on the data, the therapist can get a better feel about the severity of problems. A behavioral therapist will collect data on the intensity, duration, and frequency of marital arguments. With this data, it will be easier to tell whether clients are moving toward their goals.
3. Have the couple make a public commitment to change. By making an agreement with each other and with the counselor, the partners increase their commitment to the goals.
4. Help the couple realize that both parties are involved in a behavioral cycle, so both need to change together. This is consistent with a nonblaming atmosphere in counseling and in the relationship in general.
5. Ask clients to keep track of their own progress. In so doing, they are learning self-control and learning something about the gradual, steplike nature of change.

Treating Communication Problems

We have focused mostly on distressed or troubled couples in this section, but behavioral methods and communication training can be useful to every couple. They are useful as preventive methods for premarital couples and as relationship enrichment activities for married or otherwise committed couples. Once learned, these methods can be generalized to other relationships, including work settings, and can have a beneficial effect on the couple's social life.

Communication training may take place with the couple in the therapist's office or in a larger seminar setting with a group of couples. In the office, the therapist can adjust to each couple, whereas in the seminar, general principles of communication are taught. Typically, communication training focuses on learning very specific skills such as respect, reflective listening, negotiation, timely discussion of problems, problem solving, marital manners, overcoming mindreading, and non-verbal communication. Regardless of the setting or the skills taught, some general procedures are employed by most trainers; they begin with simple skills and build to the more complex in the following sequence. (We go into greater depth on this topic later in this book.)

Modeling Social learning theory, as described by Bandura, suggests that one of the primary ways we learn is by observing others. We learn negative communication patterns primarily from our families of origin; we can also learn better communication skills by watching them being modeled. For this reason, couples are asked to watch films or listen to tapes of couples communicating effectively. During a therapy session, the therapist may model appropriate communication by role-playing with one member of the couple while the other observes and then practices what the therapist has demonstrated.

Rehearsal A key part of learning any new skill is rehearsing, or practicing. In communication training, couples can rehearse in the actual therapy session under the therapist's supervision. In a couples group, several couples may either rehearse simultaneously or rehearse in front of the whole group and receive feedback.

Reinforcement and feedback The therapist reinforces positive communications practices after the couple rehearses by pointing out the couple's progress and complimenting each member on specific behaviors that were demonstrated. Then the therapist points out areas for improvement. Utilizing what was learned from the coaching, the couple rehearses again and receives a second round of reinforcement and feedback.

Homework Homework is specifically geared to the couple working in the clinical setting. In the communications seminar, general homework is assigned to the class and is related to the skill being discussed that week. The first item on the agenda the following week is to report on homework assignments.

Changing Reinforcement Patterns

Changing reinforcement patterns means trying to influence the low rate of positive reinforcement and high rate of punishment that often occurs in distressed couples. In behavioral couples therapy, this begins with the therapist immediately insisting on the need for reciprocal change (both partners must change) and a commitment to a nonblaming attitude. In general, the strategy is to increase positives in the relationship first, which helps to give the couple faith in the process at the onset. Behaviorally oriented therapists suggest that couples should begin by choosing several relatively high payoff, low-cost exchanges. For example, it might be very important for Barry if Linda would remember to kiss him good-bye before going to work in the morning, and it would require relatively little effort from Linda. The "Caring Days Technique" is a behavioral technique whereby couples agree to publicly commit to increasing the positives in their relationship. They post the rewards they will give to each other and objectively document their completion. The chart helps encourage the couple, as both members see real evidence of behavioral differences.

Although increasing the positives in the relationship is important, decreasing negative interactions is also vital to treating the couple from a behavioral standpoint. Most punishing responses in couples therapy are verbal "arrows" fired in anger, and communication training is the basic method most behavior therapists utilize to treat this problem. Couples learn to give compliments and reduce degrading or punishing comments. Many people are surprised to find that their common expressions are taken very negatively by their spouses, despite good intentions.

Correcting Cognitive Errors in Relationships

Couples tend to commit cognitive errors in their thinking about each other and in their ideas about the relationship. They tend to misinterpret and jump to conclusions about their partner's behavior. They see the tiniest flicker of a smile as outright mockery; they hear the refrigerator slam as a slap in the face. In individual therapy, distortions are treated by helping each individual identify his or her own errors and substitute more constructive thinking patterns. Dattilio and Padesky (1990) have written about the application of cognitive therapy to couples following Beck's lead. They suggest that cognitive couples therapy should examine beliefs about relationships in general and beliefs or cognitions about the partner specifically. Several specific beliefs may be tied together by a common theme. For example, "I have always chosen the wrong person," "Everything turns out wrong" and "I always allow myself to be used" might be three common thoughts of an individual. When we look a little deeper, we see that they all suggest an underlying view of the self as ineffective. Most cognitive therapists would try to help the individual challenge the more general thinking pattern, whether it shows up in the relationship with the partner or in one with the boss. Following Beck's ideas, McKay, Fanning, and Paleg (1994) identified the following eight basic fallacies or cognitive distortions that most frequently operate in the couple situation.

1. *Tunnel vision:* This is the tendency to see only the negative aspect of the relationship or the other person's problem behaviors and to ignore the positive aspects.
2. *Assumed intent:* Especially when couples have been together for some time, they think they know what the other is thinking or intending. On the basis of only a few words or gestures, they guess their partner's intentions. Once, during a therapy session, I asked a husband to tell me what he liked about his wife. He complimented her sense of style and dress. She reacted angrily and at length to this compliment, taking it as a veiled criticism of her tendency to spend money on clothing.
3. *Magnification:* This is the human tendency to make mountains out of molehills. Albert Ellis refers to this distortion as *catastrophizing*. Couples may describe their wedding as "a disaster" when, in fact, there were both high spots and bad moments.

4. *Global labeling:* In global labeling, one member of the couple labels the other one: for example, "She is irresponsible" or "He is a pathological liar." This fallacy takes an example of the person's behavior and uses it to sum up his or her whole personality. When a birthday is forgotten, this turns into the global label of "thoughtless."

5. *Good-bad dichotomizing:* This is the tendency to see reality and the partner in black-and-white terms, as in these communications: "While you were away everything was peaceful; now it's chaos" or "You were wrong not to consult with me, and you won't admit it."

6. *Fractured logic:* Fractured logic can be detected by client statements like "He obviously doesn't want to work on the marriage because he was so mean to my mother" or "She loves her work so much that she will probably find someone there she likes more." Fractured logic is not often expressed directly, but the implications are there in the argument. Fractured logic consists of a premise and a conclusion that are independent of each other. The therapist may point out the client's argument and identify the fracture so the client can examine his or her faulty thinking.

7. *Control fallacies:* Control fallacies can exist on both ends of a continuum. On one end, a person thinks he or she is totally responsible for all that happens in a relationship or, at the other extreme, can believe he or she is powerless and out of control: for example, "He is emotionally distant. There is no way I can have an intimate marriage" or "I can't make him happy anymore."

8. *Letting-it-out fallacy:* In brief, this fallacy involves the belief that when your partner is wrong, he or she deserves to be punished and it is all right to unleash your wrath on him or her. A corollary of this idea is that screaming and emotional violence is a necessary and justifiable way to get the partner's attention.

Let us take an example of cognitive therapy in the realm of couples therapy: Patricia and Richard have been in conflict about how to deal with the misbehavior of Patricia's adolescent son, who lives with them. Patricia's ex-husband is very much involved in the situation; he is concerned and talks with Patricia at length about the problem. Table 2.1 lists some events and each person's thoughts about the situations. This homework assignment was given to the couple as an assessment tool for the therapist and to increase the couple's awareness of their thinking patterns. The partners were asked to write down upsetting events during the week, their thoughts about the events, and their resultant emotions. In the therapy session, the therapist might help the couple identify the cognitive errors. See if you can identify some of the eight fallacies mentioned above.

You might note that this approach appears to be a treatment of individuals. Cognitive therapists help each member of the couple discover his or her nonconstructive thinking and change those thinking patterns to improve the relationship. But cognitive therapists also try to help couples sort out their distortions when they are seen conjointly (together). The therapist challenges both partners to examine the rationality or irrationality of their own thoughts and identify the errors in their

Table 2.1   Sample Homework Assignment for Cognitive Therapy

	Event	*Thoughts*	*Emotions*
Richard	Patricia is talking to her ex again.	I bet they are thinking about reuniting.	Hurt, jealous
	I come home and find Brian's books and papers in the living room.	The kid is lazy; he'll never amount to anything.	Angry
	Patricia comes home from work, talks to Brian, but doesn't ask me about my day.	She babies him. She cares more about everyone else; I'm not important.	Hurt, angry
Patricia	I came home, Richard is in our room, and Brian in his. They do not talk to each other over dinner.	I'm a failure as a wife and a mother.	Sad
	Richard asks Brian about his homework.	He's just hoping that Brian hasn't done it so he can put him down.	Angry
	I yell at Richard when he complains to me about Brian's laziness.	He was wrong. I needed to release. Maybe now, he'll let up.	Angry

thinking. The therapist does this by stopping the action during the therapy session or by asking the clients to report the "automatic thoughts" that occur when the other person is speaking.

PSYCHODYNAMIC AND OBJECT-RELATIONS APPROACHES

No one who has any experience of the rifts which so divide a family will, if he is an analyst, be surprised to find that the patient's closest relatives sometimes betray less interest in his recovering than in his remaining as he is.
Freud, 1917/1963, p. 459

The approaches in this general school of thought are bound together by their application of psychodynamic concepts to couples therapy. One branch of psychodynamic thought is called *object relations*. Nathan Ackerman, James Framo, and Ivan Boszormenyi-Nagy are some modern proponents of this approach, which has roots in Freudian concepts modified by thinkers such as Ferenczi, Klein, Fairbairn, Kernberg, and Kohut.

   The object-relations approach is not a single school of thought (Finkelstein, 1987; Kilpatrick & Kilpatrick, 1991; Scharff & Scharff, 1991; St. Clair, 1986), and although the approaches of each member of the distinguished group mentioned above are distinct, we will try to understand some of their commonalities in this section. These thinkers have tried to bridge the gap between the strictly intrapersonal theory of Freud and the growing awareness that relationships and the social context are also critical to mental health. Fairbairn (1952) was one of the original thinkers in this area, but his work makes difficult reading. A good overview of the history and major concepts of object relations can be found in St. Clair (1986).

Because object-relations theory occupies the middle ground between individual and family therapy, it is not surprising that no general agreement has been reached about whether it is best to counsel clients separately or conjointly (with their partners present). It appears that many object-relations therapists combine individual and conjoint therapy.

Figure 2.2 shows how an individual represents the self and parents as internal objects. For example, a child may have both strong positive and negative experiences with the mother; at one moment she is nurturing, the next rejecting. The child's idea or image of the mother (internal representation or object) contains contradictory experiences, which create cognitive dissonance and anxiety. To deal with anxiety, the child splits internal objects into their good and bad parts, making them into separate fantasy objects. Contradiction is reduced and equilibrium is achieved. In this case, the child splits the mother into the good mother and the bad mother representations. Because this splitting reduces anxiety, the child learns to apply this same mechanism to discrepant experiences of the self. Unacceptable (bad) and idealized (good) parts of the self become detached and projected onto others. According to the theory, many of the things we do not like about others are actually our own negative attributes projected onto those around us.

When a child reaches adulthood and becomes involved in intimate relationships outside the family, the other member of the couple is a prime target for projection. Any intense relationship brings back feelings from earlier connections and catalyzes a defensive reaction. The other member's response to this projection may be affected by his or her own unique background and upbringing. According to the theory, the interaction of these mutual projections creates most of the problems couples experience, since the partners are dealing not with their real issues but with projections of themselves and images of previous relationships.

Connected to the object-relations formulation is the notion of "interlocking pathologies." This means that, in very disturbed relationships, each member intensely needs the other person and that their internal objects have found a match; she needs him to be the father she never had, and he needs her to be weak so that he can feel strong. Object-relations and psychodynamic approaches both focus on projective identification as a primary source of disturbance in couples.

Framo's Approach

James Framo impresses those who see him work as a psychodynamic Carl Rogers. His easygoing manner and shrewd insights have made him popular among therapists. His work borrows from the object-relations theories, but it also blends with some ideas of Boszormenyi-Nagy and Bowen (see Framo, 1970, 1976). In essence, Framo sees present relationship problems as reflections of family of origin issues;

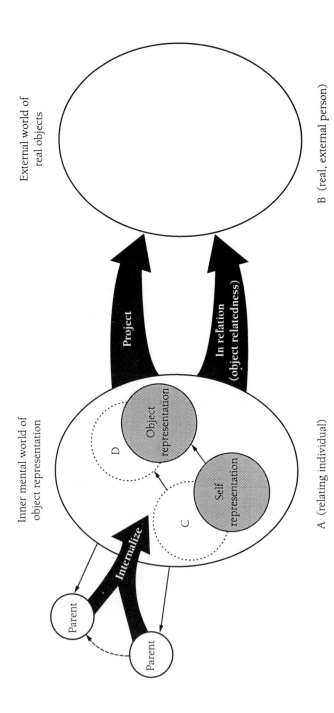

Figure 2.2 The inner and external worlds of objects. *Object relations* refers to the internal world where there are representations of the self in relation to representations of the object. These inner images may or may not accurately express objects as they actually exist in the "real" world. Person A, the actor, deals with person B in terms of his inner world, which is shaped and even distorted by his previous dealings with parents C and D. A has not only internalized his parents' interactions, expecting that this will be replicated in his own intimate relationships, but he has also identified with one of his parents and may project an idealized image onto B, thus relating with B in terms of the projected, idealized image.

Source: From *Object Relations and Self-Psychology: An Introduction,* by M. St. Clair. Copyright 1986 by Brooks/Cole Publishing Company, a division of International Thomson Publishing Inc.

we cannot see our partners clearly and we project on them because "old ghosts stand in the way" (Framo, 1990, p. 49). Framo believes in helping individuals in couples face their old ghosts by addressing the living members of their families of origin.

In a demonstration filmed by the American Counseling Association, Framo (1993) demonstrated his approach with a real couple experiencing problems in their marriage. Framo's attention turned immediately to both partners' families of origin. Both husband and wife admitted to having severely troubled relationships with their fathers, which Framo suggested they address. Framo referred to their relationships with their fathers as a "shared object," implying that both are left with similar unfinished business. He encouraged the husband and wife to meet separately with their parents and voice some of the unexpressed issues from the past in a nonblameful way to promote a stronger parent-child relationship. Framo seemed to suggest that the partners were initially drawn to each other because of similar family of origin problems, and problems persist because of unresolved issues in those core relationships.

Transactional Analysis

Transactional analysis (TA) is a form of therapy whose popularity has waned in recent years (Young, 1992). One of the reasons for its decline may be the popular, "cutesy" language used to describe its various components, such as "warm fuzzies." But TA, as promoted by its founder, Eric Berne, was one of the most easily understandable ways to explain object relations. Berne believed that parents pass on "implants" to their children, which he called "scripts," "tapes," and "injunctions." These implants were expectations and ideas about the world and the self that continued to unconsciously affect a person's behavior. Berne understood that in husband-wife interactions, "the parent" in one person was sometimes speaking to "the child" in the other. Berne's *Sex in Human Loving* (1970) and *Games People Play* (1964) point out the reasons that people, and especially couples, become involved in elaborate game-playing behavior. According to Berne, they are fulfilling childhood versions of reality or trying to receive "strokes" and other payoffs based on early learning.

Definitions of Key Terms

Following are some of the key terms associated with transactional analysis.

> *Object:* a person—not a thing—toward whom desires and behaviors are focused. An object may be represented internally or may be an actual person.
> *Object representation:* the internal mental image of an object as contrasted with the objective world.
> *Self-representation:* the internal image of the developing self. An infant begins at birth to differentiate the self from surrounding objects and, by contrast, forms an internal representation of the self.
> *Object seeking:* humans' motivation to search for and maintain contact with others; human beings are looking for intimacy. The object-relations approach's biggest

departure from Freud was Fairbairn's substitution of "object seeking" as the major motivation for human behavior, replacing the concept of libidinal drive.

Splitting: a psychological mechanism that divides a contradictory object into two or more parts. A parent who is nurturing and occasionally rejecting is parceled by the child into a two-part object, one "good father" and one "rejecting father." Splitting can serve an important defensive function, but it can also be unhealthy. When projective identification takes place, the individual is not dealing with reality but with a mental construction.

Symbiosis: the relationship between two or more people who cannot function without the other(s) (as opposed to the concept of differentiation). This is basically an unhealthy state.

Projective identification: a defense mechanism first explicated by Melanie Klein, whereby unacceptable parts of the self are attributed to another person and the other person is invited or induced to play a certain role (Siegel, 1991). It is an interpersonal process involving collusion. The domineering husband and nonassertive wife is a common example; he projects his weakness onto her and she accepts the role. According to Kilpatrick and Kilpatrick (1991, p. 216), the Freudian concept of transference, the idea of scapegoating in family therapy, Framo's notion of irrational role assignments, Mahler's term *symbiosis*, and Bowen's family projective process are all different ways of describing projective identification.

Some Premises of the Theories

Following are some of the premises held in common by the psychodynamic and object-relations theories.

1. Object seeking/attachment is a primary motivational force. We are all seeking interpersonal fulfillment.
2. Maturity means more than autonomy; it includes the capacity of becoming intimate and interdependent. In other words, growing up means allowing for appropriate regression without loss of self-respect.
3. Human beings develop from symbiotic to dependent to interdependent or individuated individuals.
4. Couples therapists who use the object-relations approach will help each member of the couple develop a better capacity for connectedness, attachment, and commitment (Finkelstein, 1987).
5. Sexual problems in marriage primarily reflect relationship problems as well as individual inhibitions and anxieties.
6. Conflicts about autonomy, attachment, and commitment are ongoing in a couple's relationship.
7. Childhood relationships with parents determine an individual's ability to function in an intimate couple relationship and deal with the issues of autonomy, attachment, and commitment.

8. Maturity is the couple's ability to meet the family life-cycle requirements.

9. Intimacy is a major motivation for becoming a couple. However, intimacy brings about fears of dependency and lack of autonomy.

10. Everyone has idealistic ideas about the intimate relationship, hoping to fulfill unmet needs from the childhood relationship with the parents.

11. Everyone is trying to balance togetherness (intimacy) and individuation (personal growth and autonomy).

12. Intrapsychic conflicts arise from experiences in the original family. The individual shapes the present relationship to mirror the family of origin as a way of trying to resolve the past.

13. By reviewing the past in individual, family, or couples therapy the individual can gain insight into his or her original conflicts and begin treating the partner as a present reality rather than as a reflection of the past.

14. Mates select each other to recover lost aspects of their primary object relations. They reexperience these aspects in the partner through projective identification (Dicks, 1967).

Problems That Couples Experience

Complementary Neurotic Patterns Based on Projections and Wishes
Neurotic is a psychodynamic term that refers to the individual's tendency to operate on the basis of projections, wishes, and defense mechanisms rather than rationality and reality. Neurotic behavior is often referred to by other theorists as self-defeating behavior.

Strean (1985) identified several couple patterns based on psychodynamic thinking.

The partner as superego This is the couples arrangement in which one partner plays the parent and the other plays the child. The "child" cannot approve of anything he or she does without the partner's approval. The "parent" in the relationship needs the partner to play the id; the "child" helps the "parent" experience id impulses. One is "stable," the other is "wild."

The partner as a devaluated self-image In this pattern, everything bad about the self can be projected onto the partner. Claiming that one has no head for money is a way of not taking responsibility for financial problems.

The partner as ego ideal "My better half" is one way of expressing the tendency to idealize one's mate. One member achieves a rather fragile self-esteem by idealizing the mate. No one can live up to fantasies of perfection, so the "ideal" eventually falls off the pedestal, bringing disappointment and conflict.

The dominant-submissive dyad In this arrangement, one member is described as sadistic or aggressive and humiliates the partner. The partner is submissive, dependent, and a martyr. From a psychodynamic perspective, the sadistic behavior is a defense against dependent feelings. The dominant member controls the self by controlling the other person.

The detached-demanding dyad   This cycle is quite similar to the classic pursuer-distancer relationship, where one member chases and the other withdraws. Here, the demanding partner is seen as dependent, and the detached one as fearing his or her own dependency needs.

Romantic-rational partnership   Sager (1976) identified several types of pathological relationships based on unmet needs. Among these is the "romantic-rational" partnership, in which one member is extremely logical and devoid of emotion and the other is prone to living in a fantasy world. The rational one provides grounding for the romantic, and the romantic one provides excitement for the rational. Neither partner develops fully.

The partner as parent   Sager (1976) recognized parent-child combinations in marriage as one of the most common pathological problems, where one partner assumes control and the other is allowed to be irresponsible and dependent. Both are meeting needs. The responsible partner needs to gain a sense of control, be viewed as "in charge," feel nurturing, or be seen as a martyr. The "child" enjoys being taken care of. In transactional analysis, this combination with a male parent and female child has been called the Big Daddy/Cinderella partnership. Again, the price paid is that one is forced to be joyless, and the other remains a child.

The "love-sick" wife and the "cold-sick" husband   This pattern was iden-tified by psychodynamic thinkers Martin and Bird (1959) as a classic pairing of "obsessive husbands" and "hysterical wives." Today, we think of this as a rather sexist understanding of the couple's relationship, not to mention an extremely pathological portrayal. In the pattern, as originally described, the woman complains that her husband is cold and unable to love, and she describes her own symptoms as "anxiety." The wife suffers from low self-esteem and requires attention from her spouse to feel worthwhile. The husband is described as emotionless with a strong ego and a tyrannical superego. In short, the husbands were thought to be rigid, and the wives unstable. The reversal of this common entanglement was the "hysterical husband and the obsessional wife." This pattern was thought to be the result of the husband searching for a "mother," that is, someone to take care of him. Psychodynamic theorists found this pattern to be specific evidence of "interlocking pathologies," meaning that certain personality patterns seek out others to meet needs and to achieve stability.

Therapy Methods and Techniques

Following are some guidelines for using psychodynamic and object-relations techniques with couples.

1. Slipp (1988) contends that one of the most important measures a therapist can take is to develop a safe "holding environment" with empathy. The therapist extends this protection to the couple in re-creating a nurturing, "maternal" environment (Seinfeld, 1993). Facilitating trust lowers defensiveness and allows the couple to deal safely with aggression and pent-up frustration.

2. The major method in object-relations psychodynamic therapy is to explore the past. The therapist ordinarily works one-on-one with each person, exploring childhood experiences and developmental history (Finkelstein, 1987). When both the relationship with the parents and the parents' own marital relationship is explored, the individual may gain insight into his or her own behavior in the present relationship. Fairbairn (1952) thought this exploration would help clients realize that everyone is basically striving to be taken care of in their couple relationship. We seek the couple relationship as a way of fulfilling unmet dependency needs from childhood. When this dynamic is interpreted in therapy, the client gains insight, through which the client is supposed to learn to accept a "normal" amount of dependency without hostility.

3. The therapist uses interpretation to help clients understand the roots of their problems. *Interpretation* is the therapist's reformulation of the clients' current dilemma in terms of its psychological meaning. For example, after examining the couple's background, a therapist might interpret the projective identification process brought forward from families of origin. Rather than interpreting the husband's behavior as "domineering," the therapist will point out that, to achieve self-worth, the husband's history taught him that it was important for him to see himself as "in charge." The therapist might then help the wife see how she colludes with her husband's projection by being submissive. By identifying the origin and describing its current manifestation, the couple is able to see that there may be more productive ways to meet their needs.

4. The dynamically oriented therapist helps couples understand their individual families of origin and how they interact. The genogram is a popular technique for this activity, but special emphasis will be placed on personal perspectives, or "representations" of parents, and on the client's view of the parents' interaction. The parents' relationship serves as an internal model for the client's own relationships.

5. Instead of couples therapy, family therapy can be conducted with the client's family of origin (Framo, 1990). This is a somewhat radical approach that James Framo has pioneered. He gathers one member of the couple and his or her family of origin for an intensive family therapy session, even though members may be scattered across the country. In this session, the individual is encouraged to deal with the real people in the family, as opposed to projections and memories. Since current problems are a reflection of older issues, one is taking these problems back to their original source. Alternately, Framo may suggest that each member of the couple meet with members of their families and attempt resolution on their own. In either case, the partner is not included. Framo's way of working with a couple would be to do this "family of origin work" and then help the couple resolve current problems. Framo says that a single session with parents and siblings, conducted with skill, determination, and care, can create more change than an entire course of individual or couples therapy.

THE BOWEN THEORY

Bowen family systems theory is best understood as an emotional relationship system made up of eight interlocking concepts. It was developed by Murray Bowen, a pioneer and major theorist in the field of family therapy. Four of Bowen's concepts are fundamental to understanding all his other ideas: differentiation, triangles, emotional system, and emotional triangles. (See the following section for definitions of these terms.) To practice Bowenian therapy with couples, each of these interdependent constructs must be understood.

All of Bowen's concepts are based on the premise that life for all species is accompanied by a chronic anxiety. The level of this anxiety is influenced by the amount of differentiation of family members. The intensity of an individual's reaction to this anxiety is based on how the person's family of origin transmitted anxiety. So although the anxiety may manifest itself differently according to one's family structure or cultural traditions, it is the same phenomenon for everyone.

Chronic anxiety in Bowen therapy does not refer to everyday worries, phobias, compulsions, or common life problems; instead, it is the automatic responses to what *might* occur, rather than to what is actually happening. Chronic anxiety is the primary promoter of all symptoms, from psychosis to cancer to anorexia. The cure and the preventive medicine is differentiation.

Bowen's theory is a systems theory, meaning that change in one part of the system shows up in other parts of the system. Bowen sees marital or couples conflict as a symptom of a system problem. Symptoms may also show up as a physical illness, emotional distancing of one partner, or the "acting out" of a child.

Bowen's unit of treatment is almost always the couple, and he would judge a marriage or couple relationship as successful when it is symptom-free. Bowen believes that no couple relationship ever gets a grade of over 70%, as he believes that no individual ever reaches more than 70% success in the lifetime journey toward differentiation. The basic goal in couples therapy for the Bowenian therapist is to promote movement to the highest level of differentiation possible in each of the partners.

Bowenian therapy is a "thinking therapy," although it in no way eliminates emotions. Bowen addresses emotionality in concepts such as "the emotional triangle," "emotional cutoff," and "emotional system." This approach appeals most to therapists who are looking to the long-term betterment of the individuals and the couple; it will be less appealing to therapists interested in immediate symptom relief. Clients who seem to do best are those who take responsibility for themselves. The focus of Bowenian therapy is on the overall emotional process, rather than on the individual content of problems.

This section was written by Judith Ann Wright, Ed.D., a marriage and family therapist in private practice in New Smyrna Beach, Florida.

Definitions of Key Terms

Some of the key terms in Bowenian theory are as follows.

Differentiation: the process of becoming emotionally independent. Differentiation involves the ability to express one's own opinions and feelings while at the same time listening to others and remaining emotionally connected. It also includes the ability to make decisions based on nonanxious thinking, rather than by simply reacting. For example, a couple with a low level of differentiation will frequently argue because both are reacting to each other in an anxious and emotionally reactive way, rather than focusing on the problem and thinking it through.

Intellectual versus emotional functioning: people are capable of making choices by using either their objective intellectual system or their subjective emotional system. These systems can operate either alone or in harmony. To make the choice, people must be able to distinguish between these two systems within themselves. The more anxious a person is, the greater the possibility of fusion between the two systems and fusion with the emotions of others. For example, if partners can remain calm in problem solving, they can think clearly and objectively. However, if too much emotionality over a long period occurs, the emotions run the system.

Nuclear family emotional system: includes all the information in a genogram. The patterns of the nuclear family's emotional system are to maintain family stability. If chronic anxiety and fusion are high, the family selects one or more of the following mechanisms to stabilize the system: (1) emotional distance between spouses, (2) marital discord, (3) emotional or physical disability in a spouse, or (4) acting out by a child. These patterns repeat from generation to generation. For example, a husband becomes a workaholic and distances emotionally in the same way his father did.

Individuality versus togetherness forces: two natural forces constantly at work in individuals and in relationships. The balance between them is constantly shifting. If one partner feels too close, he or she will create distance, and the other, feeling this distance, may experience a need for more togetherness and pursue the partner. This may cause the first partner to stop "distancing" and move toward the other.

Multigenerational transmission: the passing down of emotional responses from generation to generation, both in the nature and the degree of intensity. What happens in one generation often happens in the next. Bowen believes that people are attracted to each other at the same level of differentiation. In families, some children will have lower levels of differentiation than their parents and will seek partners who are also at this lower level of differentiation. After many generations of this lowering, a level of "no self" that characterizes schizophrenia may be reached. Bowen believes this could take as many as eight to ten generations, or fewer if severe stress and anxiety are present.

Emotional triangles: involve any three parts of an emotional system, usually composed of three people, with the dyad bringing in (triangling) a third person or a habit to diffuse the anxiety of the two-person system. For example, in marital conflict, spouses may "triangle" in a child by focusing on the child's problem and thus diffuse the anxiety of their conflict (Bowen, 1978).

Genogram: a format for drawing a family tree that records information about family members and their relationships, spanning at least three generations (McGoldrick & Gerson, 1985). This visual aid quickly points out the patterns and multigenerational transmissions of the family system. It is generally drawn during the first therapy session and then additions are made during therapy. Genograms are most often associated with Bowen's therapy but are also used by therapists of other orientations (Bowen, 1978). Genograms are described in detail in Chapter 6 of this book.

Some Premises of the Theory

Following are some premises of Bowen theory as they relate to couples counseling.

1. People are attracted to and marry or commit to someone at their own level of differentiation.
2. Couples repeat the behaviors of their families of origin and extended families, so the therapist must collect a history of at least three generations.
3. Couples conflicts or a dysfunctional partner point to problems in the family system and must be treated in that context.
4. The goal of all therapy with couples is the same: to raise the level of differentiation in both partners to the highest level possible. Couples are coached to take back the energy invested in changing their partners and concentrate on changing themselves.
5. A couple's levels of differentiation can go no higher than the level of the therapist, so Bowenian therapists must have high levels of differentiation.

Problems That Couples Experience

Chronic conflict   When high levels of chronic anxiety and low levels of differentiation are present in couples relationships, the partners will react emotionally rather than using rational thinking to solve problems. Severe conflict between the two partners is one of the most frequent symptoms of problems in the family system.

Differences in levels of differentiation   Sometimes one partner will raise his or her own level of differentiation through education or counseling, but the other does not. Bowen believed that if the difference is more than two or three levels, there will be little remaining commonality in lifestyles.

Distancer-pursuer pattern   Sometimes one partner in the relationship will distance emotionally and the other will pursue. This is often accomplished through blaming or accusing and results in conflict.

Problems due to dissimilar family of origin messages Couples often have very different family of origin messages for issues like male and female roles, money, how to raise children, and sexual issues. Each partner will fight to make the nuclear family like his or her own family of origin.

Triangulation When anxiety is high in a couple's relationship, another person or habit may be "triangled" in by the couple to ease the pressure. Examples of triangulation include extramarital affairs, alcoholism, children's behavioral problems, and in-laws.

Overfunctioning-underfunctioning pattern An overfunctioning-underfunctioning pattern may emerge, as seen in the case of a dysfunctional partner. This pattern is clearly seen in a relationship where one partner is a substance abuser, and the other overfunctions as a co-dependent.

Unresolved family of origin issues Often one or both partners left the family of origin with unresolved emotional issues involving parents. These people then find a partner with characteristics of the parent with whom they still have unfinished issues and try to work out these issues with their partner.

Therapy Methods and Techniques

A discussion of Bowenian therapy with couples must start with the description of the therapist, because a mature therapist is considered the main tool in promoting differentiation. Bowenian therapists have worked on and continue to address their own issues with their families of origin and have experienced growth in their own levels of differentiation. This is a major difference between Bowenian and other therapies.

A Bowenian therapist is a coach and a teacher. The therapist needs no specialties, as the job is always the same: promoting differentiation. Bowen directs the therapist to four main functions: (1) defining and clarifying the relationship between the partners; (2) keeping the therapist detriangled from the family emotional system; (3) teaching the functioning of emotional systems; and (4) demonstrating differentiation by taking "I" position stands during the course of the therapy (Bowen, 1978). (An "I" position stand is letting the couple know where you stand on an issue even if it goes against the grain.) It is a model for couples to be more honest and to gain the courage to differentiate.

In Bowenian therapy, couples are normally seen together. If the relationship is too filled with conflict or if only one partner wants changes in the relationship, work must first be done with the highest functioning and most differentiated partner. As one partner gains a higher level of differentiation, the other will reciprocate with more maturity.

A thorough family history of at least three generations is obtained through the use of a genogram. This is begun the first session, and additions are made throughout therapy. The therapist presents this as a research project, with the partners getting to know more about their families of origin in order to figure out their own ways of functioning and of understanding what has been transmitted through the generations. Partners are given homework assignments to return to their families of origin for more information, insight, and practice in taking "I" positions. Couples report getting to know and appreciate each other much better in this nonanxious way.

Questions and coaching are the therapist's main techniques, and the therapist takes complete control of the sessions. The atmosphere is calm and cerebral, with one partner responding directly to the therapist's questions and the other partner listening. The listening partner is then asked about the thoughts he or she had as the partner was answering the question. The therapist permits conflicts and intimacy between the partners to eliminate tension, but no interpretations are given. The therapist clarifies for the couple and insists that both partners stay focused and take responsibility for their own part of the problem. The therapist asks questions in order to point out the problems and uses words like *opinions*, *thoughts*, and *ideas* when asking for comments. Feelings or other subjective responses are avoided. Bowen thought that the magic of therapy with couples was in this externalization of the thoughts of one partner while the other overhears them.

Stages of Bowenian Couples Therapy

In the beginning stage of high anxiety, the main work of therapy is to deal with the emotionality of the couple and neutralize it. The therapist must keep from becoming triangulated, repeatedly confirming neutrality and avoiding transference-like interpretations. The therapist must listen to the content being spoken while simultaneously focusing on the emotional process.

As the original anxiety decreases through calm questioning and genogram work, one partner will move toward individuality by focusing on self-responsibility in the relationship and by beginning to accept blame for his or her own discomfort or unhappiness. The partner will then see the need for and begin to make changes in self and will give up trying to change the other.

As one spouse differentiates, the other spouse will pressure for more togetherness, which may take the form of accusations or blaming. Usually old patterns will be repeated. After several such cycles, the differentiating partner will gradually gain more strength and be able to proceed calmly with his or her own plan despite the togetherness pressures.

A period of calm will emerge after the couple adjusts to the differentiating. During this period, teaching and working on family of origin issues allows the couple to move ahead together.

When the second partner begins the differentiating process, the first partner becomes the force for togetherness. As this goes on, the cycles move faster and are not as clearly defined, but higher levels of differentiation in the partners become apparent.

When couples understand the functioning of emotional systems and display higher levels of differentiation in their relationships with their parents and their children, the therapy can be successfully concluded.

CONCLUSION

This chapter presented two rather opposing views of couples therapy, the behavioral and psychodynamic viewpoints. It also looked at the Bowen theory, which can be seen as a part of the psychodynamic approach but one that possesses original features. One idea that all three might agree on is that couples engage in repetitive maladaptive patterns of behavior that must be broken up. The cause of these patterns for the behaviorist is the client's history of reinforcement (prior learning) and the current reinforcement patterns in the present relationship. The psychodynamic thinkers would probably assert that the past is more significant than the present in understanding a couple's problems, and the Bowenians would search for the causes in the family of origin.

In Chapter 3, we discuss the structural and strategic points of view, along with the emerging brief therapies. At the end of Chapter 3, we will make a case for the integrative model proposed by this book.

3

Theories of
Couples Therapy: Part Two

KEY CONCEPTS

- Structural therapy and strategic therapy have been major forces in the history of family therapy. They have many similarities theoretically, but they are very different in technique.
- Structural therapy begins by joining the therapist with the couple. The therapist may then make changes in the couple's boundaries, their power rules, or the coalitions that may exist in the family that prevent a good couple relationship.
- Strategic therapy is aimed at "rocking the boat." Anything that can disrupt couple patterns or change their interactions is healthy. Strategic therapy is action-oriented and often uses methods that are not rational.
- Brief therapy is the fastest growing and most popular approach in today's therapy community. In marriage and family therapy, the approaches have been pioneered by the Mental Research Institute (MRI) and the Brief Family Therapy Center (BFTC).
- The MRI approach is more problem-focused, whereas the BFTC approach is more solution-focused. There are many similarities between the approaches besides the time restraints. Both are interested in changing issues that clients are concerned about, as opposed to identifying pathology. Both are ahistorical in their approach, and both work quickly to achieve change.

In this chapter, we continue with our exploration of the various theories of therapy begun in Chapter 2. Here we tackle some interrelated and very modern approaches to family therapy, all of which are still in their formative stages. We begin by looking at the structural therapy approach originally proposed by Minuchin (1974), and we compare it to the strategic approach developed by Haley. These were strong schools of thought in the 1970s and 1980s, but brief therapy has become the favorite of the 1990s (Lipchik, 1994). Although the term *brief therapy* has become somewhat meaningless because all forms of therapy have now developed a "brief" version, two major divisions of brief therapy are described here, the Mental Research Institute approach and the solution-oriented work of the Brief Family Therapy Center. At the conclusion of the chapter, we will try to draw together some of the threads from the theories we described here and in Chapter 2. These principles form the basis for the integrative approach to couples therapy presented in Chapter 4 and appearing throughout this text.

STRUCTURAL AND STRATEGIC THERAPIES APPLIED TO COUPLES

The major conflicts in a marriage center in the problem of who is to tell whom what to do under what circumstances.
Haley, 1963, p. 227

The structural and strategic schools of family therapy are distinct theoretical positions, but they contain many similarities when applied. For that reason, they have been linked and are often considered together (Friesen, 1985; Stanton, 1980; Todd, 1986). Not everyone agrees that they should be integrated (Fish & Piercy, 1987), however, because there are considerable differences in the two approaches. In this section, we will look at them both individually and as separate systems and will identify the areas where they tend to agree.

Salvador Minuchin (1974) is the figure most often associated with structural family therapy, and Jay Haley (1976) is a key theorist in strategic therapy. Both theoretical positions were originally developed for work with families but have since been applied to couples work. Strictly speaking, both viewpoints conceptualize the couple as part of the family system, and orthodox practitioners might not advocate working with the couple outside of the larger family system. From the structural and strategic viewpoints, the whole family is involved in the creation and maintenance of a problem.

Definitions of Key Terms

Following are some key terms in structural and strategic therapies.

Homeostasis: a medical term applied metaphorically to families; the tendency of a family to seek a lower level of anxiety or stability. Homeostasis is a self-regulating function, a state of balance or relative quietude during which the unit can perform some of its functions and support some of the members. Homeostasis is not necessarily a healthy state for all members.

Alignment: the alliances of two or more people in a family to achieve a common goal. Alliances are made for mutual protection and to keep secrets. Alliances are formed to maintain homeostasis.

Boundaries: imaginary lines that separate systems from each other and subsystems from the larger family. For example, the marital couple is distinct from the children. The degree to which this is made known and enforced shows the strength of the boundary. Boundaries are like membranes around a family, a couple, or a subsystem. Sometimes they are too permeable, allowing other people to interfere in the system; sometimes they are too rigid, creating too small a world for the members. Ideally, boundaries allow the couple or family system to have an identifiable life while allowing individuals to actualize as well.

Enmeshment: an excessive amount of connection and cohesion among family members. In its extreme form, there is little privacy or sense of self for individual members. Enmeshment is dysfunctional when families are over-involved in each other's lives—when families do not allow individuals to be themselves. Another way of describing enmeshment is to say that external boundaries of the family may be strong but boundaries between individuals within the family are blurred.

Disengaged: the term applied to a family in which there is a high degree of autonomy in each member of the family but there is also a lack of intimacy, self-disclosure, and belongingness. *Disengaged* is at the opposite end of the continuum from *enmeshed.*

Scapegoating: the tendency for a family to blame its problems on one member, who is then the "identified patient" or "symptom bearer." Scapegoating appears to relieve pressure on the overall system and helps the family achieve homeostasis.

Triangle: a family configuration formed when a dyad is under stress and a third member is recruited to reduce pressure. For example, a mother may seek intimacy from her daughter that she is not receiving in the couple relationship.

Joining: a term that describes both an attitude and an activity of the therapist. It means becoming a part of the family while developing a supportive and therapeutic relationship; it is the attitude of being "on their side." At certain times, the therapist may shift and "join" with an individual or a subsystem of the family when required.

Some Premises of the Theories

Following are some basic premises of structural and strategic therapies.

Structural Therapy

1. Couples relationships have three basic dimensions: *boundaries, power,* and *alignment.*
2. Boundary problems are described as enmeshment or disengagement (see definitions above). Couples need to have boundaries that allow them to experience themselves as a couple and as individuals.
3. Problems with power are due to a dysfunctional set of basic agreements about the hierarchy of the family unit, leaving some members less powerful and the others more powerful.
4. Unhealthy alliances between family members are a major source of problems. For example, some couple problems are the result of a cross-generational alliance with a child. Such an alliance may be unhealthy when it

empowers the child at the expense of one member of the couple or when a child becomes "parentified," requiring adult or spouselike responsibilities as a part of the child's family role.

5. Healthy families have clearly defined generational boundaries, with parents aligning together as the executives, especially on important issues.

6. Healthy couples have clear rules related to power. They have a workable system for making decisions.

7. Changing boundaries, alignments, and redistributing power (family structure) leads to change. Insight alone is not sufficient for change. Structural change in the family leads to change in individuals.

8. It is crucial that the therapist join with the couple or family in order to treat them. Only by joining can the therapist become influential in making the structural changes in the family. Sometimes it is said that the role of the therapist is "joining and kicking." This means that first the therapist joins the couple and then begins changing boundaries and alignments, and redistributing power.

9. Normal and expected milestones in a couple's life can create problems. Family organizational structure needs to change in response to developmental events, and new rules need to be made.

10. Couples' problems develop and are maintained in the context of family relationships. The whole family needs to be considered when dealing with a couple's problems.

11. The focus is on the here and now. The past is relevant only as it is enacted in the present.

Strategic Therapy

1. Causality is circular, and problem behaviors are part of a recursive sequence of events. It makes little sense to try to track down the culprit in a couple because both are co-creating the situation.

2. Therapist and clients are constantly influencing each other. Because therapists cannot remain neutral, the therapist's influence should be planned.

3. The therapist is a change agent. Even maladaptive behaviors maintain homeostatic balance, and changing them means "upsetting the apple cart."

4. A symptom is a communication, and the therapist's job is to help decode the message behind the behavior. When one member of the couple barricades himself or herself in the study most nights, the therapist hypothesizes that this is not just a way of avoiding the other person; it is also a message of revenge or hurt sent through this particular channel.

5. Couples form repeating patterns of responding to stress. Simply disrupting dysfunctional patterns may lead to more adaptive interactions. Insight alone is insufficient for change.

6. A person's view of his or her partner and the problem are subjective and unique. Therefore, the therapist must understand the client's particular view of reality and must adapt methods to fit that construction.

7. Therapists should be action-oriented and pragmatic; do what works.

Premises Common to Both Theoretical Positions

8. *The family is a system.* As we have described earlier, this means that all the parts of the family influence each other reciprocally. Identifying one member as the cause of family problems is inconsistent with the idea of the family system.

9. *Symptoms keep the family system functional.* For example, a symptom such as arguing over the discipline of a child may keep the parents occupied so that they do not deal with their sexual problems. This action maintains homeostasis.

10. *Symptoms are maintained by the system.* When the therapist attempts to eliminate a symptom, he or she may find that the family seems to collude in keeping the symptom going.

11. *Couples engage in repetitive patterns of behavior that can be destructive and keep the unit from achieving its goals.* When dysfunctional patterns are interrupted, the pattern does not continue.

12. *All couples (because they are families) proceed through developmental sequences through life that involve the completion of specific tasks.* When tasks for a specific stage are not completed, development is retarded. For example, a couple at the "launching stage" of development is sending its children out on their own. If children are not allowed to grow up, the family will deal with intergenerational conflict until more firm lines are drawn.

13. *The couple's current context (the present) is more important than its history.*

14. *Therapy is brief and problem-focused, and the therapist (a) is goal-oriented, (b) assigns tasks, and (c) is active and directive.*

15. *Change is more important than insight.*

Problems That Couples Face

Communication Problems

According to structural/strategic thinking, couples communication can be of two types: symmetrical or asymmetrical. *Symmetrical* means that both people do the same thing alternately; *asymmetrical* means that they take complementary roles. If both members of the couple withdraw in a fight, they are acting symmetrically. If one blames and the other placates, they are acting asymmetrically. Asymmetrical pairings lead to more conflict but are not necessarily more functional.

Couples tend to balance each other. If one is frugal, the other often spends too much. Sometimes partners can influence each other to more moderate positions. The "compulsive house cleaner" may ease up and the "sloppy" partner may get organized. Partners in conflict tend to polarize and become more extreme in response to each other. If one is too indulgent with the children, the other becomes overly strict. Sullaway and Christensen (1983) have identified the following asymmetrical pairings that are often seen as presenting problems in couples therapy:

- introvert/extrovert
- flirtatious/jealous
- assertive/nonassertive
- more involved/less involved
- repress/express emotions
- less/more devoted to partner
- dependent/independent
- relationship/work oriented
- emotional/rational
- demand/withdraw
- leader/follower
- cautious/committed

Game Playing

Friesen (1985), a structural/strategic therapist, suggests that couple patterns could be described as games similar to those defined by the transactional analysts (Berne, 1964). He identifies seven games or repetitive patterns, four of which are examined below:

"This Is War!" In this game of revenge, both try to hurt the other person more than they were hurt the last time. The strategy is to find and attack the other's weak points, including family, job, and other things that are important. Never give a compliment. This game is a dangerous one because it requires "upping the ante" each time it is played.

"I've Got the Debit and You've Got the Credit!" In this pattern, it seems that each member of the couple keeps a balance sheet, always making sure that the other person is doing his or her share. Anything done for the other person must be repaid. Early on in relationships, especially when there are young children or many responsibilities, this kind of pattern can easily emerge and is sometimes called, "I changed the diaper last time."

"I Don't Want to Discuss It!" This is a game of one-upmanship. When a fight emerges, one member of the couple disengages and remains cool, refusing to lower himself or herself to the emotional level of the other person. One member feels put down and out of control emotionally; the other feels superior and withdraws.

"Where Would You Be Without Me?" In transactional analysis, this game is called, "If it weren't for you." In that version, one player constantly complains that life would be perfect if not for the partner, who is like a millstone around the neck. As Friesen describes this pattern, a relationship often develops between someone who is competent and someone who is incompetent, ill, uneducated, or from a lower social class. The silent message behind this game is: "Because I have rescued you from your fate, I have the right to make continuing demands on you. I will remind you of my benevolence by occasionally accompanying you on visits to your dysfunctional family of origin."

Becoming Disengaged or Polarized

One common couple problem, according to the structural strategic point of view, is that of *disengagement*. The relationship is symmetrical and stable, but there is little satisfaction. This may result from a change in family development, such as when a couple with two or three young children finds that the stress of the life stage saps all the energy from the marriage. Because the two have not kept their relationship vital, they are more vulnerable to alliances with children and others who may provide them with nurturing.

Another symmetrical couple type could be called "the Bickersons," or the "polarized" couple (Todd, 1984). This is the couple that argues about everything (a symmetrical pattern—both attack). Ironically, just as disengaging does by avoiding fighting, so arguing in polarized couples prevents intimacy and prevents the couple from functioning as a unit.

Therapy Methods and Techniques

Table 3.1 shows a portion of the results of Fish and Piercy's (1987) Delphi study of structural and strategic therapy. A Delphi study is a compilation of the views of invited experts. In this case, the experts were nationally known authorities in family therapy who were asked to identify the core concepts and techniques of structural and strategic therapies. Their lists indicate several of the most representative or commonly utilized techniques in each of the two approaches. We describe several of the techniques in this list—along with a few others—in greater detail.

The lists in Table 3.1 suggest that although many of the theoretical notions are similar, there are significant differences in technique. Strategic therapists are more problem-focused and are more likely to use a variety of methods to unbalance the interactional sequence. Structural therapists are more concerned with changing the family structure—that is, boundaries, alignments, and rules—as a way of promoting long-term change.

Enactment   Enactment is both an assessment tool and a therapeutic intervention. It consists of allowing or encouraging a couple to engage in the dysfunctional behavior in the therapy setting. By observing and making the couple aware of the

Table 3.1   Experts' List of Major Techniques and Interventions of Structural and Strategic Therapies

Structural	Strategic
Joining	Reframing
Boundary Marking/Making	Obtaining an identifiable problem
Restructuring	Prescribing the symptom
Tracking	Use of client language and position
Enactment	Determining the interactional sequence and interrupting it in some way

pattern, the problem comes out into the open. Finally, the therapist encourages the development of new transactions or patterns to replace the dysfunctional ones.

Reframing   Reframing, or relabeling, is similar to the cognitive therapy technique called "cognitive restructuring." It is the art of helping a client view the problem in a different way, and it is described in detail later in this book. One version of reframing developed by the Milan school of family therapy is called "positive connotation." Positive connotation involves attributing good intentions to a partner's behavior as a way of seeing the problem differently.

The directive   A directive is an instruction the therapist gives to the couple or family to get them to behave differently (Schilson, 1991). Jay Haley (1989) developed a number of directives in strategic therapy that are designed simply to break up rigid patterns of behavior. Some directives are straightforward, whereas others are paradoxical and absurd. Some examples are:

1. *Tell the couple directly what you want them to do.* Assign a task that is absurd such as "I want the two of you to drive 17.2 miles from your home, stop the car, and find a reason for being there."
2. *Use the "devil's pact."* Here, the couple is told that the counselor has a solution to the problem, but it is difficult and arduous and the couple must agree to do it before it is disclosed to them. Normally, the couple is given time to think this over and decide whether or not they really want to solve the problem.
3. *Give the couple an "ordeal."* An ordeal is a task that is just about as difficult as the symptom and is good for the couple as well. The presenting problem becomes more difficult to maintain because of the added ordeal, and therefore the couple abandons the presenting problem. Child therapist Haim Ginnott described an ordeal that he used when his children argued and wanted him to serve as judge. He would ask them each to write a 100-word essay on his or her point of view and then he would settle the "case." Of course, the kids wandered away and found another way to settle their differences. For a couple, the ordeal may be something arduous that they have to do together, such as exercising.
4. *Assign penance or some action that will make up for guilt feelings.*
5. *Give the couple metaphorical tasks.* Here the partners are assigned a task that symbolically relates to their problem. For example, a couple might be given the job of discussing in detail how an orchestra might be run with two conductors when each is slightly different in style and in the music they like (Becvar & Becvar, 1988).

Paradoxical techniques   A variety of paradoxical techniques in strategic and structural therapy can be used when more obvious directives and suggestions do not work. One of these is called "restraining change." In this technique, a couple that is progressing very rapidly in therapy (perhaps too quickly) is given the suggestion that both should slow down the process because sudden change can be harmful (Stanton, Todd, & Associates, 1982). Such an intervention probably works to reinforce the reality of the change process and allows the couple to recognize that they have the power to change their relationship.

Structural moves or restructuring Healthy families establish boundaries between the couple and the children. Healthy couples allow each person to actualize their talents and experience a degree of autonomy. Similarly, children have the freedom to be individuals but are also part of the family, and they may be part of a sibling subsystem as well. Boundaries should be permeable enough to allow access to individuals and information outside of the family but should also enclose the family and each subsystem enough to give them a sense of unity and identity. Figure 3.1 shows these boundaries in a diagram of a healthy family structure.

Sometimes couples therapists form coalitions with the partners' parents to support the couple's relationship when it is threatened by other alliances or coalitions. Figure 3.2 is a diagram of a situation in which the mother of one partner has aligned herself with her son in order to gain power in the family. This triangle is considered to be unhealthy for the couple, and it places the son "in the middle." If the therapist decides to make a change in such a family, it would be a change in structure, or a "structural move." The therapist might choose to support the couple's relationship by asking the mother not to confide in the son. This creates a boundary between the generations and takes pressure off the son; but on the other hand, the wife or mother may feel unsupported. The therapist must then negotiate a redistribution of authority. One way the therapist can do this is to join with the wife to balance the system. System homeostasis can be maintained without supporting the current symptom pattern. Power, boundaries, and alignments can be redistributed to achieve equilibrium and equity.

Joining *Joining* was defined earlier in this chapter, but it is actually a complex method, not easily explained in a few sentences. Joining refers to the technique of providing support and a sense of being connected to the couple. Joining, though, is a two-way street; it means being accepted by the couple as a leader or guide (Colapinto, 1991). Although the therapist initially joins with both members of the

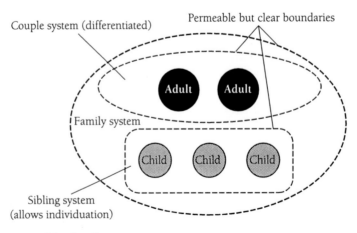

Figure 3.1 Healthy family structure

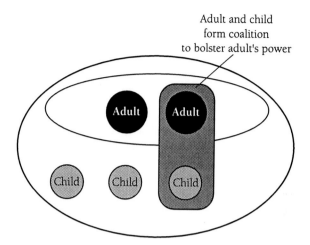

Figure 3.2 Cross-generational alliance; unhealthy structure

couple, the therapist may shift and provide more support for the member who is less motivated or more in need of nurturance.

Prescribing the symptom Prescribing the symptom is a classic paradoxical technique designed to produce the opposite effect. For example, a couple that argues a great deal is given the assignment to argue (nonviolently) twice daily at assigned times using the dysfunctional behaviors they most often employ. Both members are instructed to respond without listening, talk at the same time, or engage in any of the usual ways that they have found to be nonproductive. Arguing decreases as the couple gains control of the behavior by practicing it as prescribed by the therapist.

Pretending This paradoxical method, designed by Chloe Madanes, is intended to break a pattern by introducing absurdity. One member of the couple is to pretend to have the problem, and the other is to try to determine when the partner is truly exhibiting the symptom and when the partner is pretending. For example, if one partner is accused of not really listening when the other talks to him, he is given the assignment to "pretend" not to listen and his partner is to try to guess when he is pretending and when he is not. The purpose is to disrupt their fighting pattern and heighten their awareness of the problem.

Tracking and use of client language and position In structural therapy, *tracking* refers to the therapist's activity of closely listening and following the family's idioms, speech, and worldview. By traveling on this track, the therapist learns the family's peculiar "way of being." When the therapist issues a directive or makes an intervention, it will then be phrased in a way that brings out special meanings because the therapist is using the clients' own frame of reference (Colapinto, 1991).

In strategic therapy, the use of client language and "position" is similar to the structural idea of tracking. *Position* refers to the verbal and nonverbal ways a person communicates his or her idiosyncratic way of viewing the world. A couple has many shared ways of looking at things, and the strategic therapist identifies the clients' position (the couple's worldview) and uses it when developing interventions.

BRIEF THERAPY APPLIED TO COUPLES

If therapy is to end properly, it must begin properly—by negotiating a solvable problem. . . . The act of therapy begins with the way the problem is examined.
Haley, 1976, p. 9

Brief therapy has gained considerable popularity since 1990 because of its goal-oriented, direct, active, and creative techniques. It has also been encouraged by insurance companies and agencies, where working faster saves money. Because of this sudden acceptance and the "managed care revolution," a number of theoretical orientations have joined in the "rush to be brief" (Lipchik, 1994). Rational emotive, psychodynamic, emotionally focused therapy, solution-focused therapy, structural therapy, strategic therapy, neurolinguistic programming, and cognitive behavioral therapy all can now be applied as brief therapy (see Budman, 1992). The common features are that practitioners identify and work toward a focal problem with the individual, couple, or family, and the length of treatment is normally limited to 6–10 sessions.

Brief therapy was pioneered in individual therapy by several psychodynamic theorists, including Sifneos, Malan, and Davanloo. A more modern individual approach is the time-limited dynamic psychotherapy of Strupp and Binder (1984). The Brief Therapy Project at the Mental Research Institute (MRI) in Palo Alto, California, began in the late 1950s. This group, which originally included Don Jackson, John Weakland, and Jay Haley, led the way in the marriage and family therapy approach to brief work. In the background was the work of the late Dr. Milton Erickson, with whom Haley had studied. The MRI group gained notoriety for the creation of such techniques as the "paradox" and the "symptom prescription." Although the psychodynamic approach to brief therapy might have been as long as 40 or even 60 sessions, the MRI started seeing clients for a maximum of 10 sessions. At the heart of the approach is an emphasis on identifying a single problem to work on. In fact, it has been called the "problem-focused approach" to brief family therapy because the aim is to bring all of a person or family's resources to bear on overcoming the presenting complaint.

The next major effort in brief family therapy was mounted in Milwaukee by Steve de Shazer, Insoo Berg, and colleagues at the Brief Family Therapy Center (BFTC) (de Shazer, Berg, Nunnally, et al., 1986). There, the solution-oriented or solution-focused approach was developed. The BFTC was also influenced by Dr. Milton Erickson. This group of therapists proposes that too much time is spent searching for weaknesses rather than building on clients' strengths and abilities

(Friedman, 1992). Michelle Weiner-Davis and William O'Hanlon have written extensively about their work with de Shazer and have put forward their own ideas (O'Hanlon & Weiner-Davis, 1989). Weiner-Davis's 1992 book, *Divorce Busting*, has been a commercial success as a self-help book, but it also outlines the basic ideas of the Brief Family Therapy Institute. The book shows how to overcome marital problems by applying the principles that the solution-oriented group discovered and takes a strong stance against premature divorce. One of the most important concepts in solution-oriented brief therapy is helping clients find "exceptions," or times when the symptom is not present. When clients are able to identify those times, they are asked to determine how they created those exceptional events and then are directed to find a way to produce more of these exceptions.

A Comparison of MRI and BFTC in the First Session

There is an old maxim that states, "as the twig is bent, so grows the tree." This idea can also be applied to brief therapy because when time is limited, the first therapy session is vitally important and has a great impact on the direction that therapy will take (see Budman, 1992). One way to illuminate both the differences and the similarities of the two major models of brief couples therapy is to examine how each model looks at the first session.

Figure 3.3 shows a series of steps that will guide the first session for both the MRI problem-focused approach and the BFTC solution-focused approach. Step 6 in each approach is called the Formula First Session Task. This is a homework assignment asking the couple to pay attention to the relationship. In the *problem-focused approach*, the task is stated as follows:

> Between now and the next time we meet, I want you to watch closely, so you can describe to me next time, what happens in your relationship when this problem next comes up, that is, who does what before, during, and after the problem behavior. (Jordan & Quinn, 1994 , p. 5)

In the *solution-focused approach*, the homework is given in this way:

> Between now and the next time we meet, I would like you to observe, so that you can describe to me next time, what happens in your relationship that you want to continue to have happen. (de Shazer, 1985, p. 137)

Jordan and Quinn (1994) experimentally compared these two approaches to the first session. Among other differences, they found that clients were more optimistic after the first solution-focused session. This is thought to be a distinct advantage of the solution-focused over the problem-focused method because optimism and hope are considered to be powerful therapeutic factors (Young, 1992).

Definitions of Key Terms

Following are some key terms in brief therapy.

Brief Family Psychotherapy

Problem-Focused Approach   **Solution-Focused Approach**

Session 1   Session 1

PF Therapist
1. What problem brings you to therapy?
2. How is this a problem for you?
3. Which problem seems to be the hidden problem?
4. Who is most bothered by the problem?
5. Who is doing what to whom, when, and where?
6. Formula first-session task.

PROBLEM
IDENTIFICATION

SF Therapist
1. What would you like to change?
2. Who is doing what to whom, when, and where?
3. Tell me about a time that you did not have the problem or when the problem occurred less often.
4. If you went to sleep tonight, a miracle happened, and this problem were solved, what would you see tomorrow morning that would tell you there had been a miracle?
5. What would others notice different about you? How would you react differently?
6. Formula first-session task.

Session 2   Session 2

PF Therapist
1. Who did what to whom?
2. What is the smallest change that would show you this problem is improving?

GOAL
IDENTIFICATION

SF Therapist
1. Who did what to whom?
2. What is different about the time when you (are getting along, he gets a good grade, etc.)?

Figure 3.3   The unique focus of each of two theoretical orientations (problem-focused and solution-focused) when moving through the process of problem identification to problem specification

Source: From "Brief Family Psychotherapy," by K. Jordan and W. H. Quinn, *The American Journal of Family Therapy*, 22, 1, pp. 3–16. Copyright 1994 by Brunner/Mazel, Inc. Reprinted by permission.

Time-limited therapy: the number of sessions is predetermined at the outset of therapy. This limitation is designed to keep both therapist and client active. This is usually a six- or ten-session limit, but some therapists use planned single-session therapy (Hoyt, Rosenbaum, & Talmon, 1992).

Exceptions: (in solution-focused brief therapy): helping a client or couple identify times when the problem is not present. When both partners indicate that they cannot communicate, the solution-focused therapist might say, "Tell me about the times when you do communicate or have communicated well in the past." The couple is then asked to indicate what was different about those times compared to present circumstances.

Paradox: (paradoxical directives): instructions given by the therapist that are perceived initially as antithetical or contrary to the therapeutic goals but that are actually designed to achieve them. An important part of the paradox is that the therapist makes the directive seem rational or understandable to the client. For example, couples who are estranged sexually are sometimes asked to refrain from sexual contact. They are given a rationale that they need "a cooling-off period" before beginning therapy on the issue. When they break the rules, the problem is solved.

Symptom prescription: a directive to the client to enact the problem behavior in a controlled and limited form. A couple who complains of arguing could be given a homework assignment to argue for 15 minutes every night. Perhaps symptom prescription is effective in changing behavior because clients begin to realize that if they can produce the symptom at will they have the power to stop it.

Some Premises of the Theory

1. Sometimes a direct or linear method to solve a problem does not work; in those cases, an irrational method may be effective. The aim is to break up the pattern, whether the means for doing so is sensible or not. The techniques of paradox, symptom prescription, and ordeals are examples of these methods.

2. Problems may persist because of the client's problem-maintaining behaviors or those of others in the client's interpersonal world. If the problem-maintaining behaviors are eliminated, the behavior will change. For example, recently a couple came in for therapy and one of the major issues was that whenever they went out together, he dawdled when getting dressed and they were inevitably late. As he dawdled, she fumed, complained, and tried to induce him to hurry. The therapist suggested that her complaining was helping maintain the problem behavior by interfering with his ability to get ready on time. She was instructed not to "hurry" him and was instead to leave the house just in time to get to the event whether he was ready or not. By decreasing the arguing and building in a consequence, the problem diminished.

3. Changing one member of the family or couple can change the other people in the system. Segal (1991) described working with wives of men who had had heart attacks but who refused to alter their high-risk behaviors, such as smoking and overeating. Rather than continuing to cajole and struggle with their husbands, the wives were trained to disengage by doing estate and insurance planning with their husbands, as if preparing for their husband's demise. In some cases, this was enough to reinvolve the husbands in preventive and wellness behaviors.

4. The brief therapy method works well for reluctant clients. Reluctant clients might be described as individuals who are induced by some third party to enter the therapy relationship. Brief therapy requires a relatively short commitment time and does not require insight. Also, a tentative client is not asked to engage in a long-term intimate relationship with the counselor. Brief therapy is a more active approach than many others that many clients find less intrusive.

5. Brief therapy can help people at various degrees of readiness. De Shazer (1988) has identified several levels of motivation, differentiating among visitors, complainants, and customers. *Visitors* are not really committed to the therapy process and may be ambivalent about the need for help. They are unsure whether a problem exists and may be coming to soothe another person. *Complainants* are experiencing some discomfort but are not yet willing to take action. *Customers* are ready, willing, and able to take action to change their situation. (Compare this proposal to Prochaska and DiClemente's exciting work on the stages of change in the book *Changing for Good* [Prochaska, Norcross, & DiClemente, 1994].) The interesting implication for therapists is that we often make the mistake of treating everyone as a customer. When someone is a visitor, our best treatment may be education, bibliotherapy, or referral to attend a lecture or an AA meeting. Inducing clients who do not wish to commit to a demanding form of treatment reflects a misunderstanding of their current state of readiness.

6. The presenting complaint is the problem not a symptom of something deeper. One brief therapist is said to have remarked that the reason psychodynamic therapists do not treat symptoms is that they don't know how. This notion of a deeper "disease" is deeply ingrained in our culture and in the dynamic paradigm most mental health professionals have learned. Thus, their first inclination is to search for original causes of problems, rather than to deal with the client's present circumstances. Clients may be able to identify what caused their problem but are unable to see either how it is being maintained in the present or how to unravel it.

7. Therapy is over when there is a behavioral or perceptual change that reduces the client's pain to the extent that therapy is no longer desired. A "dent" in a problem is enough, as long as it is durable. In brief therapy, clients are not asked to eliminate a problem but instead are asked to overcome only a small part of it. Sometimes that is enough to begin a chain of events that leads to the resolution of other problems—the "snowball effect." As Milton Erickson said, sometimes it is enough to tip over the first domino (Rossi, 1980a).

The therapist never suggests that the problem will be totally resolved, only indicates that it will be significantly improved. The therapist may even indicate that there will be an "unresolved remnant" that the client can handle independently when therapy is over.

8. Goals should be formulated as positives rather than as the absence of something. A poorly formulated goal, according to this idea, would be "to eliminate arguing." A better goal might be stated as "the ability to resolve a problem through open discussion."

9. Marital therapy is identical to family therapy except that, normally, the therapist is dealing with a relationship between two people of the same generation (de Shazer et al., 1986).

10. Clients have resources and strengths to resolve complaints, and, when time is limited, it is best to rely on the knowledge they already have. For example, if a corporate executive is having trouble solving a problem with her husband, the therapist might ask her how she would deal with such a conflict at work, using the management training and negotiation skills she has already mastered.

11. It usually isn't necessary to know a great deal about the history or cause of a complaint in order to resolve it (O'Hanlon & Weiner-Davis, 1989). Brief therapy is a present- and future-oriented therapy. In the time available for therapy, it is more useful from the brief therapy point of view to see how the problem is being maintained and what sorts of things alleviate it.

Problems That Couples Face

Because of the constructivist philosophy that underlies brief therapy, the theory suggests that each couple's problems are unique. What is important is how the problems are perceived and construed by those who are in the relationship, rather than the diagnostic formulation of the therapist. Therefore, little effort has been made to identify standard patterns of interaction. Also, brief therapists, especially those of the solution-focused variety, are more interested in identifying patterns that work than in identifying those that are causing the problems. However, for our purposes, we have adapted some brief therapy material to answer this question.

Couples' Problems Are Actually Solutions

Let us take the example of a couple that is involved in a pattern in which one complains and the other withdraws. Brief therapy suggests that the complainer really does want to nag. He or she is trying to solve a problem in a way that has worked before. It is a little bit like the rat in the experimental "Skinner Box"; if the rules change and pushing the lever does not bring food, the rat begins obsessively pressing at a greater frequency until it is positively annoying. The same thing happens with a couple dealing with a persistent problem; one nags more as the other listens less and less. Suggestions that were once given full attention now fall on deaf ears. The person who is nagging is really trying to communicate, to share responsibility, or to make decisions, but the once-constructive behavior has grown out of proportion and has become a problem in itself. The couple persists in the pattern because the sequence previously solved the problem, and occasionally it still works.

Couples Aren't Really Resisting Change

Sometimes couples have forgotten to use what they know. They often have the resources and experiences in their own relationship to achieve a solution, but they are utilizing the most recent ways of interacting and have forgotten about more distant experiences of success. Therapists with a brief therapy orientation may remind couples of ways they solved the problem successfully in the past. Solution-oriented therapists may help couples remember times when they did get along and how they accomplished the feat.

Couples Seek a No-Risk Solution

Sometimes couples are looking for risk-free methods, even though risk is inevitable (Segal, 1991). Therapists must make clients aware of this tendency and help couples take risks to change the relationship. One example is called "Attempting to Reach Interpersonal Accord through Argument." This is a standard problem in couples therapy from the brief therapy point of view. The problem is actually a solution; the couple is trying to reach agreements but both partners are "stuck" because they are using arguing as the method to achieve it. They must seek a new solution that would involve leaving the safety of old methods.

Therapy Methods and Techniques

Brief therapy has spawned a variety of innovative interventions. Although there are many routine techniques like the Formula First Session Task, a variety of other procedures must be adapted through the therapist's creativity (Molnar & de Shazer, 1987). The two major technique categories are listed below, and a third group of minor techniques and variations are mentioned as well.

Changing the viewing   An underlying philosophy of brief therapy is constructivism. In a few words, constructivism is a belief about beliefs. It proposes that we each see the world through different spectacles. Constructivism maintains that truth is "socially constructed" and that no one has the real truth (Anderson, 1990). We do not have a "gods-eye view" of reality but only multiple versions, like the different perspectives of so many witnesses to a traffic accident.

To bring this concept down to a more concrete level, constructivism affects therapy in that everyone in a family will have a different interpretation of an event. Although all might agree that Father cried at the dinner table, the meaning of the event differs from person to person (see Cade & O'Hanlon, 1993). In brief therapy, therapists are not searching to identify the "real problem" but are trying to help clients construe the problems they have in a way that is solvable. This contrasts with rational emotive therapy (RET), which contends that problems will be alleviated when people become more realistic and scientific (closer to reality). According to RET, there is a right way and a wrong way of thinking, and the therapist's job is to seduce, induce, and persuade the client to accept the premises of the theory. Similarly, in the psychodynamic realm, analysts believe that there are remnants of the past that are the sole causes of present problems and that clients' ideas about these problems are defense mechanisms that prevent them from seeing reality.

The constructivist viewpoint behind brief therapy suggests that we can persuade clients to change their viewing of a problem in a more useful way. By so doing, we are not fooling clients into denying a problem when it exists; we are simply working from the premise that there is not one correct perspective. We are asking clients to question the meaning they have placed on the event and see whether an alternative point of view makes the problem more accessible to change.

Using the language of the future   Brief therapists have learned that clients more easily accept solvable constructions of a problem if they mesh with the client's worldview. Therefore, brief therapists use the client's language to enlist his or her acceptance of the changed perspective. Because the way we see ourselves is affected by the language we use, the therapist should utilize hopeful communications such as, "When the two of you are getting along better, what effect will that have on your children?" This "embedded question" has an underlying assumption of hope; the assumption is that eventually the two will be getting along better. Milton Erickson said that therapists "ought to expect to find solutions rather than passively accepting a decree of 'uncurable [sic].' Such an attitude of expectancy is far more conducive to our task of exploration, discovery and healing" (Rossi, 1980b, p. 202). Even if some things are unchangeable, focus on what is possible and changeable rather than on what is impossible and intractable (O'Hanlon & Weiner-Davis, 1989).

Finding exceptions   Identifying exceptions not only brings hope, it is also effective in helping couples immediately reduce the scope of a problem that might have seemed overwhelming. When the situation is framed as "we never get along," it is immediately improved when reconstrued as, "We get along best when we have spent some leisure time together." Exceptions also demonstrate to a couple that people can change. Having changed how the problem is viewed, couples are not looking for the flaws in each other but for the times when the other person is trying.

Following are two leads that therapists use to help couples find exceptions (Weiner-Davis, 1992):

Example 1: "Pay attention to the times when the two of you are getting along. What is different about those times?"

Example 2: "If you can't think of any exceptions recently, recall times in the past when you and your spouse were more satisfied. What were you doing differently?"

Changing the doing   Exceptions help couples change the viewing of a complaint, but there are also methods that brief therapists use to change the "doing" of it. These methods are sometimes called "complaint pattern interventions" and are similar to many strategic therapy interventions. Typical are paradoxical instructions, symptom prescriptions, the use of the surprise task, and so on. Milton Erickson once directed a couple who argued in the car to stop one block before they got home, switch places, and have the other drive the rest of the way; this was enough to decrease the couple's arguing. Habitual and rigid patterns maintain themselves, and when the routine is broken the strength of the pattern weakens. The main idea is to interrupt the pattern by manipulating the frequency, rate, timing, duration, or location of the problem. Couples are directed to add a new element or change the sequence. For example, an arguing couple may be asked to change the time of day they argue, where they argue, and how long they argue.

Changing the interpersonal context   According to the brief therapy theory, one of the most important elements that maintains the problem is the people in the couple's social world. When couples begin to grow, they may receive "Don't change!" messages from family and friends. It is not a conspiracy, but when couples really change, their relationship, parents, children, and other loved ones have to find a new place. For example, couples who find that they need to spend more time together to enhance their relationship may encounter extended family members' complaints that the couple visits less often.

Just as family members are forced to change when the couple grows, so is one member induced to change when the other member of a couple changes. In Alcoholics Anonymous, experienced Alanon members will testify that their own personal growth and self-esteem brought about changes in their alcoholic loved ones. One way this change can work in couples therapy is to ask one or both members to alter the way they are acting to see whether if it will produce a shift in the relationship. Here are a few techniques designed to change the interpersonal complaint-maintaining behaviors by changing the couple's reactions to each other.

1. *The Surprise Task.* Tell the couple, "Between now and next session, do one or two things that will surprise your partner. Do not say what it is. Your partner is to try to detect what it is you are doing. Don't discuss it with each other. We will talk about it in our next session."

2. *Do a 180.* Ask one member of the couple to react to the other person in a way exactly opposite to the way they normally react (Weiner-Davis, 1992). Let us say that relations are strained in a couple because the two partners disagree over childrearing. When the situation is analyzed, it turns out that he steps in and tries to mediate when his son and his wife argue. One way of dealing with the problem when more direct means of solving the problem have not been successful is to ask the husband to "do a 180"—make a 180° turn from the present course of action. The therapist can frame the suggestion as an experiment or as a test that may or may not meet with success. In this situation, the husband might be instructed to leave the house when the arguments occur. Alternately, it might be that suggested that he side with his wife in one of the arguments and examine the effect on the problem.

CONCLUSION

In this chapter, we looked at four theoretical orientations divided into two camps. The structural and strategic therapies held center stage in the early development of family therapy. Minuchin's structural approach advocates "joining" with a couple and then "kicking." *Kicking* refers to disrupting patterns, boundaries, and alignments. The strategic approach of Haley is more devoted to "pure change"; the couples therapist uses ordeals and other pattern-disrupting measures to get couples out of their persistent cycles.

Brief therapy is fast becoming the most popular way to describe the theoretical orientation of most mental health professionals. With the push from third-party payers, marriage and family therapists are also expected to work quickly to identify and treat specific problems. The Mental Research Institute pioneered many of the brief techniques in use today. The Brief Family Therapy Institute has furthered that work in developing solution-focused brief therapy. Solution-focused therapy has constructed novel and effective techniques and offers a positive approach that builds on couple strengths.

In reading through these two chapters about couples therapy theories, some students will be attracted to a particular point of view and will want to receive more training in that approach. Others will choose an integrative model that allows them to utilize the wide variety of therapy methodologies regardless of the theoretical origin of the techniques. In the next chapter, we explain our integrative model of couples therapy, which draws on common theoretical factors and allows students to choose techniques and interventions from a variety of therapy perspectives. The alternative to an integrative model like ours is to learn one particular model of therapy, such as object relations, and adapt it to the couples situation. Our decision to formulate an integrative model was not based on a discovery of some new truth. Instead, we were seeking to take what is best from existing theory and develop a useful way to train students who want to learn couples therapy. Integrative therapists are practical and seek an "open system," one that can accommodate new findings. The field of counseling and psychotherapy, and especially the specialty of marriage and family therapy, is dynamic. Whether we stay within the boundaries of a particular theoretical school or develop an integrative method of working, we must remain open to discovery and growth.

4

An Integrative Model for Couples Therapy

KEY CONCEPTS

- An integrative model draws on other theoretical positions, bringing together "what works" into a coherent system.
- The model rests on a circular notion of causality, which brings with it less emphasis on blaming one of the partners.
- Assessment of both past and present issues is considered to be a critical precursor to therapy.
- The model emphasizes the couple as a team and asks therapists to help couples find their hidden resources.
- For couples to be satisfied that change has occurred, both feelings and behaviors must be examined.
- The integrative model also addresses cognitive change in its emphasis on an evolving definition of the problem.
- Even when change has occurred, the couple must be trained to maintain the change.
- A major task for the therapist is to help the partners keep hope alive as they move through the process of therapy.
- The five-part integrative model moves from assessment to goal setting to intervention to maintenance to validation.

In the previous two chapters, we examined various theoretical orientations that help us conceptualize how change occurs. One of the premises of those chapters was that, at this stage in history, an integrative approach holds the best promise for identifying the practical steps in conducting couples therapy, and it allows the use of the most progressive methods from a number of theoretical positions.

From among many theoretical stances, the integrative therapist selects what is best but also what is practical (Young, 1992). The therapist's task is to determine what works, starting with the problems and goals presented by the unique situation, rather than applying the same theoretical approach to all clients (Young, 1992).

The challenge is to develop an approach that provides a coherent system synthesizing key concepts in an understandable and logical way. The integrative model proposed in this chapter and developed in this book is a structured method that draws from several theoretical positions. Many of the premises of the model are drawn from the traditional therapy schools discussed in Chapters 2 and 3. Some of the concepts are also derived from the Milan school of family therapy and the narrative approach, which are briefly reviewed in this chapter.

COMMON THREADS OF THE THEORIES

Thus far we have reviewed the ideas and languages of the most influential theories in couples work. Some practitioners accept the tenets of a single theory and proceed to practice in accordance with that perspective. Other therapists bring in other techniques, language, or perspectives from several theorists.

An integrative model, at its best, should blend several theoretical orientations in a coherent way. We have developed an integrative model for couples therapy that we apply throughout the remainder of the text. In developing this model, we have not included every tenet or aspect of every theory; instead, we have chosen specific aspects of these theories that we believe are compatible. In short, we have not created a new theory but have tried to bring together theoretical ideas, techniques, and clinical experience into a teachable and learnable model that can be used to structure the sometimes baffling experience of couples therapy. From the theories that we have reviewed (and a few others), we have identified the following eight building blocks or elements of our integrative approach.

A Circular Model of Causation

A basic premise of our model is a circular or recursive process of assessment, treatment planning, and therapeutic intervention. This idea of circularity is consistent with "systems thinking," which characterizes nearly all of the mainstream approaches to marriage and family therapy. *Circular* and *recursive* are two words used to mean that the interactive patterns of the relationship form a type of feedback-loop response system. Instead of a linear cause-and-effect view, where A impacts B and causes C, the recursive viewpoint emphasizes mutual causation of events (Landis & Young, 1994). Thus, each individual influences, and in turn is influenced by, another individual in a circular pattern: "A may cause B, but B also affects A and C and so on" (Goldenberg & Goldenberg, 1985, p. 96). Like gears in a clock, the behaviors of each person affect the functioning of the other and the relationships they have (Young, 1992). Crises, the environment, organizations, and other individuals outside the relationship also have a significant impact on the couple.

Circularity when applied to couples therapy implies that the therapist focuses on the interactions of the relationship and how the couple is affected by the continual action and reaction of each partner. For example, Roberto is not the sole cause of Marta's depression. Instead, Roberto plays basketball while Marta spends time with her mother. Roberto is angry, and Marta is hurt that Roberto is not available. Roberto states that they do not have intimate time together, and Marta expresses feelings of rejection that he does not want to be with her. All of the beliefs, behaviors, and feelings of each member are interacting factors in the problem.

Circular Questioning

Based on the premise of circular causation, circular questions are queries the therapist makes that are derived from circular thinking. Instead of asking the question, "How did the fight start?" (a linear question), the therapist asks questions that remind the couple of mutual causality, such as "What effect does fighting have on your relationship?" The question may influence the partners to examine arguing in the context of the way they relate to each other, rather than, "Who started the fight?" (Methods for using circular questioning are described in Chapter 6.)

These questions may also serve an assessment function for the therapist, who can gain information about the couple's interactions (Tomm, 1984a). The concept of circularity and circular questioning has been widely embraced in relationship therapy (Hoffmann, 1981; Keeney, 1983, 1985; Papp, 1983; Tomm, 1984a, 1984b). Sometimes just an awareness of the reciprocal relationship of behaviors may promote spontaneous change (Penn, 1982; Pallazolli, Selvini, et al., 1980; Tomm, 1984b). This awareness can allow the couple to develop a new perspective on old problems, which can lead to rapid change. When couples begin to view the problem as a relationship problem, they may better understand the need for mutual change and feel a freedom from criticism and guilt.

Blame Is Not a Useful Concept

An important starting point for the integrative model is based on the observation that each member of the couple starts with different, often contradictory, ideas about the problems in the relationship. These ideas frequently include a projection of blame on the other partner (Kottler, 1994). A principal goal of therapy is to foster a sense of mutual responsibility for the problem and mutual contribution to the solution.

We blame others to avoid our own guilt and responsibility. Although it might be self-protective to blame one's partner, it also produces a high degree of helplessness for the blamer. There is no sense of responsibility for creating a solution. We believe that a primary task of couples therapy is to define the problem "interactionally" so that there is emphasis on the reciprocal or shared nature of the relationship. The aim is to help both partners feel empowered to resolve the problems in the relationship.

Unfortunately, couples spend a great deal of time in their private lives and in the early stages of therapy using a linear approach to solving their joint problems—trying to determine who caused the problem and who is to blame. From the very beginning in the integrative model, the couple is shown that just as it "takes two to tango," it takes two to solve problems.

The Therapist's Neutrality

Neutrality is a one of the key concepts of the Milan school of family therapy. *Neutrality* means that the therapist maintains a nonjudgmental view of the problem and does not ally with either partner. It is an essential element of therapy that enables the couple to develop an objective, interactional view of the problem, rather than a blaming, critical stance. For example, if John and Alan are each blaming the other for the lack of time they devote to the relationship, the therapist would refuse to take a side but would instead help the couple examine how each can contribute to the solution.

There are, of course, some cautions to expressing neutrality when dealing with issues of domestic violence. Neutrality does not mean that the therapist either fails to take a stand against damaging behavior perpetuated by one partner or asks the couple to share the blame for the problem. Couples therapy cannot really proceed until all abuse has ceased. Couples may come to therapy to deal with later feelings of resentment and relationship-building activities, but battering, like substance abuse and a mental disorder, has to be treated as an individual problem first.

Assessment Is a Crucial First Activity

Assessment involves (1) a statement of the problem from each person's point of view, (2) an examination of family historical influences, (3) the couple's developmental stage, and (4) a review of attempted past solutions. Both Bowenian and object-relations theory recommend looking at past relationships so that both partners can recognize that they have inherited ways of interacting that may not be appropriate to the current situation. In this text, we recommend using a genogram to obtain this background information and as a quick screening instrument.

Brief therapy suggests examining what has and has not worked in the past. If we have been successful in solving a similar problem, why not implement those strategies again? Strategic therapy and behavior therapy are most concerned with looking at problem-maintaining behaviors, recognizing that problems serve a purpose. In this integrative model, we recommend assessing both past influences and present patterns to help attack the presenting problem.

The Couple Must Form a Team

The narrative approach has given new life to the idea of externalizing problems, and this approach works especially well in couples and family therapy where family or couple cohesiveness is required. *Externalizing* means that the partners learn to attack a problem together, rather than looking for the flaw in the other person. In this sense, externalizing can be seen as an outgrowth of nonblaming circular thinking (White & Epston, 1990).

Central to the team concept in our integrative model is the notion that the couple should inventory their assets as individuals and couples and recognize how these assets can be used to solve problems. This change in thinking is based on the Milan school's notion of "positive connotation" or the concept of reframing promoted by the strategic therapists. Couples are asked to see differences in their abilities and personalities as strengths in the relationship. Couples must then see that the solution to their problems lies in pooling all of their varied resources.

Both Feelings and Behaviors Must Be Changed

Most therapists would agree that behavioral change is part of what we mean by lasting change. This is a central tenet of the behavioral school, but the brief therapy and strategic therapy schools also recommend dealing with presenting problems, which are often behavioral in nature.

Affective change, or change in feeling, is also critically important to couples. Couples come to therapy wanting to feel intimacy, happiness with each other, companionship, and romance—the crucial "intangibles" of couplehood. Therapists should consider positive feeling states not as luxuries but as necessities. Couples may not believe that therapy is complete until these positive feelings have returned.

Couples Must Learn Maintenance Tasks

The behaviorists tell us that old learning is stronger than newly acquired skills. In a pinch, we are most likely to revert to old patterns unless our new behaviors are rewarded. A couple's exhilaration at dealing with a difficult problem can plummet when the first argument occurs and the partners believe that they are "back to square one." Cognitive therapy calls this "black or white" or "all or nothing" thinking. Couples must be challenged to see the progress they have made and not overemphasize minor setbacks.

Couples Must Develop Solvable Problems

For the integrative model to work, the premises must mesh and form a rational whole. As we see it, the "whole" or organizing idea is a constructivist one—that each couple comes to therapy with a perspective or construction about the relationship and its problems. The therapist's job is to guide the couple to redefine each individual's problems, not as a dissatisfaction with the other person but as a joint work project. Then the therapist helps the partners envision the problem as external to themselves and as a problem they can jointly attack. Finally, the couple is challenged to view the problem as significantly resolved yet needing continuing maintenance to prevent its return. This model suggests that, because each couple is unique, the methods and techniques used to achieve these redefining tasks will vary. The hallmark of the integrative model is that it is not wedded to a few theoretically prescribed techniques.

Therapists Must Foster Hope

Writers from Bowenian to solution-focused theories have underscored the significance of overcoming demoralization when working with couples. In our model, we see it as important initially to keep the couple in therapy. Our model builds on a nonblaming idea that helps couples overcome their negative ideas about each other. At stage 2, couples are asked to set goals. Goal setting itself gives the couple a feeling that the overwhelming problem has been identified and mapped into solvable pieces. Finally, at the end of therapy, couples are challenged to develop realistic views about change, celebrate their successes, generalize them to other problems, and congratulate each other.

AN INTEGRATIVE MODEL FOR COUPLES THERAPY

Figure 4.1 is a graphical representation of the five-part integrative model of couples therapy. The stages are sequential, and normally therapy proceeds from assessment to validation. At the center of the model is the couple's changing view of the problem. As therapy proceeds, this view becomes modified through interactions with the therapist and with each other.

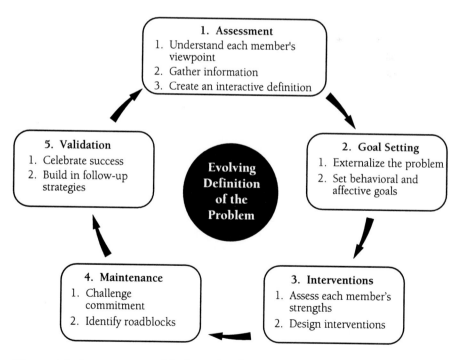

Figure 4.1 Integrative model of couples therapy

Stage 1: Assessment—"We Have a Problem!"

Understanding Each Member's Viewpoint

The initial phase of most therapy approaches is devoted to compiling the history of the couple and of the individuals and carefully formulating a description of the symptoms that led the couple to seek treatment. The therapist asks each partner to define the problem and then explores with both partners the origin of some of their ideas and the ways that they act on these ideas in their current relationship. Next, the therapist explores each person's viewpoint with an eye to combining them in an "interactive definition of the problem."

As we've mentioned before, one way to begin the assessment process is by the use of a genogram (see Chapter 6). Although there are many other assessment tools, the genogram is a quick, interactive means of understanding both past and present influences. Couples learn from the genogram, and they interact with each other as the family patterns are revealed. The couple can see how their historical, cultural, and family roots intersect and sometimes clash.

It is important also to examine solutions that have not worked for the couple in the past so that repeats of unsuccessful attempts are minimized. Attempted solutions usually have been based on what worked in partners' families of origin or what worked for them in prior stages of their relationship.

Creating an Interactive Definition of the Problem

After the therapist has obtained data from both partners' genograms and has explored attempted solutions, an interactive definition of the problem can be formulated and offered to the couple. Let us look at a brief example. Sam and Rachel have difficulty when they argue. They admit that she attacks and uses name-calling when she gets mad, and he sulks and won't talk to her for several days. In the first session, when they were asked to describe the problem, they each complained about the other person's behavior during arguments and described each other with terms like *immature* and *punitive*.

Using the genogram, the couple was able to discuss the fact that Sam's family did not openly express anger, whereas Rachel's family arguments were ways for the family to ventilate. Both believed they did not have a good model for resolving difficulties in their families of origin; one family kept everything hidden, and the other exploded but did not solve problems constructively.

When Sam and Rachel were asked about ways they had tried to solve the problem previously, they admitted that they had never seriously attempted to openly disagree with each other and try to compromise. Instead, they had waited for things to cool off, apologized, and forgot about it until the next fight. Unfortunately, fights were becoming more frequent. Through the use of the genogram, the couple identified the problem as "We don't know how to disagree"—a first attempt at an interactional definition of the problem. The phrase that summarizes the first stage of therapy and moves the couple from blaming to an interactional definition is, "*We* have a problem."

Summary of Stage 1

In summary, steps to be followed in this stage are:

Step 1: Obtain each person's definition of the problem

Step 2: Gather historical information and current behaviors and feelings

Step 3: Create a shared, interactive definition of the problem based on the information the partners have provided from their personal perspectives and other assessment procedures

Stage 2: Goal Setting—"We Have a Common Goal"

In this stage, each partner identifies the desired outcome of therapy. In other words, each is asked to decide what would be different if the problem no longer existed, to imagine life without the problem. The purpose of this stage, beyond focusing the troubled couple on a hopeful scenario, is to help transform a problem statement into a goal. One of the steps in this direction is to externalize the problem so that blame is decreased and the couple can work together. Next, therapists help clients start thinking about the problem as a goal. Finally, the couple is able to identify behavioral and affective aspects of the goal and set clear and concrete targets.

Externalizing the Problem

Externalizing means helping the couple think about the problem as separate from themselves; this puts both partners on the same team. This externalizing approach has been pioneered by Australian Michael White (1989) and is part of a narrative approach to couples therapy. The therapist begins to talk about the problem as if it is a force keeping the partners apart. Soon, couples begin to talk about the "arguing problem," "the money monster," or "the in-law dilemma." As partners externalize the problem, they can move closer together in order to conquer it. The problem can then recede in its position of importance in the relationship, and realistic goals can be set.

This notion has appeared in Japanese tradition as Kani Mushi (Tomm, 1991) and is based on the folk idea that a worm gets inside and causes the misbehavior of a mischievous child. Because it is the unacceptable behavior that is criticized, rather than the person who exhibits it, the child can retain a positive self-image and freedom from blame. In therapy, this method does not prevent people from taking personal responsibility for their actions, but it provides them with an explanation for their behavior that they can change readily by "conquering" the problem. In the examples that follow, the therapist attempts to lead the clients to externalize the problem and set a goal.

Example 1: "We have discovered that arguing over minor and unimportant issues is a concern. Can you tell me about some ways that arguing interferes with your goal of spending more time together?"

Example 2: What we have decided is that the two of you have a pattern where Nela gets jealous and Clayton's reaction is to distance himself further. The result is a cycle of increasing jealousy and resentment. What might the two of you do together to attack this jealousy-resentment cycle?"

Setting Behavioral and Affective Goals

A problem is a set of symptoms, and a goal is a vision of progress to be made. Both goals and problems are revisited throughout the therapy process. Just as the board of trustees in a company must deal with problems in production, the couple must try to solve difficulties that arise that hinder everyday functioning. But the exciting thing about managing a business is moving the company to produce a greater profit or create new products through research and development. The emphasis on goals in a couple's relationship reawakens interest in what the relationship could be and helps counterbalance the chore of dealing with problems. Very often couples get stuck on "What is wrong with our relationship?" and the relationship begins to take on a negative valence. At this juncture, the partners are asked to examine "how we would like our relationship to be."

In couples therapy, goal setting must be defined interactionally—as a shared problem. Our approach is to ask that partners identify both *behavioral* and *affective* changes they would like to see and then state them in simple and concrete terms. When such goals are defined, both members have a clear notion of what they are trying to achieve. This can counteract the hopelessness and frustration that brought them to the therapy relationship.

Here are some examples of how couples can transform problems to goals with behavioral and affective components:

> *Example 1:* "We will complete a new budget together by next week (behavioral) so that we can feel more competent (affective) as a couple and be more responsible with our finances."
>
> *Example 2:* "We will spend one night a week going out to dinner and taking a walk (behavioral) so we will feel closer to each other (affective) and have more fun in the relationship."

Most therapists believe that substantial and long-lasting change is established when corrections occur in all three areas of human functioning: the affective (emotional), the behavioral, *and* the cognitive realms. So you may be asking yourself, what about cognitive or perceptual changes? Is it not important that the couple change in their thinking and perceptions about the relationship as well? We agree that changing clients' thinking and perceptions of the relationship can be useful, but couples who come for therapy are anxious to see concrete changes. More action and less talk appears to be the first order of business. Many therapists find that perceptions change most substantially when they are accompanied by solid changes in behaviors and feelings. In Example 2 above, by spending more time together, the couple eventually begins to view the relationship more positively. In addition, our model addresses cognitive or perceptual changes directly by a constant focus on asking the couple to view the problem and the goal differently at each stage of therapy. By the end of Stage 2, the couple has moved temporarily from "We have a problem" to "We have a goal."

Summary of Stage 2

In this stage, couples are asked to change their view of the problem by:

Step 1: Externalizing the problem
Step 2: Setting behavioral and affective goals

Stage 3: Interventions—"We Have a Solvable Problem"

In this stage, two activities go hand in hand: identifying individual and couple strengths and designing interventions. First let's look at how therapists help couples benefit from an appraisal of strengths. By searching for and identifying the positive assets of each partner and how those assets have been helpful in similar situations in the past, the partners are able to view each other and the situation more positively. In addition, the therapist gets the couple to consider their joint assets. What strengths do they have as a couple? What issues have they successfully mastered that could help them in the current situation?

Identifying Strengths

The therapist may facilitate the exploration of the couple's attachment, love, nurturing, and intimacy by having the couple tell stories from past and present events.

Example 1: "How did the two of you become attracted to each other?"
Example 2: "Describe some of the most romantic times of your relationship."
Example 3: "In the story you told about how you met, what were the strengths in Jonah that you admired most?"

The couple can adapt the positive attributes from these stories for future possibilities and new outcomes. This intervention strengthens hope, a keystone of this therapeutic model. With the partners' more respectful and positive view of each other and a clearer idea of desired outcomes, the couple is able to continue to eliminate blame around the problem. The partners generate specific and concrete possibilities for the relationship as they shift from reminiscing and storytelling to a specific here-and-now plan for change.

In short, identifying the positive attributes of the relationship and its past is not only a tactic to encourage the couple, it is also a real "nuts and bolts" technique to identify who will be responsible for which changes. It evokes the best qualities of each. For example, Lela and Tim might move from a story about their ability to be romantic with each other before the children were born to a romantic picture of how it might be when the children are grown. Then they can bring the romantic notion to the here-and-now by exploring possibilities for honeymooning once a month while the children are cared for by the grandparents. They must describe exactly what they expect from each other based on the identified strengths they have attributed to each other. In this case, they must decide how they will set aside the time together, who will arrange it, who will arrange child care, and what kinds of plans they can make for spending time together.

Designing Interventions

Designing interventions is an activity calling on the therapist's expertise in selecting methods and techniques to deal with the couple's issues. During Stage 3, the therapist becomes active using techniques to help clients reach their goals, and identifying client strengths helps determine which interventions will be most effective. In Chapters 2 and 3, a number of techniques associated with the major therapies were described. Some of those covered in later chapters include:

Communication training
Use of rituals
Couples group therapy
Divorce mediation
Increasing intimacy
Referral for substance abuse treatment
Referral for sex therapy
Reframing

Summary of Stage 3

By the completion of Stage 3, couples have:

Step 1: Made shifts in behaviors, feelings, and perceptions about the relationship and each other
Step 2: Identified positive features of each other and the relationship
Step 3: Experienced successes based on the outcomes of therapeutic interventions

Stage 4: Maintenance—"We Have a Solution"

Challenging Commitment

In Stage 3, therapist interventions are designed to create movement and promote changes in the couple's relationship. Now, in Stage 4, a new set of tools is needed to keep couples from backsliding and to nurture the nascent changes that are underway. This may be one of the most critical stages in the couple's progress, because positive changes may easily be ignored when minor relapses occur. If change falters, the therapist must challenge the participants about their long-term commitment to growth. One of the ways that therapists challenge is to pose questions that ask the couple to restate commitment to the goals of therapy.

Example 1: "How big a part of you is willing to do this differently?"
Example 2: "How will the two of you keep yourselves motivated to continue to work on this problem?"
Example 3: "What will you each have to do to make the changes continue?"

Identifying Roadblocks and Pitfalls

To establish a viable maintenance strategy, the couple also must focus on the roadblocks or barriers that could sabotage change in the relationship. Once the barriers are identified, plans to prevent them from influencing the change and ways to support maintaining the change are outlined. Focusing on roadblocks or barriers has somewhat the same effect as the Adlerian technique of "spitting in the soup." When the therapist predicts relapses and "slipping," the couple will not be discouraged if there is a ready-made plan to implement. The questions the therapist asks are sometimes directed to an individual member of the couple and sometimes directed to the couple as a unit:

Example 1: "What will get in the way of your keeping up the changes?"

Example 2: "What can you do when your boss puts pressure on you to work overtime?"

Example 3: "How will the two of you handle it when Bill's mother comes to stay for the month?"

Example 4: "At various points, you are going to feel like criticizing Marie even though it is not necessary or requested. How will you handle those feelings so that you don't slip back into that old behavior?"

Summary of Stage 4

This is a critical stage in couples therapy, where the therapist utilizes any and all methods to help couples recommit to the change process. Among the easiest methods to employ are challenging questions and questions that normalize minor relapses while helping couples identify common roadblocks and pitfalls. By the completion of Stage 4, the couple has:

Step 1: Identified barriers that may impede continued growth and change

Step 2: Recommitted to the change process

Stage 5: Validation—"There Is No Problem"

Celebrating Success

Stage 5 is a time for celebration. Couples compare the goals set at Stage 2 with the current state of the relationship. Individuals must validate themselves and their partners for their success in conquering the problem as a team and for enacting new, positive behaviors. Here, the therapist underscores the importance of using maintenance strategies outside of therapy to "keep the ball rolling."

Building in Follow-up Strategies

At this stage, couples may lack confidence in their ability to handle things on their own, and the therapist's faith and conviction make the transition toward termination less difficult. Some couples will complain that the problem is not entirely eliminated. Although this may be true, sometimes it is also a symptom of anxiety at the prospect of functioning without the support of therapy. A long-term maintenance plan with the couple can include periodic visits with the therapist at 3-month and then 6-month intervals. Listed below are some therapist statements that help validate the couple's success. Even more important is asking the partners to validate their own achievements.

Example 1: "It is important to congratulate yourselves on the budget you created and followed for the past two months. It sounds like you have created more confidence in your competence as financial planners together."

Example 2: "Lee, tell Jiang what has been the most fun for you since you have been going out to dinner and taking walks together."

Summary of Stage 5

By the end of Stage 5, the couple has:

Step 1: Identified the problem as a solution

Step 2: Generalized the step-by-step approach for problem solving as a new challenge in the future

Step 3: Congratulated themselves and each other on their success

Getting Stuck

If at any time the couple gets stuck or is unclear about the direction of therapy during the therapeutic process, it may be important to return to an earlier stage of therapy. In fact, this is more the rule than the exception. One of the common reasons for reverting is that the problem the couple initially presented may have to be discarded when a more significant problem is revealed as the root of the difficulties. Reidentifying the goals or even going back to assessment issues may be necessary before proceeding to interventions.

The integrative model in Figure 4.2 graphically depicts the stages in the couple's perception of the focal problem. Moving backward means reevaluating the

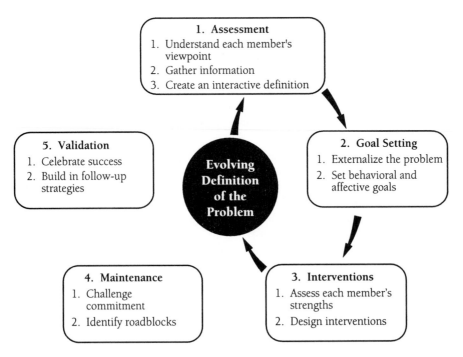

Figure 4.2 Returning to an earlier stage of therapy

problem or goal. The therapist must evaluate the couple's view of the problem at the center of the chart and then select the lower stage appropriate to the couple's needs. For example, the couple may have reached the stage of Intervention, where each is asked to look at the other partner's assets and positive attributes. Suddenly they have great difficulty in identifying these assets in each other and become negative about their relationship. Actually, they are still harboring feelings of resentment and blame, which characterizes the initial stage. The model suggests that the therapist should be flexible enough to shift gears and return to Stage 1 (Assessment). The therapist might then do a more complete inventory of the couple's issues and help the couple sort out these feelings before moving on. This "downshifting" is shown in Figure 4.2 by an arrow that travels from Intervention to the Problem Definition Stage at the center of the figure, and then back to the Assessment stage. From there, the sequence of treatment resumes its course around the perimeter of the circle. The clue or key for the therapeutic decision to return to Assessment (Stage 1) is that the couple's view of the problem has not matured enough to initiate the activities required by the Intervention stage of therapy.

"Downshifting" to an earlier stage of therapy should not be thought of as a failure, nor should discouragement be transmitted to the couple. Experience will demonstrate that all couples travel at different rates, depending on the nature of their difficulties and on the unique qualities they bring to therapy.

CONCLUSION

The integrative model is a synthesis of aspects of various theoretical perspectives with eight basic premises drawn from various schools of thought. The model provides a map for the therapist to identify the stages and steps for moving a couple from "He or she is the problem" to "There is no problem." The constructivist philosophy behind this model presumes that, as couples make behavioral and affective changes, their thinking about the problem changes.

One of the questions you may be asking is, "Must I use the integrative model to benefit from this book?" Certainly not. Although the integrative model is used in later chapters, it is mainly used to show the progression of therapy in case examples. The model is a guideline for practice but not the only guideline. Because this is an integrative approach, the book contains a wealth of methods and techniques and a synthesis of research on treatment of special couple problems.

5

The Assessment of Couples and Their Problems

KEY CONCEPTS

- Assessment is not a one-time project but an ongoing process in couples therapy. It is interwoven with treatment and is vital to achieving successful outcomes.
- We bring our own biases, assumptions, theories, and prejudices to the assessment task.
- Assessment is like a funnel with a wide variety of information pouring in and being squeezed by our constructions into useful packages that we call diagnoses or problems.
- We can choose to assess both members of the couple, the problems in their relationship, or the overall quality of the relationship.
- The integrative therapist casts a wide net, using as many sources of data as possible.
- A key assessment method for the couples therapist is the use of the interview.
- The genogram is an important assessment tool that, along with the interview, provides important historical data and information about the present family structure.
- There are a number of available assessment tools including standardized tests and semi-structured methods like imagery that can be added to the couples therapist's repertoire.

Too often we map our clients' prison, but not their escape.
Waters & Lawrence, 1993, p. 53

A course on evaluation and assessment is almost always one of the most unpopular courses in a therapist's academic training. Counselors and therapists who see couples and families seem to be even more put off by the psychological tests than other helping professionals are. A major problem is that many measurement devices seem to label *individuals* and do very little to help with the problems presented by a couple or a family. This skepticism about testing does not mean that couples therapy does not need an assessment component, however. If you begin treatment without an assessment, you are saying that all clients will benefit from the same treatment; in a way, you are supposing that all clients are the same. Those who emphasize assessment believe that differences are important.

Assessment is the way we ferret out what is unique in each individual, couple, or family so that we may apply the appropriate treatment, and an integrative model is consistent with this philosophy of difference and diversity. We believe that couples therapists must adapt to the clients' attributes, rather than forcing clients to adapt to the treatment regime. Clients differ on the basis of history, culture, adherence to traditional gender roles, readiness for treatment, and any number of factors that could seriously affect the treatment selected. Similarly, each couple is different and deserves the time that a comprehensive assessment takes.

Assessment Is an Ongoing Process

As the integrative model points out (see Figure 4.1), assessment is the first step in the therapy process (see also Ivey & Mathews, 1986). Unfortunately, a two-dimensional model like this one cannot adequately represent the fact that assessment is *not* a one-time activity of the therapist. Assessment is an ongoing process beginning with the first telephone contact, the first sight of the client, and probably the initial seconds of the first in-person encounter. We often gather important information in later sessions when clients feel more trusting and open up more.

Although assessment is continuous, there are two important points where it is critical. The first point is at initial *screening*, where the therapist is attempting to rule out serious problems such as psychosis, substance abuse, and physical violence. Following this assessment, the therapist decides whether couples therapy is appropriate or whether individual therapy, hospitalization, or some other specialized treatment might be more effective. It is through this assessment that the therapist becomes aware of the most important issues facing the couple. The second critical point for assessment in couples therapy occurs when couples therapy has been decided on and the couple has negotiated a goal statement with the therapist. Although several issues may have come to the surface in the screening aspect of assessment, once a primary or focal issue has been selected, other areas are put aside for the moment and the therapist makes a more intense scrutiny of a single issue or two. To use a metaphor, initial *screening* is like using binoculars to scan the whole horizon. But once a particular are has been selected, we engage in a more minute process of *problem assessment* that could be compared to using a microscope.

ARE ASSESSMENT AND TREATMENT REALLY SEPARATE?

To complicate things a bit further, assessment and treatment are not as separate as we like to pretend. Although it is useful in the integrative model to identify these as separate steps, in practice, assessment methods have therapeutic effects. If you ask members of a couple to write down every time they make disparaging comments about their partner during the day (assessment task), researchers tell us that couples will make fewer such remarks to each other as they become aware of what they are doing (treatment). Conversely, treatment itself often becomes assessment. Let us say we give a couple the homework assignment to read to each other nightly from a certain self-help book about marriage. When the clients return to the next session, we find that they have not done the assignment; instead, they present us with a journal of the issues they fought about during the past week. We have learned (assessed) something about the couple's response to therapist-initiated directives and what the couple sees as major problems, and perhaps we have discovered that they enjoy certain kinds of homework assignments.

To take this point about the intertwining of assessment and treatment a step further, we find that many assessment devices, such as the family genogram, are both assessment tools and intervention methods. Recall that the genogram is a pictorial representation of the client's family tree that maps out the relationships between family members. Recently, we conducted a workshop, and one of the participants revealed that she had come from an alcoholic family. At age 30, she sought individual therapy for some personal problems. During the initial session, a genogram was used and the client was able to identify long-standing problems and issues in the family and to understand something about the history of her own difficulties. She was able to relate this information to her current interpersonal problems and, after this single session, believed that she no longer needed the assistance of a therapist. Although we are not advocating one-session therapy for everyone, this client's experience suggests that assessment devices can bring about "Aha!" experiences for some individuals and couples. Similarly, Gordon (1986) reports the effectiveness of using a "dispassionate assessment" to allow couples who are contemplating divorce to reconsider couples therapy.

In light of this discussion, should we conclude that couples therapists need to become less skeptical of paper-and-pencil tests and embrace the measures of psychopathology embedded in these tools? Our answer is "No." Most standard psychological measures aimed at individuals are not worth the time when working with couples in the *problem assessment phase*. It is prudent to employ certain standardized screening tools to identify major mental disorders, substance abuse, and other issues that should be treated prior to couples therapy.

We hope that the reader will consider assessment to be a crucial and indispensable activity of the therapist. We have suggested that assessment with couples has two major parts, an initial screening and a more careful look at the particular problem. Second, we have suggested that assessment is more than testing. The therapist's interview, observations, and questions are part of the assessment process and sharpen the picture of the couple's issues throughout the therapy process. Finally, assessment can be valuable as a treatment tool as well. It can help couples become aware of positive and negative aspects of their functioning that they have ignored or that have become habituated. Although it is understandable that many marriage and family therapists have rejected traditional assessment techniques, let us not "throw the baby out with the bathwater." We need to keep an open mind to assessment methods that lead our clients to greater awareness and help us as therapists make good treatment decisions.

BIASES AND ASSUMPTIONS IN ASSESSMENT

When therapists begin a therapy relationship, they bring their own history, assumptions, biases, and prejudices with them. Mayer (1989) points out that these assumptions, biases, and prejudices affect the therapy process from the very beginning, including the assessment phase.

In addition to harboring personal biases, therapists adopt theories with built-in assumptions about human nature. If one believes that the couple's relationship is improved by treating each individual's intrapsychic conflicts, the Minnesota Multi-phasic Personality Inventory (MMPI) might be administered to both members, and the resulting data would become the basis for one or two individual therapies. If a therapist believes that all couples' problems are the result of attitudes and learning from the family of origin, constructing a genogram or family history will be the first order of business. Liddle (1983) compared various systems of family therapy on the basis of their diagnostic/assessment approaches. He points out that the assessment function is the point where theoretical systems begin to differentiate themselves. Following is a summary based on Liddle's look at the issues that various theories identify in the assessment phase.

1. The Bowen theory assesses issues such as:
   a. the family's level of anxiety and emotionality
   b. the differentiation of each person from the family
   c. the general coping ability of family members of the past three generations
2. Structural theory (Minuchin) focuses on:
   a. the organization of family rules, boundaries, alliances, and subsystems
   b. the family life cycle
   c. a search for strengths
3. Strategic theory (Haley) is concerned mainly with:
   a. the presenting problem
   b. the family life cycle
   c. specific sequences of interaction
4. Brief therapy (MRI) looks primarily at:
   a. presenting symptoms, not history
   b. observable interactions
   c. symptoms as the result of failed problem solving
   d. life's transition points
   e. communication levels, rules, and congruency

So assessment is not free of one's biases, theories, or assumptions about human nature. Besides thinking about the various theories and their perspectives on couple problems, it is important for therapists to examine their own intrinsic theories to see whether they promote a productive viewpoint or are merely "baggage." In Figure 5.1, the funnel of assessment, the diagram depicts how information obtained during assessment is filtered through our personal "lenses" that affect our diagnoses or hypotheses about a couple's problems. The following series of questions might stimulate your thinking about some of the lenses or attitudes that you bring to couples therapy. Answer by writing True, False, or Not Sure next to the question, and then explain your answer underneath. You may wish to discuss your answers with fellow learners. In your discussion, list the implications for *assessment* that arise from each statement.

Self-Assessment of Assumptions about Couples

1. If each individual is happy and self-sufficient, the relationship will be a good one. _____

2. An interracial marriage is "asking for trouble." _____

3. Most trouble in couples is due to irrational ideas or dysfunctional belief systems that clients have learned. _____

4. Most couples' problems can be treated by tracking down their roots in the family of origin. _____

5. Good couples relationships are made up of two people who are very similar. _____

6. Marriage is a sacrament and not just a legal contract; therefore, one must understand the spiritual dimension in order to help a troubled relationship. _____

7. Most couples' problems can be solved by better communication. _____

8. An "open marriage," where the couple agrees to have other intimate and even sexual relationships while remaining married, is a workable arrangement for some people. _____

9. To have a healthy relationship, partners must have an equitable or "peer commitment." _____

10. Some marriages are so troubled that a therapist should recommend divorce. _____

There are no easy or correct answers to these questions. The purpose of the exercise is to make you aware of biases that you may carry with you. How can we ever escape from them? The answer is that we probably cannot really step outside of our conceptual frameworks. We cannot truly be objective (Crosby, 1991), but we may learn to become aware of when our prejudices are affecting our actions. Here we hit upon the major problem with prejudices: we often do not know we have them. So, at the very minimum, we should become aware of our attitudes and biases by examining our own history and present belief systems. We can do this by receiving personal therapy, having good supervision, or even entering a relationship enhancement seminar with a partner. This blindness to our own point of view is the reason many therapists continue to seek supervision from a trained supervisor periodically throughout their professional lives.

ASSESSMENT USING THE INTEGRATIVE MODEL

The Funnel of Assessment

Figure 5.1 shows a funnel with information flowing from a variety of sources. Among these potential sources in couples therapy are:

1. Observations the therapist makes based on the couple's spontaneous interaction or during interactions the therapist introduces.
2. Questionnaires completed by the couple outside of the session.
3. The couple's reports regarding their behavior outside of the session.
4. Historical data from the genogram or from client histories.
5. Reports from other sources, such as family members, the courts, or police reports.
6. The results of paper-and-pencil testing.

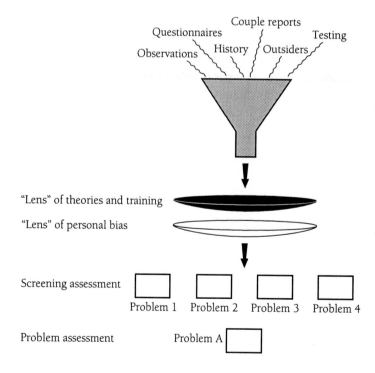

Figure 5.1 The funnel of assessment

In the next chapter, we will look at how assessment and goal setting are linked. For now, we will consider assessment as a separate enterprise during which the therapist keeps an open mind to all information flowing in and searches to gain the most complete picture of the couple's total functioning.

DIRECTIONS FOR ASSESSMENT: INDIVIDUALS, PROBLEMS, AND THE QUALITY OF THE RELATIONSHIP

Assessing Individuals

Why must we even think about the individuals if we are treating a couple? The answer is that sometimes one member's problems can be treated individually, leading to better couple functioning. Also, some unresolved personal problems can undermine the therapist's efforts with the couple. For example, a couple came into our office because of a crisis centering around the husband's infidelity. We immediately began to help the couple deal with the crisis in the relationship, trying to repair the damaged trust and support each individual. During the initial session, the wife appeared very depressed and our attention turned to her to determine the depth of her distress. The session immediately changed when it was determined that she needed to be hospitalized to prevent her from following through her planned suicide. We did not return to couples therapy for several months until the depression was under control. So, before we can successfully treat a couple, we need to determine if each individual is healthy enough to engage in the process. Specifically, individuals need to be screened for the following three major impediments.

1. Is there a safety risk? Is either one of the partners suicidal or suffering from bulimia, anorexia, or other life-endangering disorder? In addition, does the possibility of violence in the relationship exist? Rosenbaum and O'Leary (1986) suggest that interviews be conducted individually whenever violence is suspected. This allows for more open disclosure about the presence and degree of danger.
2. Is the client psychotic, severely disturbed, and unable to distinguish between delusions and reality? Is one of the partners suffering from some other major mental disorder, such as agoraphobia or bipolar disorder, that will strongly influence the effectiveness of couples therapy?
3. Is the client under the influence of drugs and alcohol to the extent that progress in the couple's relationship will be limited? Lukas (1993) recommends that the therapist ask about substance abuse in every intake session.

Although the prospect of physical danger and the presence of psychotic problems clearly must be brought under control before couples therapy begins, the issue of alcohol and drug abuse is less cut and dried. The usual "rule of thumb" is to address this issue during the first interview or by questionnaire, and then refer the individual for addictions treatment before even beginning couples therapy. It is difficult though to distinguish between those individuals who must go through treatment and those who maintain their lifestyle despite so-called "recreational use" of drugs and alcohol.

Recently we treated a couple who had reconciled after a long separation. The husband admitted to a history of drug and alcohol abuse, but we were told that he was no longer abusing these substances. We suggested that he attend AA and that she continue with Alanon. Although she did attend Alanon, he refused to participate in AA. The couple was successful in reuniting and clearing up many of the bad feelings from the past, but it soon became clear that he was smoking marijuana on a daily basis after work. He did not believe that it was a problem, but it was definitely affecting the relationship. He began to lose interest in couples therapy and in many of the maintenance behaviors that were suggested. Consequently, the relationship began to stagnate.

Drugs and alcohol, by reducing anxiety and motivation, are in direct conflict with the aims of couples therapy, which attempts to teach people to deal with their conflicts together. Alcohol temporarily relieves the discomfort and creates a behavioral syndrome (sometimes called *codependency*) in the affected others. Partners of alcohol and drug abusers take on most of the responsibilities for the household and for maintaining the relationship. This imbalance produces resentment and a parent-child instead of an equal-partners relationship.

Thus, screening for alcohol and drug use is critical, as addiction must be treated before couples therapy begins or when it is discovered. Otherwise, couples therapy may be derailed and put on hold while one of the members of the couple receives treatment for chemical dependency.

Assessing Relationship Problems

Assessment of client problems involves focusing on a particular stressor, such as sexual difficulties, problems with in-laws, parenting an adolescent, or dealing with finances. Ordinarily in the interview situation, a linear approach to assessment of problems seems the logical approach. At the heart of a linear model is the idea that if we gather enough information, we will be able to determine "why" a problem occurred. This, of course, is the basis of psychodynamic thinking: we begin to try to discover the "who, what, where, when, and how" of the problem. For example, if the couple is having difficulty with finances, it would be useful to know who is in charge of finances, what the couple's financial situation is, where and when the partners fight about it, and how the couple thinks the problem has originated. The search for a cause might lead to an understanding that one partner's impoverished family background makes him seem a miser now, and the other partner's need to acquire possessions is a symbolic way of getting love. Solving such deeply rooted problems is the individual, linear approach to therapy. A systemic approach suggests that the vain search for causes leads to blaming and rarely to a solution of the problem, because what is critical is the interaction of two people rather than simply each person's individual issues.

Assessing the Quality of the Relationship

There are literally hundreds of measures of happiness and the quality of the relationship in the literature of couples therapy (L'Abate & Bagarozzi, 1993). These measures, which are each member's self-report, ordinarily yield some overall score of general satisfaction with the relationship. Each person's score is compared with the partner's and is sometimes compared to group norms. Often, one member of the couple is satisfied and the other is not. How do we know that we are really assessing the relationship or the viewpoint of one member? Another problem with such scales is that they rarely help therapists identify specific problems. These scales also may promote the irrational idea that happiness is an enduring trait of the relationship, rather than the more realistic idea that satisfaction is a discovery one makes from time to time during life.

Attempts have been made to more clearly define what is meant by "satisfaction," but the concept remains murky (Spanier & Lewis, 1980). For example, Crosby (1991) points out that the term *stability* has been shown to be separate from the idea of happiness or satisfaction in a relationship. Stability is the couple's tendency to stay together or to maintain the couple bond. There are stable relationships that are unhappy, and there are happy relationships that are not stable. If measures of satisfaction do not show us how the couple interacts, what the partners' specific problems are, or whether or not they are likely to split up, how much usefulness can be claimed for these overall indicators?

Perhaps the most important drawback to measures of marital quality for the clinician is that they emphasize the viewpoints of the individuals in the relationship, rather than the relationship itself. One alternative is to develop observational checklists; a trained observer records data from watching live or videotaped interactions of the couple. Unfortunately, standardized observational measures are too time-consuming and expensive for ordinary clinical use (L'Abate & Bagarozzi, 1993).

Another method that has been explored is called *conjoint marital testing* (L'Abate & Bagarozzi, 1993). This is a testing situation in which both members of the couple work together on the same task. Once again, these tests have not made their way into clinical practice because of time and monetary limitations.

Notwithstanding these flaws, measures of relationship quality may still be useful to the couples therapist. They can be useful in determining the seriousness of the couples' problems and can signal improvement. Box 5.1 includes the reference for a number of the best and most concise standardized methods available. One of the best uses of the construct of *relationship quality* would be to repeat testing with a brief measure at two or three points during the course of therapy. Besides gauging progress, the results might help encourage the couple that some headway is being made.

Assessment During a Crisis

When a crisis occurs, extensive history taking and in-depth individual assessment are put on hold. Incidents of substance abuse, acts of violence, or discoveries of infidelity are the most usual crises that propel a couple into the therapist's office (Hendrick, 1995). The usual intake procedure is put aside and the therapist begins to defuse the incident. Assessment in a crisis situation consists mainly in determining what damage has been done and how to prevent imminent physical danger or psychological abuse while giving the couple support and hope. In this book, we will deal with the protocols for these three usual crises—substance abuse, violence, and infidelity—in separate chapters. At this point, let us just say that a crisis requires a brief assessment and immediate reduction of stress, rather than the normal sequence of couples therapy depicted in the integrative model.

USING TESTS AND INFORMAL TOOLS IN ASSESSMENT

With regard to choosing appropriate methods, Beavers and Hampson (1990), Grotevant & Carlson (1989), and Corso (1993) make several suggestions for the appropriate use of assessment techniques in family therapy. We have included six suggestions in the list below and modified the wording to focus on therapy couples as follows.

1. Examine the couple's needs being served and fit the assessment device to the kinds of problems the couple is experiencing.
2. Information gained during assessment should provide useful information about what areas to examine in therapy, rather than labeling the couple.
3. Choose instruments that are easy to administer, understanding that shorter is not always better.
4. Timing of the assessment is important. Use assessment instruments (especially tests and questionnaires) as early in therapy as possible while the couple is becoming oriented to the process. This allows assessment information to be used when planning treatment.
5. Use a combination of measures in order to be thorough. Use screening tests that measure a wide array of potential problems.
6. Be particularly aware of ethnic variations among clients and differences in social class, gender, and disabilities. All of these factors affect therapy, but they also influence differences from the norms that testing is based on. For example, the Marital Adjustment Scale (Locke & Wallace, 1959) uses only middle-class couples in its norm group. The scoring may not be valid with other kinds of couples.

Box 5.1 summarizes some clinically useful tests for the reader to explore. As space does not permit a discussion of each test, a reference source is given next to our brief description. We have chosen tests that represent the briefest and most psychometrically defensible ones available. Still, this does not exempt them from the six considerations mentioned above: any of these tests may be inappropriate for a particular couple.

Box 5.1
Some Clinically Useful Tests for Couples Therapy

INDIVIDUALS

The Family of Origin Scale (Hovestadt, Anderson, Piercy, Cochran, & Fine, 1985). Clients rate their family of origin on ten scales: trust, empathy, conflict resolution, positive tone, ability to express feelings, willingness to deal with separation and loss, openness of family boundaries, respect, personal responsibility, and clarity of expression.

The Myers-Briggs Type Indicator (Briggs & Myers, 1977; Briggs & McCauley, 1985). Rates clients on Introversion versus Extraversion, Intuition versus Sensing, Thinking versus Feeling, and Judging versus Perceiving.

The Cattell 16-PF (Institute for Personality and Ability Testing, 1967). Assesses 16 personality factors of individuals and comes with a computer-generated marriage counseling report that looks at similarities, dissimilarities, and potential conflicts.

SPECIFIC PROBLEMS OR STRESSORS

Scale of Marital Problems (Swenson & Fiore, 1982). Assesses problem-solving, decision making, goal setting, childrearing and home labor, relatives and in-laws, personal care/appearance, money arrangements, affection, relationships with people outside of marriage.

Marital Activities Inventory (Birchler, Weiss, & Vincent, 1975). Identifies how spouses allocate their time.

Area of Change Questionnaire (Weiss, Hops, & Patterson, 1973). Identifies specific areas and amount of change each wants.

Marital Agendas Protocol (Notarius & Vanzetti, 1983). Identifies conflict areas in marriage, expectations, blame, level of agreement about seriousness of problems.

Sexual Interaction Inventory (LoPiccolo & Steger, 1974). Assesses level of sexual functioning and satisfaction.

Golombok-Rust Inventory of Sexual Satisfaction (Golombok, Rust & Pickard, 1984). Measures global sexual functioning, impotence, premature ejaculation, anorgasmia, vaginismus.

Conflict Tactics Scale (Straus, 1979). Measures how spouses deal with conflict and express anger; can identify violence.

THE QUALITY OF THE RELATIONSHIP

Marital Adjustment Scale (Locke, & Wallace, 1959). Traditional measure of marital satisfaction.

Dyadic Adjustment Scale (Spanier & Filsinger, 1983). Overall marital adjustment, cohesion, and affectional expression, but also useful for discussion of specific problems/satisfactions.

Box 5.1 *(continued)*

Prepare-Enrich Inventories (Olson, Fournier, & Druckman, 1982). Premarital and Marriage Enrichment identifies strengths and work areas for discussion in marital preparation and enrichment courses.

Personal Assessment of Intimacy in Relationships (Olson & Schaefer, undated). Identifies seven kinds of intimacy.

Marital Problem-Solving Scale (Baugh, Avery, & Sheets-Haworth, 1982). Measures satisfaction with decision-making and problem solving in a marital relationship.

Golombok-Rust Inventory of Marital State (Rust, Bennun, Crowe, & Golombok, 1988). Twenty-eight-item assessment of overall quality of the relationship.

Marital Status Inventory (Weiss & Cerreto, 1980). Measures couple's tendency toward divorce.

Relationship Assessment Scale (Hendrick, 1988, p. 94). Seven-item global evaluation of the dyadic relationship.

Sharing Assessment Data with Clients

At the conclusion of the initial interview, the usual procedure is for the couples therapist to share with the couple the major issues or problems spotted in the assessment phase. It is recommended that couples receive a copy of the results of any testing (Boen, 1988), along with an explanation of the results. Too often, instruments are used that clients never see again. In these days of brief and briefer therapy, we must use our time and our clients' time wisely and have a good reason and goal for testing, rather than administering a standard battery.

The Myers-Briggs Type Indicator

They Myers-Briggs Type Indicator® (MBTI)® is described in some detail here for several reasons. First, it is perhaps the most popular indicator of psychological style (Fredman & Sherman, 1987). It is used in a variety of settings and for many different purposes in management seminars, team building, career counseling, and individual therapy. Very often, people come to therapy with some familiarity with the test and may even bring their previous scores or knowledge of their "type." Second, the Myers-Briggs is simple. It is based on four fairly understandable dimensions of personality or preferences: *Introverted (I) versus Extraverted (E)*, *Sensing (S) versus Intuition (N)*, *Thinking (T) versus Feeling (F)*, and *Judging (J) versus Perceiving (P)*. Various combinations lead to 16 possible personality types. Finally, the MBTI has some history in couples therapy, and the publisher provides a relationship report when both members of the couple take the test.

The MBTI Relationship Report includes more than ten pages of interpretation, including individual and couples summaries, and outlines similarities and differences on each of the four dimensions. Given a sample case of Jane and John Smith, Jane is an ENFJ and John is an ISFJ. This means that the couple enjoys *similarity* on two dimensions (F and J) and *differs* on the first two dimensions. It is this notion of similarities and differences in type that is the main thrust of MBTI interpretation. In general, similarities mean a shared viewpoint, whereas differences may suggest conflict or complimentarity.

In this section, we will outline some ways of interpreting the MBTI results to a couple. Good interpretation is based on education and familiarity with the instrument as well as on graduate or professional training. Computers make scoring easier and can provide useful information about normative data. But using computer printouts alone, without adequate training, is an unethical practice and is potentially harmful to clients. Computerized interpretation is not a substitute for training in the use of any evaluation instrument. Personality assessments in particular must be properly explained because there is greater potential for psychological damage when reports are misinterpreted. This means that a trained therapist is needed to give the proper interpretation of the scale's meaning in the context of the other scales and the client's background.

Interpreting the MBTI

An assessment session using the MBTI would begin by having each individual complete the answers separately and without input from the other partner. Usually, the instrument would be scored between sessions, and the couple would return for an interpretation session on another day. This gives the therapist time to consider the results. Provost (1993) provides one of the best sources of information about the use of the MBTI in couples therapy. Following are some of her suggestions regarding the interpretation of results with a couple.

1. Make sure the couple understands the reason for taking the MBTI and is open to the concept that both partners can learn to appreciate their differences.
2. Explain the concepts of the MBTI, the idea of preferences, and what the different key words mean.
3. After each dimension (such as Extraversion versus Introversion) is explained, ask both members of the couple to guess their own preference and that of their partner.
4. Present the partners with their actual results and discuss any discrepancies between their own and their partner's perceptions of the results.
5. Give the couple outside reading about psychological type, such as *Work, Play and Type: Achieving Balance in Your Life* (Provost, 1990).
6. Have couples complete their homework—perhaps observation of how each of them approaches a joint task—and ask that they report back at the next session. It is important to remind the partners to avoid blaming or using their own psychological type as an excuse.

What Else Can the MBTI Tell Us?

As indicated above, the MBTI can help a couple become aware of differences and similarities in their psychological types. An individual might gain some understanding of the other's uniqueness and learn to appreciate the differences as strengths rather than merely points of conflict. Both partners may see that there are different ways to achieve similar ends. Provost (1993) identifies several other ways the MBTI can be useful in couples therapy.

- Understanding their types can help couples "reframe" their difficulties. For example, a couple who fights over going out or staying home may realize that the real issue is how to find ways to balance one partner's extroverted preference and the other's introverted need for solitude. It helps both see their joint interaction as a couple, rather than focusing on one person only.
- Understanding type can help couples improve basic communication. For example, consider someone with a strong thinking preference whose partner has a strong preference for feeling. Both may fail to get their messages across as one talks about facts and opinions and the other talks about feelings and people.
- Understanding type can help couples become aware of their fighting styles. One individual with a judging style may want arguments to come to a rapid closure and resolution, while the perceiving partner may want more time to think and explore the issue before resolution.
- Understanding type can help couples and counselors identify needs associated with the partners' psychological type. For example, people vary in their need for autonomy, intimacy, and material security and in their preferences for leisure activities.
- Understanding type can help clinicians predict future sources of difficulty. For this reason, the MBTI could be used in premarital therapy, at a time when couples may not be ready to think about potential problems. Identifying and learning to celebrate differences could have the effect of helping the partners when problems do arise, rather than seeing their differences as a kind of pathology in the relationship.

Some Cautions

All personality assessments attempt to measure stable characteristics. If improperly interpreted, the results can make clients believe that their situation is unchangeable. Some possible reactions to MBTI scores are: "My partner and I are too different"; "See, he'll never change, he's an Introvert"; "She'll never be able to meet my affectional needs because she's such a Thinker." Worse, clients can come to the same conclusions about themselves—that they cannot change. In addition, it would be unreasonable to presume that similarities in psychological type are going to predict perfect compatibility. Differences in values, background, and other preferences may cause conflict even between people with the same personality type.

Living successfully in a relationship is always a matter of acceptance, appreciation, and tolerance of differences.

The MBTI was included here because it is one of the instruments best suited to couples therapy, but it should be part of a comprehensive assessment and be carefully interpreted to achieve maximum effectiveness and avoid potential harm. In the area of testing, a little knowledge is a dangerous thing. No test or assessment device should be used alone or exclusively. As noted earlier. test results can be misinterpreted or can simply be dead wrong.

Informal Assessment Tools for Couples

In this section, we consider tools for assessment other than paper-and-pencil tests. We have included a range of methods, from more structured tools such as the genogram to projective techniques like family photographs and imagery. Box 5.2 lists a number of tools we have found to be the most useful in practice. Using the genogram and questioning clients in an interview format are both informal methods of note, but because these are normally tasks of the first session, we included that

---

Box 5.2
Informal Methods of Assessment in Couples Therapy

INDIVIDUALS

The Mental Status Examination (see Trzepacz & Baker, 1993)
Questioning (See Tomm, 1987a, 1987b)

SPECIFIC PROBLEMS AND TYPES OF COUPLES

The Interview (see Chapter 6 in this book)
The Genogram (for example, a genogram of substance abuse issues in the
    couple's family of origin—see Chapter 6)
Marital History (unstructured reflections on the couple's life together)
The SII (in this chapter)
Couples Myths
Sexual Problems
    Medical Examination
    History of the Sexual Problem (L'Abate & Bagarozzi, 1993)
    The Sexual History of the Couple (L'Abate & Bagarozzi, 1993)
    Individual Sexual Histories (L'Abate & Bagarozzi, 1993)
Structural Diagrams (drawings of boundaries, alignments, and power ar-
    rangements) (Friesen, 1985)
Couples Images (Sherman & Fredman, 1986)
Family Photographs (Sherman & Fredman, 1986)
Couples Joint Tasks

material in the next chapter. More information on these methods can be located in the references provided.

In addition to those listed in Box 5.2, there are some additional assessment devices suited to couples therapy that you may wish to learn about. Each section that follows describes a separate assessment tool, and key source references are included. Some of the tools that serve a dual assessment/intervention function, like couples imagery, are described in more detail in later chapters.

Couples' Myths Assessment

Couples bring mythology and irrational beliefs to their relationship, and cognitive therapists will assess the dysfunctional belief system under which couples operate. Many of these myths surround the notion of romantic love. For example, a couple might come to believe that once romantic love has ebbed, it can never be revived. There are a number of ways to assess myths including testing and interviewing and examining favorite fairy tales, short stories, movies, and so on (Bagarozzi & Anderson, 1989).

Couples' Joint Tasks

Some couples therapists like to assign couples joint tasks to work on outside of the therapy session; the couple reports the outcome in the next session. The way in which the task is completed, organized, and scheduled tells us a great deal about the couple's negotiating style. Sometimes the therapist may ask the couple to plan a weekend getaway in order to assess the couple's communication and negotiation styles and skills. In marriage enrichment classes, couples are sometimes asked to paint a picture together or model something out of clay. Introducing the element of play does not seem to interfere with the serious intent of exposing the way the couple interacts. Not much has been written on this area, and it remains more of an informal method used by clinicians.

Family Photographs

The use of photographs in family therapy is based on several hypotheses (Anderson & Malloy, 1976; Kaslow & Friedman, 1977). Three of these hypotheses as they might apply to couples are listed below.

1. Couples tend to take photographs and films at important times during the life cycle of the relationship.
2. During stressful times, fewer pictures are taken.
3. There is a reason the couple selects certain photographs: they depict something the clients would like to portray.
4. Photographs are symbolic communication and express hidden meanings about the relationship, just as dreams and slips of the tongue give access to the unconscious.

One way of using photographs in couples assessment is the "show-and-tell" method. The couple is asked to bring in photographs to show the history of the couple or high points in the relationship, or pictures that best describe their relationship. Each member discusses the photographs selected and explains their meaning to the therapist. From the photographs, the therapist can learn about the couple's extended family, children, and home environment while getting a feeling for the nature of the relationship.

Couples' Images

Family therapist Peggy Papp uses imagery to work with couples. (This method is described in Sherman & Fredman, 1986.) Briefly, the partners are asked to close their eyes and to think about their relationship and interactions that characterize their togetherness. They are then to imagine themselves and their partner as something other than humans, something either animate or inanimate. After each member of the couple verbally describes the images, each acts them out in the therapy room. After each member of the couple has enacted his or her fantasy, the implications are discussed with the therapist. Imagery techniques yield information not obtainable in other ways because such techniques are nonrational and bypass defenses. The results can be used in therapy and provide information potentially useful in the assessment process. For example, one of our clients, Hans, imagined himself as a turtle and his wife, Marie, as a poodle. In his fantasy, she was always running ahead and coming back to tell him about what lay ahead, asking him to make a decision about which path they were going to take. He was always hurrying to keep up and did not want to make a decision until he got there himself. His fantasy revealed his perception about their two different decision-making styles.

CONCLUSION

In the opening paragraph of this chapter, we indicated that assessment is not usually thought of as the most interesting part of working with couples. We hope that this chapter shows how important good assessment is in helping clients focus in on the most important problems. In addition, we think that after reading this chapter you might see that assessment is not simply giving tests but a wider process that involves interviewing and gaining information from outside resources. The point has also been made that assessment is often based on one's theoretical orientation and one's personal assumptions and biases. Finally, we have introduced some key tools, like the genogram, and informal methods, such as the interview and couples imagery. These are points to keep in mind as we move to Chapter 6 and examine the link between assessment activities and goal setting.

6

The Initial Interview Using the Integrative Method

KEY CONCEPTS

- The initial interview is crucial to couples therapy success because it very often determines whether or not the couple will continue in treatment. For this reason, one of the first steps is to join with the couple and increase both members' comfort level.
- The second step in the first session is to continue the assessment process (described in the last chapter) by asking questions to gain information from the couple.
- In the first session, couples are asked to begin to describe the issues that brought them to therapy, and the therapist uses this information to begin fashioning an interactive definition of the problem.
- Because most couples are discouraged by the time they come for therapy, the first session should end on a positive note offering hope and giving couples concrete tasks.
- Besides the important therapeutic tasks, a therapist must deal with a number of practical and ethical issues early on, including the limits of confidentiality, the length of sessions, and the therapist's background.

You might wonder why we have included a separate chapter on the initial interview. The reason is that for many clients the first session is the only session. The attrition rate for couples is especially high. According to Nichols (1987), 30% to 40% do not return for a second appointment. Couples are often discouraged when they arrive and, unless the therapist can offer some hope immediately, they drop out.

The initial interview is a busy session. Besides gaining the couple's confidence, the therapist must complete an assessment of current and historical problems, establish fees, and complete paperwork. Because there is so much to be done, we have organized the goals of the session into six tasks:

1. Join with the couple.
2. Describe the process of treatment for the couple.

3. Make an overall assessment of the couple's problems and relationship through an interview and perhaps a genogram.
4. Begin the process of helping the couple state a solvable definition of the problem.
5. Offer hope.
6. Make some plans for the next sessions.

JOINING WITH THE COUPLE

Joining is a term that describes making contact with both members and communicating support for the couple as clients. Joining begins at the first telephone contact. It is a period of invitation, when clients get oriented to the process of therapy and get to know the therapist.

Telephone Contact

The goal of the first telephone call is to make contact with the couple, exchange information about therapy, and arrange for the initial interview (Weber, McKeever, & McDaniels, 1985; Young, 1992). It is a very important moment because both the therapist and the clients are testing each other. The clients are normally seeking a sense of trust and confidence in the therapist, and the therapist is attempting to establish rapport, determine motivation, and get a preliminary feel for the nature of the clients' difficulties. It is a time for clarification and qualification (Nichols, 1987).

During the first contact, the therapist should inform clients about fees, working hours, mode of therapy, and accessibility after hours. During the telephone call, some therapists may ask whether there has been prior therapy and, if so, what type. Most therapists are also interested in obtaining a brief description of the presenting problem. It is useful to ask the clients if they have any reservations or unanswered questions, because frequently there are unspoken fears about the nature of therapy. It is the responsibility of the therapist to make certain the couple understands that both parties must be present at the initial session.

Some therapists inquire about the referral to therapy during the telephone call. At times it may be important for the therapist to understand the role of the referral source and whether or not there will be a need to release information to other agencies during the course of therapy. If the legal system is involved and reports to the court are required, confidentiality might be discussed with the clients prior to the first session. Communicating this vital information on the telephone can prevent "no-shows"—clients appearing for the first session without the partner or without the checkbook. An informative telephone call saves time in the first session and creates a comfortable situation with clear expectations.

Greeting and Engagement

We advocate that the therapist walk into the waiting room to greet the clients. It is appropriate to shake hands with both parties, and customary to introduce oneself to the caller first because a relationship has already been established. Then an introduction to the other partner is important so that neither party feels slighted or left out.

On entering the therapy office, the clients are invited to sit where they wish for the initial interview. Some couples prefer to sit on a sofa together; others seek separate chairs. If electronic recording is to be used, the couple must be advised and sign a consent form.

Social Period

A brief social period can create a nonthreatening atmosphere for the clients and make them feel as comfortable as possible. Usually a brief conversation about the trip to the office, the weather, or any other casual comments are helpful. Fred Duhl (1986) calls this "schmoozing," and he believes that it is an indispensable aid to bonding with the couple. Of course, this activity can be overused. In fact, becoming overly casual with clients takes the focus away from their issues and tends to place the therapy relationship in a social rather than a therapeutic context. So, the social period should be limited to polite inquiries about the clients rather than self-disclosure by the therapist. The most important aspect of socializing is to warm clients up by dealing with issues that are less threatening than the ones that led them to make an appointment.

DESCRIBING THE PROCESS OF TREATMENT

Clients have a right to understand the process of treatment, and knowledge about the process helps them become more involved. Therapists have an ethical obligation to let clients know what they are agreeing to, what the chances are of success, and about the background and training of the therapist. The following 11 specific topics of procedural, ethical, and legal concerns should be covered in the initial session.

1. *Method of treatment*—specifically, whether there will be conjoint, individual, or group sessions, or a combination of more than one modality.
2. *Therapist orientation and professional disclosure*—information about the formal education and other training that the therapist has received. It is also useful to say something about the therapist's interest in and theoretical orientation to couples work. Because clients ordinarily do not know much about this area, a layperson's version is important. Some therapists provide this in a handout attached to an agreement for treatment.
3. *Length of treatment*—approximate time frame (such as one 50-minute session per week).

4. *Number of sessions*—approximate schedule. Some therapists use a ten-session format, whereas others expect to provide services for a year or more.

5. *Fees*—make certain that all fee structures are clearly defined. If there is a separate fee structure for therapy, evaluations, progress reports to the court, or deposition and witness testimony, this should be stated in the initial session.

6. *Missed appointments*—if there is a charge for appointments not cancelled 24 hours in advance, clients should be made aware in the first session, not when an appointment has been missed.

7. *Lateness*—clients should be made aware of the therapist's schedule; if clients arrive late, the therapist will use the allotted time for the appointment but will not "run over." Relatively strict adherence (short of rigidity) to this rule is important in helping clients remember that the therapy relationship is a professional one. Sometimes clients' deviations on appointment times are signals that the clients see therapy as a social rather than a working relationship. Such behavior may be the prelude to skipping appointments, missing homework assignments, and so on.

8. *Emergencies*—it is important to let the couple know whether or not the therapist can be reached in an emergency by beeper or through an answering service.

9. *Electronic recording*—it is necessary to obtain written consent by every adult present to tape a session. Clients need to be informed that they are being taped, the purpose of the taping, and that they have the right to rescind the consent for the taping at any time.

10. *Informed consent*—means getting a signed agreement for treatment. Informed consent forms indicate the possible benefits and hazards of therapy. Some consent forms tell the client a little about the therapy process and the qualifications of the therapist.

11. *Confidentiality*—clients must be made aware of the conditions for confidentiality and the exceptions to confidential treatment. Exceptions vary from state to state but normally include current abuse or neglect of a child, duty to warn and protect clients who might be in imminent danger or who intend to do harm to another, and some legal situations such as custody or divorce where records might be subpoenaed.

MAKING AN OVERALL ASSESSMENT
OF THE COUPLE'S FUNCTIONING

Observation of Couple Interactions

As Yogi Berra once said, "You can observe a lot by just watching." One way to provide the opportunity to "watch" is to leave the first part of the therapy session rather unstructured so that the couple interaction is more natural. Some therapists may even allow couples to argue over trivial issues—not simply to give the couple courage to deal with bigger problems but also to see how the couple negotiates (Crowe & Ridley, 1990).

When interviewing a couple, it is important to notice the body language of the partner who is speaking, but it is just as critical to see how the other partner is reacting. Most therapists are trained to observe individuals in terms of their grooming, gait, facial expressions, posture, gestures, voice tone, and so on. But the couples therapist needs to look at the interacting nonverbals. Does she pull away when he comes close to tears? Does he fold his arms when she mentions his family? How close do the partners sit to each other? Do they touch frequently? What can be said about the partners from the tone of their voices? One exercise to develop these observation skills is to watch tapes of couples being interviewed by a therapist. Observe the nonverbal communication between the couple with the sound turned off and see what you can guess about the relationship.

The Genogram

The genogram is a pictorial representation of the client's family tree, normally reaching as far back as the client's grandparents. The genogram was popularized by Bowen (1980) in family therapy. The Bowenian school believes that influences of the past generations are significant in the life of the individual and the couple. The genogram symbols in Figure 6.1 are slightly different than others you may have seen. We developed this set because we believe that this is the most simplified method for the beginning clinician. McGoldrick and Gerson (1985) have also developed a set of symbols that have become popular in family therapy. In most cases, they are similar to the ones in this book but are a bit more complex.

The therapist actually draws the genogram while the couple provides the information necessary to complete it. This is done on a flat surface with the couple sitting on each side of the therapist. It can be drawn at a table or the therapist can use a flip-chart arrangement so that everyone can more easily see the drawing. Ordinarily, each member of the couple is questioned separately about his or her family of origin. Sometimes the other member of the couple makes relevant comments about the partner's family.

Once the therapist has drawn a genogram for the couple, a period of discussion and questioning follows in which similarities and differences in background are examined. On the basis of the data from the genogram, the therapist develops some hypotheses about the couple and later presents these as potential goals for the couple's approval. When working with couples, the most important thrust of the genogram work is to identify how the two histories affect the expectations and rules that each member brings to the current relationship.

What to Look for in a Couple's Genogram

The Family of Origin Scale (Hovestadt, Anderson, Piercy, Cochran, & Fine, 1985) evaluates an individual's family on ten scales: (1) trust, (2) empathy, (3) conflict resolution, (4) positive tone, (5) ability to express feelings, (6) willingness to deal with separation and loss, (7) openness of family boundaries, (8) respect for each other, (9) personal responsibility versus blaming, and (10) clarity of expression (willingness to state expectations and needs). These are sometimes called *family*

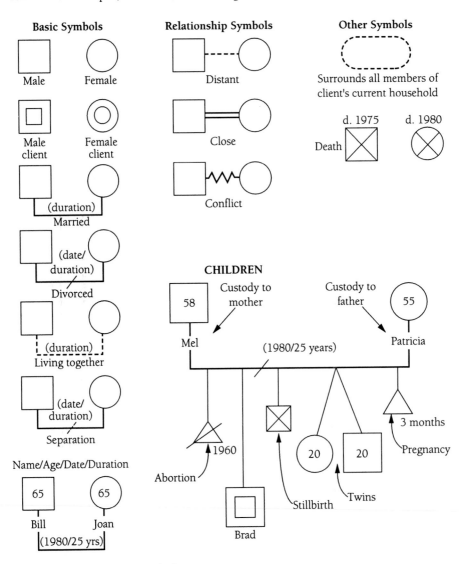

Figure 6.1 Genogram symbols

Source: From *Counseling Methods and Techniques: An Eclectic Approach*, by M. E. Young, p. 93. Copyright 1992 by Macmillan, Inc. Reprinted by permission.

rules. Beginning an exploration of a genogram by examining these ten areas would give each member of a couple and the therapist a good idea about the operation of the intersecting families of origin. Following are some other issues that might surface in a genogram and that could be useful in treatment planning for a couple.

1. *To gauge the strength of relationships with other family members besides the partner*. As you can see in Figure 6.1, lines are used to represent different types of relationships (distant, close or conflictual). Close relationships between a parent

and one of the children and a weaker, more distant relationship with the spouse might point out a dysfunctional "triangulated" relationship indicating the necessity for work on relational bonds between family members. Does one member of the couple have strong ties to parents or siblings while the other member does not? What sorts of conflicts and misunderstandings does this create? What rules are there in the relationship for keeping secrets? Does he tell his mother everything about their marriage? Is it all right if she confides in her sister?

2. *To understand the couple's history of significant relationships.* In Figure 6.1, the genogram symbols can show marriages, divorces, separations, and living together without being married. Questioning each member of a couple about past relationships very often reveals that previous experiences are affecting the present situation. Examining the repeating patterns in relationships beginning with father, to first boyfriend, to present husband would be an example of a how a woman's genogram might yield insights to aid in couple therapy.

3. *To identify family histories of significant health issues or mental disorders and disturbances.* The therapist should always ask about family history of alcohol and drug abuse. Chemical dependency counselors often darken the outside edges of each individual's circle or square to indicate such problems. Then, by simply looking at the whole genogram, the couple can see the family history. Other symbols or notations can be created to signify other diseases, such as diabetes, or mental disorders, such as schizophrenia.

4. *To point out gender role expectations.* By asking questions and writing occupations next to each circle and square, the genogram can begin an exploration of gender-role expectations that may have been handed down in the family of origin. Were women expected to stay home during the children's early childhood and work later? Were men expected to be workaholics?

5. *To understand the influence of birth order and sibling relationships on each member of a couple.* Using an Adlerian frame of reference, the couples therapist might wish to question both members of a couple on their respective birth order and any such influences that might remain from their families of origin. An only child who marries the youngest of six children might find that issues of personal property and space differ from that of the spouse. It might be revealed that ideas about the way to raise children are radically different because of the different climates in their original families.

6. *Understanding cultural and ethnic influences.* When examining a family history, the presence of different ethnic backgrounds in the couple presents opportunities for both discord and satisfaction. We have known couples where one member could not accept the differences in cultural values, ranging from kissing, to food, to holiday celebrations. We have also known couples where the spouse embraced the other's culture or religion and found it to be an exciting and enriching part of their lives. The genogram gives couples the opportunity to discuss these differences or similarities and helps the therapist discover the influence of culture and history on their relationship.

7. *To trace specific problem issues through the family or couple history.* Some of the issues that the genogram can help to unravel are values about work, preferences

for certain careers, sexual values, legal difficulties, and values about money. One couple we interviewed reported that each had opposite values about money. He was from a Czechloslavakian immigrant family and had been taught to save. He frequented second-hand clothing stores, and, from her point of view, he was miserly. She, on the other hand, had come from a wealthy family where appearances were important. Being "cheap" was considered a very negative personality trait by her family, and she was embarrassed. By exposing these historical issues in genogram work, the partners were better able to see that family of origin influences were at work in their conflict and were able to become more accepting and compromising.

8. *To examine the influence of traumatic events on the couple.* The genogram symbols in Figure 6.1 allow us to represent stillborn children, abortions, and infant deaths as well as divorces and the deaths of adults. Each of these issues can be handled as separate themes. For example the therapist might suggest: "Let's take a look at the issue of divorce in your two families. What do you think the family rules are about getting divorced?" or "How did the two of you handle the deaths of your parents?" or "When your child died, what effect did that have on your relationship?"

What the Genogram Does Not Do Very Well

The genogram can be an excellent tool, as you can see from its many uses, but the genogram tends to look mainly at historical influences. It is not as useful as a means of examining the couple's current issues. Unless you are a strict believer in family of origin theories like Bowen's, you may feel that many problems develop due to other differences and stressors that do not reach far back historically. The genogram may show what one brings from one's family but it does not as clearly show the ways a couple or a person is unique and operates differently from the family of origin.

The genogram also does not offer a way to look at relationships besides those of blood and marriage. Many people find that their most significant relationships are not within the family but are in their "adopted families" and circle of friends. In psychodrama, the sociogram was developed to look at the people and organizations that affect the client's life. The sociogram is a drawing of one's present connections to people and groups. For example, I might be a member of a particular church, a professional organization, a work team, a volleyball league, and a pottery class. I might have close friends, lovers, therapists, confidants, and ministers whose influence is stronger than that of my parents. So the genogram, when used alone, tends to focus on the history of our lives, but a more thorough approach would be to consider present relationships as well. Therapists should look for external stressors, personality differences, and extrafamilial influences and relationships that are currently affecting the couple. One of the best ways to do this is through a comprehensive interview.

Drawing a Genogram with a Couple

Figure 6.2 is a sample genogram of a couple. Each generation is represented on the vertical dimension. Horizontal lines connect couples at each end with their children, hanging like draperies on their connecting rod. Children on one side of a slash (indicating divorce) lived with or spent most of their time with the parent on

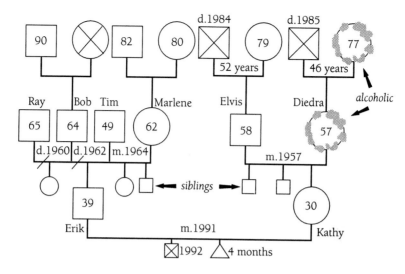

Figure 6.2   Sample genogram

the same side of this dividing mark. A skeletal genogram is depicted in Figure 6.3, which can be used to make your own genograms.

The genogram is a multipurpose assessment tool, so do not be afraid to write notes next to the symbols. These may be issues you wish to examine in later sessions or impressions about each family member or about relationships that the clients have added. The drawing can be a valuable device for explaining a case efficiently to a supervisor, and it can be a quick review for the therapist just before a session.

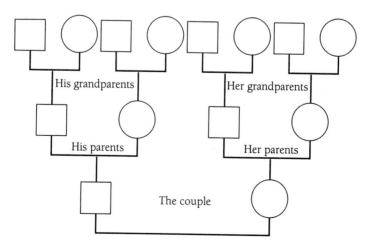

Figure 6.3.   Skeletal genogram

Questions

An assessment interview normally includes a series of questions used to assess the couple's overall functioning and their specific problems. Questioning too early and without a trusting and relaxed atmosphere can restrict clients, frighten them, and make them feel that they are in the "hot seat."

In couples therapy, questions are a valuable tool for several reasons. When the therapist asks a question of one member of the couple, the other member of the couple hears the answer. Couples experience great revelations in the therapy environment if the proper foundation of openness is laid. Secrets and hidden feelings often come out, which sometimes unleashes a whirlwind of emotions; clients may use the interview as a "safe" way to break the news that they are having an affair or wish a divorce. But positive revelations occur too. Clients admit (in front of witnesses) that they could improve; they ask for forgiveness for past wrongs, they admit their love, and they praise their partners. Willingness to ask questions like, "How sexually compatible are you right now?" signals clients that no topics are out of bounds and that open communication is the rule for therapy.

Following are a number of different types of questions based on categories identified by Tomm (1984a, 1984b). Each has a slightly different purpose or intent.

Problem Definition

Problem definition questions are constructed in order to obtain information about each individual's perspective of the problem. Often used early on in therapy, this category of questions can explore the present (What is happening in your relationship now?), the past (When did you first notice this problem occurring?), and the future (How do you foresee your life if you don't find a solution to your problem?) (Nelson, Fleuridas, & Rosenthal, 1986, p. 119). Here is an example of how a therapist might use problem definition questions.

> *Therapist:* Chanda, when did you first notice that you and Rolando did not talk anymore?
>
> *Chanda:* After he went back to school. I guess I also took a new job about that time.
>
> *Therapist:* So both events happened near the same time. How did your conversations look before you two made the changes?
>
> *Chanda:* We used to take long drives together and talk. Now we are too busy. Rolando seems to bring a lot of work home to do on weekends.
>
> *Therapist:* Rolando, did you notice the lack of time to talk about things at the same time that Chanda did?

From this interaction, the therapist was able to obtain information about the problem, about the kinds of environmental influences, and about the things the couple did when the relationship was going well. The therapist stayed neutral, emphasized circularity ("you and Rolando did not talk anymore"), and hypothesized ("it was a lack of time to talk").

Sequence of Interaction

Sequence of interaction questions are questions that attempt to determine what events precede and follow the couple's behaviors and how each person reacts to the other. A circular view is emphasized by examining the interactions related to the presenting problem of both partners (Nelson, Fleuridas, & Rosenthal, 1986). These questions lead to a clearer definition of each person's role in the symptoms of the problem. Examples of this type of question include: "Does your husband agree or disagree with your view?" "Where is your wife when you spend the day in your bed?" "When you get depressed and refuse to do your part in the domestic chores, what reaction do you get from your husband?"

Comparison and Classification

The therapist uses comparison and classification questions to help both the couple and the therapist define the intensity and duration of the problem. Beliefs, values, myths, thoughts, and feelings are explored through this type of question (Nelson, Fleuridas, & Rosenthal, 1986). Such questions might include: "How much of the time do you believe your husband ignores you?" "How long have you felt trapped in your relationship?" "Where did your idea about how a wife should behave come from?"

Interventive

Interventive questions reframe the couple's problem in a different way. These questions challenge the couple's pattern of interacting by offering new opportunities for change by (1) viewing the problem differently and (2) behaving differently with each other. The therapist might ask: "What if you looked at your partner's negativity about snow skiing as not knowing how and being fearful, rather than trying to spoil your fun? How would you handle the concerns differently?" "Chanda, if you were to help Rolando learn more about you, where would you begin?" These questions imply a different view of the problem by focusing on fear rather than on a negative attitude, or by implying a lack of knowledge, rather than disinterest.

The Assessment Interview in the Integrative Model

The assessment interview refers to both formal and informal periods in couples therapy when the therapist needs more information to further refine the definition of the problem. The interview is tied to the therapist's theoretical orientation (Lipchik, 1988a, p.xi), which determines how wide the funnel of assessment will be. Some theoretical orientations begin by immediately focusing on specific areas for exploration. For example, psychodynamic approaches use the interview to look at relationships with parents and the possible influence on the marriage. Contextual family therapists look for issues of trust and fairness in the family's relationship (Diamond, 1988), while solution-focused interviews (Lipchik, 1988b) seek exceptions and utilize the "Miracle Question." To emphasize this point, let us look briefly at the structural school of family therapy (Minuchin, 1984).

The structural school looks at couples as families consisting of two people, so both therapy and assessment follow the same principles used with larger families. The structural family therapist would probably begin the assessment task by investigating at least four areas.

1. How well does the couple deal with the partner's relationships with their families of origin?
2. How good are they at coping with being together and operating separately?
3. How much intimacy has the couple established?
4. In what ways have the partners divided authority and responsibility?

Because structural therapy emphasizes enmeshment/disengagement as a major construct, therapists look for this in the couple's relationship. The degree of enmeshment or alienation is derived primarily from the interview (see Wilk & Storm, 1991).

As integrative couples therapists, we are willing to spread the net a bit more widely. We believe that togetherness/separateness may be an issue for a couple, but it may not be. This is the difference between an integrative viewpoint and one that is more strictly tied to a specific theory. The integrative or eclectic point of view is, we think, more client-oriented. The client's constructions of the problem are more crucial than the therapist's theoretical viewpoint. As Sperry (1989) points out, couples of the 1990s are older, more culturally diverse, more dysfunctional, and more multisymptomatic than were couples in the past; consequently, "marital therapists have had to expand their repertoires of both assessment and treatment modalities to adequately tailor their therapy to spouse and couple. In short, marital therapy is becoming more couples-centered" (p. 547).

How the Integrative Therapist Conducts a Couples-Centered Assessment

As the funnel of assessment (Figure 6.4) shows, we recommend gaining as much information from the six main sources of data. We recommend: (1) screening to evaluate the mental stability of each member of the couple; (2) screening with a genogram to understand the context and history of the couple's relationships; and (3) focusing on specific stressors and problems through an interview. Here are some other suggestions:

If possible and appropriate, talk to individuals close to the couple who may have some insight into the couple's daily life.

Use a paper-and-pencil test when the definition of the problem is unclear or complex or as an intervention tool to help a couple become more aware of some problem being considered for the problem list.

Use the assessment interview to gain information about individuals, their problems, and the type and quality of the relationship. This is a conservative and more time-consuming approach, but a comprehensive assessment saves valuable time in treatment.

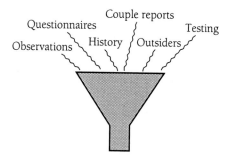

Figure 6.4 Funnel of assessment

A Checklist for the Initial Interview

Box 6.1 is a checklist to help the beginning therapist organize assessment information during the initial session. The first section is simply a reminder to address the administrative and legal issues. The remaining sections remind the therapist to briefly assess the presenting problem, each individual, and the couple and make an ending evaluation about the plan for treatment and the suitability for couples therapy. As you can see, the data can be obtained through a variety of instruments or through the interview questions.

BEGINNING TO BUILD A SOLVABLE DEFINITION OF THE PROBLEM

When an initial assessment is completed, it is critical to spend at least a few minutes dealing with the specific problem that brought the couple to treatment. After looking at all the issues that have to be addressed in the interview, it seems ironic that relatively little time is spent on the couple's reason for coming for therapy. Experienced therapists know that a lot of preliminary work is needed, for without a good assessment, therapy can proceed in a totally unproductive direction. For example, we once treated a couple whose presenting problem was that the wife was having an affair. Because the husband was a well-dressed, prominent businessman, we took his claims at face value and launched into dealing with her denial of infidelity. We realized in the second session that the husband was delusional and needed treatment for a mental disorder.

Even when the initial session is filled with legal details and assessment questions, at least a third of the session should be set aside to get a first impression of the presenting problem from the viewpoint of each member of the couple. Because this will be the first time the therapist hears the problem, it may be too early to offer any suggestions or develop a well-defined interactive definition of the problem. If the issue has persisted over some time and the partners are polarized, it will not be productive to try to get them to come together too quickly. Instead, it may be more useful after careful listening to offer the couple hope for the

Box 6.1
Initial Interview Checklist

Check each topic after discussing with clients.
 1. method/modality of treatment   _____
 2. therapist orientation   _____
 3. length of treatment   _____
 4. number of sessions   _____
 5. fees   _____
 6. missed appointments   _____
 7. lateness   _____
 8. emergencies   _____
 9. electronic recording   _____
10. informed consent   _____
11. confidentiality   _____

INSTRUMENTS USED, NOTES, STEPS TAKEN

Presenting Problem (Who, What, Where, When, and How Questions)
Specific behavioral sequences
Solutions that have been tried
Previous therapy obtained
Each person's account of the problem
Crisis that brought about therapy
Outsiders' views of the problem

Individual

Genogram
Mental status (when a mental disorder suspected)
Substance abuse
Violence potential (self or other)
Family history
Personal health
Personal style
Other

The Couple System

History of relationship
Overall satisfaction of the couple
Intimacy and affection
Adaptability to change
Ability to communicate
Family of origin issues
Boundaries

Box 6.1 *(continued)*

Power arrangements
Roles
Decision-making styles
Observations about the couple's overall satisfaction
Observations of behaviors during the session that illustrate aspects of the
    couple's relationship

Evaluation

Motivation for therapy
Couple's status regarding divorce/separation
Suitability and readiness for couples therapy

---

resolution of the problem and assign a task that helps both move toward a shared definition.

OFFERING HOPE

As the session draws to a close, a few words from the therapist can keep the couple motivated for therapy and begin to chip away at the demoralization that plagues the early sessions. These statements take the form of summaries of the important content, feelings, and/or meanings with the addition of an optimistic statement by the therapist. Here is an example of a summary that, in context, might help a couple look forward to the next session: "The issues that we have talked about today are serious. We talked about how you two will be able to relate in the aftermath of the affair and the financial problems that you can't seem to agree on. While this has been going on for some time, I feel very hopeful that the two of you will be able to resolve this. You're both committed to the task, and in my experience an affair does not necessarily mean the end of a relationship. It can be a new beginning. Once you two are communicating better and new agreements have been hammered out, I believe the financial issues will not be difficult to solve."

ASSIGNING TASKS

A task or homework assignment is useful for two reasons. First, it provides a concrete direction and goal for the couple to accomplish before returning to therapy. Second, it provides a reason for the couple to return and report on their success or difficulty with the task. Very often, clients need this kind of encouragement in the first few sessions to help them overcome the discouragement they feel.

For the most part, tasks should be designed with the couple's unique needs in mind. This is where the therapist's creativity comes into play. A standard first session task might be "Each person should write down all of the things they like about the other person," or "Write out some things you would like to do as a couple in the next five years." These tasks get couples thinking about the positive rather than the negative aspects of the relationship.

CONCLUSION

By the time many couples come for therapy, they are frustrated and discouraged. The therapist must "join" with the clients, inviting them to enter a therapeutic relationship and providing a sense of security and support. The therapist also describes the process of therapy to the couple, educating them as to the normal course of therapy. At the same time, the assessment process must be initiated. The couples therapist tries to cast the net of assessment as widely as possible, including other sources of information besides the couple's own reports. Without a thorough assessment, it is possible to mistakenly deal with only superficial issues or to miss crucial signs of substance abuse, violence, or major psychopathology. A genogram is a useful tool for gaining an overall idea of the couple's background. It can be completed during the initial session and referred to later in treatment.

Arriving at an interactive definition is the fourth major task of the first session. Although it cannot always be accomplished so quickly, the therapist begins to train the couple to see where areas of concern overlap. The therapist is actively involved in this process, taking the concerns of each person and melding them with his or her professional training.

Joining with the couple, orienting the couple, assessing, and arriving at an interactive definition serve their own purposes, but together they also engender a feeling of hope and confidence in the couple. The therapist encourages the partners to be hopeful while warning them that change may be difficult.

The final task of the first session is to make plans for the next session. Often this involves an experiment or an awareness activity to focus both members on the relationship as they prepare to set goals for the future. Concrete tasks encourage the partners to believe that they are responsible for the outcome and keep them thinking about the session throughout the week.

7

Goal Setting and
Treatment Planning with Couples

KEY CONCEPTS

- As the assessment phase closes, the couple's first task is to trade in each individual version of the problem and develop an interactive definition.
- Diagnosis, as we define it, is a collaborative process between clients and therapist in which the therapist's theoretical knowledge and experience blends with the clients' needs to identify the key problems or goals.
- DSM-IV diagnostic categories for couples' problems focus on symptoms or impaired functioning by a person in a relationship.
- DSM-IV "V" codes and adjustment disorder diagnoses are categories that encompass some of the problems that couples face, but they cannot be used as diagnoses of a relationship.
- Marriage and family therapists tend to use their own diagnostic categories to describe dysfunctional relationships.
- The funnel of assessment and treatment planning is a way of visually depicting the process of gathering information and refining it through interaction with clients until a set of solvable goals is reached.
- The interactive definition of the problem is a key feature of the integrative model because it is this negotiated goal that drives the treatment plan.
- There are a number of practical questions that therapists must face when devising treatment plans, such as, "Which problems should be addressed first?"
- One helpful notion in developing goals is that all clients are at various states of readiness, and sometimes the partners' readiness must be heightened before they can receive the maximum benefit from therapy.
- When interactive definitions are formed, the therapist's job is to transform these problems into goals or positive statements of how the couple would like the relationship to develop.
- The integrative model focuses initially on "cognitive" change, getting clients to see that they are both contributing to the problem and that they can team up to make a change.

- Finally, couples want to reach concrete behavioral change and they want to experience positive feelings or emotions about the relationship. These behavioral and emotional goals have to be addressed to ensure client support for goals over the long term.

In Chapters 5 and 6, we looked at both formal and informal methods of assessment for couples. In this chapter, we will try to link the assessment process with what is usually called *diagnosis* and *treatment planning*. Some therapists do not like these two terms because they imply a medical model, and so prefer to say, "identifying problems and goal setting." We will start out in the traditional direction by describing various methods of diagnoses used in couples and family therapy, and then we will present our own ideas from the integrative model that are much more consistent with a nonmedical paradigm. Figure 7.1 shows the integrative model with the goal setting stage highlighted.

FORMS OF DIAGNOSIS

The *Diagnostic and Statistical Manual* (DSM-IV)

In Chapter 5, we identified *assessment* as the general term to describe the gathering of information about clients from all six sources of data (refer to Figure 7.2 on page

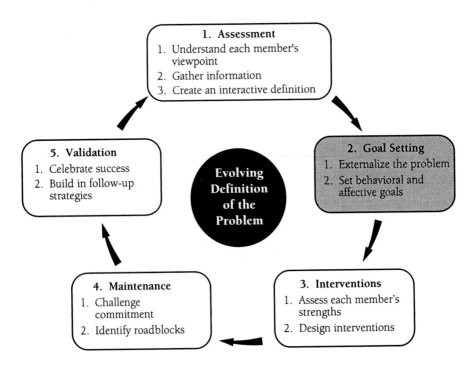

Figure 7.1 The integrative model of couples therapy

120). *Diagnosis*, on the other hand, is a transformation of data; it is the art and science of grouping findings into categories. The term has unfortunate medical implications because it suggests that two cases of a mental disorder have the same or similar features and nearly identical treatments.

DSM-IV, the most recent *Diagnostic and Statistical Manual* of the American Psychiatric Association (American Psychiatric Association, 1994) is a listing of all the major mental disorders and the criteria for assigning a person to a category. A *mental disorder* is defined as a set of symptoms or a syndrome (a disease) that interferes with social or occupational functioning or creates significant distress. It is important to note that in DSM-IV, only an individual person can be described as having a mental disorder. Families and marital relationships cannot be diagnosed as pathological because they involve more than one person. Karl Tomm, a seminal thinker in family therapy, proposed that the DSM-IV list a number of "PIPs," or *pathologizing interpersonal patterns*, such as abusive relationships. Unfortunately his and similar suggestions were not included in the recent DSM revision, but Florence Kaslow (1996) recently published a book of family diagnoses.

Conditions or "V" Codes on DSM-IV

"V" codes are DSM-IV diagnoses for issues that are a focus of clinical attention but that do not reach the level of a mental disorder. The capital letter V appears before the numbers in the diagnoses, which indicate that a *person* (not a couple) can have a "relational problem" or a "problem related to abuse or neglect." The political issue connected with this category is that V code diagnoses are not normally eligible for insurance reimbursement, regardless of the seriousness of the abuse or relationship problem. Therapists who treat couples are being encouraged by the third-party payment system to identify mental disorders in individuals and treat them individually, rather than solve them as couple problems. Box 7.1 shows the DSM-IV "V" code diagnoses most often used to diagnose couple problems in an individual.

DSM-IV Adjustment Disorder Diagnoses

The adjustment disorder is an actual mental disorder that arises in response to clear psychosocial stressors. To be classified as a disorder, it must appear within three months of the stressor's appearance, and the client must also show a level of distress that exceeds what would normally be expected from this stressor. There must be impairment in job, social, or academic functioning; and the symptoms must not last longer than 6 months nor be caused by bereavement. Box 7.2 lists the adjustment disorder diagnoses. Any of these are possible diagnoses for an individual with couples problems.

To make this diagnosis on Axis I of the DSM-IV, the therapist must also code the stressors on Axis IV. Couples problems are generally categorized as "problems with the primary support group." Here is an example of a four-axis diagnosis of a fictional client who is experiencing depression as a result of marital separation:

Box 7.1
*DSM-IV "V" Codes for Relational Problems
and Problems Related to Abuse or Neglect*

V61.9 Relational Problem Related to a
Mental Disorder or General Medical Condition

When the client's problem is caused by interacting with a significant other who possesses a medical problem or a diagnosable mental disorder.

V61.1 Partner Relational Problem

When a person shows clinically important symptoms or whose functioning is negatively affected by the relationship with a spouse or partner. Communication problems may or may not exist.

V61.20 Parent-Child Relational Problem

When the client shows clinically important symptoms or is negatively affected in functioning by problems with a parent or a child.

V61.18 Sibling Relational Problem

When the client's functioning is negatively affected or shows clinically important symptoms as a result of the way siblings interact.

V62.81 Relational Problem Not Otherwise Specified

Problems in a relationship not covered in the other categories of relational problems.

PROBLEMS RELATED TO ABUSE OR NEGLECT

V61.1 Physical Abuse of Adult

This includes spouse abuse and elder abuse. If the person is the victim rather than the perpetrator, the diagnosis numbers 999.5 are specified.

V61.1 Sexual Abuse of Adult

This is the category for rape or sexual coercion. If attention is on the victim, the therapist must specify 995.81.

ADDITIONAL PROBLEMS THAT MAY BE
THE FOCUS OF CLINICAL ATTENTION

V62.89 Phase of Life Problem

This catchall can be used when the client shows important symptoms or is negatively affected in functioning by a change in life circumstances. These circumstances can include marriage, separation, or divorce.

Box 7.2
Adjustment Disorders in DSM-IV Related to Couples Problems

309.0 With Depressed Mood (tearful and sad)
309.24 With Anxiety (nervous, worried)
309.28 With Mixed Anxiety and Depressed Mood (a mixture)
309.23 With Disturbance of Conduct (the client violates rights of others or
societal rules)
309.4 With Mixed Disturbance of Emotions and Conduct (may be depressed,
anxious, or both with conduct disturbance)
309.9 Unspecified (for example, withdrawal from social contact)

Axis I 309.0 Adjustment Disorder with Depressed Mood
Axis II V71.09 No Diagnosis
Axis III None Known
Axis IV Problem with Primary Support Group (marital separation)

Family Therapy Diagnoses

Although most couples therapists will tell you that they shun diagnostic formula-tions, marriage and family therapy as a profession has its own diagnoses. Just because the diagnosis is made for a family or couple does not mean that it is not a label or that it is not stigmatizing and confining. Marriage and family therapists often use special terms like *schism, skew, triangulation,* and *enmeshment* (see Chapters 2 and 3) as labels for unhealthy relationships. The notions of "dysfunc-tional family" or "co-dependent relationships" are diagnoses applied to a family in the same way that "neurosis" came into common parlance in earlier times. On the other hand, the marriage and family therapy field has sought to identify interac-tional patterns between people rather than blaming specific individuals, and more emphasis has been placed on the patterns of family interactions. As Jurg Willi (1982) suggests, couples and families "collude" in creating their problems. In addition, there has been a tremendous effort made to avoid the medical terminology that identifies couples, individuals, and families as "sick."

Diagnosing Problem Patterns

Diagnosis is a transformation of data from specific bits to labels that suggest larger patterns. Patterns emerge from all forms of assessment including the interview, the SII, and the genogram. The notion of a pattern suggests that it is a recurring behavioral sequence involving two persons who both play parts in the problem. Listed below are a number of commonly observed couples patterns.

1. *The parent-child relationship.* This relationship is characterized by one partner's taking care of the other and assuming the bulk of the responsibility for

most maintenance tasks. The "child" may have physical or mental disorders. Such a pattern is often present when one partner is a substance abuser. A lesser form might be called the responsible/irresponsible relationship.

2. *Siamese twins.* In this pattern, the partners are so involved with each other that they have no life outside of the relationship, have few friends, and exercise little autonomy.

3. *Victim-victimizer.* The victim-victimizer pattern is typical of some long-term abusive relationships. The treatment for this pattern is normally individual therapy for the victimizer and supportive therapy and assertiveness training for the victim before addressing the relationship issues.

4. *Pursuer-distancer.* This is a classic pattern in which one member of the couple is always seeking more intimacy than the other seems to want. When the pursuer moves toward the partner seeking closeness, the distancer moves farther away. It is a frustrating experience for both members of the relationship.

5. *The A-frame relationship.* In this pattern, both members of the couple lean on each other, supporting each other like two sides of the letter A. Each has strictly defined roles typical of traditional couples, but each is "lost" without the other. In contrast to the "Siamese twins" couple, it is an asymmetrical relationship. Both partners may have separate lives but are dependent on each other in some significant way.

6. *The parallel relationship.* Sometimes called the "marriage of resignation," couples sometimes develop a pattern of distancing themselves and leading nearly completely separate lives. The relationship may be stable, but the partners do not experience much caring, intimacy, or friendship.

Besides these commonly observed patterns, we identified a number of patterns associated with particular theoretical orientations in Chapters 2 and 3. They are listed again here.

Couple Patterns Observed by Various Theorists

I. Behavior therapy
   A. Maladaptive communication patterns
      1. Coercive exchanges
      2. Withdrawal
      3. Retaliatory exchanges
      4. Cross-complaining (summarizing self syndrome)
   B. Low rates of mutual reinforcement/high rates of mutual punishment
II. Psychodynamic theories
   A. Complementary neurotic patterns
      1. Spouse as superego
      2. Spouse as devaluated self-image
      3. Spouse as ego ideal
      4. Dominant-submissive dyad
      5. Detached-demanding dyad
      6. Romantic-rational partnership
      7. Spouse as parent
      8. "Love-sick" wife/"cold-sick" husband

III. The Bowen theory
  A. Chronic conflict pattern
    1. Distancer-pursuer pattern
    2. Triangulating
    3. Overfunctioning-underfunctioning pattern
IV. Structural/strategic theory
  A. Asymmetrical pairings
    1. Introvert-extrovert
    2. Flirtatious-jealous
    3. Assertive-nonassertive
    4. More involved–less involved
    5. Dependent-independent
    6. Others
V. Transactional analysis
  A. Game playing
    1. "If it weren't for you"
    2. Many others

DIAGNOSIS AND TREATMENT PLANNING IN THE INTEGRATIVE MODEL

Table 7.1 lists five key therapist activities that are involved in completing the assessment and goal-setting phases of the integrative model. Notice that the first step refers to the six sources of client information. Figure 7.2, the "Funnel of Assessment" (previously presented in Figure 5.1), shows the kinds of information that the therapist tries to gather in the assessment phase. In this phase, each member of the couple has had the opportunity to express his or her own viewpoint. As assessment activities are completed, however, the therapist challenges the couple to combine the viewpoints into a single problem or two. We could compare this to

Table 7.1 Key Therapist Activities in the Treatment Planning Process

Stage	*Activity*
Assessment	1. Therapist obtains information from six sources
	2. Therapist obtains each individual's view of the problem
	3. Therapist constructs an interactive definition of the problem with the clients
Goal Setting	4. Therapist helps clients refine definition
	(This is a precursor to Step 5. Externalizing is another step in this stage, but it is not strictly treatment planning. Its main purpose is to join the couple and to help them view the problem as external and as something to conquer.)
	5. Therapist helps clients change problems to create behavioral and affective goals stated in a solvable form

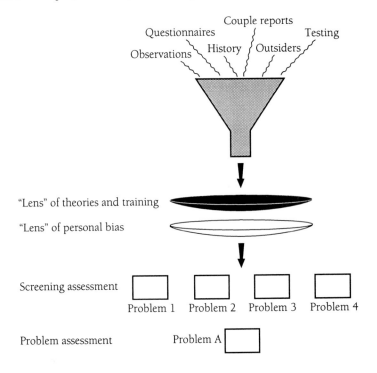

Figure 7.2 Funnel of assessment and treatment planning

looking through binoculars. Each lens provides a different viewpoint, but when both lenses are viewed together, a wider, three-dimensional picture emerges. Similarly, in the assessment phase, each member's perspective is recognized, but the assessment process is not complete until a joint vision of the problem is identified (see Figure 7.3). The therapist's role at this phase is to take the clients' concerns and use his or her knowledge and skills and the results of the assessment to help the couple achieve the most useful and solvable statement of the problem available. The therapist guides the clients to find a constructive way of looking at their difficulties—a way that leads to resolution of problems rather than further confusing, pathologizing, or discouraging the clients. This positive outlook is a key feature of the integrative model elaborated in this book.

In constructing an interactional definition of the problem, the therapist feeds back to clients the essence of their individual perspectives on the problem using foundational counseling skills like paraphrasing and reflecting feelings (Ivey, 1994; Young, 1992, 1998). Meanwhile, in the therapist's mind, the raw assessment information is being transformed into larger concepts such as patterns, games, or common problems, depending on one's theoretical orientation. The therapist is developing hunches about what is and is not working in the relationship and what needs to change to create a significant change for the better.

Figure 7.3   The goal-setting process

Although we believe that clients' goals are the centerpiece of the treatment plan in the integrative model, the therapist's input into the construction and definition of these goals is crucial. The therapist is an expert in human relationships and is a partner in the creation of the interactive definition. The integrative model is founded on the premise that therapy should begin with the client's definition of the problem, but that creating an *interactive definition* is the result of a confluence of three perspectives: those of each partner and that of the therapist or therapists involved (see Figure 7.3).

Case Example: Bill and Wanda

Perhaps the process of arriving at an interactive definition is best grasped by looking at a case example. We have chosen the example of Bill and Wanda, whose treatment plan is described throughout this chapter.

Bill and Wanda, both in their early thirties, have been married for 7 years and have come for therapy to deal with Wanda's affair with a co-worker 6 months ago. The couple has been arguing unproductively for several months. Wanda feels pressured, and Bill is anxious and mistrusts her. The couple seem to have the most difficulty when they have been apart for some time. Bill usually initiates troublesome discussions when he becomes agitated after ruminating over the past. Wanda "closes down" when confronted and becomes uncommunicative. After the first session, the therapist formulated the following hypotheses or preliminary diagnoses.

1. Bill and Wanda are experiencing a pursuer-distancer type of pattern; he attacks and she withdraws.
2. Bill feels weak and ineffective, while Wanda feels guilty.
3. The couple is socially isolated (having moved recently).
4. Wanda's mother is very involved in the couple's life and supports Wanda, blaming Bill for her affair.
5. The couple has difficulty dealing with finances.
6. The couple reports several years of a positive and mutually supportive relationship that deteriorated about 1 year ago.
7. They share several joint interests including backpacking and photography. Some of their best times have been during their wilderness adventures.
8. They are very concerned that their teenage son is smoking marijuana.

Deciding Which Problems Should Be Addressed First

Couples who come for therapy typically have multiple problems. Which are the most important? As we indicated earlier, crises involving physical risk, mental disorders, or substance abuse are normally dealt with first. But many couples like Bill and Wanda have no such issues, and the therapist is confronted with several options. The integrative model suggests first dealing with the issues that the couple feels "ready, willing, and able" to attack. "Ready and willing" refers to motivation; "able" asks the question, "Do the clients have the necessary skills to complete the goal?" Box 7.3 lists a number of guidelines that therapists can use to think about priorities in goal setting.

Ready and Willing

Although we think we know what is best for our clients, they may not be willing or ready to accept our goals for their lives. We have learned that the greatest chances

---

Box 7.3
Goal-Setting Guidelines

1. Choose goals that the couple is ready, willing, and able to achieve.
2. Tackle crises first. As Maslow points out, you cannot deal with higher-order needs, such as intimacy, when you are being evicted from your apartment.
3. Advocate for goals that lead to general improvement rather than goals that are Band-Aids.
4. Set goals that represent the presence of something rather than the absence of something. Make goals simple—things that the couple can really do and feel.
5. Translate vague words into action and connect with feelings. For example: "How do you expect to feel when you find you are spending more time together?"
6. Reframe therapy as a joint project that requires hard work, rather than as a painful medical procedure. The couple will see this as a familiar learning process, not as "magic" performed by the therapist.
7. Make sure that the goals are important by asking the couple, "How will we know when therapy is completed?" The answer should include completion of the majority of therapy goals.
8. It is all right to tell couples you are searching for an interactive definition and a goal for therapy. Enlist their help.
9. Assume that therapy is going to be a success. In your discussions with clients, use terminology such as *when and yet.*

---

for success and change is to adopt those goals that are important to the clients. For Bill and Wanda, we may believe that resolving issues related to the affair are the most crucial to their general well-being. But it is absolutely imperative that the problem initially identified is one that the couple is ready to attack. If Bill and Wanda are determined that their key issue is a teenage son's smoking marijuana, this would probably be the very place to begin.

Six levels of change   The emphasis in therapy literature that is now being placed on readiness signals a shift in the way that we have conceptualized the change process. Prochaska, Norcross, and DiClemente (1994) have developed a six-part model based on research about how clients reported they made lasting changes. The model is circular and proposes that change takes place in six successive levels.

1. In the first level, "Pre-Contemplation," clients feel resentful and angry when it is suggested that they have a problem. Their reaction is "I can handle it!" They lack awareness of the issue, which we could call denial.
2. At the "Contemplation" level, there is some dawning awareness that a problem exists but also a feeling of confusion about what to do. The client is anxious and slightly uncomfortable but not quite ready to change: "I'm stuck!"

3. At the "Preparation" level, the client knows that change is necessary but is unsure how to begin. "I'll stop drinking tomorrow" is a familiar phrase associated with this stage.
4. In the "Action" level, the client makes a commitment to change and takes some action to change the problem but is very scared about the new territory.
5. At the "Maintenance" level, the client is dealing with the fear of relapse while experiencing some of the rewards of having made a significant change.
6. Finally, "Termination" takes place when maintaining change is nearly effortless. Even though there are temptations to return to earlier behaviors, the change lasts.

The model goes much further than this outline. It proposes specific therapist activities at each stage that help clients move toward change. For example, two clients who had been married for only 6 months recently consulted us because they were concerned that they did not know how to make something productive come out of their disagreements. Normally they would get into a spat and it ended as they both became angry and gave each other the "silent treatment." They were not interested in couples therapy because they said that they were happy in their marriage and did not feel that they needed that kind of assistance, but they wanted to work on "better communication." The couple was seen twice and was given a set of videotapes about communication and negotiation. This level of treatment (education) was in keeping with their minimal level of readiness for therapy (contemplation). They did not wish to make a third appointment, but we recommended that they come back if problems reemerged.

Are you buying, or just looking?   Steve de Shazer (1988) made an important conceptual breakthrough when he announced the "death of resistance." De Shazer and his colleagues at the Brief Family Therapy Center felt that lack of progress in therapy is often blamed on clients through use of the term *resistance*. Instead, de Shazer believes that clients are at different stages of motivation that he describes as having three levels. He calls some clients "Visitors," some "Complainants," and some "Customers." Visitors lack motivation and often arrive at the therapy appointment at the behest of some third party. Complainants are experiencing discomfort and understand the need to change but are unwilling to take the necessary steps. Customers are those who come to therapy ready to take action. De Shazer's view, like that of Prochaska, Norcross, and DiClemente, is that therapists must select interventions based on the client's state of readiness. In general, visitors need education, and complainants need to become more aware of how the problem is affecting them so they can better see the need for change. Customers are ready to respond to the suggestions to change.

Ripeness is all   Barry Dym (1995) has elevated this concept of readiness to the central feature of his work with couples. In his book *Readiness and Change in Couple Therapy*, Dym cites a long tradition in family therapy, religious customs, and groups like Alcoholics Anonymous that support the simple truth that people are most likely to change when they are ready. As Shakespeare said, "Ripeness is all!"

According to Dym, a relationship is comfortable when it is stable. As long as things are stable and discomfort is minimal, the couple is unlikely to change. Dym compares trying to change a stable couple to trying to budge a 400-pound sumo wrestler who is standing firm. Dym proposes that readiness to change comes about only when the couple is off balance or in a state of disequilibrium. The disequilibrium may already be underway when the couple enters therapy, often because of a crisis or a new life situation or life cycle stage. Dym's insight is that during the assessment and goal-setting phase of therapy, we should be aware of what issues clients are ready for and begin with the "hot issues."

Applying this point to our case example, Bill and Wanda may not be *ready* as a couple to address all seven items on the list of problems. Bill has his favorite issues and Wanda has hers. They may not even be willing to confront those the therapist believes are most important. On the other hand, in the goal-setting phase, the therapist encourages the couple to set goals that both people seem to be ready for. Because chances for success are greatest when readiness is high, we can bring about early success that helps to overcome initial skepticism and helps build hope.

Helping the Couple Decenter

Getting couples to identify a common issue is probably the most difficult part of couples therapy. For one thing, couples may be angry, hurt, or vengeful. They often see the therapist as the judge who is going to find their partner as guilty and themselves as innocent. The skills called for at this point in couples therapy are not so much negotiation skills as skills in listening and reflecting thoughts and feelings. Negotiation implies that we give and take in a compromising, businesslike fashion, but what is really needed is for each member of the couple to understand and validate the other person's concerns. *Decentering* is a word taken from the moral development literature that means the ability to transcend one's own point of view. Similar to empathy, it means learning to "walk in the other person's shoes." For example, a couple came in with the following difficulty: the husband was very jealous and believed that his wife was being unfaithful to him. He had no evidence beyond his suspicions, but he was adamant that the infidelity issue must be solved. She was angry and hurt but relentlessly stuck to her story that he was unduly suspicious. Therapists can easily get trapped into seeking to determine who is telling the truth, but the real task is to construct a "joint truth" that can be approached productively. In this case, the partners were able to rename their problem as the distrust-distancing pattern and began to work on it in therapy. In order for this to work, both partners must have the opportunity to express themselves (get past overwhelming feelings) and to feel fully understood. Often, it is necessary to cover the same ground over and over and to stop and check each person's understanding, because often each one believes that he or she has the proper perspective. For example:

problem." As the therapist begins introducing budgeting and negotiation exercises, the couple balks. Bill and Wanda believe that the major issue is that they have different basic values. They are able to express and accept each other's point of view, but when it comes to finances their priorities are very different. This information from a couple may make a beginning therapist panic over the thought of abandoning the way the problem is being viewed and embracing a whole new concept. Eventually, we become comfortable with the fact that this is part of the process of refinement of the problem that lies at the center of the integrative model.

Recall that one of the assumptions of the integrative model is a *constructivist* philosophy; the therapist is trying to help the clients construct a workable goal based on a shared perspective. It is not a compromise but a "new-promise," meaning that the new goal is a novel way of thinking about the problem. The therapist is under no illusion that he or she is able to determine "the truth." If it seems that the clients want to call the problem "agreeing on financial priorities" rather than "managing money better," the therapist respects this change because it is just as useful in achieving the goals of therapy. Clients reword problems to make them fit better into their framework and worldview. As long as the refined problem is constructive and solvable, the therapist must remain flexible and adapt as the couple's picture of the problem evolves.

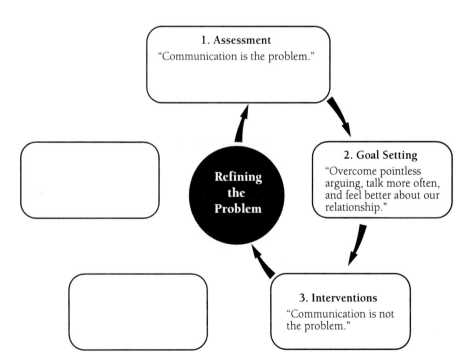

Figure 7.4 Refining the problem: Returning to an earlier stage

SETTING GOALS

Our experience in couples therapy suggests that most couples seek counseling when they are demoralized and "at the end of their rope." Instituting hope is an important healing activity of the therapist (Frank & Frank, 1991). Having set clear and achievable goals, clients immediately feel a sense of relief and can become more involved in the change process. Reaching even small goals makes them feel encouraged that they are finally out of the rut of endless arguing or distance that has characterized their relationship. Although goal setting is central to our integrative model, other theories vary regarding the degree to which clear goals are stated, negotiated, or discussed with clients.

Transforming a Problem into a Goal: Cognitive Change

During the 1960s, a very effective television advertisement for the Peace Corps asked viewers to decide whether a glass of water was "half full" or "half empty." This is an intriguing idea because we know that both statements are true; but which viewpoint is the most constructive and hopeful way of looking at the situation? Similarly, in the integrative model, we begin by allowing couples to have their "say" and to identify the troubling issues confronting them; we allow them to talk about the half-empty view of their relationship. We do this because we need to understand the severity of the problem and they need to feel understood. But it is easy to become bogged down in blame and recriminations. Eventually, we ask couples to transform their problems into goals: to identify not what is missing in the relationship but what they want to have. Here is an example.

Interactive Definition 1
"When we argue, it escalates into name-calling and we end up saying things that hurt each other without solving the problem."
(Viewpoint: This is what is wrong with our relationship.)

Goal 1
"We want to be able to keep our arguing on the topic and stay with it long enough to solve the problem."
(Viewpoint: This is what our relationship could be if we are successful.)

Choosing the Kinds of Goals

Because many clients present with multiple problems, it is often difficult to decide which to deal with first. Although we have suggested that "hot goals" are best, there are some other guidelines for deciding the ordering of goals that might be helpful when reflecting on a treatment plan for a couple (see Box 7.3).

When goals are established, the integrative model recommends breaking them down even further into behavioral and affective components. This fits with the com- monsense notion in therapy that real change involves change in all three areas of human functioning: cognitive, behavioral, and emotional. Figure 7.5 shows the interaction of cognitive, affective, and behavioral change. Regardless of where we decide to change behavior—emotions or cognitions—a change in one produces changes in the other. For example, people who quit smoking (a behavior) feel pleased, happy, and confident (emotion) and see themselves as having more self-control (change in perception).

Cognitive Components

Cognitive change in our model comes about through the process of reconstructing the problem situation in interactive "goal language." As clients change their view from blaming to a "joint work project," they have made an important shift in their thinking. The collaborative reconstruction of the problem between therapist and clients is a shift in perception that continues as the view of the problem evolves. The next step is then to make sure that clients actually change their behavior and feelings about each other and the relationship.

Behavioral Goals

Couples come to therapy hoping for the best but they are often skeptical that things will really change. They want and need to see tangible results. Most therapists (not just behaviorists) see behavioral change as an important sign of real change. Even Freud admitted that sometimes clients must get up off the couch. But one of the most important reasons to focus on observable change in couples therapy is to keep the couple's hopes alive. Seeing new behaviors in oneself or one's partner engenders hope and optimism. Success breeds success.

When setting goals, behaviorists suggest making goals quite specific and observable so that there is no question that they have been reached. In couples therapy, a couple may want to have a goal of spending more time together. In setting a behavioral goal, the therapist tries to get the couple to be simple and specific. An example of a specific behavioral formulation of the couple's goal to spend more time together might be stated as "We will spend two evenings per week going for a long walk in our neighborhood."

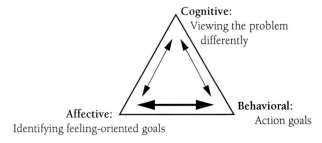

Figure 7.5 Interaction of cognitive, affective, and behavioral change

The Role of Emotion in Couples Therapy

Before describing affective goals, a discussion of the role of emotion in couples therapy is warranted. Emotions are often seen as the enemies of the relationship. The equivalent of the Four Horsemen of the Apocalypse for marriage have been described as critical anger, contempt, fearful defensiveness, and sullen withdrawal (Gottman, 1991). Couples become involved in creating cycles of emotional inter-action, as when one person ends up feeling angry and the other defensive. These patterns do not seem to resolve themselves, and couples find it very difficult to change these patterns on their own (Johnson & Greenberg, 1994).

Aside from trying to escape from the throes of negative emotions, couples want to regain the initial good feelings that they had about their relationship and about their partners (Pierce, 1994). They do not simply want their partner to stop annoying habits, they also want to feel some of the old attraction, closeness, contact, and intimacy. In fact, the quality of a couple's emotional contact is a better predictor of whether they will stay together than is how much they fight. It appears that even if couples do not resolve their issues during disagreements, they tend to stay together if they are able to remain in emotional contact and not become defensive and distant (Gottman & Krokoff, 1989). In sum, emotions appear to be significant factors in couples' decision to stay together, and emotions can form an important source of dissatisfaction that brings couples to therapy.

Next we turn to the therapist's role in evoking clients' emotions for the purpose of bringing about change. Through reflecting feelings and helping clients focus on their emotional reactions, therapists help couples give vent to strong affect by expressing sadness, grief, anger, and even joy. The experience of emotional arousal and the consequences of expressing feelings form an important curative factor in all forms of counseling and psychotherapy (Frank & Frank, 1991; Young & Bemak, 1996). This phenomenon has been referred to by various names, including *catharsis* and *abreaction*. In the therapy session, therapists often encourage clients to express deeply held feelings, hoping that this unburdening will bring about new awareness and a sense of relief. Techniques from psychodrama and gestalt therapy have been widely used for this purpose.

In the family therapy field, Virginia Satir (Satir, Banmen, Gerber, & Gomori, 1991) made experiencing and transforming feelings a major part of her theory. Satir was aware that when one member of a couple expressed strong emotions, it had an effect on the partner. Emotion-focused marital therapy (EFT) (Greenberg & Johnson, 1988) recommends that couples be asked to disclose their previously unacknowledged thoughts and feelings about their partner. As a result, partners experience a change in their view of the other person when shown this hidden side (Denton, 1991). The partner who expresses feelings receives the benefits of emotional release and startling self-awareness, while the other partner has the opportunity to become aware of the other's viewpoint and to develop empathic closeness. Of course, strong negative emotions expressed toward the other partner can be hurtful rather than beneficial. It is the therapist's job to encourage the expression of emotions when it is clear that they will either lead to greater

ress an important issue, or lead to greater understanding for the couple.
cal for a person to hear how another's actions hurt them, but it may be
ive to hear the juicy details of an affair with its attendant emotions.

sence of the therapist—aside from providing a safe environment—
somehow makes the expression of strong feelings more of a landmark experience, just as affirming wedding vows "before witnesses" becomes a watershed event in a relationship. When one partner's feelings are evoked by the therapist, the other partner is able to take a less defensive stance. Because the emotions are not aimed at the partner, he or she finds it easier to accept and understand them.

To summarize, emotions play an important role in couples therapy. Negative emotional cycles propel couples into therapy and are a primary source of dissatisfaction; good feelings, intimacy, and closeness help couples weather difficult storms. Evoking emotions and allowing the partner to see underlying feelings seems to be a powerful method or technique to help couples regain closeness. Finally, we have seen that couples come to therapy to feel better about their relationship, not just to accomplish behavioral goals. A prescription for a better relationship thus includes planning for and expecting better feelings about the relationship.

Affective Goals

Thus, the integrative model recommends including affective or emotional goals when behavioral goals are formulated. For example, a couple wants to manage finances better, but both members also want to feel more in control and more positive about their ability to solve problems as a couple. Another couple wants to improve both partners' sexual satisfaction, but they also want to experience feelings of closeness, not just more orgasms. In the integrative model, we recommend setting clear goals for therapy, so that as each goal is reached the couple feels the renewed sense of being on a winning team. Couples do not wish to accomplish only behavioral goals; they also want to be happy with each other.

The emotional goals, facilitated by the therapist, can be clearly stated as part and parcel of the desired outcome of therapy. We now present a dialogue with our fictional couple Bill and Wanda. This session depicts how a therapist moves a couple from (1) viewing each person's version of the problem; (2) to constructing an interactive definition of the problem; (3) to changing problems to goals; (4) to establishing behavioral and affective goals.

Case Example: Bill and Wanda (continued)

Bill and Wanda have been working on the lack of trust in the relationship since Wanda's affair with a co-worker. The couple has changed the problem into the goal of leaving the past behind. But because the past still haunts them, it was deemed useful to discuss the specifics of where, why, when, and how the issue arises—that is, to do more assessment and gain a more refined version of the problem.

> *Therapist:* So, we were talking about how you two get into fights, usually after work, is that right? You get into fights when Bill has been home alone for a while. Tell me about that.

Bill: Well, yeah, I've been at home, thinking about the past, you know, and getting myself worked up. And then when she comes home and I am almost looking for something—some way that she is lying. And she just acts mysterious, like it doesn't bother her.

Wanda: I get the third degree.

Therapist: What do you mean, Wanda?

Wanda: Well he starts in with the questions. "Who were you with after work?" "What did you do today?" et cetera, et cetera, and then I just clam up.

Therapist: Right now I would like to sort of trace the way in which this problem surfaces. But remember, just because we identify a beginning and an end to your pattern, that is really artificial. Couples interact all the time, so I don't want you to think that just because we start with Bill, for example, that he is to blame for the problem. It takes two people to create it. So let me understand the way you two set up the distancing problem. Let's call it that because that's how it ends up. You are both confused and distant. Right?

Bill: Right.

Wanda: All right, but if he wouldn't start, things would be a lot better.

Therapist: Well, right now, that's what I want to avoid—blaming. (*Pauses*) OK, it happens like this: Wanda comes home, probably a little wary, and Bill, who has been brooding and alone, starts asking leading questions because he is feeling jealous and suspicious. Wanda feels guilty and angry because Bill's first contact with her is to start asking questions. The result is that you two are distant and mistrustful. And what you want is to be closer (*interactive definition of the problem*). Is this right?

Wanda: Right.

Bill: Yes.

Therapist: So, how would you like it to be?

Wanda: I would like us to have fun again.

Bill: I am not sure we could.

Therapist: But is that what you want too, Bill?

Bill: Sure.

Therapist: Give me an example of what that would be like—what would you be doing.

Wanda: Well, we would be going out together, or we would just spend a night together without bringing up that tired old subject.

Therapist: How's that, Bill?

Bill: Yeah, I would like that. We would be able to have a normal discussion about her job and my job without ending up in a fight.

Therapist: OK, I think I see that. You'd like to be able to have a discussion about work and end up feeling good about it. And you'd like to do something different so that you could feel closer. Am I on the right track?

Bill: Yeah.

Wanda: I don't think we are ready to have a normal discussion about work yet. I don't trust Bill not to blow his top. It will just end up like before.

Therapist: OK, if it's agreeable to you, Bill, we'll put that part off for now and concentrate on finding a way for you to get out or do something different so that you can feel that you're on the same team again.

Wanda: Just comfortable again.

Therapist: All right, so my understanding is that this week, on two occasions, you two will try to find something to do together during which you'll try to relax and just be comfortable with each other. I might suggest that each of you choose one of the activities but both of you strive to have fun and relax with each other. When we get back together next week, we'll see how it's going.

At the end of the session and with the therapist's help, Bill and Wanda have:

1. Negotiated an interactive definition of the problem: "We have a 'distancing' problem."
2. Changed the problem to a goal: "We want to be closer and have more fun together."
3. Added behavioral and affective components: "On two occasions this week we will agree on something that will allow us to feel relaxed and comfortable with each other."

CONCLUSION

Treatment planning when working with an individual normally involves assigning a diagnosis once assessment has been completed. The treatment plan is then dictated by this formulation of the problem. In the integrative model, our focus is on getting the couple together as a team to meld their individual complaints and jointly attack a mutual issue called "the interactional definition of the problem." Because this is a more solution-oriented, positive approach, the therapist guides the couple to translate this problem into a solvable goal, a vision of what the future would hold if the problem were solved. To reach that vision, the couple must articulate behavioral steps and feeling outcomes that will tell them when the goal has been reached.

TWO

COMMON ISSUES IN
THE LIFE OF THE COUPLE

8

Treating Communication Problems: Issues and Skills

KEY CONCEPTS

- Good communication is essential for solving problems, sharing information, and supporting each other in the couple relationship.
- The history of couples therapy includes a strong influence from social learning theory and other skills training approaches.
- Besides communication training, couples need skills in learning to negotiate and to increase the amount of positive interactions.
- Nonverbal communication plays a special role in couples' communication and can accentuate couples' messages or create a roadblock.
- There appear to be gender differences in communication that may play a role in the ways partners misunderstand each other.
- Self-disclosure is an interpersonal skill that some couples need to address if they wish to be more intimate.
- The linear model of communication allows us to look at the key features of sender-receiver and feedback in couples' communication patterns and begin to examine the importance of the intent and the impact of messages.
- Communication is misunderstood because people are indirect in their sending of messages. They also play games, manipulate, and erect smoke screens with communication.
- Often communication is disturbed because there are hidden agendas that the couple needs to address directly but that have not been brought out into the open.
- Communication can be assessed in several ways, such as using inventories, identifying problem patterns, and videotaping.
- Communication barriers are standard patterns that experts have identified that couples can use to examine their own interactions.
- Positive communication skills can be learned in group formats or can be taught in ordinary couples therapy sessions.

- Several packaged communication training programs for couples are available at many marriage enrichment seminars.
- Therapists using the integrative model of couples therapy set specific behavioral and affective goals for each couple regardless of the format of the training.

Communication is the currency of the intimate relationship. On a very practical level, communication allows couples to discuss and solve problems and to exchange important information. For example, partners who cannot disclose their feelings toward each other will have difficulty discussing sex. If they constantly use blaming as a method for problem solving, they will have difficulty navigating the course of parenthood. Couples who cannot bring disagreements to agreements often end up in cycles of unfinished business that are repeated for years. However, when couples have open lines of communication, they can utilize each other for support and as a sounding board for personal and work problems.

While recognizing the benefits of good communication, much of the focus in couple therapy is on breakdowns and impasses. Figure 8.1 shows a ranking of marital problems reported by family counseling agencies in the 1970s. Nearly 87% of the couples in therapy indicated that they had communication problems. Both therapists and couples say that communication is the most common and destructive problem in troubled marriages (Jacobson, Waldron, & Moore, 1980).

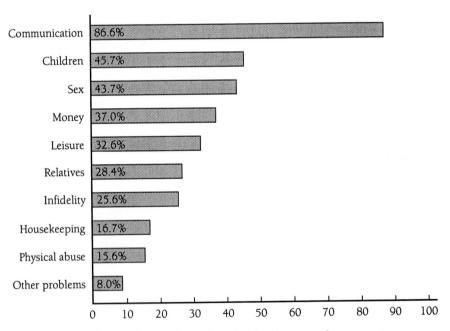

Figure 8.1   Rankings of marital problems by family counseling agencies

Source: From *Progress on Family Problems: A Nationwide Study of Clients' and Counselors' Views on Family Agency Services,* by Dorothy Fahs Beck and Mary Ann Jones. Copyright 1973 by the Family Service Association of America. Reprinted by permission.

Looking at this the other way around, we discover that when couples have other kinds of problems they develop communication problems, too. Couples tend to communicate less when they are having a serious problem, and because less information is exchanged, possibilities for misunderstanding increase. It is truly a "Catch-22." Communication can heal problems between people, but when couples are troubled their communication becomes impoverished in both quality and quantity and they become less able to use the tools that can help them.

A major emphasis in communication enhancement is to help couples see that communication is a set of skills that can be learned. These skills can be provided in workshop and group formats (Crowe & Ridley, 1990). From these programs, it has become clear that three separate aspects or skill sets can be identified: communication training, behavioral exchange training, and problem-solving or conflict resolution training (Chasin, Grunebaum, & Herzig, 1990). In Chapter 2, we spent some time reviewing the behaviorist ideas about exchange training (increasing reinforcers in the marriage) and introduced the "caring days" technique, in which couples identify things that they find rewarding and then provide rewards to their partners. In Chapter 10 we will address problem solving, negotiation, and conflict resolution. In this chapter, we will confine ourselves to the skills involved in increasing communication and eliminating behaviors that disrupt the workings of a relationship.

Focusing on communication training alone is a little artificial, as most couples groups and training sessions with a single couple include all three of the major skill areas. But communication is an important enough issue to earn this separate treatment. In this chapter, we will discuss the barriers to good communication and methods to teach couples how to develop positive behaviors and avoid communication blocks. Finally, we will review some of the communication skills programs that work for couples in group settings, and we will see how these skills can be taught to individual couples in office sessions.

Questions to Consider

1. Suppose that you are married, living together, engaged, or involved in an intimate relationship. On a scale of 1 to 5 with 5 being the most difficult, rate each of the following topics on how uncomfortable it would be to discuss the issue with your partner:
   a. Your feeling that your partner spends too much money.
   b. Your need to spend more time together.
   c. Your sexual preferences.
   d. Your partner's sexual preferences.
   e. Your need to have privacy.
   f. Your negative feelings about your partner's family.
   g. Your partner's personal cleanliness.
   h. Your partner's bad habits.
   i. Your worst fears.
   j. Your past relationships.
2. If you needed to talk to your intimate partner about one of the more difficult issues listed above, what might stop you from bringing up the problem? Discuss your answers with fellow learners.

3. Draw three concentric circles on a sheet of paper. Place a dot in the center of the innermost circle. Think of the outer circle as acquaintances, the second ring as friends, and the inner ring as your closest confidants. What sorts of things do you discuss with the acquaintances versus with friends and confidants? How many people are in this inner circle? Are you able to confide everything to people in this group, or do you keep many things to yourself? What prevents you from including more people in your inner circle? Compare your answers with members of the opposite gender. Do you see any patterns or differences?

4. Do you think there might be other ways of increasing communication in couples rather than teaching them new skills? Write down some things you might have done to improve the quality of a relationship that did not involve either person learning a new behavior.

THE HISTORY OF COMMUNICATION IN COUPLES THERAPY

As early as 1956, Gregory Bateson had noticed that dysfunctional families had dysfunctional communication patterns. Among the first to be identified was the "double-bind." The double-bind is exemplified in the old joke about a parent who buys the son two shirts. When he tries on the blue one, the parent asks, "What—you didn't like the red one?" In the double-bind, no matter what you do, you can't win. Such communications lead people to frustration and withdrawal in intimate relationships.

Family therapist Virginia Satir extended the work of the "communication school" of family therapy and popularized it among therapists (Satir, Banmen, Gerber, & Gomori, 1991). One of Satir's main contributions was her focus on changing families' communication patterns instead of on "healing" their personalities. This was a real paradigm shift from the psychodynamic viewpoint that was built on identifying the interlocking pathologies of family members.

Eric Berne (1961), the founder of transactional analysis (TA) in the 1960s, focused therapy on the transactions, or exchanges of recognition and affection, between people and the elaborate games involved in getting attention and intimacy. He diagrammed communication patterns between client ego states and saw bad communication as mainly "crossed transactions," and good communication as coming from "complementary transactions." For example, complementary Adult-to-Adult transactions are good for exchanging information (Q: "Do we have enough money to pay the bills?" A: "Yes, we do"); Child-to-Child transactions are necessary for a couple to have fun together. A "crossed transaction" exists when one member sends a message like "What do you want for breakfast?" (Adult to Adult) and the other replies (crossing the transaction), "Why should you care?" (Child to Parent). Berne got us to look at the *intentions* and the payoffs involved in elaborate communication games.

Behaviorists have had a major impact on the development of communication training for couples by taking communication training from the therapy room to the classroom. Weiss (1975), O'Leary and Turkewitz (1978), and Gottman and associates (1976) contributed to research and training by identifying the specific skills involved in better communication for couples and in conducting research on the effectiveness of such programs.

Recently, Gottman (1994) turned his attention to the communication patterns associated with marriages that succeed and those that fail. His research suggests that successful couples maintain a 5 to 1 ratio of positive to negative interactions. Gottman compares this conceptualization to testing the pH balance of soil; no matter how much acid is added to the soil, the pH remains the same if a neutralizing amount of alkaline is thrown in. When a couple's negative interactions increase beyond this magic 5 to 1 ratio, the relationship destabilizes. This formula accounts for an enigma we often encounter: volatile couples who fight a lot but stay together. According to Gottman, stable relationships of this type have counterbalancing helpings of passion and positive interactions.

Gottman then asked, "What are stable couples doing that maintains this balance?" He found that stable couples, although they expressed negative feelings, were much less extreme when doing so. Overall, they showed less contempt, were less critical, and were better listeners. But more important, these couples showed their "positivity"; they openly expressed positive feelings.

COMMUNICATION FUNDAMENTALS

Nonverbal Communication

Therapists have long known that nonverbal communication can be as powerful as the words people use. One reason is that nonverbals convey the emotional tone of communication. Mehrabian (1972) found that about 7% of the total emotions conveyed are by verbal means, 38% are vocal, and 55% are facial. Nonverbals add the punctuation to our verbal statements; saying you are concerned and then putting your arm around someone can accentuate your message. Emotional intimacy is communicated largely through nonverbals. Therapists intentionally face clients squarely, show mostly open postures, and maintain eye contact for the purpose of increasing intimacy and facilitating their clients' self-disclosure.

Earlier, we pointed out that distressed couples communicate less when they are having problems. This is also true in nonverbal communication; distressed couples use far less eye contact than do those who are not having problems. Virginia Satir often asked couples to pay attention to their physical messages. She felt that when sending a message to the partner, the nonverbal aspect can communicate sincerity and "anchor" the verbal message. Satir would sometimes demonstrate this to couples by asking them to sit back-to-back and discuss a problem. She then showed them the contrast by asking them to sit eye-to-eye, hold hands, and repeat the verbal message.

Nonverbal messages can also be used to manipulate, to dominate, or to create distance in a relationship. A too-common family pattern is when one member is a "rage-aholic," using aggressive nonverbals such as loud voice tone and angry postures to get what he or she wants. By the same token, one member may use the "silent treatment" to escape from the intensity of a relationship or to punish the partner.

It has often been said that we can't *not* communicate. Although we are constantly communicating, we are not always aware of the messages that are going out. Very often one member of a couple is not aware that his or her communication style is aggressive or has some other effect on the partner. By watching videotapes or receiving other kinds of feedback, couples can become more aware of the messages they are sending.

Nonverbal behavior can also contradict what the sender is saying, revealing that the sender is not congruent. People can be saying one thing but meaning another with their nonverbals. Recently a college administrator we know held a session on "two-way communication" during which he gave a lecture and did not ask for comments. Although he was "talking the talk," he was not "walking the walk."

A final point about nonverbal communication is that it is ambiguous. Sometimes crossed arms mean that I am not open to listening to you; at other times, it may mean that the room is cold and I am warming myself. Couples can easily misinterpret the their partners' nonverbals. Research suggests that couples who are having problems—"distressed couples," as they are called in research studies—often interpret all kinds of messages more negatively than the partner intended. This must also be true of nonverbals. Sometimes the raising of eyebrows, tone of voice, silence, or an inflection can be enough to set off an argument when one member of a couple reads the nonverbal as extremely negative despite what was intended. A good example is the ways couples communicate about sex. Couples may use words to initiate or refuse sexual interaction, but nonverbals are used more frequently than verbal methods (Sprecher & McKinney, 1993). Given that nonverbal communication can be ambiguous and that the sexual relationship may be imbued with tension and embarrassment, misunderstandings can quickly develop. When communication about sex is more satisfactory, the couple judges the sexual relationship and the relationship as a whole as more satisfactory (Cupach & Comstock).

Gender Differences in Communication

Much has been made of male/female differences in communication. Whatever one's evaluation of the pop psychology book *Men Are from Mars, Women Are from Venus* (Gray, 1993), this volume has struck a chord with an American public that believes that men and women do not communicate well because of their different communication styles. Deborah Tannen (1994), in her book *Gender and Discourse* (1994), addresses these differences in a very scholarly way. One of Tannen's contentions is that men communicate to exchange facts (report talk) and women communicate to maintain relationships (rapport talk). These two different agendas cause confusion. When she says, "Sit down, I want to talk to you," she may mean, "Let's be close for a minute." His response is likely to be, "What do you want to talk about?"

Self-Disclosure

We often define our relationships as either close or distant. By *close*, often we mean the degree of self-disclosure that exists in the relationship. Self-disclosure normally deepens over time in a relationship, but sometimes it develops rapidly. Self-disclosure in a relationship means sharing one's emotions as they are felt, but it also includes such things as admitting to bad habits; sharing aspects of one's past; and sharing one's hopes, dreams, and ambitions (Waring, 1988). In couples, there appears to be a positive relationship between disclosure and marital satisfaction (Hendrick, 1981). Because of the relationship between intimacy and self-disclosure, many marriage enrichment programs try to improve relationships by helping couples disclose more to each other.

Self-disclosure has been considered to be important both to the well-being of relationships and as a general barometer of mental health (Jourard, 1964; Pennebaker, 1990). On the other hand, we find that disclosure is not always helpful and can be destructive (Gottman, 1994). Unrestrained self-disclosure can cause severe damage; many wrongs are perpetuated by telling the brutal "truth." Although sharing too many negatives about the relationships can lead to dissatisfaction (Levinger & Senn, 1967), self-disclosure is more likely to cause a problem in a relationship when it is restricted, leading to a lack of intimacy and misunderstanding.

Individuals and couples vary in terms of how much intimacy and disclosure they desire. Fitzpatrick (1988) has identified three patterns of disclosure in relationships. *Traditionals* are couples who are very interdependent. They share many things, but when conflict arises, they communicate nonassertively. *Independents,* on the other hand, also share a lot but have separate lives, and they tend to be assertive and confrontive in their communication. Finally, *Separates* are much less interdependent, are limited in their assertiveness with each other, and avoid open conflict. Any of these patterns may keep the couple in a state of homeostasis and allow for the degree of closeness that the couple desires.

Women are more disclosing in same-sex friendships than men are and, in general, have closer relationships. Research suggests that American women disclose more throughout their lives than do their male counterparts (Hendrick, 1995). In this culture, it is acceptable for girls to shed tears, whereas such expression for a teenage boy would be considered weak. Hendrick (1995) claims that penalties for self-disclosure of emotions are also higher for adult men than for adult women. Crying on the job or losing one's temper carries a greater stigma for a male, so men learn not to express affect. Male images of success and strength show men not as performing despite fear and self-doubt but as like James Bond, heroes who laugh in the face of death. This "strength" becomes a problem in a marital situation where the woman highly values self-disclosure and wants it from a man. In the typical case, the man values it less and so produces less disclosure than the woman would like.

The Linear Model

One well-known conceptualization of the communication process is the *linear model*. This model is useful because it simplifies a single set of communications and allows us to look at each as if it occurs in a linear/temporal sequence: he says, she says; he responds, she responds. In reality, verbal and nonverbal messages simultaneously flow back and forth between sender and receiver. While she is speaking, he is turning away; she responds to that and changes her message. Although it is important to recognize this back-and-forth flow, it is difficult to depict, so we use the linear model because of its simplicity and teachability.

The linear model suggests that there are listeners and receivers, messages, channels, and feedback loops. These elements are shown in Figure 8.2, and the model is very simply explained in Thomas Gordon's book *Parent Effectiveness Training* (1975). The model indicates that a sender originates a message and sends it through a particular channel to the receiver.

A *channel* is the way a sender encodes a message, and encoding is affected by the sender's past experiences. For example, one might learn to send an "I" message rather than a "you" message. An "I" message like "I get annoyed when I see those dirty dishes piling up" is likely to be better received than is "You are a filthy slob." But the channel someone chooses is often based on the person's beliefs and family history. In one couple we worked with, the wife came from an Italian family where great emphasis was placed on being honest and "calling a spade a spade." The husband came from a rather quiet Maine Protestant family. When she expressed, he was surprised to find that she did not quietly confide her concerns but instead engaged in name-calling and explosive outbursts of emotions. The way she sent her messages of anger was based on her cultural and family history, and she could not understand why this was so unpalatable to her husband. After all, what she said was "true" and that was how everyone in her family acted. People encode their messages and send them through familiar channels, assuming that decoding will be easy. For example, a husband once said to his wife, "You are a good person to be away from," which was a confusing channel for his communication. He was trying to express that he felt comfortable when he was away from his wife and looked forward to seeing her on his return. She decoded it as "I like being away from you."

One of the biggest problems in decoding the messages of others is that messages can become confused by "noise." *Noise* is anything that gets in the way

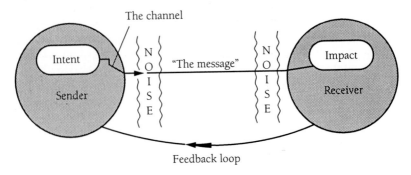

Figure 8.2. The linear model of communication

of understanding the content, feelings, and intentions of the message. One source of noise is internal. Just as in a radio broadcast, we cannot hear the message when static is interfering. We cannot hear intimate messages when we are listening to thoughts and past experiences that distort other people's messages. Noise is shown in Figure 8.2 as outside of the Sender and the Receiver, but in reality noise is anything that interferes, including loud sounds in the environment, a partner's hearing disability, one person's preoccupation with other matters, each one's perceptions and cognitions, and any past experiences that make it hard to read the intention of the message. As we said before, cultural and family background provide noise and filter the messages coming in from others.

The fact that there is noise in human communication makes a feedback loop necessary. A *feedback loop* is actually "metacommunication," or communication about communication. The feedback loop is a statement by the receiver to the sender asking for confirmation about the sender's message.

"Am I hearing that you do not intend to go to the party with me?"
"Are you saying you want to be alone right now?"
"What I am picking up is that you would rather invite your family here for Thanksgiving than go to my parents' house."

Feedback is a nonblameful restatement of the message heard that asks for confirmation. Feedback statements are best constructed so that they do not make the other person feel defensive. Sometimes what appears to be feedback is really angry communication designed to retaliate.

"You couldn't care less about me, could you?"
"You don't want to spend any time with me, do you?"
"You hate my family, isn't that true?"

The questions in these examples are rhetorical; they pretend to ask for confirmation but they are really expressing anger. This is what makes intimate communication so confusing. We respond to the verbal message "You hate my family, isn't that true?" by saying, "I like your family" rather than responding, "You feel hurt and angry about my plans to spend Thanksgiving with my side of the family." Very often, the *feeling* is the real message, not the factual content.

Feedback: The Way Out

The emergency exit from confusing cycles of bad communication is to focus on the feedback loop (see Figure 8.2). According to Gottman and associates (1976), feedback is "when the listener tells the speaker about the impact a message had" (p. 2). By comparing *impact* and *intent*, we can see where miscommunication occurred.

Case Example: Levon and Maria

The example of Levon and Maria illustrates a simple but common miscommunication sequence that allows us to examine impact and intent.

Levon: I don't think the party is going to be any good.

Levon's statement is chosen as a way of easing into a difficult conversation. He may be afraid to say "I don't want to go to the party tonight" or "I feel more like going to a movie." These are his intentions. He chose a channel that he thought would open up conversation without committing himself to a course of action. In other words, Levon's *intent* was different from the message he sent. Figure 8.3 shows Maria and Levon's exchange in terms of impact and intent.

Maria: (Option 1) You don't want to spend any time with me, do you.

Maria feels angry, and instead of asking for feedback in a nonblameful way, she accuses Levon, hoping he will feel guilty. Perhaps she is retaliating because the impact of his message was that she feels hurt. The *impact* on Maria's side was based on the confusing message she heard, but she perceived it in a much more negative way than was intended.

Maria: (Option 2) Are you saying you don't want to go to the party with me?

Using the feedback loop as shown in Figure 8.4, Maria evoked the message Levon was really sending (see Figure 8.5).

Levon: No, I am just tired. I want to stay home.

Now that Maria better understands Levon's basic message, they are on the road to clear communication. Although they may not have solved the problem about whether they are going home or going to the party, some of their needs are more out in the open. Much of the work in communication training is aimed at teaching couples this process: to stop the action, obtain a clear idea of the intent and impact of messages, and then work out reasonable compromises.

Manipulations and Games

Sometimes communication is manipulation, in which one member of a couple sends a message designed to produce an emotional state in the other member. For example, if Levon feels guilty, he may accede to Maria's wishes. The problem with this "persuasive" communication is that it raises Levon's defenses and it gets off the topic of going to the party and onto the topic of how much they care about each

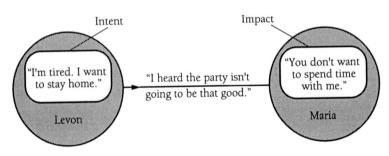

Figure 8.3. Intent and impact: Poor communication

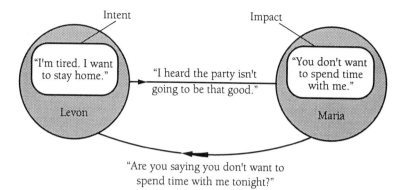

Figure 8.4. Giving feedback

other. The therapist must watch for these "games," as Eric Berne called them. They can be elaborate ways to get attention or bring excitement into the relationship. In short, there is a payoff. But a side effect is less intimacy, since one partner feels manipulated.

Hidden Agendas and Underlying Issues

The impact of Maria's response to Levon's message may seem an overreaction to an outsider. Why must she be so unreasonable? But Levon's message may have particular meaning for Maria. There may be a hidden agenda or underlying issue. For example, Maria may be feeling ignored *in general*. Because the couple has not solved this problem, it emerges whenever the couple tries to communicate. It is not just *this* party that she is responding to, but all the times Levon has not wanted to go out with her. Once communication has clarified the original intent of Levon's message, the couple must then evaluate why this message had such an impact on Maria. Is this a problem that the couple needs to put on their list of issues to be addressed in therapy?

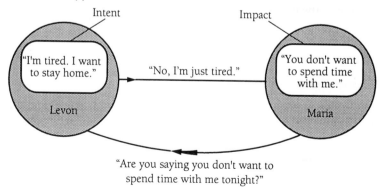

Figure 8.5. Responding to feedback with clear communication

Indirectness and Culture

Why do people send such indirect messages? Why can't Levon tell Maria that he is tired in the first place? Very often the answer lies in one's upbringing. Tannen (1986) claims that people choose indirect channels because they are afraid of the effect their words will have on the other person, so they drop hints to test how the other person feels. Levon may fear that if he says he is tired, either Maria will go to the party without him or she will be angry and he will have to contend with that for the rest of the evening. So, rather than expressing his feelings, he tests the water with his initial statement.

Politeness is a cultural matter. Tannen (1994) has suggested that the stereotype of Jewish people as "pushy" may have derived from their culture's directness and confrontive communication style that conflicts with the more indirect Anglo-Saxon style. I vividly remember telling a story to a Jewish friend during which I claimed to have erected "hundreds" of fence posts during my childhood in the country. The friend interrupted my story and asked for a realistic accounting. Now in my Appalachian culture, communicating disbelief is considered to be extremely rude. One accepts the word of another person (even hyperbole such as this) without comment because any other response is tantamount to calling that person a liar. Even indirectly suggesting that someone is a liar is using "fightin' words." However, my friend did not know the cultural meaning of her comment; to her, directly questioning the other person was a natural part of the give and take of a friendly conversation.

Another example that comes to mind was related by an Indian acquaintance. Within his North Indian culture, one did not make direct requests of parents. Such a thing would be met with silence and would be considered very unkind because it implies that the parents are not taking adequate care of their children if the children have to request something. Consequently when as a child this acquaintance wanted a radio, he planned a strategy of hint-dropping to his father that extended over several days. One day, he would say, "You know, there are many interesting broadcasts about current events on the radio." Another day, he might have related the fact that a friend with a radio had cited one of the programs in a school term paper. Finally, one day his father told him that he had chosen a radio and that it could be picked up at a certain shop. This may seem an elaborate way to send a message, but it maintained the respectful relationship between parent and child, and the message was communicated.

Cultural problems in communication often occur because of a different use of nonverbals. We are all familiar with the fact that certain nonverbal gestures in one country have opposite meanings in another. But communication, verbal and nonverbal, is full of many nuances that are not so easy to detect. Voice tone, volume, speed, and word choice all convey special culturally specific meanings (Tannen, 1986). Recently, I found myself becoming annoyed at an acquaintance from Germany. When I asked him about various aspects of his country, he very often responded, "Of course!" These words and intonation in the United States suggest that the speaker is correcting the other person for asking such a stupid question. This was not the intention of this person's message, however; he had learned "Of course!" as a synonym for the word *Yes*. It is a challenge for a couple to communicate when the partners come from different cultural roots. It is also a challenge for therapists to understand the communication patterns of couples whose backgrounds differ significantly from their own.

ASSESSMENT OF COMMUNICATION PROBLEMS AND STRENGTHS

There are three avenues to the identification of couple communication strengths and difficulties. One method is to look at questionnaires such as the Primary Communication Inventory (PCI), a 25-item self-report inventory (Navran, 1967). Some of the screening instruments listed in Chapter 5 contain communication scales. A second direction is observational coding systems, wherein videotaped records of a couple's reactions are examined and coded to analyze communication. A third and more commonly used assessment is to look for standard maladaptive patterns, identified by couples experts.

All three assessment methods have their shortcomings. Research suggests that classifying both self-report and communication patterns into types fail to get at the real nuances when compared with the videotapes of couples trying to communicate (Baucom & Adams, 1987). Not all couples' communication problems fit very neatly into the categories we identify. But observational coding is far too time-consuming for a clinician, and a short sample cannot be relied on to reflect how the couple really communicates. Both methods tend to ignore the cognitive aspects of the communication. What did each person intend by the message? What did each perceive the intentions of the partner to be?

One way out of this issue is to use screening inventories and discuss the results with the couple as a starting point. We recommend educating couples on the common communication problems or standard patterns, but we also try to get a handle on the unique ways that a particular couple both fails and succeeds in communicating. One way to do this is through the use of videotape as an assessment tool.

Videotaped Assessment

The presence of a video camera in the therapy office sets everyone's nerves on edge, even the therapist's. If the presence of a video camera is introduced as a natural part of therapy, then clients will be more receptive. One way to do this is to have the camera in the room with the lens cap on for several sessions before actual taping takes place. Then begin taping early on in the session. When some particularly good interaction between the couple has been filmed, the tape can be stopped, perhaps halfway through the session, and played back for the couple to view. One way to get clients to look at intentions and perceptions is to stop the tape and ask the following kinds of questions.

"What were your intentions when you said . . ."
"Tell your partner what you mean by . . ."

"Were you suggesting a change, or were you trying to hurt your partner?"

"Was this statement constructive or destructive?"

"How effective were you in getting your point across? What ways would work better?"

"If you were going to use a listening response, what would you have said instead?"

Here are some actual examples from a recent session.

"Fred, when Sara said, 'Just like always, I have to take care of everything,' how did you feel?"

"Sara, you perceive yourself as having to take care of all the difficult tasks. When you say to Fred, 'I have to take care of everything,' what are you requesting from Fred?"

"Sara, can you think of another way of expressing how angry you are and asking for a change?"

Who Should Receive Communication Training?

Another important aspect of assessment in communication training is to determine which kinds of couples ought to be included and which should be excluded from such training. The existence of a substance abuse problem is a reason for exclusion, since the couple will not benefit under these circumstances. And if there is violence in the couple relationship, communication training is only a Band-Aid approach and so would not be appropriate. Violence must be treated separately, and communication training can begin only when the violence has ceased. Even then, communication training is often best in a facility like a domestic violence center, where couples with similar problems can join together. Also, communication training is usually a waste of time for couples who have recently experienced an affair. That wound will need some healing before couples can benefit from communication training (see Chapter 12).

COMMON COMMUNICATION PROBLEMS IN COUPLES

This section describes some of the common roadblocks to communication—sometimes called "negative skills"—that researchers and couples therapists have identified. A good communication program will help couples identify the patterns to be eliminated as well as help them build "positive skills." We suggest that therapists help clients understand the importance of moving away from blame early in such training. Otherwise, clients may use these patterns to lash back at their partner by pointing out the other person's communication shortcomings.

Gottman (1994) thinks that most negative communication patterns fall under the following four broad categories, which he calls the "Four Horsemen of the Apocalypse."

1. *Criticism versus complaint.* This problem exists when couples attack the person rather than the behavior. Usually this takes the form of an accusation: "I can't have any fun because you don't like to dance." Alternatively, a complaint might be: "I really enjoy dancing. I wish you and I could dance more or take dancing lessons."

2. *Contempt.* The difference between criticism and contempt is the *intention* to psychologically wound or hurt your partner. Insults and name-calling, hostile humor, mockery, and contemptuous body language are the signs of contempt.

3. *Defensiveness.* When defensiveness sets in, the couple is not acting as a team. Both partners deny responsibility, make excuses, and use methods like cross-complaining. Couples at this stage have a difficult time solving problems because they leave many things hanging when they walk away in frustration.

4. *Stonewalling.* When couples reach the point of giving up, one member may turn into a "stone wall" and remove himself or herself from the conversation. Turning into a stone wall conveys contempt and is both a retaliation and a gesture of helplessness. Many people stonewall occasionally during the course of a relationship, but habitual stonewalling can become a serious problem.

Specific Maladaptive Communication Problems in Couples

Mind Reading　Mind reading occurs when one member of the couple consistently acts on the perceived intent of the other person without utilizing the feedback loop.

> "I didn't even tell you about the free tickets to the ballet because I knew you wouldn't want to go."
>
> "I could tell by the look on your face that you didn't want to eat at that restaurant."

Mind reading occurs in couples who have known each other for a long time and in those who have been together a short time. It is a short-circuit in the communication process because one person is reacting to a message or even a nonverbal cue, such as an uplifted eyebrow, without checking on its intent.

The Panel Discussion　The panel discussion is a tendency for partners to be excessively rational in their discussions so that the underlying feelings are not expressed. People who communicate this way often are in dual-career partnerships, are highly educated, or merely place a great deal of value on being civil and avoiding conflict. Counseling involves helping them express and reflect their feelings.

> *Vincent:* "The thing that is the most troublesome is that you never call me and tell me when you are going to be late. I don't know how to plan the evening. *(Intent: I am annoyed and lonely)*
>
> *Denise:* I suggest that you assume that if I am not home by 7:00, you can make plans that don't include me. *(Impact: I feel angry and pressured)*

Being Right The more unhappy a couple is, the more both partners believe that they are "right" and are justified in their viewpoint (Noller & Vernardos, 1986). Although inflexibility can be the problem of individual members, it can be seen in both members, with each person trying to be right.

The Summarizing Self Syndrome, or Cocktail Listening Like people at cocktail parties, some partners rehearse what they want to say and simply wait until the other person stops talking instead of listening to what is being said (McKay, Fanning, & Paleg, 1994). The summarizing self, or SS, syndrome, identified by Gottman (1994), is another way of describing this interaction. It pertains to couples who continue to reiterate the same complaint without reacting to the partner's statement. The result is that the conversation goes nowhere.

Renee: I said "ABC."
Manny: I said "XYZ."
Renee: But I said "ABC."
Manny: But I said "XYZ."

Cross-Complaining Cross-complaining is answering the other person's complaint with one of your own.

Partner 1: I wish you would not spend so much money on golf.
Partner 2: Well, I wish you wouldn't invite your mother over every week.

A cross-complaint sounds like a response to the other person's complaint, but it is a defensive reaction rather than an attempt to solve the original issue on the table.

Incongruent Messages Incongruent messages contain positive and negative aspects or verbal and nonverbal messages that do not carry the same meaning. For example, one member of a couple verbally encourages the other person to talk while continuing to watch television.

The "Stinger" Pattern The stinger is an incongruent message containing a positive statement with a criticism at the end: "Sure, you want to spend a lot of time with me now, but why couldn't we have done this five years ago?"

Name-Calling and Nonsupportive Statements It seems obvious that character assassination and questioning of the other person's motives and abilities disrupts communication and decreases trust. Unfortunately, this is the norm in many families. People who grew up in such families bring this kind of communication pattern to their other relationships and must become aware of the damaging nature of such insults. Communication training helps these individuals and couples express their feelings rather than using invectives, and learn to abandon "being right"—a belief that is often behind name-calling and insults.

Not Hearing the Positives A common cycle in many distressed couples occurs when compliments, praise, and recognition are not heard. Instead, one or both members of the couple hear only the negative aspects of the communication. Therapists like to "stop action" when they find that couples are responding only to the negative aspects of the messages. Couples can then be made more aware of the intent and impact of their communication.

Kitchen Sinking When a couple begins an argument on a certain topic, sometimes other unresolved issues are brought up. Without some restraint, everything but the kitchen sink is complained about at once.

Positive Communication Skills

Perspective Taking Perspective taking is the ability to understand another person's point of view. Perspective taking simply asks that we understand another's thinking and intellectually put ourselves in another's place, and it seems to be important to good relationships. Research suggests that, in distressed marriages, men are often low in perspective taking (Long, 1993). This skill combats several negative communication practices, including "being right" and the SS syndrome.

One way of teaching this skill is to explain it as a role-playing assignment. The couple takes an example of a recent disagreement, and then Person A tells his or her perspective. Person B summarizes A's perspective again and again until Person A feels that Person B has understood. Person B then gives his or her side of the story until Person A can paraphrase it adequately. Then they reverse roles and reenact the argument; Person A argues Person B's point of view and Person B argues Person A's point of view. At the end of the exercise, the couple may have a better handle on how to solve the problem because each person now understand the needs and perspective of the other (Young, 1992).

The Speaker-Listener Technique In the speaker-listener technique, partners take turns playing each role. Listeners cannot become speakers until the speakers indicate that they have been properly heard. Then the partners switch roles. Couples are given the following instructions:

When you are a speaker, you:
Describe the problem without laying blame
Stay on one topic
Express your feelings
Don't insult or criticize the other person

When you are a listener, you:
Pay careful attention
Don't interrupt

Try to understand the speaker's perspective
Use good listening nonverbals
Reflect and paraphrase for accuracy (use the feedback loop)

The Floor Technique   The floor technique is designed to give couples feedback on the impact that their communication has on the other person (Gottman et al., 1976, p. 5). Couples first decide on an issue they wish to discuss, and then they label three index cards: one says, "The Floor," another says "POSITIVE," and the third is labeled "NEGATIVE." Whoever holds "The Floor" card is the speaker and can talk without interruption until finished. The speaker may hand over The Floor at any time if asked. The listener holds up the "NEGATIVE" or "POSITIVE" cards to let the speaker know the impact of the current message. When the listener holds up the "NEGATIVE" card, this often leads to a change of floor because the speaker now wants to get feedback on what was negative about the message. It is useful to stop the action at these points and see why intent and impact are not matching. We have found that this technique is initially best practiced with the therapist present, serving as a referee and coach.

Giving Affection, Praise, and Admiration to Your Partner   In Chapter 2, we reviewed the importance of increasing the positives in the relationship. When couples are troubled, they stop noticing the positives altogether. Ask couples to notice the positives, the way the other person is trying, instead of noting only what is lacking in the relationship.

Editing: The Art of Being Polite   Earlier we cited research (Birchler, Weiss, & Vincent, 1975) claiming that we are more polite to strangers than to those closest to us. *Politeness* in this context does not mean "walking on eggshells"; it means editing out the negative aspects of one's message and learning to pare it down to include only things that are constructive. Gottman and associates (1976) recommend nine rules of politeness, as summarized here.

1. Be direct: Say what you can do and want to do.
2. Show appreciation in a sincere and positive way.
3. Be considerate and courteous.
4. Show interest in the other person's activities. Listen and ask questions.
5. Say things that you honestly feel and that might be important to your partner.
6. When you think you were wrong, admit it but don't criticize yourself, as this requires that your partner offer support.
7. Keep your focus on the present, not the past.
8. Let your partner finish speaking before you respond.
9. Try to understand your partner's point of view, needs, and desires.

Editing is the skill of looking at one's own statements and determining whether they follow these nine rules of politeness. Couples can review transcripts, see videotapes, or give written responses to stock situations in order to learn to edit their responses according to the rules.

COMMUNICATION TRAINING PROGRAMS

Couples communication training is best done in a group setting. Therapists can design their own methods or choose from a variety of prepared materials (L'Abate & Weinstein, 1987). Alternatively, couples can attend marriage enrichment or relationship enhancement programs. These programs vary widely in their quality and intent, and many are not, in fact, communications skills training. Some are affectively oriented and help couples feel better about their relationship, often conducted within the context of a specific religious denomination. Therapists must investigate these programs before a referral is made to determine whether they will address the issues a couple is facing.

The Prevention and Relationship Enhancement Program (PREP)

The PREP program began in 1980 at the University of Denver and has its origins in the work of Gottman, Notarius, Gonso, and Markman (1976). It has gone through several revisions and is now the best researched of any couples enrichment program. The long-term studies (3- and 4-year follow-ups) seem to show that couples who have gone through the program are more likely to stay together than are couples in control groups, and they show less negative communication (Markman, Renick, Floyd, Stanley, & Clements, 1993). The program is skills-based but also considers getting the proper attitude set for couples. It asks couples to view improving their relationship as skills that can be acquired. It asks them to consider small modifications and build on successes. PREP uses research data to convince participants that real improvements are possible.

Basic Principles of the PREP Program
Some of the major topics addressed in the program include:

> The intent-impact model (Gottman et al., 1976).
> Effective speaking and listening (Speaker-Listener Format)
> Destructive and constructive styles of communication
> Giving specific feedback
> Examining expectations that may affect the relationship
> Hidden issues behind the surface topics
> The role of fun in maintaining the relationship
> Problem solving
> Team building: positive ways to increase intimacy and commitment
> Spiritual values of honor, respect, intimacy, and forgiveness
> Communication in the sexual relationship
> Practicing and maintaining skills

Format

The program utilizes two formats: the extended format and the large group. In the extended format, 4 to 10 couples attend 6 weekly sessions lasting between 2 and 2½ hours. Brief lectures are given on the topics listed above. Later, every couple is given a "communication consultant" who coaches them when they practice skills together in a separate room. In the large group format, up to 60 couples come together for the lecture portion that extends over 1 weekend. Couples normally stay at a hotel and practice the skills on their own in their rooms (Floyd, Markman, Kelly, Blumberg, & Stanley, 1995). A PREP book can be purchased (Markman, Stanley, & Blumberg, 1994), and the course is available on two videotapes that couples can view in their own homes.

Relationship Enhancement (RE)

Guerney and associates (1986) developed a relationship enhancement program based on a psychoeducational model of therapy. They believe that most human problems can be reframed as skills deficits.

Basic Principles of the RE Program

The program involves training in the following areas.

1. Expressive skills (teaching couples appropriate self-disclosure)
2. Empathic skills (teaching listening and reflecting feelings)
3. Mode-switching skills (learning to change from listener to speaker, depending on who has the problem)
4. Problem-conflict resolution skills (creative problem solving, negotiation, and compromise)
5. Self-change skills (self-monitoring and setting personal goals)
6. Helping others change skills (supporting the other person's goals)
7. Generalization-transfer skills (using skills learned in other interactions to help the couple relationship)
8. Teaching supervisory skills (training others in a social environment to use good communication skills so clients can practice and use these methods)
9. Maintenance skills (relapse prevention skills, helping clients practice problem solving and use preventive measures such as relationship enrichment activities)

Other Programs

Practical Application of Intimate Relationship Skills (PAIRS)

Not all programs for couples communication and relationship enhancement are based on behavioral or social learning theory. The PAIRS program is an eclectic blend of experiential, psychotherapeutic, and educational elements (Gordon, 1990). It is run by therapists who conduct a 12- to 16-session program that meets weekly, with monthly follow-up sessions. Interestingly, the program accepts singles as well as couples and is aimed at helping people develop self-awareness, couples awareness, communication skills, sexuality/sensuality awareness, fair-fighting skills, and negotiating skills.

Association for Couples in Marriage Enrichment (ACME)

ACME is a unique marriage enrichment organization. Married couples who have been through the program and have received additional training facilitate weekend enrichment courses for couples. During these weekends, the couples address problem solving, communication, intimacy, spirituality, and sexuality. The attendees first work together as a group and then split into couples to discuss each topic.

Marriage Encounter

Marriage encounter programs similar to ACME are now conducted under the auspices of several religious denominations. They vary from a single weekend meeting to sessions over several months. They also vary in the degree to which professional therapists or therapists are involved. To find out more about these programs, look at the World Wide Web on the Internet. You will find home pages for marriage encounter in the following denominations: the Roman Catholic Church, Lutherans, Seventh-Day Adventists, United Methodists, United Church of Christ, Jewish Marriage Encounter, and others.

CONDUCTING COMMUNICATION TRAINING IN THE THERAPY OFFICE

As we said before, group communication training is likely to be the most effective medium for couples. Couples benefit from the group process, feeling a sense of cohesion and less alone in their struggles. They begin to see that the problems they are facing are quite common, and the instruction is more easily swallowed because it is not aimed directly at them. Still, there are many times when such training must take place in the therapy office because there is no suitable group available—for monetary reasons or a hundred other practical issues. Following are some suggestions for working in an office setting with a single couple (based on Young, 1992).

General Considerations

The therapist needs to have a trusting relationship with the couple if the training is to be effective. Couples are fearful that the session will disintegrate into unproductive squabbling. Establishing a good relationship in the beginning will help the couple see the therapist as neutral and will prevent one member from feeling "picked on."

The therapist also needs to promote hope. Couples may lose courage when they find themselves back in the same old patterns, even with the therapist present.

The therapist must be encouraging and reframe apparent setbacks as part of the normal progression.

One good way to start is to help the couple see the process as educational and conducive to the development of skills, just as it is promoted in the group session. Therapists can use a workbook or other publication for homework such as *Couple Skills* (McKay, Fanning, & Paleg, 1994). This workbook approach will help make sure that all the needed skills are covered and can provide ready-made homework assignments.

Every session can be structured in the same way.

1. The therapist requests that each member of the couple report on what progress was made on last week's skill during the homework assignment.
2. The therapist requests any information about recent successes the couple has had in any aspect of communication.
3. The therapist introduces a new skill by briefly giving a rationale and then demonstrating it with one member of the couple in a role play. For example, if the skill is "paraphrasing," the therapist asks one member of a couple to describe a recent problem and then gives good listening and paraphrasing responses.
4. After a brief discussion of the demonstration, couples are asked to practice the skill using a real-life situation, if one can be identified. During the couple's interaction, the therapist acts as a coach, intervening and asking the couple to try again with the corrections. The therapist also praises the couple for good skill demonstrations.
5. The therapist gives couples feedback and encouragement on their progress so far. A homework assignment is given, which might include an outside reading or writing assignment or might be a practice session to take place at home.

Regardless of the specific skill the couple is working on, the therapist gives feedback to the couple in the following manner.

- Letting them know when they are off the original topic
- Engaging in a negative pattern such as SS syndrome
- Interrupting monologues and getting the silent partner to intervene and respond
- Helping couples notice when there is an imbalance in the amount of communication between the two partners
- Helping each person speak for himself or herself and send "I" messages, rather than expressing the partner's opinions
- Helping couples learn that when complaints are made, they should be turned into requests
- Preventing couples from bringing up past issues that are irrelevant to the issue at hand
- Helping the couple become aware of each partner's nonverbal messages
- Helping partners encourage each other to speak

- Helping couples increase their feeling vocabulary and express and respond to feelings

Suggestions for the Therapist

- Ask the partners to face each other in the session.
- Spend a short time observing the couple's interaction over a common problem without interrupting. Videotaping can be useful here.
- You will have to repeat suggestions over and over again. Be persistent.
- Pay attention to nonverbal behaviors.

Suggestions for the Couple

- At home, talk to each other, not through in-laws, friends, or children.
- Make sure that you are in the right place and have enough time to communicate (cut out whatever "noise" can be controlled).
- Use "I" statements rather than accusatory "You" statements whenever possible. Instead of saying, "You are always coming home late for dinner," try "When I don't know when you're coming home, I don't know whether to wait or eat alone and I don't like waiting." The elements of a good "I" statement include a nonblaming description of events and the tangible effects it has on you, the sender of the message.
- Develop "beltlines" in your communications. Beltlines are agreed-upon rules for "fair fighting," meaning that during a fight certain topics are off limits. These boundaries are set by the couple themselves. For example, one couple may need to rule out name-calling; another may need to eradicate references to one partner's mother. Both partners know what the other one's "buttons" are; setting beltlines is an agreement not to push them.

CONCLUSION

Communication training is part of a set of interventions therapists can use when they have assessed that troubled interaction patterns are a major problem. In this chapter, we limited ourselves to discussing methods of assessing and intervening with couples who want to improve communication. Two other associated topics are increasing positive exchanges in relationships and dealing with conflict. These topics are addressed elsewhere in the book.

Therapists using the integrative model will use assessment tools to understand the difficulty and obtain an interactive definition of the problem from the couple. Couples need to set goals in communication training, such as, "We want to be able to discuss our work problems with each other occasionally (behavioral goal) so that we can let off some tension and enjoy being at home together (affective goal)." If couples do not set goals, it is very possible that they will attend enrichment weekends and communication classes but will not notice improvements. It is possible to accomplish these goals in a group setting if proper arrangements are made to have individual coaching on specific problems or to ask each couple in the group to define a specific goal. This same process can be transferred to working with a single couple in the counselor's office.

9

Intimacy and Sexuality

KEY CONCEPTS

- Intimacy and sex are interlocking concepts, but it is possible to have one without the other. Generally, couples want both in their relationships.
- There may be gender differences in the way that intimacy is expressed, which may lead to misunderstandings.
- Three key elements of love are passion, commitment, and intimacy.
- Therapists assess the degree of intimacy in the couple's relationship and help them enhance closeness.
- Most sexual problems and dysfunctions are based in the couple's emotional struggles. Because some dysfunctions are medical problems, it is always important to have sexual problems medically checked before treating the problem in couples therapy.
- Sex therapy is a specialty that requires special training. Couples therapists should understand the causes and treatments for the major sexual dysfunctions.
- Therapists assess the couple's current sexual functioning by taking a sexual history and using a sexual genogram.

INTIMACY

Defining *intimacy* has received a great deal of attention because it has been identified as an essential factor in human relationships. In relation to a couple, Waring (1980) defines couples intimacy as composed of the following eight elements.

1. *Affection*—the degree to which feelings of emotional closeness are expressed by the couple
2. *Expressiveness*—the degree to which thoughts, beliefs, attitudes, and feelings are communicated within the relationship

3. *Compatibility*—the degree to which the couple is able to work and play together comfortably
4. *Cohesion*—a commitment to the relationship
5. *Sexuality*—the degree to which sexual needs are communicated and fulfilled
6. *Conflict resolution*—the ease with which differences of opinion are resolved
7. *Autonomy*—the couple's degree of positive relationships with family and friends
8. *Identity*—the couple's level of confidence and self-esteem (p. 23)

Gender Issues

Intimacy is still influenced by a patriarchal relationship structure that is usually biased in a power differential favoring men. Traditionally, men controlled the money that provided power over their spouses. Because perceived equality is a key ingredient for the development of intimacy, the lack of it does not promote fairness and support for both partners.

According to Tannen (1990), men traditionally value independence over emotional intimacy, and women are better than men at creating and maintaining intimate connections. It has been said that men use communication to preserve independence and maintain their status, whereas women use conversation more often, to express and create intimacy (Gilligan, 1982).

Different values are placed on emotional disclosure for men and women. For example, women have been socialized that it is permissible to cry and talk about hurt and disappointment, whereas men have been told to be quiet and stoic when they hurt or are disappointed. In general, women are comfortable talking about personal issues, and men typically do not easily disclose. This does not mean that men are opposed to or cannot learn greater openness; they are simply unfamiliar with the methods of disclosing and have been taught to fear the consequences.

Because of the stereotype that women are more active in seeking closeness and intimacy with their partners, the woman is often identified as the pursuer where emotional issues are concerned. The man has been characterized most frequently as the distancer in such relationships. For example, a woman may be more inclined to initiate talks about feelings, love, hurts, and other personal information or inquiries in an attempt to feel more connected with her partner. A man may be more inclined to turn his feelings inward and protect his self-esteem by refusing to talk on a personal level or to refocus a conversation to more concrete issues with less emotionality. The more often a woman may push to talk or follow the man from room to room in an attempt to initiate conversation, the more he is apt to leave the room or become angry so the conversation will be discontinued. In other words, the more she pursues, the more he distances.

Although the "dance" in which they engage may be divided along these traditional gender lines, it is often the case that the man is the pursuer and the woman, the distancer. Interestingly, when the female stops pursuing, the male may begin to move toward her. This change in the usual behavior creates a space or opportunity for obtaining desired results of closeness as one partner changes the step of the dance.

Both partners participate in the "dance of intimacy" out of fear. For the pursuers, the fear is that they will be rejected or abandoned if they do not push for closeness. Men are primarily distancers either because they fear that they will be engulfed or overwhelmed by an emotional female or because they fear that they may reveal too much information that could potentially harm them or trap them in the future (Bowlby, 1973).

Sternberg's Triangular Model of Love

Sternberg (1986; cited in Weeks and Treat, 1992) has postulated a triangular theory of love based on the components of passion, intimacy, and decision/commitment. The theory suggests that the amount of love one person experiences is based on the strength of the three components. Furthermore, the type of love each person experiences is relative to the interaction of the three dimensions, shown in Figure 9.1. It is theorized that stable, loving relationships contain all three components of passion, friendship, and commitment.

Intimacy, Passion, and Decision/Commitment

Intimacy includes self-disclosure and feelings of connection and emotional bonding with each other, but passion involves erotic interest in another (Harvey, 1995). The energy leading to romantic love, physical attraction, and sexual feelings (Sperry & Carlson, 1991) can be described as *passion*. Passion may be present quickly for some couples, but it can wane in a long-term relationship. Intimacy develops over the course of the relationship and often includes a decision of loyalty to the relationship. The decision/commitment component refers to the decision to be with one partner, to deny any other partners, and to maintain the relationship above all else.

Therapeutic Interventions

Therapists must assess the couple's degree of intimacy, motivations behind fears, avoidance strategies, and distancing techniques before a plan can be devel-

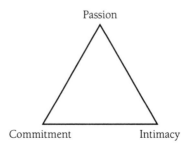

Figure 9.1   Sternberg's triangle of love

Source: From *Couples in Treatment*, by G. Weeks and S. Treat, p. 103. Copyright 1992 by Brunner/Mazel, Inc. Reprinted by permission.

oped to increase the levels of closeness and connection in the relationship (Watzlawick, Weakland, & Fisch, 1974). Box 9.1 lists some suggestions for helping couples become more intimate. A genogram can also be used to uncover expectations about gender roles, communication patterns, and male-female modeling in the partners' families of origin. After the messages and patterns have been identified, couples learn how they can communicate effectively and reduce anxieties and distancing behaviors through the use of behavioral, modeling, rehearsal, and contracting techniques. As trust develops, couples regain a sense of empathy for each other, rather than distrust and disharmony (Zimmer, 1987).

The achievement of a healthy balance between fusion (too much togetherness) and separateness also increases intimacy and promotes clearer boundaries for the couple. In therapy, couples practice role reversals to develop a greater appreciation for their partners, and they learn to view each other in a new way previously hidden behind the routine behaviors of daily living (Bach & Wyden, 1969; Stauffer, 1987). Couples must also acquire healthy conflict skills so that both can trust their partner, thus increasing self-disclosure and feelings of connection (Atwood & Dershowitz, 1992; Atwood & Weinstein, 1989).

Case Example: Amy and Greg

Amy and Greg have been married for 6 years. During the first year of their marriage, they lived with Amy's parents because Greg had been laid off from work

---

Box 9.1
Suggestions for Helping Couples Develop Intimacy in Therapy

1. Help partners assign good intentions to each other while they strengthen their intimate relationship.
2. Teach them active listening and how to paraphrase, summarize, and reflect feelings as they attempt to understand each other.
3. Explore gender myths and resentments.
4. Teach them to use "I" statements and to avoid blaming each other.
5. Help the couple understand that difference is a positive factor that keeps the relatonship alive and interesting.
6. Help the couple create time to talk and problem-solve as well as time for play and relaxation.
7. Encourage expression of feeling as a key ingredient in solution-focused discussions.
8. Eliminate unfair tactics from their conflicts such as blaming, diversions, silent treatments or negation, grocery-listing complaints, interruptions, humiliation tactics, and mixed messages.

Source: From *Solving Problems in Couples and Family Therapy*, by R. Sherman, P. Oresky, and Y. Roundtree. Copyright 1991 by Brunner/Mazel. Reprinted by permission.

and was having a difficult time finding another job. There was a high level of stress in the relationship during this time. Amy's parents argued frequently and expressed all their emotions freely. Greg had difficulty with the open expression of feelings since his parents had not been affectionate in front of him, nor had they argued openly.

Two years before the couple came to therapy, Amy's mother died. Amy had been very close to her mother and had visited her and confided in her often. Shortly after her death, Amy and Greg began to fight more frequently. They came to therapy with issues of increased conflict, feelings of "drifting apart" emotionally and physically, and confusion about how to be intimate with each other.

Application of the Integrative Model: A Problem of Intimacy

Stage 1: Assessing the Problem

From Amy's perspective, the problem is the unresolved conflict between the partners and her feelings of being unheard and unimportant. Greg described the problem as his difficulty feeling close to Amy and increased feelings of distance and fear of closeness. After exploring the patterns in their families of origin, they realized that they each brought different ideas about intimacy to the relationship.

Greg recognized that his desire to distance himself during conflicts stems from his discomfort with his own emotions. Living with Amy's parents had allowed Amy and Greg to deflect their feelings from each other and create distance. Amy became aware that her overinvolved relationship with her mother contributed to the distance she and Greg created. Greg reported that he never felt "good enough" in Amy's mother's eyes and so he distanced from Amy when she spent time with her mother. They never discussed the issue at the time of conflict.

Amy and Greg now see that they "let a lot of things get in the way of being connected and close to each other." Amy notes that when they have tried to solve the situation by talking, it always turned into an argument and remained unresolved. Greg reports that he has tried to "fix" the relationship by creating space from arguments by walking away, but he acknowledges that this action has only created more distance.

Stage 2: Goal Setting

Amy and Greg agree that they learned how to be intimate from their families and that they now desire to create their own definition of intimacy so that they can eliminate the distancing, learn to communicate clearly and problem-solve successfully, and feel more connected. They are hopeful as they realize they have the power and knowledge to make the changes.

Amy and Greg are able to accept joint responsibility for the solution once they reframe the problem and view it as a roadblock on a highway that they must go around, rather than as an obstacle that impedes their journey. They are able to view their problem as their inability to overcome the roadblock; in attempting to do so, they had gone in different directions trying to find a way around it. Now they are excited about traveling the highway together and about finding a better way to navigate around the roadblocks together.

Stage 3: Adopting New Perceptions and Behaviors

Greg, a draftsperson, is organized and creative. Amy works as a technician in a veterinary clinic and is required to make quick, sound decisions and display a caring attitude at all times. Together they are adaptable and have worked well together in other areas, such as teaming up for road rallies when sharing responsibilities for mapping a route is critical. Amy and Greg report that they feel most connected and intimate when they work side by side cooking dinner and then share the meal talking quietly. The therapist offers a perspective that, for most couples, different ideas about how to create and maintain intimacy will present roadblocks, but the better the couple is able to see them clearly and anticipate them, the easier it is to navigate around them *together*.

Stage 4: Maintaining New Perceptions and Behaviors

Greg and Amy report that they really enjoy the feelings of being closer and connected and are hopeful for continued improvement. Amy feels more important in Greg's life, and Greg feels safer sharing his thoughts and feelings with Amy. They are both aware that there are obstacles that may attempt to interfere with these new feelings and behaviors. Greg knows that if he begins to guess about Amy's motives or keeps feelings to himself and does not share with Amy, he will build resentments. Amy knows that she must monitor her communications and that if she becomes accusatory or blaming she risks stilted couple communication. The two are also aware that both of them are responsible for the solution. They both will need to identify clues that indicate they are not feeling as close as they would like.

Stage 5: Validating New Perceptions and Behaviors

The couple realizes that their hard work has paid off. Greg likes spending time with Amy and is feeling more relaxed. Amy feels more secure and accepted after recognizing that Greg will not abandon her. Because of these connected and united feelings and the open, clear, and solution-focused communication, the partners feel comfortable enough to use their new skills to discuss their financial concerns and their sexuality. They feel confident about success with these other relationship issues because they have new tools with which to problem solve and to express their true feelings. Greg and Amy like the growth and change and have accepted that the relationship will be in a constant state of change and will always require their attention and nurturing (K. Schoening & J. Schoening, personal communication, May 1995).

Considerations for Working with Intimacy Problems

This checklist can be used during the assessment stage to address important issues related to intimacy.

1. Is the couple aware of the messages both partners received from their families of origin regarding the expression of intimacy?
2. Are the partners willing to explore the myths of gender expectations and negotiate an equitable relationship, rather than allow one partner to have all the power?

3. Can the partners communicate about the ways in which they would like to demonstrate closeness and attempt to meet each other's needs?

4. Are the partners willing to self-disclose and trust their partner with their feelings?

5. Can the couple learn problem-solving skills and conflict resolution to promote solutions?

6. Is the couple willing to share responsibility for problems and solutions in the relationship?

7. Can the couple create a healthy balance between a strong self-identity and a couple identity?

8. Are both partners able to value the other's contribution to the relationship?

9. Is the couple willing to create time together to nurture their relationship?

10. Does the couple provide romantic situations to promote a continued "honeymoon" period throughout the relationship?

SEXUAL ASPECTS OF RELATIONSHIPS

Love, intimacy, and sexuality are interrelated aspects of a close relationship that influence each other in both positive and negative ways. For example, if love and intimacy are high, sex is most likely satisfactory. If the level of intimacy is low, sex may seem mechanical or purely physical, without emotional responsiveness. Although it is possible to have good sex without intimacy and love, the best sexual relationship occurs within the context of love (Hendrick, 1995). Often sexuality is a presenting problem couples express when they come to therapy, and it is usually related to a problem of intimacy in the relationship, rather than to a physical problem.

SEXUALITY AND THE COUPLE

Sexuality refers to a holistic concept based on both personality and sexual characteristics, including biological, psychological, and social attributes (Weinstein & Rosen, 1988, p. 1). In sexuality therapy, the therapist helps the couple explore conjointly their sexual feelings, values, responsibilities, needs, and behaviors (Weinstein & Rosen, 1988, p. 1). Social influences such as multiple family constellations, changing sex roles, dual careers, media exposure to sex, and a high frequency of substance abuse all play a role in couples' sexual satisfaction, responsiveness, and sexual performance and affect the degree of sexual intimacy in their relationships.

Social Issues and Sexuality

One of the most important factors for couples to consider is that sexual problems are not necessarily internal conflicts manifested in the sexual relationship, nor are they necessarily physical dysfunctions. Most often problems are a result of environmental influences that affect couples' emotional state and interfere with healthy sexual functioning (Leiblum & Pervin, 1980). Life circumstances such as the death of a loved one, family illness, job stress, the birth of children, or economic worries may precipitate the onset of sexual problems. Similarly, hurt feelings, anger, hostility, and jealousy directed toward a mate can adversely affect a sexual relationship.

Communication and Sexuality

Cupach and Metts (1991) have identified two central concepts that underlie couples' communication: (1) a couple's quality of communication is closely linked to the quality of the relationship; and (2) a couple's skill in communicating about sexuality is instrumental in maintaining sexual satisfaction and general satisfaction in the relationship (Harvey, 1995). Clearly, if partners are able to be direct and honest in their relationship, there is less likelihood that ambiguous messages and other unclear communication patterns will develop.

In addition to communication, there are practical and ethical considerations in sexuality. The practical functions include the "where, when, and how often" aspects of sexual relations that must be determined, particularly if there are rigorous demands on the couple's time. For example, couples with small children or dual-career couples may find it necessary to plan time to be intimate. Ethical considerations relate to fairness in the relationship. Specific issues include deciding which partner will initiate lovemaking, what each will give up in order to make time for the other, and what both will do to keep the relationship exciting and passionate.

The Development of Sexual Problems

Sexual problems, like other relationship problems, often develop as a consequence of vicious cycles of imbalance in the partners' styles of loving—in particular, their sexual styles (Roughan & Jenkins, 1990). Early in the relationship (the honeymoon stage), couples rarely experience desire problems. As the relationship develops and external factors such as work and children intrude, one or both partners may find themselves less physically available for each other. If only one is more removed, the other may feel hurt and attempt to entice the other to respond more sexually.

If the imbalance persists, couples may become more polarized and experience hurt, disappointment, and frustration. One may tend to blame the other for the lack of sexual intimacy so that neither is interested in initiating the sexual relationship. These vicious cycles can continue to escalate until either they reach a crisis and create resolution to the problem or there is a breakdown in the relationship. Sometimes the relationship becomes stalled because neither partner wants to risk the breakdown. The couple may decide to retain the unsatisfactory relationship indefinitely or until another crisis brings the problem to the forefront (Roughan & Jenkins, 1990).

Dysfunction or Problem?

It is difficult for a couple to establish a satisfying sexual relationship if there is a diagnosed sexual dysfunction. If a dysfunction exists, couples can explore options to improve their love relationship either through couples therapy, self-help manuals, physiological changes such as a new medication, or learning techniques to enhance lovemaking and ameliorate the problem. It is important to seek a medical opinion from a qualified physician before any diagnosis or treatment is initiated.

Often the problem is not physiological but is emotionally based. These sexual difficulties can include differences in the partners' sexual preferences including frequency, setting, time of day or night, sexual positions, fore or after play, degree of passion expressed, and type of communication employed by each partner (Karpel, 1993).

THE PROCESS OF SEXUALITY THERAPY

Assessment and Diagnosis

Determining whether a couple has a sexual dysfunction or a sexual problem has important implications for therapy. Sexual dysfunctions require medical attention and the services of a highly trained professional experienced specifically in treating dysfunctions. Treatment strategies for sexual dysfunctions are usually behaviorally based. In many instances, a combination of psychotherapy and behavioral strategies are utilized. If the partners experience no difficulty in the desire, excitement, or orgasmic phases of their sexuality, then a dysfunction is probably not present. A sexual problem or unresolved relationship problems should then be considered (Heiman, LoPiccolo, & LoPiccolo, 1976; Kaplan, 1983). Specific questions about sexuality must be asked to determine the diagnosis. Some common general content areas for questions include (Leiblum & Rosen, 1984):

1. Current sexual function and satisfaction for both partners.
2. Family of origin message and sexual practices for both partners (see sexual genogram).
3. Relationship history that includes major events in the relationship such as divorce, separation, pregnancies, deaths, and so on.
4. Effects of contraception, pregnancy, illness, medication, and the aging process.
5. Current sexual concerns and relationship concerns.

Once the presence of a dysfunction is discerned, the couple should be referred for a medical evaluation and to a licensed sex therapist. If a relationship problem is determined, then couples therapy can be directed toward the development of goals to include increased sexual pleasure and responsiveness.

All therapists, whether or not they are experienced and qualified sex therapists, must be familiar with the most prevalent sexual dysfunctions in order to determine the course of treatment. In addition, after couples have undergone treatment for a particular sexual dysfunction, they may require therapy for relationship issues that have surfaced. Thus, therapists must also be familiar with treatment procedures.

Sexual Genogram

A sexual genogram is a useful assessment tool for collecting information about both partners' family of origin messages and critical events in their sexual development (Hof & Berman, 1986; Duhl, 1981). (See Chapter 6 for information on use of the genogram.) Also, a time line can be created, with the years of the couple's relationship noted at regular intervals on the line. The therapist can then ask the couple to describe sexual satisfaction and problems at each point in time.

Goal Setting for Sexual Problems in Therapy

To reduce the partners' feelings of blame and guilt, the goals for sexuality therapy must include a shared definition of the problem. Goals can include changing the intimate time the partners spend together, challenging negative messages from their families of origin or the relationship, or making specific changes in their sexual behavior.

MALE AND FEMALE SEXUAL DYSFUNCTIONS

In this section, we will identify the most common sexual concerns that couples bring to therapy, as well as some of the most common methods of treatment. (We would like to acknowledge the contribution of J. Palelog to this section.)

Male Dysfunctions

Erectile Dysfunctions

Inhibited male orgasm, more recently referred to as *erectile dysfunction*, is the continued or repeated delay in achieving or maintaining an erection sufficient for the purpose of intercourse (Lefrancois, 1993; Weinstein & Rosen, 1988). With primary erectile dysfunction, the man is never able to achieve an erection sufficient for intercourse. With secondary erectile dysfunction, a man has at one time in his life been able to achieve an erection but, for some reason, is now unable to do so. With situational erectile dysfunction, the man is able to have sexual intercourse in some circumstances but not in others (Weinstein & Rosen, 1988).

Causes   Male erectile dysfunction is caused by physical factors, such as fatigue, diabetes, medication, low androgen level, narcotics or alcohol, and neurological diseases. Physical causes can occur alone or in conjunction with other psychological factors like anxiety or guilt, excessive maternal or paternal dominance in childhood, or inhibitory religious doctrines (Kosch, 1982; LoPiccolo, 1985; Spector & Carey, 1990).

Treatment   The goals of treatment for erectile dysfunction involve: (1) removing the man's fears about sexual performance, (2) helping him be an active participant in the sexual experience, and (3) relieving the woman's fears about the man's performance. Usually asking the couple to refrain from sexual intercourse removes the fear of performance so that the couple can focus on giving and receiving pleasure in other situations. This step is called *sensate focus,* and it provides a relaxed atmosphere for the couple to engage in pleasurable acts without a goal of intercourse. Later, the couple is instructed to assume a female-superior position, manipulate the penis to a semi-erect state, and then manually insert the penis into the woman's vagina. Initially, the woman thrusts and slowly stops so that the man may begin to thrust. Sometimes the partners are instructed to stop if an erection occurs, but eventually they learn to maintain intercourse with the goal of pleasure, rather than an erection (Masters & Johnson, 1970; LoPiccolo & LoPiccolo, 1978).

Premature Ejaculation

Premature ejaculation is the inability to control ejaculation. Ejaculation occurs before the individual wishes it because of recurrent and persistent absence of reasonable control during sexual activity. When a man believes he has ejaculated too quickly, he becomes frustrated and develops a fear that the pattern will continue (Weinstein & Rosen, 1988).

Causes If primary premature ejaculation exists and the man has never experienced control during sexual experiences, it is unlikely that the problem is organically based. On the other hand, with secondary premature ejaculation, where there has been a prior history of control, the problem may be caused by medication or other physiological factors. Psychological causes such as power struggles, unconscious anger, or low self-esteem may also affect the ejaculatory control (Leiblum & Rosen, 1989).

Treatment If the couple's problem is premature ejaculation, the squeeze technique is prescribed after the couple completes sensate focus exercises. The woman is instructed to stimulate the man to full erection and to immediately apply pressure to the penile glans, with her thumb on the frenulum and the first and second fingers adjacent to each other on either side of the coronal ridge. This effectively eliminates the man's urge to ejaculate.

During the next step, the woman brings the man to an erection two to three times while in a female-superior position. Thereafter, the woman inserts the penis into her vagina and remains motionless. If the man feels the urge to ejaculate, the woman uses the squeeze technique again. Then, the woman initiates low-level thrusting in a nonthreatening way. As the man maintains prolonged ejaculatory control, the woman can thrust more vigorously (Masters & Johnson, 1970; Weinstein & Rosen, 1988).

Retarded and Retrograde Ejaculation

Retarded ejaculation is the man's inability to ejaculate and achieve orgasm during intercourse. With primary retarded ejaculation, the man has never experienced ejaculation during intercourse; with secondary retarded ejaculation, the man was previously able to ejaculate during intercourse but is now unable to do so.

Causes   Physical responses are rarely the cause of retarded ejaculation. Psychological factors include a subconscious fear of being injured, anxiety, problematic relationships, trauma during early sexual experiences, or inhibitory religious practices (Leiblum & Rosen, 1989).

Treatment   Sensate focus is the first step in treating this problem. The woman manually stimulates her partner so that she can be viewed as a pleasure-giver. The woman manually stimulates the man just short of ejaculation and then assumes a superior position and inserts the penis into her vagina. She initiates thrusting until the man ejaculates. If he does not, she returns to manual stimulation and repeats the procedure (Masters & Johnson, 1970).

Common Female Sexual Dysfunctions

Inhibited Sexual Desire

Inhibited sexual desire is a deficiency or absence of desire for sexual activity or fantasy. Although men can experience this problem, it is more common among women. There are two subtypes of this dysfunction: (1) primary—those who have never experienced sexual desire, and (2) secondary—those who have had an interest in sexual activity but for some situational reason no longer feel desire, or those who feel desire in certain circumstances but not in others (Weinstein & Rosen, 1988).

Causes   Physical causes for inhibited sexual desire include alcohol, narcotics, and antiandrogens and diseases that affect testosterone and pituitary functioning (Kaplan, 1979). Psychological causes can be prior negative conditioning related to sexual experiences (Masters & Johnson, 1970), such as rape or incest in early childhood. Negative messages from parents regarding sexual practices like masturbation or oral sex can also affect adult sexual functioning. Other causes are sexual anxiety stemming from lack of knowledge, unrealistic expectations, guilt, or performance concerns (LoPiccolo, 1985; Weinstein & Rosen, 1988).

The presence of desire also depends on biological drive, adequate self-esteem, previous positive experiences with sexual activity, a suitable partner, and a positive relationship in other areas with a sexual partner (Leiblum & Rosen, 1989). Unresolved issues in a relationship such as affairs can also lead to unsatisfactory sexual functioning.

Treatment   Often, problems of inhibited sexual desire require relationship therapy to address the issues preventing the woman from desiring sexual activity with her partner. Intrapsychic issues from her past or current issues regarding intimate time together, finances, children, work, or other factors may be dealt with in therapy. Once those issues are resolved, the partners must make time for sexual activity together. Sensate focus exercises and general physical, nonsexual touching is a good way to begin creating desire. Later, more erotic sexual touching should be initiated, leading to intercourse or other forms of sexual pleasure. Communication between the partners about what they like and dislike is a part of this process (Leiblum & Rosen, 1989).

Orgasmic Dysfunction (Inorgasmia)

A woman suffering from inorgasmia shows signs of sexual arousal yet does not experience orgasm (Weinstein & Rosen, 1988). There are three subtypes of inorgasmia: (1) primary—the woman has never reached orgasm, (2) secondary—the woman has previously achieved orgasm but is currently unable to do so, and (3) situational—the woman can achieve orgasm under specific conditions, such as through masturbation.

Causes Physical causes include hormonal patterns, drugs (such as alcohol), antidepressants, alpha adrenergic agents, nerve damage, and advanced diabetes. Psychological factors include lack of sexual knowledge, poor communication about sexual needs, guilt, fear of losing control, overt anger, and unconscious motivations (Weinstein & Rosen, 1988; Leiblum & Rosen, 1989).

Treatment Sensate focus exercises followed by stimulation of the woman's genitals by her partner in a nondemanding position is initiated early in treatment. Continued touching combined with communication about pleasurable feelings follows as the woman is able to feel a warmth and security with her partner. If all proceeds well, intercourse follows, with the woman in a superior position with her partner. Sexual play should ensue, interspersed with periods of rest. Finally, lateral positions and prolonged periods of sexual activity that may result in orgasm are initiated. Other conjoint treatments including anxiety reduction, sexual training, and continued relationship therapy may also be indicated (Masters & Johnson, 1970; Weinstein & Rosen, 1988).

Vaginismus

Vaginismus is defined as a disorder in which an involuntary contraction of the muscles of the vagina prevents intercourse. Penile entry may be difficult and can be very painful for both partners; sometimes entry is not possible at all. In some instances, even the use of tampons and pelvic examinations are impossible without pain. Other women have reported that although penile penetration is impossible, they are able to use tampons or engage in sexual practices that include digital penetration (Kaplan, 1983).

Causes Endometriosis, vaginitis, herpes, pelvic tumors, childbirth, and surgical injuries of the genitals are some of the physical causes of this dysfunction (Kaplan, 1983; Weinstein & Rosen, 1988, p. 22). Psychological causes include social factors related to religious practices, fear of pain, or a partner's repeated erectile dysfunction.

Treatment   After a thorough medical examination indicates a diagnosis of vaginismus, the woman can use dilators to increase her ability to open her vaginal muscles and reduce her anxiety about intercourse. The dilators come in graduated sizes and are used in the privacy of the couple's home under nonstressful conditions. Sexual intercourse is not attempted until the woman has success with the dilators, usually at least 6 weeks into the program (Weinstein & Rosen, 1988).

OTHER PROBLEMS IN THE SEXUAL RELATIONSHIP

Sexually Transmitted Diseases (STDs)

Sexually transmitted diseases are serious and painful and can cause significant damage to the sexual and reproductive organs if left untreated. Sometimes there are no outward signs or symptoms of the disease. STDs are spread during sexual activity, usually through intercourse, oral sex, and anal sex. Most STD germs live in warm, moist areas, so they are often found in the mouth, rectum, vagina, vulva, penis, and testes.

Couples who report any symptoms should be referred immediately to a medical doctor or clinic for treatment. Although there are more than two dozen diseases referred to as STDs, the most common are chlamydia, gonorrhea, and herpes.

Acquired Immune Deficiency Syndrome (AIDS)

AIDS is caused by the human immunodeficiency virus (HIV). HIV is an organism that appears to mutate rapidly, so it is difficult to treat. At present, the disease is incurable and fatal. It is transmitted through the exchange of body fluids, principally blood and semen, but it can also be found in vaginal fluid, breast milk, and menstrual blood. The HIV virus breaks down the immune system, creating a susceptibility to common infections and unusual cancers. An infected person may be symptom-free for years, but is still contagious. In the final stages of AIDS, a person may exhibit symptoms of prolonged fever, weight loss, diarrhea, and swollen glands. The transmission of HIV can be prevented through abstinence, monogamy, use of condoms, and, for intravenous drug users, avoiding the sharing of needles.

Alcohol and Sexuality

Although traditionally alcohol has been regarded as by some as a powerful facilitator and disinhibitor for sexual behavior, it has some destructive and detrimental consequences (Briddell & Wilson, 1976; Leiblum & Rosen, 1984; Wilson, 1981). Alcohol use can be associated with impairment of erectile response as well as the impairment of communication necessary to understand each partner's needs. In addition, alcohol diminishes the intensity of a woman's orgasm and can depress her arousal. Certainly, chronic use of alcohol has a negative effect on the relationship since it promotes denial, poor communication, and poor coping styles for resolving relationship problems.

Childhood Sexual Abuse and Therapy

When treating a couple in which one partner has a history of childhood sexual abuse, key questions concern identification of the problem, the effect of the therapist's gender, the modality of treatment (individual, conjoint, or group), and the process of interventions (Wilson & James, 1992). Organic sexual dysfunctions may be present and must be diagnosed by a medical doctor. Specific sex therapy may be indicated, in addition to relationship therapy.

If individual therapy is recommended, the couple may return after sex therapy to resolve the relationship conflicts. If possible, it can be useful to provide treatment for both partners so that the nonabused partner can learn about the effects of the abuse on the partner and can learn specific triggers that may reenact or recall the prior abuse. Sometimes a certain touch or phrase can trigger the recall.

A goal of treatment is to help the couple identify ways in which the problem currently affects their relationship negatively. Interventions to ameliorate the situation may include communication techniques, sensitivity training, behavioral strategies, and intimacy development enhancement.

Checklist for Sexual Dysfunction Treatment

1. Does the couple report a sexual dysfunction or a sexual problem?
2. Have appropriate questions been asked to ascertain the problem?
3. How willing or open is the couple as the two discuss their sexual relationship?
4. Have they explored their sexual messages from their families of origin?
5. Is there significant blaming by one partner, or do they both accept responsibility and desire change together?
6. Do they have correct sexual knowledge in order to understand what they desire?
7. Is there excessive use of drugs or alcohol or other medications that may have an impact on sexual functioning?
8. Has either partner experienced any childhood sexual abuse?
9. Do the partners appear willing to address their sexual problems conjointly?

ETHICAL CONCERNS FOR THERAPISTS TREATING SEXUAL ISSUES

Only experienced and qualified therapists should treat sexual dysfunctions. An appropriate referral should be made once a diagnosis or tentative hypothesis is ascertained. To be certified to treat couples for sexual problems in their relationship, many states require that therapists complete a certain number of academic hours of training in sexual issues.

It is important to remember the caveat "first, do no harm" and take all presenting concerns seriously. Couples must never be told that the problem is "all in their heads" or that they are making up problems. All concerns are to be taken seriously and treated respectfully by the therapist. At no time should the therapist promote a sexual practice or side with one partner on the appropriateness of a sexual action. Clearly, the partners must determine how they wish to express themselves sexually. If a conflict exists, the therapist's goal is to help the clients problem-solve and negotiate successful resolutions to their sexual problems (Hill, 1992; Westheimer & Lieberman, 1988).

Case Example: Charlotte and Frank

Charlotte is 24 years old, and Frank is 26. They were married while Charlotte attended college, and she is currently in graduate school. Since Charlotte began graduate school, Frank has been working two jobs in order to make ends meet financially. Charlotte also works full time and maintains a full class load. They have no children and they have not had sex for 3 months.

Application of the Integrative Model: Working with a Sexual Problem

Stage 1: Assessing and Obtaining an Interactional View of the Problem

Frank complains that Charlotte is too busy and never wants to have sex. Charlotte asserts that Frank does not understand how stressed she is. An interactional view is that the two have allowed themselves to overload and they have not found a way to create intimate time together.

Stage 2: Goal Setting

The therapist developed the following goals with Frank and Charlotte.

1. Charlotte and Frank want to create more time together for cuddling and being close, as well as for sexual activity.
2. They will set aside 2 hours a week to share their thoughts and feelings and the events of their lives so they will feel more connected to each other.
3. They will do some long-range planning and create future goals to be implemented when school has ended. This will provide a sense of anticipation and hopefulness for the relationship.
4. They agree to wage battle against the time clock and create more balance in their lives. School, career, and couple time will be reapportioned so they can feel a sense of control of their lives.

Stage 3: Adopting New Perceptions and Behaviors

The couple noted Charlotte's skill at creating time management plans for her co-workers. Frank is more flexible and can create blocks of time if he is aware in advance of the need to do so. The two practice a written time management plan they have created, then they plan one "sabotage" of a work or school time when they will sneak away together for couple time. This way, they do not feel so controlled by their schedules.

Stage 4: Maintaining New Perceptions and Behaviors

Frank and Charlotte agree that the priority must be on maintaining the couple relationship. School and career are necessities and responsibilities that must be achieved, but that cannot dominate their lives. They agree to each take a turn planning and implementing fun time in the relationship.

Stage 5: Validating New Perceptions and Behaviors

They compliment each other on taking control of their lives and vow not to let the time clock regain control. They are eager to use the same system to plan their future once school is over. Charlotte's planning and Frank's flexibility and fun-loving nature will keep them on the right track. Finally, they decide to reevaluate their success every 3 months (J. Najafian, personal communication, May 1995).

CONCLUSION

Emotional and sexual intimacy are at the core of most couple relationships. Decision making and intellectual processes also play a part but are less significant, particularly in the honeymoon stages of the relationship. Social factors such as family messages, religion, career, childrearing, and financial stressors also have an impact on the couple's intimate life.

Many people have been hurt and have a fear of closeness. As couples, these partners often create a dance of closeness and distance so that they do not become intimate with each other. Distancing occurs from fear—fear of being hurt, of anger, of dependency, of loss of control, and of rejection by one's partner.

Sexual problems may be evidenced when partners fear intimacy and do not feel connected to each other. It is important to distinguish a sexual problem from a sexual dysfunction, because problems are often created from the relationship and dysfunctions may be organically based. A thorough medical examination is necessary to rule out organic causes. Other factors such as childhood abuse, inhibitory religious practices, family messages, or a series of unsuccessful extramarital affairs can create sexual dysfunctions.

Therapists must determine an appropriate referral, when necessary, but must also be knowledgeable about sexual dysfunctions and their treatments if they are to be helpful to couples who have experienced or who are currently experiencing these problems. Specificity and empathy are two of the most valuable tools a therapist can possess when working with sexual problems. These tools can help therapists provide an arena for couples to set goals and attempt new methods for achieving emotional and sexual intimacy in their relationships.

10

Conflict:
Negotiation and Resolution

KEY CONCEPTS

- Conflict within the couple is a natural function of differences. Conflict cannot be avoided, but it can be managed to produce positive negotiated outcomes.
- Conflict can result from tension caused by forces external to the couple, as when economic conditions lead to conflicts over finances.
- Conflict also occurs when one member of the couple perceives inequity or experiences an imbalance in rewards.
- Anger can be a signal of underlying problems. It can also be a manipulation. Constructively dealing with anger prevents abuse and violence.
- Verbal abuse can occur with or without physical violence. It involves criticizing, name-calling, and belittling the partner.
- Physical violence in the relationship is a cue to separate the partners and treat each individually. Power and control issues for the male batterer must be dealt with.
- Strategies such as reframing, use of metaphors, relationship contracting, and role reversals may be employed to deal with a couple's conflicts.

An intimate couple relationship includes the challenge of learning both how to be connected and how to be different. It is in the process of maintaining connection and expressing the differences that conflict occurs. Conflict situations arise when varying degrees of independence and interdependence are required for couples to cooperate and make joint decisions (Wall & Nolan, 1987). Expressions of differences can be defined on a continuum of responses ranging from mild disagreement to violent conflict (Rapoport, 1974; Smith, 1971). Partners who are ineffective in addressing their differences tend to be more dissatisfied in their relationships than are partners who are more effective (Rands, Levinger, & Mellinger, 1981; Ting-Toomey, 1983). In several studies, distressed couples report higher levels of conflict, negative affect, complaining, and withdrawal as compared to their non-distressed counterparts (Markman & Notarius, 1987; Markman, 1991). Because

178

the inability to resolve conflicts leads to the breakdown of intimacy, it is important to better understand conflict and to help partners learn to manage it more constructively (Cahn, 1992).

Research suggests that some kinds of conflict are more harmful to the relationship than are others. For example, the more intensely heated the conflict (in terms of physiological arousal), the more likely the couple is to break up within a 3-year period (Cahn, 1992; Gottman, 1991).

SOURCES OF CONFLICT

Social Context

Change is an inevitable process that can either present opportunities for adaptation and growth or lead to defensiveness and withdrawal. Either way, change is initially stressful for individuals and relationships. The changing relationships and roles within the relationship present challenges for couples today. Social changes such as dual careers, shared parental responsibilities, economic stressors, and societal mobility are also potential sources for conflict (Guerin, Fay, Burden, & Kautto, 1987).

Situational Stress

Sometimes foreseen and unforeseen events require adaptive or coping behaviors. Although the resulting anxiety does not stem from the relationship, it can trigger conflict (Gilbert, 1992) Chronic illness, death, aging parents, financial crisis, or child-related problems are often conflict triggers. The degree and intensity to which stress is evidenced depends on the couple's conflict-coping skills.

Perceptual Differences Theories

One reason conflict develops is that two parties view a situation differently to begin with. Conflict starts with perceptual differences and is expressed in emotions and behaviors. There are basically two types of perceptual theories: motive-centered and action-centered models. *Motive-centered* definitions view psychological states as the cause of conflict, whereas *action-centered* orientations view behavior as a central focus.

Equity Theory

Equity theory provides the conceptual framework to link perception to conflict behaviors (Adams, 1965; Levi-Straus, 1969; Murstein, Wadlin, & Bond, 1987). An individual's perception of fairness in the relationship is determined by an appraisal of the outcomes. In other words, a person looks at what he or she is getting out of a relationship and what the partner is receiving. If one perceives the relationship to be inequitable or unbalanced, psychological tension results, and tension leads to conflict. In a dual-career couple, one member may, for example, perceive inequity in the distribution of household tasks, giving more free time to the other partner.

Exchange Theory

Exchange theories explain that conflict arises when one partner in a relationship is dissatisfied with the exchange achieved and uses hostility as the ultimate bargaining move (Scanzoni, 1979). Exchange theory as applied to interpersonal relationships suggests that conflict is the result of looking at a psychological balance sheet: how much I am putting out compared to what I am getting in return (Murstein, Wadlin, & Bond, 1987). Each partner wants to maximize the rewards and minimize the costs (Brown & Christensen, 1986). The relationship is maintained by the provision of rewards to both partners ("I'll scratch your back if you scratch mine"). Some of the rewards that couples exchange include money, goods, services, love, status, and information (Argyle & Furnham, 1983).

Attribution Theory

Attribution theory suggests that people's responses to a problem are very often based on their ideas about what caused the problem. Attributing the cause of a problem to one's partner and not taking personal responsibility for conflict is a common way of feeling better about oneself without resolving the conflict (Baucom & Epstein, 1990). Field studies and laboratory experiments on conflict have found that when people perceive that they have some control over the resolution of the problem, they are able to cope more effectively with negative events (Langer & Rodin, 1976; Schulz, 1976).

Behavior/Event Theories of Conflict

In contrast to perceptual theories, behavior/event theories of conflict contend that it is important to understand the *action* of each partner during conflict and then seek new behaviors to manage the conflict (Patterson, Hops, & Weiss, 1975; Satir, 1964; Turner, 1970). Successful management of the conflict includes clarifying rights and obligations, setting interpersonal boundaries, promoting shared decision making, and using open communication (Coser, 1956; Deutsch, 1973; Simmel, 1950; Sprey, 1971; Vuchinich, 1984). A situation that illustrates this theory is a partner who belittles and criticizes, while the other just leaves the room rather than verbally confront the behavior. Instead of resolving the conflict, the partner leaving the room only increases the conflict. The focus of behavior theories is to change the behavior of both partners.

Negotiation Theory

Negotiation theory has some relevance to understanding the causes of couples conflict. Negotiation theory indicates that conflict is the result of failed bargaining strategies (Scanzoni & Polonko, 1981). Bargaining strategies and tactics such as verbal persuasion may be ineffective in a relationship (Scanzoni, 1978; Straus, 1979). The negotiation behaviors themselves then, rather than the underlying needs, become the reason for the conflict. An example of these behaviors is seen in the relationship of Gustav and Anella. Anella would like Gustav to remain home during the evenings, so she rewards him for staying home with sexual activity. She is attempting to meet her needs of having him home with her by offering more sexual play as a solution that benefits both of them. If she is unsuccessful, Anella might begin to complain when Gustav goes out with his friends, thereby pushing him more toward his friends. She might then retaliate by decreasing sexual activity as a way of punishing him for being unwilling to accept her solution to the problem.

Developmental Theory

According to developmental theory, conflict results as a couple experiences stress at predictable and unpredictable stages of development. It is during transitional phases in the family life cycle that conflict in relationships will most likely emerge. The more problematic the transitional issue is for the couple, the more intense the conflict. For instance, a couple who have just borne their first child may come to therapy complaining of increased distance and disagreement in their relationship. Both partners feel hurt and are confused about why their relationship is deteriorating at such a happy time for them. As their confusion grows, their anxiety increases and they begin to misunderstand each other.

VERBAL CONFLICT

Conflict and Anger

Conflict and anger are intimately related. Many of us fear anger because it associated with losing control and being destructive, but anger is a signal and is one worth listening to. It can be a message that we are hurt, that our rights are being violated, that our needs or wants are not being adequately met, or simply that something is just not quite right (Lerner, 1985). It is not anger that is the problem but how we express it.

Couples can be taught to deal constructively with anger in their relationship. For most of us, our style of anger comes from two sources: from experiences with the partner and from the family of origin. An anger genogram might be used to understand the family of origin perspective, or the following questions may be asked to explore the couple's typical ways of dealing with angry feelings:

1. What is anger?
2. What does it mean when you are angry?
3. What does it mean when you are angry with your partner?
4. What does it mean when your partner is angry?
5. What does it mean when your partner is angry with you?
6. How do you respond to your partner's anger?
7. How do you respond to your own anger?
8. How do you let your partner know you are angry?
9. How long does your anger usually last?
10. What other feelings are associated with anger?

Questions to Ask for an Anger Genogram

1. How did your parents deal with anger or conflict?
2. Did you see your parents work through anger or conflict?
3. When members of your family got angry, how did others respond?
4. What did you learn about anger from each of your parents?
5. When a parent was angry with you, what did you feel and do?
6. When you got angry, who listened or failed to listen to you?
7. How did members of your family respond when you got
8. Who was allowed and who was not allowed to be angry in your family?
9. What is your best memory about anger in your family? Your worst memory?
10. Was anyone in your family ever seriously hurt when someone got angry?

This genogram reveals patterns in the family, including the expression or inhibition of anger, and can assist partners as they attempt to learn how these patterns affect the way they currently deal with conflict.

Anger as a Manipulation or Defense

Many times anger is used as a defense against hurt and pain; it also may be used to give a person a sense of power and control, as in abusive relationships. Sometimes a partner uses anger to create distance in a relationship, to punish, or to be left alone.

Anger can function in a healthy way when it is a signal that boundaries are violated. For example, one partner might become annoyed when the mother-in-law repeatedly calls in the evenings during dinner. Anger can be a signal that one partner has violated the other's freedom (Weeks & Treat, 1992).

Sometimes anger can serve as a motivator for resolving differences. It can be viewed as a barometer indicating that there are underlying unresolved feelings that must emerge. Anger can be a helpful reminder to deal with such deeper issues as hurt, fear, disappointment, or self-reproach (Wile, 1993).

Withdrawn Partners

One common conflict style is withdrawal. Sometimes this affects the relationship, and both partners become demoralized and back away. Withdrawn partners suppress their thoughts and feelings. They fear humiliation or do not feel entitled to their feelings. They may also be fearful that by expressing the conflict they will hurt their partners, or that it will lead to an unmanageable argument. These fears are often based on experiences in the family of origin or repeated unsuccessful attempts to resolve conflict with their partners.

Alternately, some individuals are seen as withdrawn by their partners because they have fewer social needs, or perhaps they have little faith that they can solve problems through negotiation. Others have learned that withdrawal is a powerful tool to control their partner and so use it to establish the classic pursuer-distancer relationship with their mate (Wile, 1993).

Consider the situation with Dave and Sandy. During her childhood, Sandy's mother told her that "men cannot be reasoned with" and that "it is better to pretend you agree and then just do what you want to do." She was also told that if she persists long enough, "men will break down and give you what you want." Dave, on the other hand, watched his father leave the house each time there was any tension. It is easy to understand how Sandy has become the pursuer and attempts to get what she wants through tactics rather than by negotiating with Dave. It is also apparent that Dave is following in his father's footsteps; he goes to the other room and watches television each time there is conflict. Because neither of them has seen positive problem solving modeled in their families of origin, they are playing out the patterns from their early childhood training.

In addition to identifying anger and withdrawal as indicators of verbal conflict styles, we must look at other behaviors that can vary in their intensity and duration.

Characteristics of Verbal Abuse

Verbal abuse is hurtful and attacks the abilities of the partner. It can be manifested by overt, angry outbursts or may be very covert and couched in sincere terms that only the abused can discern. It is insidious and manipulative. Verbal abuse is also unpredictable, and it can be expressed in double messages. Finally, verbal abuse becomes the problem in the relationship, rather than just the process of disagreement. For example, when a couple is having a disagreement about money and one or more of the abusive tactics is employed, the issue no longer is about the money but is centered on the way one partner treats the other (Evans, 1992, pp. 73–79). Verbal abuse is characterized by the following behaviors:

1. Discounting the partner's ideas
2. "Put-downs" disguised as jokes
3. Blocking and diverting
4. Accusing and blaming
5. Judging and criticizing
6. Trivializing the partner's viewpoint
7. Threatening
8. Name-calling

Verbal abuse can be associated with physical abuse and couple violence if the couple cannot manage conflict in other, more appropriate ways. Verbal abuse inhibits the couple's intimacy, communication, and problem solving. For example, Ryan and Allyson have been having a disagreement about Allyson's forgetting to pick up the dry cleaning for the week. Gradually, as Ryan continues to berate her, he accuses her of being stupid and a worthless human being. He also insinuates that he is not getting ahead at work because she is not a "good enough wife." Allyson cries and promises to do better. This verbally abusive interaction could be considered a kind of coercive cycle described in Chapter 2; the abusive behavior is rewarded by one partner "giving in."

CONFLICT ISSUES AND PATTERNS

Control, Power, and Equity

The major conflicts in a marriage "center in the problem of who is to tell whom what to do under what circumstances" (Haley, 1963, p. 27) and who is to have the power. The couple makes rules and assign roles regarding who is to control each situation. Control issues center around resources such as space, money, and children (Deutsch, 1973), and couples often get involved in win/lose struggles over these topics, rather than negotiating their differences. If one partner "wins" more often, the other may feel worthless, frustrated, and angry. Consider the situation of Ken and Babs when they entered therapy. Ken has a job that requires that he travel most of the week, and he has been working like this for three years. Babs has made a life with her female friends when Ken is away and is not always at home when he calls her. Ken has become angry and has insisted that Babs remain at home and wait for his call each evening. Ken confides that he feels unimportant in Babs' life and wants to regain control of his relationship by this symbolic act, indicating her subservience. The therapist's job in such situations is to help couples understand the sources of these feelings and then learn to negotiate new rules rather than act on outmoded ones.

Blame

Blame is an attribution that the other partner is the cause of the problem. Thus, blame is a form of denial about one's own responsibility for the conflict. Rather than lead to productive negotiation, blame sidetracks the couple on the issue of what or who caused the problem.

The following four methods of blame have been identified as contributors to relationship distress (Strong & Claiborn, 1982; Weeks & Treat, 1992).

1. *Justification* is the practice of assigning negative behaviors to external situations: for example, "I cannot help the way I act" or "It is your fault I got angry and broke the vase. You shouldn't get me so upset."
2. *Rationalization* is the practice of denying one's behavior as harmful: for example, "I did it for your own good" or "I have to leave home without telling you where I am when you act like that."
3. *Debilitation* refers to statements indicating that one is helpless because of the other's behavior: for example, "I go crazy when you do that and I can't help it" or "You kill me when you act like that in front of my friends."
4. *Vilification* is when the other person is made the villain by attributing negative intent: for example, "I know you try to feel superior to me so you make jokes in front of your friends" or "I know you don't want your family to like me so you tell them stories about me to make me look bad."

Often, one partner blames the other to protect his or her self-esteem. Blame makes us feel temporarily better about ourselves. Pointing out another's faults seems to affirm our own "goodness" (Johnston & Campbell, 1988). All of these tactics interfere with solution-focused discussions between partners and instead foster avoidance, retribution, anger, and withdrawal.

Triangulation

When couples experience repetitive, polarized conflict, the struggles can become so great that they may attempt to ease the distress by drawing in a third element to the disagreement. This method, discussed briefly in an earlier chapter, is referred to as *triangulation*. The third element of the triangle can include excessive work, in-laws, friends, drugs or alcohol, children, or an affair (Dym & Glenn, 1993).

Triangulation is an avoidance strategy with destructive consequences (Prosky, 1991). One typical avoidance pattern of triangulation is "scapegoating, " or shifting the focus to an innocent person as a way of lessening the intensity of the couple's conflict (Minuchin, 1974). The scapegoat may be a boss, a parent, or a social agency. Scapegoating can have devastating effects on children and fails to solve the real problem.

Another pattern involves one partner forming an alliance against the other partner. For example, a client may try to get the therapist to intervene in a conflict with a partner, rather than dealing with the issue alone. If the therapist becomes a go-between, the tension is lessened but the couple has not learned to deal with conflict. This pattern provides more power but creates less opportunity for conflict resolution because the other person feels "ganged-up on."

A very common pattern is to get one's emotional or sexual needs met through an affair, rather than by addressing the problems of emotional distance or sexual dysfunction in the marriage (Guerin et al., 1987). Chapter 12 includes a more detailed discussion of some ways to manage this kind of triangle.

Interactive Conflict Patterns

Another way of looking at conflict in a couple's relationship is to examine common conflict patterns. When the couple identifies the pattern, both partners can then begin to stop themselves when they see it emerge and implement better negotiating strategies. Listed below are a few of the most common patterns:

Pursuer-Distancer

This pattern evolves in couples when one partner becomes the aggressor in the relationship and constantly moves toward the other by attempting to involve him or her more intensely in the relationship. There are several ways to pursue. Initiating discussions or conflicts, overplanning the partner's time, following the partner throughout the house, initiating sexual interaction, or "overcommunicating."

On the other hand, the distancer remains aloof from the relationship and commits little time to the activities planned, retreats for privacy in the home, deflects conversation if it becomes too intense, and finds excuses to divert sexual attention or intimate verbal communication with his or her partner. Together, these styles create a "dance" in which both partners contribute to a lack of closeness and intimacy in the relationship. Often, each will blame the other and fail to see the pattern they have fallen into.

Reminder-Procrastinator

Also known as the overfunctioner-underfunctioner or overinvolved-underinvolved pair, this duo presents as one responsible partner who must remind the other to be responsible. Usually, the procrastinator eventually retreats from duties until reminded many times. This procrastination allows the person to underfunction in the relationship, yet he or she becomes resentful when the other partner nags. The more reminders given, the more dependent the procrastinator becomes. This "dance" promotes resentment and anxiety in the reminder and resentment and rationalization in the procrastinator.

Parent-Child

Similar to the reminder-procrastinator, this interaction is based on a critical "parent" attempting to place the other in a more submissive position in the relationship by criticizing, punishing, withholding praise and positive comments, or demanding certain tasks or responses of the other partner. The "parent" is angry and feels justified in treating the partner as an infant. The "child" is often characterized by exhibiting withdrawn or rebellious behavior or helpless responses to the "parent," rather than maintaining a position of responsibility and equality. This cycle is destructive because each behaves in a way that requires the other to remain in the undesired role, rather than change.

DEVELOPMENTAL STAGES OF COUPLES CONFLICT

One way of looking at conflict is in terms of how it escalates. Couples can be thought of as progressing to higher stages of conflict when they consistently fail to negotiate problems. The higher the stage, the more severe the conflict and the more intervention is required.

Stage One

This stage involves a minimal degree of conflict and is usually present in couples who have been married or together for a short time. Conflict has generally not persisted longer than 6 months and has not created resentment or significant tension in the relationship. Most of these couples are preclinical, but they will respond to psychoeducational approaches in therapy. Without significant anger present, they are able to assimilate information to produce change.

Stage Two

Couples in stage two are typically experiencing chronic conflict lasting more than 6 months. Communication between the partners is open, so both can express their dissatisfaction; however, blame and triangulation increase. Couples continue to spend time together and have fun, but resentment is evident. As a response to stress, the couple may exhibit patterns of the pursuer-distancer, the reminder-procrastinator, or the parent-child. Therapy during this stage focuses on lowering anxiety and stress and reestablishing self-focus in place of partner blame.

Stage Three

These couples present with severe conflict that has persisted well over 6 months with periods of intense anxiety and stress. Blame is evident, as well as polarization and power struggles. Anger and control are primary issues and may be diverted temporarily by increased triangulation of other parties or events. These attempts are an effort to reduce the conflict when it is most stressful. Communication is closed and trust is low. Therapy in this stage is centered on reducing the polarization and emotional reactivity and on reestablishing trust. This requires that any toxic issues be shelved temporarily until the couple has reduced blame and can utilize some degree of problem solving in the relationship.

Stage Four

Couples in stage four are characterized by the extremes of all the dimensions of relationship stress. That is, communication is poor, power struggles and blame are high, criticism is intense, self-disclosure is absent, and triangulation—which may be in the form of an attorney—is evident. Relationship therapy is not indicated because anger is so high. Instead, therapy may focus on negotiating concrete parent-children issues or the partners' reactions to the divorce process. Mediation, rather than an adversarial process, is the treatment of choice (Sperry & Carlson, 1991), as it can provide a more successful disengagement from the relationship.

VIOLENCE IN THE COUPLE

During periods of intense conflict in relationships, many couples experience varying degrees of violence. If violence is evident, individual therapy for each member, rather than couples therapy, is required. It is the therapist's duty to assess the propensity for violence and make an appropriate referral. If one partner is abusing the other, the first issue is to make sure the abused partner is in a safe place, such as a shelter, and has notified authorities.

Scope of the Problem

Every minute in this country, four women are beaten by their husbands, boyfriends, or former spouses (Marino, 1994). Domestic violence causes more injuries to women than car accidents, muggings, and rapes combined. The term *domestic violence* refers to a cycle of destructive thoughts, feelings, and actions that often involves physical battering accompanied by psychological, sexual, or property violence (Viano, 1992). Most acts of violence are carried out by men toward their female partners. However, 5% of married men are abused by their wives (Marino, 1994).

Definition of Battering

Battering is a pattern of behavior in which one person establishes power and control over another person through fear and intimidation, often including the threat or use of violence. Battering occurs when batterers believe they are entitled to control their partners (see Figure 10.1). Battering includes emotional abuse, economic abuse, sexual abuse, manipulation of children, exercise of male privilege, intimidation, isolation, and a variety of other behaviors designed to maintain fear, intimidation, and power.

Recognizing a Potential Batterer

The following warning signs of a potentially violent relationship can help clinicians identify the profile of an individual who has the propensity for violence. The terminology used reflects the fact that most batterers are male and most victims are female.

1. Experienced physical or psychological abuse as a child
2. Had father who battered his mother
3. Displays violence toward other people
4. Uses guns for protection from other people
5. Loses temper frequently and more easily than necessary
6. Commits acts of violence against objects and other things, rather than people
7. Uses alcohol excessively
8. Displays unusual amount of jealousy
9. Expects partner to be present or available at all times
10. Becomes enraged when he gives advice and it is not taken
11. Appears to have a dual personality
12. Exhibits a sense of overkill in his cruelty or kindness
13. The partner is afraid of his anger; preventing him from being angry becomes an important part of the partner's behavior
14. Has rigid ideas of what people should do, usually determined by male or female sex-role stereotypes

Batterers tend to possess other identifiable characteristics including depression, anxiety, low self-esteem, dependence, paranoia, dissociation from their feelings, poor impulse control, antisocial tendencies, and hostility toward women (Viano, 1992). They need a close relationship, but they fear the intensity of a relationship and the possible loss of control.

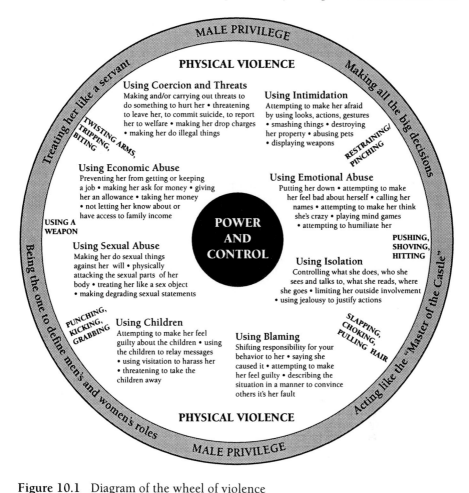

Figure 10.1 Diagram of the wheel of violence

Source: From the *Wheel of Violence*, developed by the Domestic Abuse Intervention Project, modified by Paula Basil, M.A., L.M.H.C. Reprinted by permission of the Domestic Abuse Intervention Project, 206 West Fourth St., Duluth, MN 55806.

Passive abusers tend to gravitate toward assertive women. Sometimes abusers are resentful of their victims' life achievements. They may be jealous of the amount of education their partner has received or jealous of the amount of money made. Overall, the abuser perceives the victim of abuse to be more efficient in life, often as a result of the abuser's low self-esteem (Marino, 1994).

The Cycle of Violence

The cycles of battering are tension building, explosion, and love, and these cycles increase in duration and intensity and may also increase in frequency. It is not possible to predict the length of each cycle or the degree of damage that will occur the next time. In other words, just because an abuser has never used a knife, it is not safe to assume that the abuse will not reach that level the next time. Situational events, stages of life, and the partner's response all affect the timing and the acts committed.

Tension-Building Stage

In this stage, the victim (we will assume "she") begins to sense the man's edginess and begins to smooth over minor issues. She denies her anger and believes she can control the situation. He knows his behavior is wrong and is fearful she will leave him. She reinforces his fear by withdrawing so she will not set him off. Tension rises. Some women report they begin to provoke attacks after a while just so they can "get it over." Provocation, in their mind, is a sense of control of the situation.

Explosion Stage

The abuser does not understand his anger and does not want to hurt his partner, he just wants to "teach her a lesson." He knows his rage is out of control but justifies it by her actions. Women may feel safer during this stage and may release their own anger and fight back. This is the shortest stage, which can last from a few hours to about 2 days. Women commonly deny their injuries, sometimes to soothe the batterer or because they are embarrassed and cannot accept the seriousness of the situation.

Love Stage

Both partners welcome this stage. The abuser is remorseful and fears his partner will leave him. He acts charming and manipulative. He believes that he can control himself and that he will not behave that way again. He convinces her and others that he is sincere. The victim wants to believe him because he is being nice to her and she wants to recapture the picture of love they once had. He acts dependent on her and says he cannot live without her. She begins to feel responsible for him as well as for her own victimization. She receives what she wants with overkill. He brings home flowers and candy, does errands, and may plan a vacation they have been discussing. They look toward the future and believe the abuse will not happen again. Unfortunately, as this stage progresses, tension begins to build again (Walker, 1991).

Reasons Women Stay or Return to Abusive Situations

Following are some of the reasons women may tolerate abuse from their partner.

1. She has low self-esteem; she thinks she deserves the abuse she has received.
2. She models her mother's behavior and considers it normal for women to be battered.
3. She believes she does not have enough money or other resources to leave.
4. She fears the abuser will find her and hurt or kill her.
5. She is dependent on her abuser's decision making and does not think she can manage by herself.

6. She loves him and believes she can change him.
7. She feels embarrassed to admit she has been abused.
8. Her abuser has agreed to seek therapy.
9. He "only gets abusive when he drinks."
10. She believes she has control of the situation ("he only hits me when . . .")

Therapy for Batterers and Victims of Domestic Violence

Once the therapist has assessed the presence of violence, couples therapy should cease. The overall goals are (1) to stop the violence, (2) create safety for the battered, and (3) help the abuser interrupt the violent cycle. Only then can couples therapy be reestablished.

The Batterer

The focus of treatment is on the cessation of the violence by teaching the batterer new skills for dealing with anger control, problem solving, and assertiveness. Old cognitive patterns are replaced with more effective ones. In addition, issues of self-esteem, jealousy, substance abuse, impulse control, and feelings toward women are addressed. Group and individual treatment are the methods of choice, and couples therapy cannot be reestablished until a safe environment has been created.

The Abused Woman

Discovering a plan for the victim's physical safety is the first priority. She should live apart from the batterer until he has acquired new skills and she has a safety plan in effect. She must accept the seriousness of the situation and understand that he will not stop the abusive behavior on his own. She must accept that the abuser does not understand what is happening and has displaced anger and rationalization, so he will not accept responsibility for his actions.

Group or individual therapy provides an arena for her to tell her story and have her feelings regarding the seriousness of the situation validated. Therapists can help her accept responsibility to protect herself when she is in danger and to recognize that danger. She should not be "rescued" but should be supported by the therapist. Treatment focuses on identifying her strengths, understanding how violence has affected her life and her behavior, and teaching her problem solving and assertiveness. She can look toward the future knowing that she may need to take care of herself economically and emotionally if he does not change. She should not be involved in couples therapy until she has accomplished these tasks and until the abuser has made significant changes. If he does not, she may desire assistance with divorce issues.

NEGOTIATION AND PROBLEM SOLVING FOR COUPLES

Decision making and conflict resolution for couples have been based to some extent on concepts and assumptions basic to negotiation theory (Scanzoni & Polonko,

1981). The aim of negotiation is to attain a convergence wherever there is a conflict of aims, goals, or behaviors (Rubin & Brown, 1975). Each partner utilizes strategies or tactics to optimize the reward opportunities. The reward can be intrinsic (a feeling of rightness) or extrinsic (better couple relations).

Couples who experience successful joint decision making are able to focus on the issue without bringing in extraneous arguments and feelings that would impede the process: for example, hurt feelings from other unresolved problems, anger, or current situations. Decision making requires that each partner feel a sense of equality and that input for the decision is valued by both parties. Use of "I" statements, uninterrupted time to speak, and the acceptance that the outcome (solution) may be an accommodation of both person's perspectives are essential components of the process. Rules for fair fighting must be established in relationships if that is to be part of the decision-making process. In addition, conflict training and couples contracting can be helpful interventions to produce positive negotiation and solutions for partners.

Conflict Training

Conflict training involves a shift from an emphasis on the individual to a view of the couple in which the individual is only a part (Cahn, 1992). Engaging in couples communication skills training (see Chapter 8), learning a problem-solving model, and adopting principles of solution-focused discussions are all part of effective conflict training.

Problem-Solving Model

Successful problem solving is based on the partners' shared view of the problem and shared responsibility for its solution. These following steps for solving relationship issues increase the likelihood that a positive outcome will be forthcoming.

1. Clearly define a joint definition of the problem.
2. Brainstorm multiple possibilities for solutions to the problem (no idea is too unrealistic or too absurd).
3. Narrow the possibilities to three (one that one partner chooses, one that the other chooses, and one that is mutually agreed-on).
4. Prioritize the possibilities (rank-order).
5. Choose one possibility with the understanding that, if it does not work, the second will be attempted.
6. Decide the particulars (who, what, when, where, how). Each person's responsibility for the outcome must be clearly stated, rather than assumed.
7. Do it!
8. Evaluate the effectiveness of the solution attempted.
9. If the situation isn't resolved, try the second option.

This model allows both partners to participate in the formulation and resolution of the problem in a nonblaming process. Ideas are not "bad" or "stupid"; they either work or do not work.

Fair Fighting

When couples air their differences, certain rules must be established to protect the productivity of the disagreement and the feelings of each individual. A fair fight begins with the person who perceives a problem making an introspective assessment of feelings and beliefs associated with the issue.

During the first part of the fight, feelings must be expressed. Second, rules must be established so that blaming and name-calling are eliminated. Third, time and place must be established so that full attention is given by both parties. Fights should not be hurried; they can be broken into segments, if necessary. Finally, after resolution is completed, the same issue should not resurface when there is a new problem to solve (Weeks & Treat, 1992). These steps ensure the safety of the interaction, so that each person continues to feel valued and the relationship can be free to grow and flourish.

CLINICAL INTERVENTIONS

Reframing and Framing

Reframing, or relabeling, is a technique used to change a negative meaning into a positive one. It consists of changing the frame of reference against which a given event is considered or judged, thus changing the meaning and value judgment of the event without changing the facts (Paolino & McGrady, 1978; Sherman & Fredman, 1986).

After observing the couple's language, worldview, and solutions to the problem, the therapist can feed back the pattern of behavior in a different, positive frame of reference or context so that the clients can see it differently. Seeing it in another way should offer new possibilities and help the couple think and feel differently about it. In turn, this may trigger optimism in approaching the situation (Sherman & Fredman, 1986).

Interestingly, the behavior reframed is the same behavior that the client has defined as symptomatic (Weeks & Treat, 1992). For example, partners who come to therapy because they fight too much can see their problem differently if the clinician says: "You two must have a lot of passion for each other as your fights are so intense. There seems to be a lot of caring or you wouldn't bother to fight."

With this reframing of the event, it is possible to wonder what it would be like if the partners showed their passion in different ways. Determining those ways can be a goal of therapy and a positive attempt at problem solving.

Yet another example of a positive reframe is demonstrated in the case of Christophe and Celeste. Christophe complains that Celeste begins to cook whenever they start arguing. When she cooks, he becomes even more annoyed. Celeste explains that she does not understand why she cooks; perhaps it is a way to keep herself from saying something she will regret. The therapist might reframe her behavior to suggest that cooking is her way of showing Christophe she loves him, even when they are fighting. Celeste likes this idea and further states that she feels that she is doing something positive for the relationship. Christophe can now look at her cooking as a way that Celeste shows she cares, rather than as a way to avoid a disagreement. By creating a positive explanation, the two can then determine whether or not they want to continue to handle disagreements this way. The blame and frustration are diminished, and they can look toward positive resolutions in problem solving.

Using Metaphors

A metaphor is a way of speaking in which one thing is expressed in terms of another, thereby casting new light on the character being described. The metaphor used in counseling couples must be congruent with the problem situation and must provide a possible solution in that context. Friedman (1990) explains that metaphors or fables give the "reader or listener distance from his or her own real life encounters. Yet, through the distance they provide fresh perspectives on familiar human foibles."

Types of metaphors include metaphorical stories, fables, anecdotes, and short stories; analogies, similes, and relationship metaphors; tasks with metaphorical meanings; metaphorical objects; and artistic metaphors. Metaphors are also used because they are usually more interesting than direct messages and so can appeal to the receiver's imagination. Metaphors can be constructed to help clients try things or think about things in ways they have not viewed them before. Because metaphors are indirect, they can offer clients new perspectives in a less threatening way.

To effectively use metaphors for couple problems in a family context, the therapist must join successfully with the clients and have an understanding of the issues involved. The therapist then constructs characters equivalent to the actual clients. Table 10.1 shows the elements of a story about a client family with an anorexic daughter and other family problems. From this outline, a story might be constructed about the metaphorical family as a way of getting the couple to face the family problems objectively (Rosenbaum, 1992).

The therapist must also plan how to use the metaphor to help achieve the desired outcome. Because the solution cannot be apparent, the metaphor must demonstrate how the characters representing the real-life subjects made the changes that enabled them to overcome their problems. This is the *connecting strategy* (Gordon, 1978); the story indirectly introduces ways the partners can deal effectively with their dilemma.

To conclude the metaphor, the therapist can either help the couple see how their own behaviors are similar to the ones in the story or can leave them to think about the meaning and implications of the story and discuss it at a later time.

Contracting

In an attempt to understand relationship conflict, Sager (1976) described marital conflict as a clash of different marital contracts. These contracts are a way of portraying the partners' expectations and beliefs in the relationship.

Table 10.1 Sample Use of Metaphors in Therapy

The significant events of the case must be represented by equivalent events or incidents in the story. This, of course is possible only when a full assessment of the case has been completed.

Real Family	Metaphorical Family
Carol will eat only vegetarian foods and is showing signs of anorexia.	Prince Christopher will eat only grains and vegetables and is getting very thin.
Linda is overinvolved with Carol's life.	The Queen and Christopher engage in many activities together, and the Queen has high expectations for the Prince.
Linda and Stu fight over Carol's work with the homeless.	The King and the Queen fight over the Prince's work with the peasants.
Linda and Stu fight in front of Carol about her work with the homeless, and Carol withdraws.	The Prince hears the King and Queen fight over the Prince's work with the peasants. He leaves and goes to a nearby village.
Linda and Stu do not have a life together without Carol.	The King and Queen do not know how to relate to each other without the Prince's presence.
Carol and Stu do not have a good father-daughter relationship.	The King and the Prince do not understand each other or have a good relationship.

Source: Adapted by permission of the author from "The Use of Metaphor," by J. Rosenbaum (1992). Unpublished manuscript, Counseling Department, Stetson University.

Relationship contracts help couples negotiate problems in an explicit, rational manner. They are based on bargaining or exchange theory. In other words, "to get what I want, I must be interested in what you want and accommodate with you" (Sherman & Fredman, 1986). Contracts are behavioral in form and require that both parties participate in the discussions and subsequent creation of the contract. The case example of Maria and Kimberlee describes a situation involving a good faith contract; their contract is illustrated in Box 10.1.

Case Example: Maria and Kimberlee

Maria is a 37-year-old single mother with a full-time job. Her daughter Kimberlee is 17. Kim's father is described as a "deadbeat dad" whose whereabouts have been unknown since Kimberlee's birth. Maria initiated a request for family therapy, stating that "Kimberlee is out of control." Maria wants the two of them "to be close—like we used to be."

Maria describes the family as one in which tension has recently increased. Kimberlee does not come home or let her mom know where she is most weekends. Kimberlee, according to Maria, also skips school three to four times a week and is not completing her chores at home. Maria believes this change in behavior is associated with Kimberlee's new friends.

Kimberlee describes her family situation as extremely strict and punctuated with frequent screaming matches between mother and daughter. She believes that her

---

Box 10.1
Example of Good Faith Contract
Resulting in Extrinsic Rewards with Case Study Family

Maria and Kimberlee both agree that the following specific tasks will be carried out in good faith by each member of this contract as it is specifically stated in writing below.

It is understood that Maria

- Will come home by 5:30 three times per week
- Does not speak with Kimberlee for the first 20 minutes she is home
- Will not make any derogatory remarks about Kimberlee's friends

It is understood that Kimberlee

- Will keep the bathroom and her own room as clean as agreed upon by Maria and Kimberlee in session
- Must attend school four out of five days a week
- Must call home by 10:30 on weekend evenings to let Maria know where she is, what time she will be home, or an appropriate friend's house at which she will be staying

Signatures: _____

_____

---

mom is too strict and is trying to live her life through her daughter. Both agree that tense feelings at home are associated with Kimberlee's absence from home and her avoidance of household responsibilities. Maria states that she also has been remaining at work long after the required hours in order to avoid a confrontation with her daughter. They agree to define their expectations and negotiate a new set of rules so they can "get along better" and establish more positive feelings between the two of them. The therapist helps Maria and Kimberlee develop a contract (Box 10.1) so the expectations will be clear and specific.

Role Reversals

The use of role reversal in couples therapy helps each partner see the other's reality from a different perspective. When each is placed in an alternative role, it is easier to exercise self-control and view the situation in a more objective manner. This deflates the need to be right or wrong that so frequently produces conflict in the couple.

When one partner "walks in the other's shoes," he or she may feel more empathy and may understand the problem in a different way. Concomitantly, the other partner may view himself or herself as if in a mirror, because the self is seen through the other's perceptions. Thus, new insights are created.

A role-reversal strategy to encourage couples to consider viewpoints other than their own can be accomplished by having partners switch places, symbolically and physically. The partners might switch their seating arrangement and each take on the behaviors of the other. The therapist instructs both partners to communicate as if they are the other person, stating the other's views, even if logically they do not agree with them. Looking through a different lens can provide insight about the other person's belief system or behaviors and feelings. Finally, the partners should switch back to their real selves and process with each other what it felt like to be in the other's shoes and what they learned by the experience.

Bratter (1974) describes role reversal as driving a car 50 miles per hour and then shifting it into reverse to go the other way. It disturbs the equilibrium and provides a context for change. In couples therapy, the technique can be most effective in examining reciprocal roles such as pursuer-distancer, rescuer-scapegoat, parent-child, or other repetitive patterns that cause conflict.

Case Example: Morena and Saul

Morena and Saul have been married for 3 years and have been experiencing increasing conflict about Saul's hobby of collecting antique cars. Not only is it a very expensive hobby, according to Morena, but the time he spends working on them and purchasing them cuts away much of their couple time. Recently, Saul has rented a garage in which to store the cars, making him even less accessible to his partner.

Morena has begun to argue with Saul and is spending more time in the library researching careers in the travel industry. Saul will not discuss her career because he believes she will be away from home too frequently. Morena has recently met Tobias, a travel consultant who has offered to train her and allow her to travel with him on familiarization trips.

Application of the Integrative Model

Stage 1: Assessing and Obtaining an Interactional View of the Problem

Initially, Saul reports that Morena is being very hostile about his time away from her and has begun to nag and complain when he is at home. He admits that he likes to get away from the house when she is acting so negatively. Morena complains that Saul is spending more time with his cars than with her. She claims that she is bored and would like to have a close relationship but does not know how to get back on track. Saul indicates that their sexual activity has been almost nonexistent.

After they each explain their frustrations, both agree that they would like to get closer and negotiate the time they will spend together. Morena wants to plan special dates; Saul extends the idea by including intimate time with more sexual touching as part of their new couple commitment.

Stage 2: Goal Setting

Together, Morena and Saul formulate the following goals:

1. They will plan time for talking and dating so they can feel closer again.
2. They will have regular planning meetings so they can negotiate the time they will spend on hobbies as well as the time together, in order to feel more included in each other's lives.
3. Morena will research the travel opportunities and discuss them with Saul before any future plans are made. They will feel more capable of problem-solving when they complete this task.
4. The couple will plan a vacation independent from any auto rallies so they can be more adventurous and romantic with each other. The vacation will provide an opportunity for a more connected feeling and more playful spirits.

The couple begins to refer to their problem as the "3-year marriage blahs," and they are determined to overcome their boredom and renew their interest in each other.

Stage 3: Adopting New Perceptions and Behaviors

In this stage, one of Morena and Saul's tasks is to negotiate and implement a written contract on their couple time. In addition, they have organized a trip for a romantic week in the Caribbean islands. Finally. they have determined to spend 30 minutes per day communicating with each other about their feelings and concerns for their relationship.

Stage 4: Maintaining New Perceptions and Behaviors

Both partners discuss each person's responsibility to continue working on the problems and vow to hold each other accountable if the day ends without "talk time." They decide to confront each other if the weekly date is not made a priority and discuss at a couple meeting what they have planned for the upcoming weekend.

Stage 5: Validating New Perceptions and Behaviors

Morena and Saul congratulate each other on their renewed commitment and identify Morena's free spirit and sense of adventure as their barometer if they should get off track with their plan for fun time together. Saul, the more serious-minded of the two, will gently remind them if they do not uphold their contract in every aspect. They also realize they need more time to address the sexual issues of their relationship, and they have confidence that they can begin to work on the issue because they have been so diligent in this endeavor. (See Figure 10.2 for an overview of the therapy process.) Both determine to return to therapy in 3 months to assess their progress.

Considerations for Working with Couples in Conflict

1. Determine the causes of relationship stress and view it from an interactional perspective.
2. Assess the style of conflict each partner uses and attempt to design interventions that interrupt the pattern.

3. Assess the capability for violence in the relationship and cease couples therapy if violence is present.
4. Be aware of the destructive nature of verbal abuse and educate the couple of the destruction, if appropriate.
5. Assess the degree of power and control each person possesses and help both move toward an equitable relationship to promote problem solving.
6. Help the couple reduce blame by learning more useful communication skills.
7. Understand the stages of relationship conflict and provide appropriate interventions for each stage.
8. Know the cycle of violence and refer the batterer to individual or group therapy.
9. Assist the battered victim with a protective plan and a plan for individual or group therapy.
10. Use a psychoeducational approach to help clients learn fair fighting and problem-solving skills.
11. Be aware of the need for specificity with any relationship contracting.

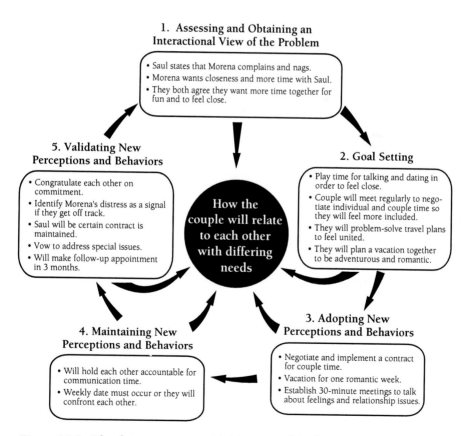

1. Assessing and Obtaining an Interactional View of the Problem
• Saul states that Morena complains and nags.
• Morena wants closeness and more time with Saul.
• They both agree they want more time together for fun and to feel close.

5. Validating New Perceptions and Behaviors
• Congratulate each other on commitment.
• Identify Morena's distress as a signal if they get off track.
• Saul will be certain contract is maintained.
• Vow to address special issues.
• Will make follow-up appointment in 3 months.

2. Goal Setting
• Play time for talking and dating in order to feel close.
• Couple will meet regularly to negotiate individual and couple time so they will feel more included.
• They will problem-solve travel plans to feel united.
• They will plan a vacation together to be adventurous and romantic.

How the couple will relate to each other with differing needs

4. Maintaining New Perceptions and Behaviors
• Will hold each other accountable for communication time.
• Weekly date must occur or they will confront each other.

3. Adopting New Perceptions and Behaviors
• Negotiate and implement a contract for couple time.
• Vacation for one romantic week.
• Establish 30-minute meetings to talk about feelings and relationship issues.

Figure 10.2 The therapy process with Morena and Saul

12. Be familiar with reframing, use of metaphor, and role reversals as potential interventions to reduce conflict or channel it in more constructive ways.

13. Remember, conflict is necessary; it produces change. It is the negative way in which some couples conflict that is deadly.

CONCLUSION

Once the couple is able to understand that conflict is a normal part of a relationship, both partners can begin to examine the way in which they disagree. As long as violence is not present, couples can learn effective problem-solving skills to encourage long-term solutions. In addition, they can identify destructive interactional patterns and interrupt them for better results.

The therapist can assist the couple explore the aspects of blame, power, and control and determine how these concepts influence their relationship. During the assessment stage, the therapist can identify the stage of marital conflict in which the couple is currently functioning and design interventions based on the nature of the conflict.

Strategies such as reframing, use of metaphor, relationship contracting, and role reversals may be employed to facilitate change with conflicted couples. As couples learn fair-fighting techniques through communication exercises and practice problem-solving through the use of a model, they will be able to express their feelings, identify the stress or source of the conflict, and collaboratively create solutions without blame or inequities of power in the relationship.

11

Divorcing Couples

KEY CONCEPTS

- Therapists use divorce stage theories to assess and design effective treatment strategies.
- Each partner may progress through the stages of divorce at a different rate.
- An integrative model of couples therapy helps provide the couple with a shared description of the presenting problem so that blame is not necessarily a central issue of the divorce experience.
- An integrative therapy model provides a systemic view of the couple's divorce process.
- Mediation and rituals are two specific intervention strategies to help couples complete the divorce process.

SOCIOLOGICAL CONTEXT: THE PREVALENCE OF DIVORCE

The number of relationships ending in divorce has almost tripled in the last 40 years (National Center for Health Statistics, 1984), and evidence suggests that half the marriages of today's adults will terminate in divorce (Glick, 1984). Among divorcing adults, 65% of the women and 70% of the men are likely to remarry (Glick & Lin, 1986; Norton & Moorman, 1987), and it has been projected that well over 50% of those who remarry will divorce again (Glick, 1984). On the basis of these statistics, therapists can assume that a majority of the couples presenting for therapy will personally experience divorce or be affected by the divorce of a family member.

DIVORCE STAGE THEORIES

One way of understanding the divorce process is through divorce stage theories. It is important that therapists understand the dynamics of divorce and the stages through which couples progress in order to assess and design interventions for the couple. For example, the issues for a couple exploring the possibility of divorce will be very different from those of partners who have been emotionally detached from each other for a long period of time and who may primarily be seeking assistance with the issue of child custody.

Making the Divorce Decision

Internal Stressors

The decision to divorce is a result of the extreme internal stress of at least one partner, which may be influenced by unmet needs or goals, poor coping styles in handling life events, or the inability to communicate feelings to the other partner. These factors can affect one or both partners' ability to manage conflict and negotiation in the relationship.

External Stressors

In addition to internal difficulties within the couple or individual, couples may experience a variety of external stressors on the relationship. Some of these stressors involve career, community, and extended family. For example, the wife may be angry with the husband because he will not support her career by attending the charity events she organizes in the community. The husband claims it is not his style, while she believes it is critical for her career advancement. Over many months, she becomes resentful and more withdrawn in the relationship. Communication becomes strained and she spends more time at the office. Her husband complains, but eventually it becomes easier for him to be involved in his own activities. Finally, after a year and a half, she decides that she wants a divorce.

As trivial as the issues may seem, this is not an uncommon scenario. What therapists need to remember is that it is not usually the issue itself but the way in which couples attempt to resolve the issue that leads to a deterioration of the relationship. In this case, the partners did not seem to negotiate the relationship very successfully, nor did they manage conflict well. Gradually the relationship eroded without either of them attempting to reconcile the differences. The wife may have become dissatisfied first, but clearly the husband played a role in the erosion of the marriage, even though he may not have wanted a divorce.

The decision to remain in a relationship or seek a divorce is clearly the responsibility of the couple, not the therapist; ethical standards (AAMFT, 1988) prohibit therapists from making such a choice for the couple. The therapist's role is to help couples make decisions about divorce. To be effective in this role, therapists must understand divorce stage theories and the experiences of each partner as they progress through the stages.

The Stages of Divorce

Couples are often at different stages as they consider the possibility of divorce. Most divorce stage theories focus on the emotions and experiences that each partner must resolve in order to progress to the next stage in the process. Although there may be a sequence of stages through which individuals generally progress, a particular person may repeat the stages, skip them, or experience them simultaneously. The intensity and duration of the stages may vary from person to person, and emotions experienced during a particular stage may resurface in other stages or during intense crisis periods in the lives of the divorced couple.

DEVELOPMENTAL MODELS OF DIVORCE

Differences between the developmental models of divorce are generally described in terms of points of emphasis (Landis, 1991). Some models focus more on the emotions each individual experiences, while others emphasize thoughts and behaviors. Most models that emphasize feelings or behaviors hypothesize a sequence that typically progresses from denial to anger to depression and finally to acceptance (Crosby, Gage, & Raymond, 1983; Kaslow, 1984) within a 2- to 3-year time period. Generally the sequence of feelings and behaviors is described as three phases: (1) predivorce decision-making stage, (2) divorce restructuring stage, and (3) postdivorce recovery stage (Kaslow, 1984; Sprenkle & Storm, 1983).

The Three Stages of Divorce

Predivorce Decision Making
In this stage, one or both partners experience a growing dissatisfaction about the relationship. Usually one partner begins to daydream or make plans for the future that do not include the other spouse. The dissatisfied partner may investigate the legal process of divorce and discuss the possibility of divorce with friends and family members.

Divorce Restructuring
This stage includes addressing the economic realities of divorce, the logistics of where each partner will live, and coparental and custodial issues if the couple has children. The result may be confused feelings as well as fear, loneliness, anger, and at times elation.

Postdivorce Recovery
It is during this stage that individuals begin to explore new life experiences, new identity, and new love objects. Although it can be an exciting period, it can also be characterized by ongoing regret or long-term resentment.

A Diaclectic Model of Divorce

Kaslow and Schwartz (1987) have proposed a comprehensive, eclectic model of divorce that organizes behavioral dynamics, stage theory, and the emotional responses to divorce. Their model, highlighted in Table 11.1, includes five elements:

Table 11.1   Diaclectic Model of Stages in the Divorce Process

Divorce Stage	Station	Stage	Feelings	Actions and Tasks	Therapeutic Interventions
	1. Emotional Divorce	1	Disillusionment Dissatisfaction Alienation Anxiety Disbelief	Avoiding the issue Sulking and/or crying Confronting partner Quarreling	Marital therapy (one couple) Couples group therapy
Predivorce A time of deliberation and despair		II	Despair Dread Anguish Ambivalence Shock Emptiness Anger Chaos Inadequacy Low self-esteem Loss	Denial Withdrawal (physical and emotional) Pretending all is okay Attempting to win back affection Asking friends, family, clergy for advice	Marital therapy (one couple) Divorce therapy Couples group therapy
	2. Legal Divorce	III	Depression Detachment Anger Hopelessness Self-pity Helplessness	Bargaining Screaming Threatening Attempting suicide Consulting an attorney or mediator	Family therapy Individual adult therapy Child therapy
During Divorce A time of legal involvement	3. Economic Divorce	IV	Confusion Fury Sadness	Separating physically Filing for legal divorce Considering economic arrangements Considering custody arrangements	Children of divorce group therapy Child therapy Adult therapy

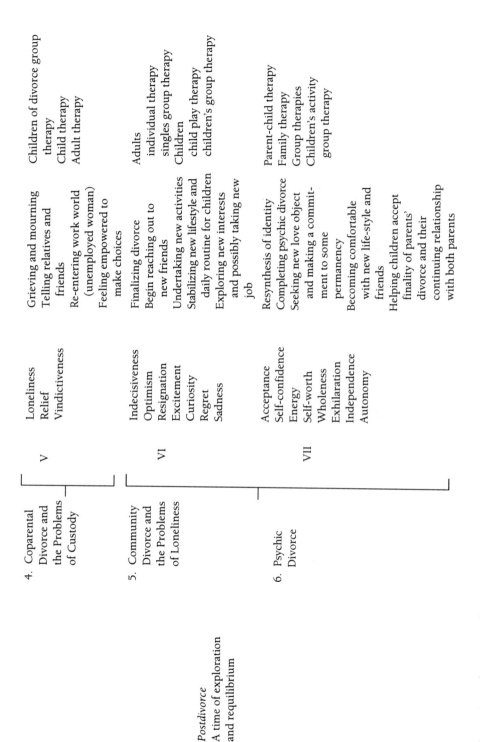

4. Coparental Divorce and the Problems of Custody	V	Loneliness Relief Vindictiveness	Grieving and mourning Telling relatives and friends Re-entering work world (unemployed woman) Feeling empowered to make choices	Children of divorce group therapy Child therapy Adult therapy
5. Community Divorce and the Problems of Loneliness	VI	Indecisiveness Optimism Resignation Excitement Curiosity Regret Sadness	Finalizing divorce Begin reaching out to new friends Undertaking new activities Stabilizing new lifestyle and daily routine for children Exploring new interests and possibly taking new job	Adults individual therapy singles group therapy Children child play therapy children's group therapy
6. Psychic Divorce	VII	Acceptance Self-confidence Energy Self-worth Wholeness Exhilaration Independence Autonomy	Resynthesis of identity Completing psychic divorce Seeking new love object and making a commitment to some permanency Becoming comfortable with new life-style and friends Helping children accept finality of parents' divorce and their continuing relationship with both parents	Parent-child therapy Family therapy Group therapies Children's activity group therapy

Postdivorce
A time of exploration and requilibrium

Source: From *The Dynamics of Divorce: A Life-Cycle Perspective*, by F. Kaslow and L. Schwartz, pp. 30–31. Copyright 1987 by Brunner/Mazel, Inc. Reprinted by permission.

1. temporal sequence
2. stations of divorce
3. intrapsychic dimensions
4. behaviors/events
5. therapeutic implications

Temporal Sequence

This element refers to the developmental stage through which the partners progress and the time frame typically required to progress through the stage. Most often, both partners do not experience the same rate of dissatisfaction or feelings associated with the disillusionment of the breakdown of a relationship.

Stations of Divorce

Stations include various aspects of divorce, such as emotional reactions, legalities, economics, coparenting, community reactions, and internal reactions of each partner (Bohannon, 1973). Often these stations are intertwined so that partners are reacting to intense emotional stress at the same time that they are receiving pressure from extended family, friends, or attorneys.

Intrapsychic Dimensions

These aspects encompass the feelings and emotional reactions each partner experiences during the stage of divorce. These feelings and reactions range from disillusionment, despair, shock, emptiness, anger, hopelessness, confusion, loneliness, excitement, regret, acceptance, independence, and autonomy.

Although certain stages of the divorce might be most often characterized by particular feelings, dramatic shifts in feelings and experiences can create a "roller coaster" effect. For example, when one spouse first tells the other he or she wants to separate, there may be initial reactions of panic, anger, fear, or shock that can later turn to excitement and back to hopelessness in a matter of minutes or hours.

Behavior/Events

These elements refer to the actions taken or tasks in which the individual engages during stages of divorce. Some of these actions might be sulking, crying, confronting the partner, bargaining, threatening, grieving, making new friends, telling relatives, exploring new interests, and stabilizing new relationships. Behaviors are also quite confusing, as one may vary from pretending that all is fine, to consulting with an attorney, and then to attempting suicide, all in a 24-hour period. It is a time to expect the unexpected.

Therapeutic Implications

Different interventions may be more or less appropriate at different stages of divorce. Interventions include marital therapy, couples group therapy, divorce therapy, individual adult therapy, child therapy, family therapy, parent-child therapy, and group support therapy for adults or children. For example, relationship (couples) therapy would most likely be useful during the predivorce decision-making stage while the couple formulates a plan. Later, family therapy to help the children understand what is happening may be indicated. Once the divorce has occurred, group therapy for either partner or for the children may help individuals address their feelings of hopelessness and fear and to begin to formulate plans for the future.

Application of Divorce Stage Models

As discussed earlier, it is particularly useful for the therapist to understand divorce stage models, as both partners may not have agreed on the decision to divorce and may be progressing through different stages during the decision-making process. One partner may have agonized over the decision to divorce for quite some time and may have experienced the disillusionment, anguish, and emptiness characteristic of the predivorce decision-making period. These feelings, however, may be unknown to the other partner, who may be shocked when the other announces he or she wants a divorce. Furthermore, the unknowing partner may perceive the other as cold, uncaring, impulsive, or unfeeling if he or she has detached and appears ready to take action, such as a physical separation or filing for divorce. The therapist's primary role is to help the couple communicate about the decision to divorce, even when both partners do not appear to have the same goals for the relationship.

Therapy and the Divorce Stages

During the predivorce decision-making stage the couple begins to consider divorce as an alternative to the ongoing marital conflict. Usually this decision has been made after the couple has struggled for some time, either alone or with each other. Guerin, Fay, Burden, and Kautto (1987) identified four developmental stages of marital conflict to describe the couple's decision to divorce.

Stage 1 typically occurs in the early years of marriage. In this stage, the relationship is characterized by open communication and a minimum amount of conflict. Negative reactivity toward each other and criticism are at low levels, and so therapy is not usually sought during this stage of conflict. Instead, couples attempt to negotiate their differences in a healthy way as they form their new relationship.

Issues such as how to spend time with each other, budgeting, in-law contact, career, and other household roles and rules are addressed. Most encounters between therapists and couples at this stage are through psychoeducational programs or marital enrichment courses sponsored by local churches, civic groups, and schools (Guerin et al., 1987).

In *stage 2*, the couple defines marital conflict as a problem. Couples in this stage experience anxiety and emotional arousal and fight openly with each other. Communication remains open, but there is more criticism and struggle for control. Although there may be some thoughts of separation or divorce, therapy more often is sought to address marital issues in an attempt to reconcile the differences.

If the therapist will be seeing the partners separately, it is important for the therapist to discuss confidentiality issues with the couple before the sessions begin so that secrets do not emerge in individual sessions that cannot be expressed in joint sessions. A good rule of thumb is for the therapist to tell both partners that all information brought forth in any session is to be considered joint information and can be shared with each other in a conjoint session.

A useful approach at this stage is a short-term couples group. This modality seems to help reduce the couple's tendency to cling to past hurts and battles and make excessive demands on each other and instead begin to create excitement and joy once again in the relationship (Kaslow & Schwartz, 1987). If couples are able to resolve their differences and address historical problems, they will not progress to the point of divorce therapy.

Stage 3 is characterized by a dramatic emotional climate in the relationship. Anxiety is high. At times, one partner may appear to take an opposing view just to fuel disagreement. The level of criticism is high at a time when both spouses have an impaired ability to communicate over day-to-day events. One or both partners may be bitter, and their lives run parallel courses as they pursue their own interests with minimum interaction (Guerin et al., 1987).

Couples at this stage experience confusion, ambivalence, and denial, and one partner may pretend that everything is fine while attempting to win back the spouse's affection. Chaos, confusion, inadequacy, and failure are prominent feelings (Kaslow & Schwartz, 1987, p. 28). Often individuals turn to their families and friends for emotional support or to enlist their help to induce the other partner to stay in the relationship.

Conjoint couples therapy is the treatment of choice at this stage until it is relatively clear that the relationship will end in separation or divorce. The role of the therapist here is to help the partners clarify their confused feelings, help them determine any possibilities for the resolution of their difficulties, and help them make a decision that will be in the best interest of all parties involved. Custody may be a major issue during this stage, particularly if each desires primary custody of the children. Children can become pawns in the battle of divorce if custody disputes become the central focus.

Therapy can be difficult at times during stage 3 because of the intensity of emotions the couple expresses. The therapist's initial goal is to reduce the anger, blame, and criticism the partners direct toward each other in the session so that the couple is able to make some decisions for the relationship. The therapist must also help the partners validate their own pain and must instill hope for the emotional survival of both parties. If the partners are able to cooperate and focus on a solution that will attempt to address the "best interests" of all parties involved, they may begin to feel empowered to make their own choices and experience more self-respect as they take responsibility and exercise choices for their futures (Kaslow & Schwartz, 1987).

It is also appropriate in this stage for the therapist to refer the couple to mediation for the resolution of their issues. Mediation is the resolution of issues with the assistance of a neutral third party, to reduce the couple's anger that is sometimes fueled by an adversarial court battle. (This intervention will be outlined later in this chapter.) If mediation is not utilized and conflict remains high, adversarial legal proceedings are usually pursued. The couple may feel depressed, helpless, and pessimistic as the negotiating and problem resolution is now in the hands of attorneys, who may fuel the amount of anger, despair, and conflict by virtue of their adversarial positions (Palmer & Landis, 1989; Landis, 1991). The division of possessions, decisions over parental arrangements, and the loss of one's life dreams are very painful experiences for all involved.

Therapists must be aware that individuals can move from feelings of intense anger and retribution to extreme sadness and anxiety very quickly and without any apparent provocation (Landis, 1991). It is important to make couples aware of these dramatic mood swings and help them identify ways of managing these feelings when they arise. For example, one partner knows that when the other parent comes to pick up the children for contact time, a prolonged discussion ensues leading to anger and frustration; that partner might plan in advance to have the children ready and then immediately leave as soon as the children are in the other's care. A further plan might be to go to a movie with a friend so that the loneliness and frustration are not exacerbated by staying in the house and brooding.

Finally, *stage 4* is marked by extreme conflict. One or both parties have usually engaged an attorney at this stage, and it may be most useful at this time to refer both parties to individual therapy. Continuing to see the couple conjointly is beneficial only if both are willing to work on unresolved joint issues affecting their children or the dissolution of their marriage. It is not recommended for the same therapist to retain either one of the parties for individual therapy. Confidentiality issues could be confusing in circumstances where both parties have been prior clients, and any information about the therapy sessions requested by one partner requires a release of information form signed by both parties.

Another complication would be if one party believed that the therapist sided with the other partner. The result may be a malpractice suit. At the very least, the therapist is faced with being subpoenaed by one party and becoming involved in a legal battle over what information can be used in court.

Because the divorce process can be a very chaotic time for most couples, it is important that the therapist have a clear model for addressing the couple's needs. These needs can be addressed by the use of the integrative model outlined in Chapter 2.

THE INTEGRATIVE MODEL AND DIVORCE THERAPY

The following case example concerns a couple that comes to therapy during the predivorce decision-making stage. The partners are engaging in behaviors indicative of late stage 2 or early stage 3 of relationship conflict (Guerin et al., 1987). At this stage, emotionality is high, communication is low, and there is an excessive amount of blame directed at each partner.

Case Example: David and Marcy

David and Marcy have been married for 6 years. David initially makes the appointment on the advice of his best friend, after confiding that Marcy had been working 50 to 60 hours per week for over 2 years and at times has been sleeping at the office after a long night of work. David reports that there is no excitement in the relationship and that the two have little in common. Sex has been almost nonexistent, and David has been the primary caretaker of the children for too long. He admits that he is lonely and would like female companionship, even if it is not with Marcy.

Marcy emphasizes that she loves her work and gets a lot of satisfaction from it, something that she does not experience as a wife and mother. She blames David for not being available to her because he is either playing with the children or playing tennis at the local club. Marcy is not interested in maintaining the relationship and would like to work out a separation so that the children, ages 3 and 5, will be minimally traumatized. David, on the other hand, would like to resolve their differences if at all possible.

Application of the Integrative Model: Divorce Therapy

Stage 1: Assessing and Obtaining an Interactional View of the Problem

During this stage of assessment, the therapist obtains information about each partner's perception of the problem. This is accomplished by the use of circular questioning. As both parties describe their version of the problem, the therapist gathers data about their families of origin and some of the early messages and interactional styles they brought to the relationship. This information may be useful later as the couple examines the early messages they have received from their families and identifies the personal strengths they have each developed to cope with life events.

David sees Marcy's work and apathy about the relationship as the problem; Marcy views David's lack of excitement and diverted interests with the children and tennis as the focus of the problem. The therapist helps the couple begin to see an interactional problem so that they can share in the solution by jointly owning the problem. One interactional definition tentatively advanced is: "It seems that both of you are lonely in your relationship and that you are seeking other ways to fill that loneliness. You both seem to have lost touch with each other to the point that one of you is ready to separate."

The therapist proceeds to obtain more information about the duration of the problem, the partners' commitment to trying to resolve the problem, others who are affected by the problem, and alternatives to a decision to separate. David claims that the children are afraid they will not see their parents anymore if their parents divorce. As the therapist finds out more about the couple, the couple explores attempts that have been made in the past to resolve the problem.

David states that he has tried to get Marcy more involved with the children and has tried to plan a family vacation together. He says that he also tried to teach Marcy to play tennis so they could play together, but she claims that it hurt her arm and the weather was too hot. Marcy believes she tried to involve David more with her work-related activities that she says he found boring. They said that the only time they agreed on activities was when they participated together in a school carnival for the children.

Stage 2: Goal Setting

During this stage, the therapist asks David and Marcy to identify specifically what their lives would be like if the problem were solved. It is important to help the couple see the new picture of the relationship interactionally, rather than as individually focused. It is not clear yet whether the focus will be on helping the couple stay together or helping them separate successfully; that decision is to be made solely by the couple, not the therapist. If the focus is on the couple remaining together, Marcy's statement that "David needs to spend more time with me away from the children" could be restated as "David and I need to find specific ways to spend time together as a couple and as a family with our children."

At the conclusion of this stage, the decision is made whether to continue with marriage therapy. David and Marcy decide to continue. The therapist then asks each partner to be more specific as they identify possible goals. David and Marcy identify the following goals:

1. They will set aside one night per week to pursue an activity together to infuse some excitement and joy in their lives. They will provide a babysitter and take turns planning the activity.
2. David and Marcy will sit down with the children and plan five activities they would like to do as a family and then plan a time schedule to complete the activities so that they feel more connected to each other.
3. The couple will spend time together talking about their intimate relationship and will set aside time at least once a week for a one-on-one activity, such as massaging each other, to increase their mutual pleasure in the relationship.

These goals could be more extensive, but now let us assume that Marcy and David do not wish to work on the marital relationship. Instead, they would like to discuss a separation with the therapist. First, the therapist helps the couple understand what has led to their decision to separate and what barriers they have encountered in attempting to resolve the conflicts. The therapist can also help the couple be direct in their communications to the other so that there is a minimum of mixed messages and game playing about leaving the relationship. The couple must also entertain the challenge, "Is there anything that can be done to save this relationship?" Usually this question spawns conversation about deep-rooted notions of love and intimacy.

If the couple is not interested in pursuing the relationship, or even if one is somewhat interested but the other is not, the therapy will begin to move in a different direction. Both parties must be invested in making the relationship work or there will be conflicting interests between the parties; it takes two to make the relationship work.

Therapy is now oriented toward helping David and Marcy explore and express their feelings about the divorce and the arrangements for the children. Goal setting with the couple now might be more like the following:

1. David and Marcy will discuss how they envision their lives as coparents and will develop a plan on paper before they talk to their children. This plan will help them feel more confident when they talk to their children and will help give them more direction about their future.
2. David and Marcy will talk with their children conjointly and answer any questions they can without blaming the other. The children will feel more secure as their parents describe what they can expect with regard to parental contact, where they might live, what school they'll attend, contact with grandparents, and so on.
3. David and Marcy will attend mediation sessions and will contact attorneys to finalize plans they make. This process will help feel more collaborative rather than litigious as they separate their lives as marital partners.
4. Each individual will pursue friends and family to help feel supported during this time. Neither person will blame the other in front of family or friends.
5. Divorce therapy will continue for at least five sessions to help them express feelings and say goodbye to the marriage.

Specific goals for the couple during this stage help provide a focus and instill hope for a more positive coparenting relationship. A general goal or outcome statement might be "David and Marcy will seek all methods and support available for the two of them to divorce in the most collaborative, nonblaming manner possible so that they will feel more hopeful about the future and their children will feel more secure with the changes in their lives."

Stage 3: Adopting New Perceptions and Behaviors/Interventions

At this stage, the therapist facilitates a conversation as the couple draws on the strengths both partners possess individually and as a couple to divorce successfully. Strengths in this case might include the ability to work on the school carnival together even when they were fighting, David's ability to be creative to find solutions, or Marcy's negotiating skills to find a middle ground. It can be useful to help the couple create their own story about how they want to parent their children and live their lives separate from each other. A conversation initiated by the therapist may progress like this:

Therapist: David, you said earlier that you two were able to work on the carnival together. Tell us what you saw as the most cooperative thing you did to make that happen.

David: Well, I took some time off and wrote a schedule of each event and who needed to perform each task.

Therapist: So, you were very clear about what you saw as each person's responsibility for the carnival events. How did you check that out with Marcy and come to an agreement?

David: She looked at the schedule and made some changes based on her time frame and how she thought it might run more smoothly.

Therapist: Is that how you see it, Marcy, that you were able to have a written plan and then make changes together to create a final plan?

Marcy: Well, basically. David is very good at planning a project but sometimes he forgets about child care needed to implement his ideas.

Therapist: So you were able to help him make a plan that worked because you had more familiarity with that aspect of the plan.

Marcy: Yes, it went real well.

Therapist: I wonder if it would be possible now for the two of you to make a plan to include a parenting schedule flexible enough for all of you with your careers and with the children's activities.

David: I could make a chart of all the activities and a weekly time plan, and then Marcy could look at it to see what might be useful and where it might break down.

Therapist: Marcy, would you be willing to do that so that you could each have a part in the parenting schedule?

David and Marcy seem able to work things out. However, if the partners seek mediation at this stage, they focus on collaboration, not litigation.

Stage 4: Maintaining New Perceptions and Behaviors

In this stage, the focus is on how the couple will continue to work together even when they have issues with each other. Questions to each about how much each wants to be successful with the divorce, how much each is willing to be different, or how much each is willing to give up the old picture and create a new one are helpful for underscoring the idea that often one part of us would like to be different, whereas another side would like to remain the same. One part of us would like to blame and be resentful, but another part would like to be cooperative. Therapy helps the couple acknowledge the inflexible reactions while emphasizing the flexible, creative side that exists in all people.

During this stage, questions are designed to help the couple identify the barriers or "pulls to the old pattern." For example: "What do you each need to do to ensure that the plan you have created will work?"; "What will prevent success for you now?"; or "What do you need from others to make this happen?" are effective questions to provoke thought about the barriers.

David and Marcy identify their work schedules, Marcy's mother, and David's bitterness as obstacles that get in the way. The couple begins to discuss what they will do when work interferes, what Marcy might say to her mother if she is negative, or what possibilities exist for David, such as a support group or special friend to confide in when he feels bitter. The more specific the couple is as they identify barriers and solutions to the barriers, the more potential for resolution they create.

Stage 5: Validating New Perceptions and Behaviors

In this stage, the task is for the partners to restate their goals for therapy and define their successes. David and Marcy have attempted to resolve their differences in therapy, have attended mediation, have identified their support systems, and have talked to the children together about the divorce without blaming each other.

The outcome statement directly addresses the statements they made in stage 2 as they defined their goals for divorce therapy. Both partners validate their collaborative success as well as their personal contributions to the successful resolution. Marcy says, "I am happy that we have been able to work together and that David has been so helpful about the scheduling," and David replies, "It seems like we really have a plan to work together for the children. I think Marcy has been very accommodating in making sure my parents see the children when they come down to visit." (See Figure 11.1.)

Ending therapy in a positive manner continues to provide the partners hope for the future that they will be able to work together on a variety of issues that arise. They are given a sense of accomplishment in the midst of grief, loss, and change. Although the feelings of grief and loss are dealt with only minimally in this model, this is not meant to suggest that these feelings are not central to the divorce process.

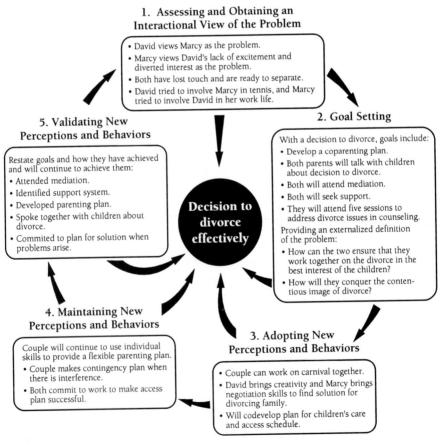

Figure 11.1 The therapy process with David and Marcy

Rather, it suggests that much of the individual feeling or grief work needs to be done individually. The focus of therapy in our case study, as stated in the goals, was to work together to parent the children effectively.

Considerations for Therapists

Following are some guidelines for therapists engaged in counseling couples on divorce.

1. Determine the stage of divorce each partner is experiencing and help the couple accept the differences.
2. Assess the stage of marital or relationship conflict including frequency, duration, and intensity.
3. With the couple, determine joint as well as individual goals for therapy.
4. Design treatment plans based on the needs of both partners.
5. Assist the couple in the identification of support systems for each partner during the divorce process.
6. Help both members of the couple identify appropriate therapeutic resources for each partner. These resources may include individual, family, or group therapy or community support groups.
7. Restate goals of therapy and define the achievement of success.

Therapists in training can identify the appropriate therapeutic goals and treatment strategies for a couple by using a role-play situation in the classroom to practice the "fit" of the goals, treatment plans, and therapeutic style of the integrative model we have outlined. At the conclusion of the exercise, each class member can offer feedback based on the following guidelines.

Feedback Questionnaire

1. How well did the therapist assess the current stage of divorce and clarify the stage for the couple?
2. To what extent did the therapist assist the couple in defining the problem interactionally?
3. To what extent did the therapist address each partner's individual needs?
4. To what degree did the therapist assist the couple in identifying goals for therapy and a clear definition of success?
5. How well did the intervention strategies employed by the therapist help the couple move toward stated desired outcomes?
6. To what extent did the therapist make appropriate referrals?

INTERVENTION STRATEGIES

During the course of divorce therapy, therapists can employ a variety of interventions to facilitate change. These interventions must be selected according to the unique characteristics of the couple. This section discusses mediation and rituals of separation because they may have specific application to divorce and separation issues. It is important to remember, however, that these interventions can also be used in other situations, depending on the couple's needs.

Mediation

Mediation is a process designed to assist separating couples in conflict to reach an agreement privately, confidentially, and informally. It employs the skills of a neutral and impartial third party, the mediator, who helps the individuals make their own decisions by providing necessary information, clarifying issues, helping them explore alternate solutions, and suggesting possible accommodations. Issues often mediated include child custody, primary and secondary residential parenting, child support, alimony or spousal support, division of assets, and taxes (Palmer, 1993).

Goals of Mediation

The goals of mediation are to (1) reduce anxiety and other negative effects of the conflict by empowering the parties involved to devise a cooperative solution that best fits their needs and the needs of their children, (2) prepare the parties to anticipate and ultimately accept the consequences of their own decisions, and (3) promote an agreement for the future that all parties involved can accept (Palmer, 1993).

Advantages of Mediation

Mediation minimizes the potentially traumatic emotional and psychological effects of the adversarial process. Discussions between the parties can often proceed quickly, and an agreement can be reached in just a matter of one or a few sessions. For issues concerning children, the sessions are structured with the best interests of the child in the forefront of the discussion and in such a way that each partner can emerge a winner. Finally, mediation is much less expensive than traditional litigation proceedings.

What Mediation Is Not

- It is not therapy.
- It does not circumvent the legal system, as both parties are encouraged to seek individual legal counsel at appropriate times.
- It is not primarily educational; rather, it is an interactive process with the primary focus on decision making, the establishment of a memorandum of understanding, and the development of a plan of action for the future.
- It is not arbitration. In arbitration, the couple authorizes a neutral third party to decide on a binding resolution of the issues. In mediation, the couple—not the third party—decides on the agreement that will govern the partners' relationship with each other in the future.
- It is not conciliation. People often use the two terms interchangeably; however, conciliation is a process whereby the couple meets with a neutral third party in an effort to work out the marital problems in order to continue the marriage. Mediation takes place after the couple has agreed that the marriage is over.

If Mediation Fails

If mediation does not bring about an agreement between the parties, any statements made during the sessions by any of the parties remains confidential. This means that a mediator cannot be forced to testify in court about the mediation process. If the parties cannot agree, the mediator will notify the court that agreement is not possible but will not comment or recommend further.

How Mediation Works

The process of mediation begins by an order of the court or by agreement of the parties. The mediator, though neutral and objective, plays an active role by assisting the parties in working toward their own settlement agreement. The parties are educated regarding what information is needed to achieve a fair agreement. The mediator clarifies and organizes details, prompts discussion and cooperative communication, and manages conflict. The purpose of the mediator is to help the couple identify issues, develop bargaining proposals, and conduct negotiations with the goal in mind of arriving at a settlement that best suits both partners' needs.

During mediation, the mediator uses such skills as managing conflict, referring the parties out for an expert opinion or advice, and sometimes just "directing traffic." Throughout the mediation, the mediator's function is to keep the parties task-focused and mindful of the purposes, procedures, and scope of mediation.

The mediator does not make any decisions for the parties but facilitates the couple's own decision-making processes. When the issues have been resolved, the mediator drafts a memorandum of agreement. After review and approval by the parties, it is given to their attorneys for legal implementation.

The Therapist's Role

The therapist who is providing services for one or both parties seeking a divorce or modification can refer the couple to a certified mediator, who will work with the couple on settlement of the issues relating to children and division of assets. The therapist may continue to see the couple for other therapeutic services, but the therapist should not attempt to mediate for either client while the couple is seeking therapeutic services. Therapy and mediation are two distinct services. It is important for therapists to be aware of mediators in their communities so that appropriate referrals can be made. We should note that a therapist can be a trained mediator. Training requires the completion of a prescribed course with some practicum experience, and in some states training is governed by specific laws. It is not appropriate, however, for therapists—even if they are trained mediators—to provide mediation services once a therapy relationship has been established, as mediation and therapy must remain distinct services.

The Attorney's Role

The mediator's role is neutral and is not a substitute for independent legal advice. The mediator does not represent either party but focuses on helping the parties reach their own agreement, so each party is urged to seek independent legal counsel throughout the mediation process. Although the decisions reached in mediation are made by the parties, it is important that they be informed decisions.

Attorneys may attend the mediation sessions, and at all times the parties are permitted to communicate privately with counsel. Upon completion of the mediation, the mediator will submit the memorandum of agreement to the parties' attorneys. If necessary, the attorneys will draft a settlement agreement from the terms of the memorandum for filing with the court.

The Cost of Mediation

The mediator's fee is usually determined on an hourly basis, and both parties are encouraged to share in the expense. The court may set the fee and determine the party responsible for payment when mediation is ordered. Occasionally, when the parties are indigent or qualify for financial assistance, low-cost services may be available. The important thing to remember is that mediation can be, and frequently is, less expensive in the long run, both financially and emotionally.

Who Uses Mediation

Mediation is for parties who have made the decision to dissolve the marriage but who cannot agree on any or all of the many issues involved in the dissolution. Occasionally, mediation is used if the parties decide to separate for a period of time, when separation might result in a dissolution. Frequently parties have found mediation valuable in resolving differences that arise even after a dissolution has been rendered. These postdissolution problems usually involve issues related to children (Palmer, 1993).

Rituals for Separation and Divorce

Traditionally, rituals have been associated with repetitive or symbolic behaviors designed to address a life event in a meaningful way for the individual or couple. Rituals can also be one of the most powerful socialization mechanisms throughout the life span (Laird & Hartman, 1988). Through rituals, we define and reaffirm our traditions and ourselves. Although rituals may employ language, they also take us beyond the conscious and cognitive domain to a more subconscious domain of myth, metaphor, and symbol. Rituals imply action and, being executed in the present, reflect the past and shape the future at one and the same time (Laird & Hartman, 1988). They can help individuals and couples express and create new realities without conscious awareness and can enable and impose change (Myerhoff, 1983). As rituals are enacted beyond our conscious awareness, they can be most effective for working with couples on issues of divorce.

Often in divorce, people become fearful and rigid and are reluctant to change. Both parties are confronting many new events, emotions, and situations in their lives, and there is a tendency to hold on to the life and behaviors from the former marriage, even when it is not feasible to do so. For example, Maya has always celebrated her birthday with Raoul at her favorite restaurant. This year, as a newly divorced person, Maya wanted to continue the tradition with one of her friends. But after the dinner, Maya was very disappointed at the emptiness she experienced. Maya may be stuck in determining how she would like to commemorate occasions now that Raoul is not a part of her life. With the help of her therapist, she is able to identify a new tradition for her birthday that will elicit new meaning in her life without Raoul.

This is an example of how rituals can be powerful interventions in therapy when utilized to help clients effect change and provide alternatives to life situations. Rituals provide therapists a mode for helping people master life transitions, alter relationships, and construct more meaningful self-definitions (Laird & Hartman, 1988). They include a plan created by the therapist with the client to change a pattern in the present or the future.

Consider the following when creating a ritual:

1. Understand the context for the event that requires a ritual; did it come from the family of origin or from the past behaviors of the individual or the couple?
2. Explore in detail with the individual or couple the old behaviors associated with the event and meanings ascribed to it.
3. Identify with the individual or couple the new context or manner in which they want to commemorate the passage of an event.
4. Identify the meaning the individual or couple would like to attach to the event.
5. Create a new behavior or way to commemorate the event that would ascribe new meaning to the event.
6. Explore with the client the barriers or "blockers" for the completion of the task or ritual.
7. Evaluate the effectiveness of the new behavior and meaning of the behavior for the individual or couple in the past, present, or future, modifying the ritual accordingly.

Case Example: Kim and Lia

Kim and Lia are newly divorced. Kim initiated the divorce, and Lia was devastated. Finally, after 7 months, Lia is going to visit the mountain cabin she and Kim had built during their marriage. Lia is taking her sons, Tyler and Stan, but she does not know what she will do without Kim to help her with them. Lia has considered asking her mother or a girlfriend to go with her, but she is concerned that she will get upset and does not want to be burdensome to anyone. She knows that she should be "getting on with her life" but feels uncertain and stuck. Lia has just begun to see a therapist and has decided to discuss her impending trip in her next session.

Intervention

After a thorough assessment, goal setting, and treatment planning with Lia, the therapist decides to help construct a ritual for Lia while she is on her vacation in the mountains. Because Lia was accustomed to Kim's company on the long drive to the cabin, she ordered a novel on audiotape that she could look forward to listening to on the drive while the children were sleeping. Lia also made plans to have an old friend stop and spend one night with her on the way home. Lia was most concerned, however, about the mementos that she and Kim had accumulated over the years in the cabin. Of particular importance was the arrangement of dried flowers they had collected on one of their hikes in the mountains.

As the therapist discussed with Lia the possibilities for change through a ritual, the following suggestions were made:

1. Lia will ask her friend to accompany her on the hike that she loved so dearly, but this time they will hike to a different destination on an unknown trail.
2. Lia will decide on a transformation for the dried flower arrangement and will carry out the plan while in the mountains.
3. Lia will mark the transformation by some repetitive behavior or symbol while on the vacation.
4. Lia will select one friend with whom to share her feelings about her experience.

After much collaboration, Lia, with the therapist's assistance, decided to take her friend Carlita on the trip with her. She advised Carlita of her plan to hike to a different location from the hike she previously took with Kim. Lia also decided to talk with Carlita about her fears and sadness about returning to the place she and Kim had shared so fondly.

After much deliberation, Lia devised a ritualized experience to mark the passage from her marriage to life as a single person. Lia was to take the dried arrangement and make a colorful potpourri, placed in three plastic bags. Next, the children and Carlita were to accompany Lia on a hike and picnic in the mountains. While in the mountains and as the children were resting in their sleeping bags after lunch, Lia was to disperse the potpourri throughout the hills, rocks, and streams. Finally, Lia would bury the vase in which she had arranged the flowers deep within the mountainous area. Through the ritualized transformation of the flowers Lia had cherished with Kim, Lia chose to free them by returning them to their very origin, much as she hoped to feel after her divorce.

Symbolically, the burial of the vase meant the death and unavailability of the receptacle that had held the precious mementos, much like the end of her marriage. Having Carlita along during the hike signified the need for old friends, past experiences, and current events to ascribe new meanings to her present life.

This intervention has the potential for far-reaching effects if constructed with the client in a meaningful way. Each ritual must be unique for the individual or couple so that the clients will experience the new meaning and symbolism. Input from the client is crucial because it is the client alone who understands the meanings associated with particular events from the past.

CONCLUSION

With almost half of all marriages ending in divorce, this is a critical area of learning for all therapists. The five-stage integrative model and its application for working with divorcing couples was reviewed in this chapter. The model includes (1) assessing and obtaining an interactional view of the problem, (2) goal setting, (3) adopting new perceptions and behaviors/interventions, (4) maintaining new perceptions and behaviors, and (5) validating new perceptions and behaviors.

In addition, two specific intervention strategies have been adapted for this particular population and were described in this chapter. Mediation was discussed in depth because clients often go through mediation and participate in therapy simultaneously. Rituals and their usefulness for progressing from one stage of divorce to another were also described. Finally, a case example was used to illustrate how this strategy can be used by therapists to help divorcing individuals or couples.

12

Infidelity in Relationships

KEY CONCEPTS

- Extramarital affairs, or affairs outside a committed relationship, are common, and when discovered they are among the chief reasons for the breakup of a relationship.
- People enter into affairs for a variety of reasons. Desire for sexual novelty and a wish for intimacy are two important motivations.
- Society's code of silence about sexuality and media images support romantic ideas about affairs.
- Affairs do not necessarily mean the end of the couple relationship.
- The therapist must help bring ongoing affairs out into the open, being careful not to support one member's desire to keep the affair hidden.
- Therapy with couples who have experienced an extramarital affair has two distinct phases: an emergency period, and a separate time when key couple issues are faced.
- Getting over an affair, when it can be done, takes months or years. Patience and professional support are required.

Affairs promise so much: an opportunity to pursue dreams that have been dormant, to come alive again, to find someone who truly understands. Their hidden promise is pain.
(Brown, 1991, p. 3)

A friend recently purchased an antique oak bed at an auction, and one of its romantic features was the well-preserved bullet holes in the headboard just above where someone might have lain. The bed is a good conversation piece, but at the same time it is a grim reminder that intimacy can be betrayed and that love can turn to murderous rage. Infidelity is emotional dynamite to a relationship and many, if not most, affairs precipitate a breakup. Affairs exhilarate the unfaithful partner and can cast the other into a living hell. The unfaithful partner feels guilty

222

and happy at the same time, while the other feels unattractive, used, and angry for having been so trusting. The couple in crisis spends long hours arguing, has many sleepless nights, and often experiences wild mood swings and irrational outbursts.

When one is going through this roller-coaster of emotions, the situation appears hopeless and the relationship seems to be "dead on arrival" at the therapist's office. But, as Simone de Beauvoir said, a relationship is not like a chain that is broken; people are connected by a hundred individual threads. When the tornado of an affair hits a relationship, there are still connections that can form the basis of a new relationship if the therapist and couple can find them. Couples can come back from the brink and forge a new relationship.

The couples therapist must remember that there is hope for the relationship if both people are willing to be patient. In addition, the partner having the affair must be willing to change, the other partner must be willing to forgive, and the couple must confront the issues that may have given rise to the affair. These are four big "ifs." These "ifs" and the fact that the affair can blossom again at any moment, causing a new cycle of pain, are what makes working with affairs among the most challenging issues in couples therapy.

WHAT CONSTITUTES AN AFFAIR

Extramarital sex is the usual definition for an affair, but this may be a male-oriented definition according to Glass and Wright (1992). They identify three types of affairs: emotional involvement, sexual involvement, and a combined type. According to Glass and Wright, emotional involvement is the essence of an affair to most women. They point out that "emotional affairs" are damaging to relationships even if sex is not involved. The line between a close friendship and an emotional affair is difficult to draw, which is probably the reason the former are not included when the percentages of people having affairs is reported.

Frank Pittman, who wrote the influential book about men's affairs called *Private Lies* (1989), indicates that the definition of whether an affair has taken place is based on the couple's definition of the contract. Although a partner may not have had a sexual affair, time, interest, and intimacy may have been spent on another person. Such situations must be dealt with as affairs if they break the couple's agreements or threaten the primary relationship.

In this chapter, we will refer to the partner who has formed an intimate relationship with a third party as the "unfaithful partner." We use the term *other partner* to refer to the member of the couple who is not involved in an affair. The use of these terms is designed to be as neutral as possible to avoid assigning blame.

The Prevalence of Affairs

A recent study of marriage and family therapists (see Moultrup, 1990) revealed that nearly half of their clients came to treatment for issues associated with affairs by one or both partners. There are a variety of estimates about the current percentage of married people having affairs, but most suggest that around 60% of men and

45% of women are willing to report that an affair has occurred sometime in their marriage (cf. Glass & Wright, 1992). Brown (1991) suggested in her research that about 70% of all marriages experience an affair. In summary, more than half of marriages experience an affair and nearly half of the couples seek therapy on the heels of an affair. Given these statistics, it seems incumbent on all therapists working with couples to be informed about this issue.

Types of Affairs

So far, we have learned that an affair may be sexually based, emotionally based, or a combined type (Glass & Wright, 1992). The way to determine the type is to ask the unfaithful partner about his or her justifications for the affair and look at his or her thinking patterns. The reason for trying to identify the type is that sexually based affairs are easier to end, and emotionally based ones are a bit more difficult. The combined type is the most difficult to disengage from because it offers excitement, reward, and the fantasy of "true love" waiting just around the corner.

Brown (1991) classified the most common affairs seen in clinical practice in terms of the goal of the affair.

1. *Conflict avoidance affairs:* The issue is frustration and the couple's inability to deal with conflict.
2. *Empty nest affairs:* The couple's relationship is unfulfilling after children leave home.
3. *Out-of-the-door affairs:* Concocted to induce the other partner to end the relationship, thus avoiding taking responsibility for ending it.
4. *Intimacy avoidance affairs:* Response to feelings that, after several years of marriage, intimacy has become overwhelming. An affair puts more comfortable distance in the relationship. Both members of the couple may have an intimacy-avoidant affair.
5. *Sexual addict's affairs:* Entered into to make sexual conquests and involving an element of daring.

(Note that Brown uses the term *infidel* to refer to the unfaithful partner and *spouse* instead of *partner*.)

According to Brown, each type of affair requires different handling. Table 12.1 shows typical characteristics, recommended therapy, and possible outcomes of each affair type.

Frank Pittman (1989) has taken a different angle. Whereas Brown tends to see at least three of the four types as couples problems, Pittman does not believe that relationship problems necessarily precede affairs (Pittman & Wagers, 1995, p. 305). Rather, some types of affairs are simply caused by one person's willingness to have an affair. Pittman's clinical experience revealed four basic types of affairs, viewed in terms of the unfaithful partner.

1. *Accidental infidelity.* These are unplanned trysts that are not based on a love relationship. They occur when alone, when traveling, when there are problems at

Table 12.1 Characteristics by Type of Affair (Extramarital)

	Conflict Avoidance	Intimacy Avoidance	Sexual Addiction	Empty Nest	Out of the Door
Gender of Infidel	male or female	male and female	male	male	female or male
Age of Infidel	20s and 30s	20s and 30s	any	40 and up	any
Length of Marriage Before Affair	less than 12 years	less than 6 years	0 years	20 or more years	less than 15 years
Theme of Affair	avoid conflict	avoid intimacy	individual feels empty	family and shoulds vs. wants	avoid facing ending of marriage
Duration of Affair	brief	brief	brief	2 or more years	6 months to 2 years
Level of Emotional Involvement in Affair	minimal	minimal	none	great	some
Presenting Affect of Infidel	guilty	angry and chaotic	grandiose and/or seductive	depressed	uninvolved
Presenting Affect of Spouse	angry but nicey-nice	angry and chaotic	denial	depressed	angry
Interaction Pattern of Couple	conflict is deflected	continual conflict	separate lives	troubled communication	Infidel uninvolved, Spouse angry
Who Presents for Therapy	Infidel or couple	couple	Infidel or Spouse	couple, Infidel, or dumped Spouse	couple or dumped Spouse
Primary Treatment Mode Initially	couple	couple	individual	individual	couple
Prognosis for Resolving Issues	very good	very good	poor	good	good
Probability of Divorce	low	low	low	above average	very high
Best Outcome	solid marriage	solid marriage	family in recovery	revived marriage or divorce	resolve issues of ending marriage
Worst Outcome	other affairs or divorce	other affairs or divorce	damaged family and public humiliation	empty shell marriage or divorce	unresolved loss

Source: From *Patterns of Infidelity and Their Treatment*, by E. M. Brown, p. 30. Copyright 1991 by Brunner/Mazel, Inc. Reprinted by permission.

home or when the partner is unavailable because of medical problems, pregnancy, or some other reason. Some affairs are not necessarily the result of a bad relationship, according to Michele Weiner-Davis (1992); they are the result of bad judgment. Some are "one-night stands" engaged in after the consumption of too much alcohol. Even so, trust has been lost and must be rebuilt.

2. *Philandering.* Philandering is making a career of engaging in affairs, almost like a hobby. As mentioned earlier, male philandering according to Pittman is to avoid the control of women. It is a hyper-masculine behavior that defines all relationships with women as potentially sexual and all relationships with men as competitive. Female philanderers are thought to be searching for Mr. Perfect. Both male and female philanderers live with a certain amount of danger, and these "dangerous liaisons" are more exciting because of their illicit nature.

3. *Romantic affairs.* Romantic affairs have to do with falling in love. Pittman claims that romantic affairs are conducted by "romantics." Romantics do not fall in love with someone who fulfills their dreams; they fall in love when their real life becomes insipid and they are "not quite ready for suicide" (Pittman & Wagers, p. 304). Very often one person is involved in the affair romantically, and the other is using it for sexual variety. When two romantics team up, they may abandon their other relationships for their "love." Pittman claims that romantic affairs are often the ones that end in explosions with enough hurt to go around for everyone involved.

4. *Marital arrangements.* In these situations, both partners have openly or silently agreed to have affairs on the side. It is a way of establishing distance in the relationship while maintaining some of the perquisites of marriage. An example of this situation is the businessman having a 20-year relationship with his secretary. Marital arrangements can also include permanent separations, as these triangles can work as long as the lover or lovers make no demands that the arrangement be modified. Pittman also identifies other more exotic and volatile arrangements such as revenge affairs, flirtation/jealousy patterns, and other, more bizarre agreements that seem to be made for the purpose of arousing the other partner.

WHY PEOPLE HAVE AFFAIRS

Obviously, a single answer to this question will not do; there are as many answers as there are couples involved. Reasons often given by the unfaithful partner include a feeling of entitlement, that he or she deserves to be happy, that the relationship has been bad for a long time, or that the partner is no longer attractive. Fisher (1992) speculates that people have affairs to get attention; as a search for autonomy and independence; or to feel special, desired, or more masculine or feminine. Still others want to prove they are still young in a "last chance" affair.

The other partner often tries to analyze why his or her partner had the affair, attempts to determine what went wrong in the relationship, and may blame him- or herself or the third party involved. This partner's thinking is skewed because there is a tendency to want to protect the unfaithful partner.

Concerns for protecting one's partner and introspection into the causes of the affair are usually lacking in the unfaithful partner, who is afraid to think—afraid to examine the affair very closely for fear that, like a mirage, it may evaporate. Our experience is that both the other partner and the unfaithful one are protecting themselves from feelings of guilt, low self-esteem, and depression. The reasons given for the development of the affair will come out as therapy progresses, but they may not be evident in the first pronouncements.

We will present some research that tries to shed light on these issues, but all these data are self-reports and retrospective. The real reasons may not be known to the unfaithful partners but may in fact be self-serving defensive reactions aimed at protecting their self-esteem or justifying their behavior. Pittman and Wagers (1995) have trouble taking any "justifications" seriously because these usually tend to blame the other partner or the relationship. Pittman and Wagers find it difficult to see how the affair solves these problems effectively. They reported one justification by a woman who felt that her husband's unwillingness to dance gave her the right to sleep with anyone who would dance with her.

Buunk's 1980 study of couples in the Netherlands asked unfaithful partners to indicate the reason for their involvement in an affair. Reasons included a need for intimacy, need for variety in a relationship, emotional independence, sex-role equality for women, need deprivation in the marriage, partner approval, and social context. Social context characteristics that women reported as influencing their first extramarital affair included peer influences: knowing someone involved in an affair and talking to that person (Atwater, 1979).

Various studies have added to the list of reasons given, but it was not until Glass and Wright's (1992) study of justifications that an attempt was made to identify and pull the many threads together. In a study of about 300 middle-class, educated travelers at an airport, Glass and Wright looked at 17 justifications for affairs reported in the literature, and then made a factor analysis of the results. Four factors emerged. The first was a *sexual factor*, which included novelty, curiosity, and excitement. Factor II was *emotional intimacy*, involving understanding, companionship, and enhancement of self-esteem. Factor III was labeled *extrinsic motivation*, which referred to reasons such as career advancement and getting even with a spouse. Factor IV was called the *love dimension*, which included getting love and affection and "falling in love." To simplify, there is support for clinicians' rule of thumb that there are sex-centered justifications and love-centered justifications.

Gender Differences

Glass and Wright (1992) found that men were more approving of affairs for sexual reasons, whereas women approved more of affairs that had emotional justifications. Their research supports previous data suggesting that men engage in affairs more frequently, start earlier in a marriage or relationship, and have more partners than women do. While men are more likely to have an affair, over the past decade evidence has accumulated that younger women are participating in affairs at higher rates than are their partners (Lawson, 1990). Regardless of age, women are more likely to have emotional affairs without sex. According to Glass and Wright (1992), women who are satisfied sexually in their relationship are less likely to have an affair, whereas men have affairs despite the quality of sex in their primary relationship.

Among the most interesting analyses of why men have affairs is the work of Frank Pittman (1989). One of his hypotheses is that the philandering type have affairs to escape the intimacy they equate with domination by a woman. Male socialization has imprinted the image of a "real man" as being autonomous, independent and a "stud." Men must live up to the "Playboy philosophy" that means having more than one sexual partner. To be faithful, in some ways, is seen as enslavement. In various parts of the United States, men engage in activities such as softball, fishing, bowling, and poker to provide an escape from the pressure of an intimate relationship. In other words, it is a protest against the domestication needed to raise children and preserve societal institutions. These activities are not simply to enjoy the company of other men, because often these relationships are quite shallow. Similarly, men are not usually seeking intimacy in an affair; they are likely seeking sex, escape, and excitement. Thus, having an affair decreases the pressure some feel in the intimacy of the primary relationship. Kell (1992) suggests that many men would prefer two partial relationships to a more intimate, single relationship.

Romance: Threat or Menace?

One of the main reasons people give for having an affair is that they "fell in love." First, they indicate that they "fell out of love" with their original partner. So love or romance is reportedly something that one can fall in or out of rather rapidly and uncontrollably. Romantic love was not dreamed up by European courtiers, as is sometimes thought; this notion of romantic love has been with us throughout history and has been discovered in 78% of 168 cultures studied by anthropologists (Jankowiak & Fisher, 1992).

One term being used to refer to romantic love is *limerence*. In her book *Love and Limerence*, Dorothy Tennov (1979) interviewed 400 men and women and found that the condition of infatuation (love sickness) had specific characteristics. One element is that "the beloved" takes on a "special meaning" or becomes the center of a person's life. As infatuation progresses, intrusive thoughts of the beloved invade waking consciousness. Everything reminds the person of the beloved. Depending on the strength of the obsession, many reported that 85% and more of their thoughts were directed to the love object. In addition, Tennov found that love is not blind; the beloved's faults are acknowledged but are considered unique and "part of his/her charm."

But limerence is love sickness. Besides its obsessive nature, it is imbued with fear; there is constant fear of loss and fear of appearing less than perfect when meeting with the beloved. Other feelings include fear of rejection, worrying anticipation, and longing for the beloved to reciprocate feelings of affection. In W. Somerset Maugham's great work *Of Human Bondage*, he chronicles the love sickness of a young man who becomes obsessed with a pasty, rejecting woman. Her anemic looks become beautiful to him, and he fights against the irrational aspects of these feelings. He lives a life of fear and anticipation as he becomes more and more cut off from other relationships and even comes to hate himself for this delusion that has taken over his life.

A key feature of romance is that it does not remain at the same strength it had at its first appearance. Shakespeare has said that love that alters is not love. Thus, romance or limerence is not lasting; it can barely last two years before the beloved begins to lose that glow. Either suddenly or slowly, romance fades. Most people who have been together a long time have a good perspective on romance, knowing that romance will reappear at intervals but the real constant is mature love—what we call affection or friendship. They recognize that there is a beautiful madness when romances first flares up, but many such relationships have no lasting fuel and quickly die out.

Societal Factors

Social context reasons or societal factors are often given short shrift in the literature on affairs (Vaughan, 1989). It is understandable that clinicians are more concerned with helping the anorexic or bulimic client rather than attacking the media's glorification of thinness, even though advertising certainly has an impact on this disorder. In the same way, the decision to have an affair is influenced by those around us and by our social conditioning. For example, the code of secrecy about sex and extramarital affairs is respected by friends, family, and even therapists at times. In this society, the facts are that sex is a taboo subject and that affairs thrive in secrecy. If the affair can be brought into the open, much of the glamour and destructiveness can be avoided.

Another aspect of this problem is the glorification of love and romance in the media, from magazines to soap operas. Our ideas about what we should have in a relationship are shaped by these unrealistic portraits of "true happiness." *The Bridges of Madison County* was a national best-seller that was eventually made into a film. Despite the fact the book was panned by critics, it enthralled millions who yearn for the excitement, romance, and sexual fulfillment portrayed. Such fictional works morally justify the behavior of the participants because they are "in love," thus providing justifications for others who want to identify with the star-crossed lovers. Perhaps the more realistic picture is found in an older story: the fall of Camelot and the ruin of three lives is blamed on the revelation of an affair between Guinevere and Lancelot. The tale may have been concocted as a moral lesson, but it has survived through the ages because there is another side of the affair story that needs to be told; romance and lust can be a Pandora's box and not the panacea touted by fairy-tale endings.

Cultural Differences

Little has been written on the cultural differences in how European Americans, African Americans, and Hispanic couples, for example, deal with affairs. To say a little about each of these three major cultural groups would probably provide more stereotypical than useful data for the clinician. Good information would be enlightening because the meaning of adultery in each culture is bound to be very different. In addition, culturally acceptable ways of dealing with these kinds of situations and specific family patterns might tell us a lot about the expectations couples have about divorce and the possibility of reconciliation. At this juncture, each therapist should try to gain a better understanding of how infidelity is viewed in the cultural context of the individuals involved. Especially in bicultural couples, experiences of infidelity could have widely different meanings.

Most of the research in this area has been limited to identifying various social arrangements in which affairs are sanctioned within the society. In the United States, this has existed in marriages that were arranged to suit political ends. It was accepted that politicians would marry someone whom they can stand beside in the photographs while privately carrying on affairs.

Even in societies that condone affairs, there are safeguards to protect the partners from jealousy. For example, the Kuikuru, a small group in Amazonia, has an arrangement in which all adults carry on between 4 and 12 affairs at a time. Everyone in the village is aware of the relationships and discusses them openly; however, husbands and wives never confront each other with their knowledge (Fisher, 1992). Fisher concludes that "there is no culture in which adultery is unknown, no cultural device or code that extinguishes philandering" (p. 87).

HELPING PEOPLE DEAL CONSTRUCTIVELY WITH AFFAIRS: PRACTICAL ISSUES

Is an Affair the End of the Relationship?

An affair often signals the end of a marriage. Pittman and Wagers (1995), using data from their clinical population, estimate that 90% of first marriages that break up involve some form of infidelity. Pittman and Wagers believe that this grim truth is not often acknowledged by the people involved, including therapists. Couples develop elaborate self-protective reasons for divorce that they use simply to explain the breakup to other people. "Sure I had an affair, but by that time, the marriage was over anyway," Certainly affairs can be a method used to exit a relationship while thumbing one's nose at a partner. But the revelation of affair can also be the cause of an irreparable tear in a good relationship that makes the slope to divorce even more slippery.

For whatever reason, the revelation of an affair seems to have different effects on men and women, Pittman and Wagers (1995) suggest that men who appear in therapy at this stage seem to be more emotionally devastated on the average than do women whose partners are having an affair. Brown (1991) indicates that women's affairs are much more likely to upset the marriage, and Lawson (1990) found in her research that a woman's revealing an affair to her husband is tantamount to ending the marriage. Possibly this difference is because men see their affairs as based on sex, whereas women indicate more often that there is a serious emotional involvement.

Michele Weiner-Davis, in her book *Divorce Busting,* identifies a number of illusions or irrational beliefs that prevent people from rebuilding their relationships. Illusion 5 is "My Spouse Had an Affair, the Marriage Can't Work." Arnold Lazarus (1985) calls this Myth 3, "Extramarital Affairs Will Destroy a Marriage." According to Weiner-Davis, the crisis of an affair is an opportunity to reform the relationship. Saying that the marriage is over is one easy way to end the pain, but it is not necessarily the only avenue. Weiner-Davis points out that many couples find new solutions to bad relationships that were at the root of the affair.

Can We Help People Fall Out of Love?

One of the situations that confronts couples therapists is trying to help a couple when one member is deep in limerence with a third party. Perhaps we need to help clients face the fact that romance is an everyday phenomenon and that there should not be so much stock placed in its power or appearance. If we can convey this idea to someone who has fallen in love and explain it as more like a case of mononucleosis, we would have a chance of fighting some of the irrational and obsessive thinking that the person in the affair is experiencing. Pittman and Wagers (1995) recommend treating such a person as if he or she is "manic." People suffering from manic highs often do not wish to take medication to end their mania. We confront the same problem of motivation when trying to address the person who is having the affair. This person is having the cake and eating it too by holding on to the security of the primary relationship while experiencing the exhilaration of the affair. This is why the unfaithful partner wants the affair to remain a secret and tells lies to maintain this position.

Should the Therapist Keep an Affair a Secret?

A good rule when seeing one member of a couple is to get a written understanding at the initial session that the therapist will not keep important information about one partner secret from the other. This is consistent with American Association for Marriage and Family Therapy Code of Ethical Principles (1991), which states that, without a written release, it would be unethical to release information about one family member to another.

In the event that the unfaithful partner wants to be counseled alone and confidentially, the therapist should inform the client that although individual therapy about the affair is possible, any couples work would have to be done with a different therapist. The obvious reason for this condition is that there cannot be productive couples therapy when therapist and client collude to hide something from the third person present. It restricts the therapist's ability to explore all aspects of the relationship, and the strong conflicting emotions erect a barrier between the therapist and the other partner.

If we are working with an individual who wishes to end an affair, we have three goals to accomplish:

1. Help the individual find a way to reveal the affair to the partner.
2. End the third-party relationship.
3. Refer the individual to couples therapy.

These three tasks are listed in order of priority. Many individuals having affairs do not come to therapists necessarily to end the affair. They may be experiencing some guilt and anxiety that they hope the therapist can take away or they may be looking for a place where they can leave their partner if the relationship collapses. In general, they want to maintain the status quo as long as possible. The therapist, on the other hand, must advocate for change.

When Should Affairs Not Be Revealed?

Most therapists agree that there are very few situations in which the unfaithful partner should not be instructed to level with the other partner (Brown, 1991; Pittman & Wagers, 1995). Among these rare situations are the following scenarios.

- When there is potential for physical violence; one partner is unstable, has a history of volatile and violent behavior, or has threatened violence.
- When the divorce proceedings are rather far along and the revelation could bring about destructive litigation. Here, the purpose of revealing the affair is to force the other partner to initiate a divorce (a manipulation). This is what Brown (1991) calls an "out-of-the-door" affair.
- When the affair is ancient history. This situation requires a judgment call on the part of the therapist. One rule of thumb is to help the unfaithful partner reveal affairs that explain current marital problems or have an impact on the present relationship. Revealing ancient affairs may also be an "out-of-the-door" strategy. Even if the person wants to reveal a very old affair to relieve his or her guilt, the matter should be carefully considered. It may mean creating months of pain for the other partner so that the one who had the affair can feel less guilty. Very often this is a moot point, as ancient affairs may already have been revealed at the time the current affair came to light.

When It's Not Certain That an Affair Is Taking Place

A common scenario is when a couple comes for marital therapy and the therapist suspects an affair. The possibility may have been suggested by one partner but the suspected partner denies it. One alternative is to conduct individual sessions with each member of the couple, with the understanding that the essence of these meetings will be shared with the other member. During the session with the one suspected of having an affair, the therapist confronts the person in the following way: "I know that you are having an affair. It is affecting the couples therapy session and we need to find a way to resolve this problem by bringing it to light." Because people having affairs are unlikely to admit to suspicions, sometimes this tactic helps move the process past the denials. When the person admits to an affair, a plan for a joint session to reveal the affair is made. If the person wishes to do this privately with the other partner, the therapist coaches the person on how to do this in the least harmful way possible. A follow-up appointment for the couple or for the other partner following the revelation should be set up because one or both parties will need support as the postrevelation crisis develops.

Guidelines for Revealing an Affair

Whether the affair is revealed privately with the partner or during a couples session, some directions by the therapist can help the process.

Directions to the Unfaithful Partner

• *Be patient; getting past the affair will take at least a year.* There are no exact time limits, and in fact, the revelation may cause a problem in the relationship that may never be repaired or may take years to get over. But not telling the partner can create long-term difficulties and a worse situation when the partner finds out accidentally.

• *Be as honest as you can, but try to avoid making comparisons between the third party and the partner.* The partner may ask for such comparisons about attractiveness, penis size, sexual performance, and the like. Total honesty can be taken to an extreme. There is no need to compare sexual satisfaction between the other party and the partner. One woman told her husband that he was like an old sweater and her lover was like a new silk shirt. Nobody wants to be an old sweater.

• *Don't blame the partner for the affair; take responsibility.* It is important for the other partner to hear that the unfaithful partner is taking responsibility for the behavior and that the infidelity was wrong. What the partner needs to hear is that the other recognizes this as a personal problem and is not trying to justify the affair.

• *Try to avoid the small details.* The large details include who, when, and why but not necessarily how and what. Graphic details of the sexual activities and where they took place can be damaging. For example, if the partner is told which motel was used, the issue will resurface every time he or she drives by. This is an issue of compassion; although the unfaithful partner may feel less guilty after purging all the information, the partner will be left with haunting images for years. If asked for information that might be hurtful, the unfaithful partner can put off giving this information until the couples therapy session, letting the therapist handle the extent of revelations. Some therapists recommend letting the partner write down a list of every question he or she needs to have answered. Rather than getting all the answers immediately, the questions are all answered by the end of couples therapy.

• *Don't expect to get trust or forgiveness right away.* The unfaithful partner cannot really imagine how devastating the news of an affair can be. Simply admitting one's error will not gain instant forgiveness. Forgiveness must come in its own time when it is sincere and the crisis is past. We cannot decide to start trusting a person again just because it seems to be the rational thing to do. Trust builds over time, and when it has been breached, it remains fragile. The partner displays distrust and suspiciousness as protection against being hurt again.

Guidelines for the Other Partner

• *Get support.* The partner will need a great deal of support from close friends, but bringing family into the picture is a risky matter until divorce proceedings are underway. If the couple stays together, family members may carry resentment for years, even after the affair has been forgiven and the relationship has been rebuilt.

• *Watch out for paranoia and becoming a detective.* After being lied to, suspiciousness is a natural consequence. But the other partner should beware of letting the affair take over all of his or her life. Searching for clues of continued infidelity increases the obsessiveness and retards the healing process. For example, some partners go through the other's pockets, wallets, or purses or stalk them. The only way to prevent someone's infidelity is to be with the person 24 hours every day. Some partners try to do just that, but the simple fact is that a person cannot prevent an affair if the other wishes to continue it. One choice is to spend the rest of life as a detective; the other is to ensure survival, whatever the future brings. This second choice means that the partner focuses energy on healing the self, not on reforming the mate. Either the partner will change or the relationship will end at some time. It does not work to merely protect oneself from hurt; one must develop a life that can withstand an affair and a termination of the relationship.

• *Take care of yourself.* In addition to the preceding suggestion, the other partner needs to take good physical care. Some people find it difficult to eat, their mouth may be dry, and they can take in only liquids; a stunned depression may take over. The partner should be warned that there will be times when eating is difficult and to eat more when hungry. Exercise is important too. Signs of major depression or adjustment disorder with depressed mood should be noted and referral should be made for a medical evaluation if needed. In our experience, about 5% of situations require medication or hospitalization of one partner after revelation of an affair.

THE INTEGRATIVE MODEL AND COUPLES THERAPY

We view an affair as a crisis in the relationship that has two phases: the emergent phase, and the longer-term issues associated with reconstructing and reinventing the relationship. The crisis of revelation is often what brings a couple to treatment. The unfaithful partner may offhandedly confirm the partner's suspicions, creating an unexpected ultimatum or separation. In many cases, people discover their mates *in flagrante delicto*, and their subsequent violent interactions bring them to therapy. Another, more common, scenario is when the suspicions are brought into the therapy room and the guilty party denies the affair but admits to having some kind of relationship with a third party; only later is the full extent of the affair revealed.

Figure 12.1 is another depiction of the integrative model of couples therapy. Because of the intricacies of dealing with an affair, we will present a case study that shows the progression from the emergent phase to the normal stages using the integrative model.

Case Example: Clarice and William

Clarice and William are an African American couple who have been married for 6 years and have a 2-year-old child. The couple came for therapy when Clarice found out that William was having an affair with a co-worker. William is a vice principal at a junior high school, and the woman involved, Donna, is an unmarried faculty member. According to William, the affair had been going on for about a year and had started when they found themselves together at a bar during Friday Happy Hours. Their first sexual encounter had occurred as an "accident," but they continued the affair after that. Clarice found greeting cards in William's briefcase from Donna that suggested a personal relationship. Clarice threatened to leave William and divorce him if he didn't break up with Donna immediately. William agreed, and Clarice listened on the extension phone while William relayed his decision to Donna. When the couple came for therapy, the affair had been known for about 5 days.

Emergency Period: The First Four Sessions

In the first few minutes of the first session, the therapist took a brief history of the marriage to get some background and found that this was the couple's first reported affair. William indicated that he was relieved that the affair with Donna was over and

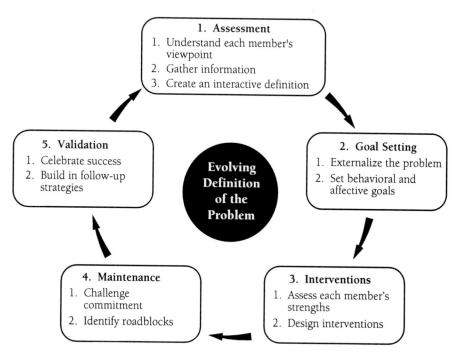

Figure 12.1 Circular model for integrative couples therapy

he regretted the pain caused to Clarice. He indicated that he wanted the marriage to work and felt that the problems in the marriage had caused his decision to have the affair.

Clarice responded that she agreed things had not been going well but pointed out that she did not feel the need to have an affair. In summary, Clarice was openly expressing a great deal of hostility and had threatened to go over and "have it out" with Donna. Clarice appeared agitated at times and tearful at others, and indicated that she had not slept in several days. When the affair was revealed, Clarice had slapped William and had thrown her wedding ring at him.

During the first session, William was calm, appeared sad, and looked down as he spoke. One of his chief concerns was that Clarice would confront Donna in a public place and the affair would become common knowledge at the school. William also felt guilty about the way that Donna was being treated in the situation, and he wanted an opportunity to talk with her, something that Clarice was decidedly against.

The therapist spent most of the session eliciting the feelings of each member of the couple and providing support to Clarice. By the end of the session, the therapist had obtained a written contract from Clarice and William indicating that there would be no confrontation of Donna and no further violence in the relationship. Clarice indicated that she no longer had any desire to confront Donna. On William's part, he was to make no personal contact with Donna and was to be truthful. It was agreed that he would send a letter, that Clarice could read, indicating his regrets. Finally, the therapist worked hard to instill hope in the couple that the relationship could continue, that couples overcome such problems, and that no drastic measures needed to be undertaken at this moment. The therapist told Clarice that William has the power to correct this problem if she will give him the opportunity. Clarice was encouraged to obtain support and take care of her physical health. The couple was to call before the next session if any problems arose.

The second and third and sessions of couples therapy were more of the same. The therapist's major effort was to try to keep the situation from exploding, either by William contacting Donna and lying about it or by some kind of physical altercation between Donna and Clarice or between Clarice and William. During these two sessions, Clarice was taking a mild tranquilizer prescribed by her family physician, which improved her ability to sleep. Clarice said that she was willing to work on putting the marriage back on track but that she was still dealing with a lot of anger. William reported that he had received an angry reply letter from Donna, who wished to meet him in person. He had declined and shared the letter with Clarice.

During the fourth session, William complained that all of the couple's waking hours were spent taking care of their son or talking about the affair. Clarice worked part-time but spent the rest of the day at home with their child. She said that by the time William got home, she was "bursting" with fear and suspicion and needed to talk. The therapist encouraged Clarice to tell her two best friends about the situation and to call them on alternate days for support; William agreed to this plan. The therapist reassured the couple that things were proceeding well and helped the couple arrange time to talk about the issue—about 30 minutes a day, immediately after William arrived home—so that their entire time together was not consumed by the affair.

Application of the Integrative Model: Infidelity

Stage 1: Assessing and Obtaining an Interactional View of the Problem

In the assessment phase, it may be useful to utilize Brown's or Pittman's typology to characterize the affair. For William and Clarice, Brown would see theirs as a conflict avoidance scenario, and Pittman would characterize it as a romantic affair.

Each Person's View of the Problem In the fifth session, William and Clarice spent some time indicating what each felt were the major issues in the relationship apart from the affair. Clarice indicated that the couple spent very little time together and that William found ways to avoid intimacy and contact with her. In a moment of anger and honesty, William complained that Clarice was boring and that all she talked about was the baby and what her friends said. He missed the excitement in the marriage and felt that the relationship was "in neutral."

Family of Origin Issues Genograms for William and Clarice revealed that William was the oldest of five children and had always been very responsible. His father had left his mother when the children were in high school, and even before that he had been known as a philanderer. William met Clarice in college while she was recovering from a severe auto accident. She believes that William was responsible for helping her through that difficult period. As time went on, they continued in an overfunctioning-underfunctioning relationship. Clarice worked only part time even before their child was born; William took care of all the finances and made most of the decisions. As William discussed his genogram, he indicated that, as much as he hated to admit it, his father's behavior was coming back to haunt him.

The genogram for Clarice revealed that Clarice's father was an alcoholic and that she was the youngest of three children. Clarice had supportive grandparents whom she believes were instrumental in her upbringing. Clarice's mother is "very religious," and Clarice does not feel she can go to her mother for support because of their religious differences. There was a great deal of conflict in Clarice's home while she was growing up, and she said that she was determined not to live in such a situation herself. This is what she finds so hard about the present situation; she feels that she is going back on the promise she made to herself.

Interactive Definition The sixth therapy session was spent pulling together the couple's complaints into a joint statement of the problem. In essence, both felt that the relationship had lapsed into a set of responsibilities, that both had stopped trying to be attractive to each other, and that both were more like roommates than lovers. The therapist asked them if this problem had ever occurred before, and they admitted that the issue had surfaced about 3 years earlier when Clarice was pregnant. However, at that time, they spent more time together, went on a long weekend to the beach, and started designing their dream home together. They both recalled that period as a good time in the relationship.

Stage 2: Goal Setting

In the seventh session, the couple reported having had a rocky week. Although the two still agreed on the joint definition of the problem, William had become distant and appeared sad, which heightened Clarice's suspicions. In the session, William admitted that he had been thinking about the relationship with Donna but had not contacted her. The therapist confronted William by asking him how much energy he was putting into the marriage, compared with thinking about the affair. The therapist then identified this stage as a normal transitional state before the marriage gets back on track. The therapist expressed optimism that things would soon improve and that it was necessary for the couple to continue along the present lines until a breakthrough occurred. By the end of the session, the couple had agreed on a set of joint goals for the marriage. They envisioned a relationship in which Clarice was more of an equal partner in the marriage and in which both members of the couple made an effort to confront boredom and monotony in the marriage rather than avoiding it.

In the eighth session, the couple reported some relief, feeling that they had enjoyed a good week and had spent time together every night after the baby had gone to bed. Then, when William said he realized that he didn't really listen to Clarice's opinions when she expressed them, Clarice lashed out, saying that William had better get used to hearing her opinions because from now on the decisions in the family would include her input. The therapist reinforced this breakthrough by indicating that this was the major change that had been expected. The therapist externalized the problem by indicating that the couple had joined together to attack the boredom problem and that it had taken both of them working together to allow Clarice's voice to be heard. William would have to listen and Clarice would have to speak loudly and clearly. The major accomplishment of this session was that the couple seemed to have changed their perspective from a self-centered to a couple-centered one.

Stage 3: Adopting New Perceptions and Behaviors/Interventions

The next session started off with the therapist asking the couple what strengths each member had that would help overcome the boredom and the problem of excluding Clarice from the decision-making processes. The therapist suggested that Clarice talk about William's strengths and that William identify Clarice's. The couple agreed that Clarice was a very organized person who liked to check out all of the options before making a decision. William seemed to be the more spontaneous of the two and had the ability to make work fun and to keep them laughing.

The two were then asked to write down two or three things that they felt were assets or supports in the relationship. William indicated that the relationship's stability was a great support to him; his home life was ordered, predictable, and a safe haven after a stressful day. Clarice indicated that some of the best times in the marriage came when they took on a joint project, such as the landscaping the back yard. The therapist asked if this landscaping task had used the best assets of the individuals and the relationship. William remembered that Clarice organized the project and he added many of the creative touches, including a small waterfall. More important, they had felt good about the finished product and had fun doing it.

The two were then asked if they could turn these same strengths to the problem at hand, creating a more exciting relationship and a better balance of power. Surprisingly, the couple said that they had decided to plan a monthly getaway for the next twelve months. The therapist attempted to build on this plan and incorporate the couple's goals into the process. Clarice was to make the basic arrangements with regard to scheduling the time and place and making sure finances would allow for the trip. William's job was to add a touch of creativity to each mini-vacation.

During the session, the therapist noticed that Clarice was rather silent and that William was doing most of the talking. Although Clarice did not appear depressed, the therapist assessed a basic communication pattern of the couple related to the problem of Clarice's lack of power in the relationship. The pattern appeared to be that William often expressed strong opinions, and Clarice was either silent or went along with William so as not to cause waves. When Clarice was questioned about this pattern she said, "I think it comes from my family; there was so much fighting, and I don't want to live like that." About half of the session was spent in discussing how Clarice might learn to disagree with William without causing an argument.

At the session's end, the couple was given the following homework assignment. At least once a day, Clarice was to tell William how she was feeling using "I" statements (see Chapter 8). William was to reply with a listening response rather than disagreeing or trying to change Clarice's feeling. This was intended as a preliminary attempt to change the couple's communication problem, which seemed to be based on Clarice's fear of fighting and William's tendency to not listen to Clarice's opinions.

Stage 4: Maintaining New Perceptions and Behaviors

As therapy progressed, the couple began to see how their individual behaviors affected each other. It was perhaps William who had the first insight when he said, "I think I was trying to avoid arguments by making all the decisions." Their arrangement, where he decided and she suppressed her feelings, was coming unraveled. At this point, they were asked to identify what things they could do that would maintain the changes that were occurring and what things might send them back to their old pattern. They came up with the following list, with some help from the therapist.

Things That Will Help Us Change
- If Clarice continues to express her opinion to William when a problem comes up, and if William listens.
- If we can finish an argument and come to a decision together.
- If we can continue to have new experiences together that are fun.

Things That Will Keep Us from Changing
- If Clarice agrees just to avoid a fight and William lets her by taking over the decision-making process.
- If William gets so involved in work and doesn't try when he gets home and Clarice does not mention it.
- If we stop trying to fight the boredom and let the relationship get back in a rut.

Stage 5: Validating New Perceptions and Behaviors

After two sessions working on maintenance behaviors and helping the couple anticipate the tendency to relapse, William and Clarice were told that they were greatly improved and that the next session could be scheduled in about three months. Clarice, especially, seemed nervous about such a long hiatus, but they were assured that they could be seen immediately if something came up.

When the couple came for the follow-up session, both partners indicated that the changes they had begun were holding. After some discussion, it appeared that there was a change in the communication and decision-making processes and that they both felt the relationship was more fun and exciting than it had been in years. The therapist encouraged them to celebrate this change and to look for ways to continue this upward trend by seeing how their teamwork could address future problems. William and Clarice also felt that their sexual relationship was much better than it ever had been, which they attributed to better communication.

Although the two were mostly upbeat, they had to admit that the affair was still a problem in the relationship. Donna (William's lover) had sent him a message that Clarice had been driving by her house after school. Clarice admitted that she still had moments of suspicion and jealousy that she tried to suppress, but she felt she had to talk about it. When she talked to William, he felt guilty and then got angry because he felt unable to alleviate her unhappiness. Because it had been seven months since William had announced the affair, it seemed to them that little progress had been made. The therapist indicated that normally one year is needed before the spouse can stop bringing this issue up in the relationship and get over the hurt and suspiciousness. The therapist suggested that Clarice consider one year to be a time limit when she would cease bringing up the past to William, as long as there were no future incidents of infidelity. Clarice said that she was ready to stop now but that she needed some guarantee from William that she would not be hurt again.

The therapist spent some time explaining to Clarice and William that there were no guarantees about these things. Instead, the therapist asked Clarice what she would do if she discovered that William was having a new affair. She said that she would leave him immediately, move in with her sister, and file for divorce. The therapist tried to promote the idea that the only way she could absolutely guarantee that it wouldn't happen again would be to leave at this point in time. Otherwise, she would have to take a risk and express her doubts and negative feelings to her close circle of friends. Clarice appeared angry at first, believing that William was getting off too easy. Rather than try to persuade Clarice to stop bringing up the affair, the therapist suggested a strategy. Each time either one of them mentions the affair, that person is to pay the other person one penny. They were also to discuss the reasons for bringing up the subject. At the next therapy session, they were to bring in their proceeds. Another session was scheduled in three months.

CONCLUSION

In this chapter, we addressed one of the thorniest problems in therapy: how to deal with an affair. Most of the writers in this field believe that couples can survive the affair if they are willing to face it and to improve the relationship. But with all this hope, there is the ever-present specter of divorce or separation. The affair is seen by the spouse as an insult and a rejection. Both members of the couple become defensive and focus on themselves rather than on the relationship. It is a difficult task to open people to new hope in a relationship where they have been severely hurt. Many affairs that are revealed in therapy end in divorce.

Despite their tremendous impact, affairs are quite common, probably affecting the majority of couples. People engage in affairs for sex, for romance, for intimacy, to avoid intimacy, to advance themselves in jobs, and for a variety of other reasons. U.S. society promotes romantic ideals in television, films, and books. These irrational ideas and mistaken beliefs about the importance of romance give people justification for affairs and tell them that, somewhere, "the grass is greener."

The literature on this topic suggests that couples therapists cannot keep information about an affair secret when it is revealed by one member of a couple except under extreme circumstances. Therapists must help their clients face these secrets and deal with the outcomes. The beginning therapist can easily fall into a trap of agreeing to keep a client's confidentiality and then being faced with conducting couples therapy with this secret in the background.

Helping couples deal with an affair is a delicate business. It involves dealing with a crisis or emergency period before the couple can even begin to think about reconstructing the relationship. This is a period filled with doubt and pain that has to be gone through. Even when the initial crisis is passed, the issue will periodically reemerge and slow down the therapy process, sending each member of the couple running for cover. The therapist's job is to help couples who want to stay together to cope with events after the affair has been exposed. The affair must end, and eventually the other partner must stop bringing it up. These are the two major hurdles that are easier said than done. The therapist's role as one who instills hope is never more tested than in dealing with an affair. But couples find that if they can weather the affair, they may address deeper issues in their relationship and build a new and stronger foundation.

THREE

SPECIAL CHALLENGES

13

Counseling Couples
with Alcohol Problems

We chose to look at couples' alcohol problems rather than at substance abuse as a whole because alcohol affects so many relationships. One counselor we know likes to joke that "if it weren't for alcohol, we would be out of a job!" Alcohol is the drug of choice for our society. It is legal and extolled as beneficial despite the fact that it disables millions. It is touted as a tranquilizer on soap operas, sold as a sign of masculinity in beer commercials, and designated as a mark of sophistication in wine and whiskey ads. Recently a young woman considering marriage told us that she wanted to serve alcohol at her wedding because people "can't have fun without it." Teetotalers are ridiculed. Young people do not have to wait for peer pressure to drink; the whole society is pushing them to use alcohol. Not many can resist this advertising blitz.

ALCOHOL AND THE COUPLE

Alcoholism can be considered the most serious health problem in the United States. It affects the physical health of the alcoholic and the mental health of millions of families. The effects of growing up in an alcoholic family can linger into adult life. Despite the efforts of Alcoholics Anonymous to change the view of alcoholism from a weakness to a disease, the public perception is that alcoholics drink to escape their troubles and either do not want to quit or simply can't control themselves. Consequently, their families and affected others feel a sense of shame and helplessness. The families contribute to the cycle by denying the problem, covering it up, and "enabling" the alcoholic. All family members are affected by drinking, and the partner probably bears the greatest burden.

Alcoholics are just as likely to be married as anyone else is, but they are more likely to be divorced (Nace, 1982). In fact, alcoholics have a higher divorce rate than do groups with any other psychological disorder (Reich & Thompson, 1985).

Even if the couple stays together, alcoholics have more problems and greater distress in their marriages than do other couples (O'Farrell & Birchler, 1987).

Looking at it from another angle, the emergence of marital problems often *precedes* relapse when abstinent alcoholics return to drinking (Maisto, O'Farrell, Connors, McKay, & Pelcovits, 1988). However, marital support seems to be highly conducive to a strong recovery and is predictive of success in treatment (Finney, Moos, & Mewborn, 1980; O'Farrell et al., 1990). Alcoholics who are also assigned to marital and family therapy while undergoing alcohol treatment are less likely to drop out of treatment (Noel, McCrady, Sout, & Fisher-Nelson, 1987). In short, alcoholism and marital problems can exacerbate each other, and a good relationship can aid recovery.

ASPECTS OF ALCOHOLISM

Terminology

Alcoholic

It is traditional for speakers in Alcoholics Anonymous groups to begin by saying their first name, followed by ". . . and I'm an alcoholic." Recognizing one's problem is considered by therapists and substance abuse treatment workers as an essential first step. Anyone who has a problem with drinking needs treatment, whether they wish to call themselves alcoholic or not. Referring to oneself as an alcoholic indicates only that the person has reached the stage where he or she is no longer in denial and is taking responsibility for the problem. We generally use the terms *alcoholic* and *alcoholism* in this chapter—rather than *problem drinking*, *alcohol abuse*, or *dependence*—simply for convenience.

Codependency

The term *codependency* was coined during the 1970s when many people realized that they needed help dealing with alcoholic individuals in their lives. By 1990, more than 20 books on codependency were on the market (Kaminer, 1990). Codependency has been described as the inability to see oneself as separate from the alcoholic (Wing, 1992). Alanon is a support group designed to help codependents enter the recovery process, and Adult Children of Alcoholics supports those who grew up with alcoholics in their families.

The term *codependency* has come under attack, perhaps because it has been overapplied and has become synonymous with *nonassertiveness*, thus losing its original reference to someone in an alcoholic relationship. Many clinicians reject the term because it carries with it the language of "disease" inherent in 12-step programs, suggesting that codependents are never cured but are recovering for life, just as the alcoholics are. It has been suggested that although treatment for the partner is also necessary, the term *codependency* need not be used. Marriage and family counselors tend to shy away from labeling individuals, and instead focus on the family system that is supporting drinking.

Alcohol Dependence and Alcohol Abuse

The fourth edition of the *Diagnostic and Statistical Manual* of the American Psychiatric Association (1994) differentiates between alcohol dependence and alcohol abuse. Both are mental disorders, but dependence is more severe. A diagnosis of *dependence* requires at least three of the following symptoms: loss of control, physical tolerance and withdrawal, unsuccessful attempts to cut down, excessive time spent drinking or recovering from drinking, interference of alcohol with social or occupational functioning, and use of alcohol despite knowing that physical and psychological consequences will ensue. Note that alcohol dependence can be diagnosed with or without physical dependence, withdrawal, or tolerance.

Alcohol abuse is "problem drinking," which includes failure to fulfill major roles in work and family life, drinking repeatedly such that there is a potential for harm (drunk driving), recurring legal difficulties, and continued drinking despite social or interpersonal consequences caused by alcohol ingestion. Some clinicians and researchers feel that dependence, abuse, nonproblem alcohol use, and abstinence are points on a continuum, rather than separate disorders (McCrady & Epstein, 1995). Patterns of abuse vary, and people move from one point to the next. The important point is that just because someone is not diagnosed as alcohol dependent does not mean that the drinking problem does not need treatment.

Abstinence and Sobriety

Two other important terms are *sobriety* and *abstinence*. Abstinence means completely refraining from drinking. Sobriety, on the other hand, has taken on a positive connotation, meaning a rewarding lifestyle without alcohol.

THE COUPLE RELATIONSHIP THAT SUPPORTS ALCOHOLISM

Referring the Couple for Alcohol Treatment

A recent study of couples who came for marital therapy in Australia showed that 20% of the men could be classified as alcoholic and that four-fifths of the couples reported arguments about alcohol consumption (Halford & Osgarby, 1993). Alcohol problems were associated with more severe marital distress, more progress toward divorce, and greater physical aggression by the men. Although alcohol abuse differs among cultures, this study suggests, that when couples come for marital therapy, a considerable number come with alcohol in the background of the relationship. Proceeding with marital therapy alone may not suffice to deal with this tenacious addiction.

When a therapist determines that one member of the couple needs treatment for alcohol addiction, a referral is made to an inpatient facility for detoxification and treatment. At that time, couples therapy is suspended and the therapist helps the couple make the kinds of practical arrangements needed to cope with the alcoholic's absence. For example, if the partner needing treatment is a full-time mother, the couple may need help in thinking about who will "fill in" when the spouse is working. If she works outside of the home, who will tell her boss? What story will be given to family and friends about her absence?

Couple Patterns That Support Alcoholism

Couples fall into patterns where the alcoholic member's addiction allows the other person to care for the alcoholic, an asymmetrical relationship. This caretaker arrangement does not help the alcoholic gain insight, nor does it help the codependent achieve self-actualization, since both are centered on their too-significant other. An analysis of genograms of codependents shows that they often come from alcoholic families where this kind of behavior is normal. This is not to say that the spouse of an alcoholic wants the spouse to remain addicted. Living with an alcoholic has significant negative consequences, and spouses of alcoholics are more likely than others are to experience physical and psychological problems (Moos, Finney, & Gamble, 1982). Unlike the effects of crack cocaine addiction, the deterioration due to alcoholism takes place over years rather than months. The spouses and families habituate and adapt to the alcoholic's behavior.

Besides habituation, another reason alcoholic relationships become stabilized is that they support unspoken agreements. An example is, "I won't make you deal with your drinking, if you won't make me deal with my obesity." A recent award-winning film, *Leaving Las Vegas,* depicted this kind of arrangement between a man who decided to drink himself to death and his prostitute girlfriend. He needs company while he kills himself, and she needs someone to nurture who will not make her face the fact that she is despised by society. In this dark movie, the collusion of two individuals that allows them both to destroy themselves is a disturbing look at how one dysfunctional behavior can support another.

Other common patterns include an arrangement where the partners cease to have any interaction with each other and stay together out of convenience, fighting only occasionally about the drinking issue. If money is not a problem, such arrangements can go on for decades. Often couples share alcohol or other addictions and develop a lifestyle based on their shared drinking. Aftercare for the couple following treatment often means constructing a completely new relationship when the primary source of interaction is eliminated.

How the Partner Can Help the Alcoholic

Partners of alcoholics can best help by seeking their own treatment, because recovery demands changes in both partners. One of the best avenues for this kind of help is Alanon, the support group for people who live with alcoholics. In the beginning, most people who go to Alanon meetings are searching for ways to change their alcoholic partners, but they soon find out that they need to work on themselves instead. Alanon helps the family members, especially husbands and wives, to stop enabling the alcoholic spouse. One woman described to me her life before and after Alanon. She told me that when her binge-drinking husband came home drunk, he invariably picked a fight with the kids, vomited, and passed out on the living room floor. She would get him to bed, clean up the mess, and quiet the kids. The next morning, he would remember nothing, she would be silent, and the kids would avoid him. He was bewildered and she was angry. Through Alanon, she learned to stop "cleaning up his messes." She developed a plan to take the kids to her friend's house when he came home drunk. After the third time he woke up alone amid a mess on the living room floor, he agreed to seek treatment for his problem.

We do not mean to give the impression that the sole goal of Alanon or any treatment for so-called codependents is to induce the alcoholic to stop drinking. Spouses of alcoholics very often believe that once alcohol is gone from the marriage, harmony will return. Rather, the goal of Alanon and other codependency treatments is to help the "affected others" develop a healthy lifestyle for themselves. It is true that an alcoholic's best chances for recovery are where the partner is not "walking on eggshells" or centering his or her life around the drinker. But it is equally important for codependents to begin their own process of treatment and self-examination, whether or not their partner starts down the road of recovery.

Synchrony in Recovery

We often see couples in therapy some time after one member has been released from a treatment facility. Often, the major problem is that they are not "in sync." Sometimes the alcoholic is farther down the road to recovery than the partner is; often it is the other way around. Wing (1992) identified four stages in the progression of goals in alcoholic recovery.

1. *Denial:* refusing to admit a problem with alcohol.
2. *Dependency:* alcoholic's goal focuses on maintaining something, such as a job or the marriage.
3. *Behavior change:* goals are directed at personal recovery and self-growth.
4. *Life planning* (aftercare issues): goals regarding marriage, family, career and education come to the fore after sobriety has been maintained for a few months.

Wing asks the question, "What happens in the relationship when the alcoholic and the spouse are at different stages?" She suggests that many conflicts result when the partners are "out of sync" and that there is relative harmony when stages are coinciding. When the partner is ahead of the alcoholic, pressure on the alcoholic to change is maximized; when the partner is a stage or two behind the alcoholic, there is little or no pressure to change and some pressure to regress. Two frequently encountered conflicts are the denial-dependence relationship and the denial–behavior change relationship. If, for example, the partner is in denial and the alcoholic is in dependency, there will be little motion toward behavior change and little impetus to make the commitment to enter a treatment program. When the spouse is in denial and the alcoholic is in behavior change, there is little support for recovery.

Wing indicates that when either partner is in denial, the couple shows little interest in joint treatment because there is no shared problem. Individual confrontation-oriented treatment may be necessary to move a person from the denial position. Referring back to Chapter 6 and the notions of stages of change according to Prochaska, Norcross, and DiClemente (1994), educational interventions may be the only treatment someone at this stage will accept. Many alcohol treatment facilities provide tapes, run educational groups, and use assessment sessions to educate alcoholics and family members. It becomes possible to treat couples conjointly when they are in the dependency phase because fear motivates them. But couples in the behavior change phase are the most responsive to couples therapy, which is aimed mainly at helping the couple cope with treatment and its immediate aftermath. When both members are in the life planning or aftercare stage, the major work in couples therapy can be accomplished, with the aim of helping them develop strategies for a better relationship, rather than focusing entirely on maintaining sobriety.

The Systems Approach toward Alcoholic Behavior

Systems theorists, like those described in Chapters 2 and 3, have traditionally looked at symptoms such as alcoholism and asthma as signals of underlying dysfunction and stress that serve to maintain the family system. The term *alcoholic system* is often used to refer to families that are in denial and are adjusting to the alcoholic. Normally the aim of systems theory is to treat the system rather than the symptom bearer, that is, the alcoholic or asthmatic.

Research conducted by Steinglass and associates over several years has supported the systems approach (Steinglass, Bennet, Wolin, & Reiss, 1987; Steinglass, Davis, & Berenson, 1977; Steinglass, Weiner, & Mendelson, 1971). As these researchers understood it, alcoholism can serve either as a signal of underlying dysfunction or as an organizing principle around which the family stabilizes. They found that one of the difficulties in such systems is that sobriety leads to instability, and so there is pressure to return to the familiar homeostatic state. This finding addresses the question that everyone who works with couples and families always faces: "Why does everyone seem to return to unproductive relationships despite their determination to change?" Steinglass and associates have suggested that, besides offering familiarity and stability, alcoholism allows these families to express feelings that were not allowed during sobriety. Therapy with alcoholic families and couples in recovery, then, would be aimed at enhancing emotional expression and improving relationships among family members, which would support changes.

The AA Approach and the Systems Approach

Alcoholics Anonymous and Alanon tend to focus on each individual's recovery and generally do not favor family or couples therapy as the treatment for alcoholism. Most marriage and family therapists today support this approach to some extent. It is certainly true that little progress is made in marriage therapy when one member of the couple is actively alcoholic. The difference in the two approaches may not be so much about whether couple or family treatment *is* needed but *when* it is needed.

AA believes that alcoholism is a chronic disease and that the solution to an alcoholic's problems is found in the simple statement "Don't drink, and go to meetings." Although most disease-concept-oriented treatment centers are now including spouses and families earlier in treatment, there persists the notion, based on the experience of alcoholics in AA, that focusing too much on one's relationships can distract one from developing a high-quality recovery.

The orthodox family systems approach suggests that the cause of alcoholism is a dysfunctional family system and that marriage or family therapy may be effective in treating the family's problems associated with alcoholism. There is little support for this kind of treatment today, and we are unaware of any therapists who practice couples or family therapy when one member is in crisis or denial. That approach is too risky, creating more discouragement to family members. What, then, does couple or family therapy have to offer to alcohol treatment? Although most treatment programs do not utilize couples therapy until recovery is fairly well established, others are beginning couples work immediately after detoxification. Behavioral marital therapy has been shown to stabilize and support sobriety during the initial months following treatment if it is combined with continuing treatment for alcoholism (McCrady, Paolino, Longabaugh, & Rossi, 1979; O'Farrell et al., 1990).

The Problem Drinker

What if the person is a problem drinker but not an alcoholic? Before prescribing a medication, physicians sometimes refer their patients to a specialist, such as a cardiologist, to make sure that the patient's heart is healthy and can tolerate the treatment. By this analogy, couples therapists should be willing to postpone treatment when they suspect alcoholism and first have the necessary assessment taken. It is often more effective to refer the individual to an alcohol treatment facility for a screening. Regardless of whether alcohol treatment is initiated, the screening can get the couple to contemplate the seriousness of the alcohol problem.

In borderline cases where alcoholism cannot be clearly diagnosed, treatment for alcohol problems can still be advised. In such cases, alcohol is probably still a problem in the relationship, and solving that problem can be insisted on before couples therapy begins. Often the couple disagrees on the importance of the drinking behavior. In the classic scenario, the drinker claims that the partner is exaggerating the drinking, and the partner claims that the drinker is minimizing it. One therapist we know tells her clients, "If alcohol is not a problem or an addiction for you, I would like to try something. I'd like you to experiment and see if you can eliminate alcohol entirely for 6 weeks. If you can, then you probably don't need treatment. If you can't, then I'd like you to agree to go into a program." Usually, when the couple returns, the problem drinker has failed and has many excuses. This therapist's ploy sometimes works to make both members of the couple aware that the drinking is out of control. In some cases, it helps propel the problem drinker into treatment.

Zweben and Barrett (1993) recommend getting couples to work together to assess the costs and benefits of drinking in their lives. Box 13.1 contains an outline of brief couples treatment. This treatment protocol was used in mental health centers with clients who had low to moderate alcohol problems. The program required that participants have no major psychiatric disorders, have alcohol as a primary concern, have a moderate score on the Michigan Alcohol Screening Test,

---

Box 13.1
Outline of Brief Couples Treatment for Alcohol Problems

A. Assessment interview and screening (one session)
   1. Preparing the client for change
   2. Owning the change process
   3. Gathering information
      a. Michigan Alcoholism Screening Test
      b. Time-Line Follow-Back Drinking Interview
      c. Alcohol Dependence Scale
      d. Inventory of Drinking Situations
      e. Situational Confidence Questionnaire
      f. Revised Marital Happiness Scale
      g. Spouse Hardship Scale
B. Team conference (one meeting of professional team)
   1. Reviewing assessment and preparing personalized feedback and advice to the couple
   2. Formulating drinking goal based on individualized assessment
   3. Preparing strategy for use by counselor in feedback session
C. Feedback session (one meeting)
   1. Identifying the severity of the alcohol problem and issues associated with alcohol use
   2. Establishing a consensus about change
   3. Setting drinking goals
   4. Requesting a period of abstinence
   5. Delaying a commitment to change
   6. Enhancing a commitment to change
   7. Maintaining a commitment to change
D. Follow-up session 2–4 weeks later (one or two sessions)
E. Emergency session (if necessary)

Source: From "Brief Couple Treatment for Alcohol Problems," by A. Zweben and D. Barrett. In *Treating Alcohol Problems: Marital and Family Interventions*, by T. J. O'Farrell (Ed.), p. 356.

and have a partner willing to participate in all aspects of the program. As the outline indicates, the program lasts about six sessions.

In the first session, the couple is interviewed, the alcoholic is assessed, and the couple's commitment to therapy is reinforced. A unique aspect of the program is the team conference. Here, the therapist reports the findings of the therapists who have reviewed the couple's situation, presenting the team's suggestions about appropriate goals of treatment. Then an initial treatment goal is established, which may or may not be abstinence, though normally a 3-week period of abstinence is prescribed. The next session is spent on firming up these goals, considering maintenance, and addressing relapse prevention. Follow-up sessions continue this process.

THERAPY TECHNIQUES

Arkin, Lewis, and Carlson (1990) offer the following three major goals or treatment strategies for therapists seeing an alcoholic or an alcoholic couple.

1. Interventions aimed at supporting the alcohol user into changing.
2. Interventions aimed at improving the quality of the couple or family relationships.
3. Relapse prevention for the alcohol user.

These three interventions could also be considered phases of recovery for the couple. The first is a treatment phase for the alcoholic, the second is an adjustment phase for the family, and the third is a lifestyle-building phase that promotes sobriety and prevents the alcoholic's relapse into drinking. These distinctions seem to be a good way to organize our thinking as we describe some techniques for working with couples experiencing alcohol problems.

Interventions to Support the Alcoholic's Change

Zweben (1991) studied therapy with resistant alcoholics that involved conjoint sessions with alcoholics and their partners. The partner's role was to share and receive information about the severity of the alcoholism, acting as a "witness" rather than as an active participant. Partners were urged to attend to their own issues in another setting. It was found that, during this process, the partner becomes educated and minimizes his or her interference with the treatment goals. Also the partner provides support and constructive feedback. When partners were involved, the alcoholics did better in treatment and showed less relapse potential. Zweben found that the partner's involvement in the alcoholic's treatment is most helpful when the relationship bond is strong and the partner is far enough along in recovery to put aside personal issues during the alcoholic's sessions.

The Therapist's and the Spouse's Conviction

The scenario with the highest probability of success is a couple who presents as a unit deciding that the couple wants to go in the direction of recovery (Arkin, Lewis,

& Carlson, 1990). But this situation is relatively rare. More often it is a matter of dealing with a partner who is acutely aware of the problem and the alcoholic who is still denying.

How do you convince someone to go into treatment? No matter how severe the alcoholic's condition, there is always some measure of ambivalence about the necessity of treatment. Once it is clear to the therapist that treatment is necessary, it is important to convey a clear message to the alcoholic and partner. Individually or during the couple's session, the therapist enlists the partner's aid to maintain pressure on the alcoholic.

At some point, the partner begins to realize the personal costs associated with the alcoholic's going into treatment, such as: "I'll be taking care of the kids myself"; "Treatment will be very expensive"; "Everyone will know"; or "I don't want my spouse to suffer in that cold environment." Such thoughts can easily waylay the decision to force the alcoholic into treatment. But once the partner has decided to do so, the therapist must help the partner remain firm and deliver a strong message to the alcoholic, who is already wavering. The alcoholic should not get the idea that the therapist or spouse is not sure whether treatment is needed or that the treatment can be handled in some other way. The person struggling with an alcohol addiction is looking for a way out. The partner's support is important, but so is the partner's determination not to allow the alcoholic to go untreated.

"The Intervention" Technique

It is often said that people do not stop drinking because it sounds like a good idea; they stop when they hit bottom. This bottom is caused by the pressure from those around them and their life circumstances. The most powerful motivators are hospitalization caused by physical effects of alcohol, threatened loss of job, and threat to the couple relationship. If the partner is able to communicate that the relationship cannot continue with alcohol in the picture, this provides great leverage for change.

"The Intervention" is an alcohol treatment technique that has been developed over the past 10 years. It involves bringing family and friends together for the purpose of confronting an alcoholic about his or her behavior and how it is affecting everyone. Specifically, the people invited to the "intervention" are those who have witnessed the drinking behavior and its consequences, such as older children, friends, and family members. The aim is to get the alcoholic to agree to treatment, but these interventions have high risk. They may propel the drinker to seek treatment or they may alienate the person from the nonalcoholic support system. In many cases, it is a last-ditch effort after other means have failed.

Total Disengagement

One method for putting pressure on the alcoholic to change is to counsel the partner to totally disengage and not react to the alcoholic's behavior. Although the partner is not to become cold and indifferent, efforts should be focused primarily on developing a positive lifestyle with or without the alcohol abuser. The partner agrees to no longer shelter the alcoholic, enabling that person to face the consequences of drinking. This approach is recommended by Alanon. Because it is difficult and often involves breaking long-term behavior patterns, peer support from Alanon is extremely helpful.

Partner Involvement with Drug Therapy

Antabuse and similar drugs are best used with individuals who have repeatedly relapsed following treatment. In this circumstance, abstinence can be supported by a drug that causes nausea, vomiting, and extreme discomfort when alcohol is ingested. In fact, one can actually become dangerously ill when these two substances are combined. Besides providing a powerful motivator not to drink, with Antabuse, lapses are accompanied by immediate punishment, creating a classical conditioning scenario in which alcohol ingestion becomes associated with nausea and pain even when the drug is discontinued.

Compliance with Antabuse is a problem. Alcoholics on their own are likely to forget or purposely discontinue use, but both compliance and abstinence are positively affected when the partner administers the daily Antabuse. In fact, couples can learn to make it a kind of ritual. One couple we know turned it into a part of their contact over breakfast; she would get the Antabuse and place it next to his juice or coffee. Both described this action as a sign of caring rather than as nagging.

Interventions to Enhance the Quality of the Relationship

When one member of a couple stops drinking, there is an initial period of disequilibrium and confusion in the relationship. Often the nonalcoholic partner does not trust this "new person" and is reluctant to relinquish control of finances or family responsibilities just because the person is now sober. The codependent feels less important, has to give up "being strong," and always worries about relapse. There may also be residual anger covering hurt and feelings of betrayal. On the other hand, the alcoholic may be struggling with guilt, shame, and anxiety, and the alcoholic's need to focus on his or her own treatment may appear self-centered. Both partners can feel that their efforts are unappreciated.

Together, the partners struggle with a fear of conflict and a tendency to suppress feelings as family tensions build. Before the relationship difficulties can be faced, each person normally needs to work through some personal feelings (McCrady & Epstein, 1995). AA and Alanon meetings allow partners to work through these issues on their own, but eventually the two must face each other and deal with present problems; the repressed conflict must eventually emerge.

The therapeutic methods for enhancing relationships are not much different for couples with alcohol problems than for other kinds of couples. Methods include (1) couples therapy focusing on goals that would bring back pleasure and positive experiences for the couple, (2) a "recovering couples" group, and (3) coping and communication skills training groups for alcoholics and their spouses using a psychoeducational format.

Pleasing Behaviors

O'Farrell (1987) described an exercise called "Increasing Pleasing Behaviors" which helps strengthen the relationship by reestablishing the partners' confidence in each one's good intentions. Each person draws up a list of five things the partner has done that demonstrated good intentions and that were pleasing. Then each partner draws up a second list of things done that were not pleasing but that were done with good intentions. It is important that the good intentions are described. Each partner then reads the two lists aloud and a discussion ensues. The reading of the first list acts as a positive catalyst and encouragement for change. The second list suggests a new way of looking at the partner's behavior. Perhaps those around us do things we don't like, but their intentions are good. One of the problems in many relationships is that partners jump to conclusions about behaviors without recognizing the intention behind the action. Couples need to know that when people are defensive, they often feel that the partner's behavior is directed at them. Finally, the couple looks at the good intentions/not pleasing list and brainstorms alternative behaviors that would be pleasing.

The "Recovering Couples" Group

Shields (1989) described a recovering couples group that can be effective as early as one month following sobriety when each member of the couple continues in AA/Alanon treatment and is fully committed to the relationship and to recovery. Couples who are engaging in severe emotional or physical abuse or making suicide or homicide threats are screened out. Shields suggests a group size of five to six couples. Group therapy for recovering couples is not much different from other group approaches for couples except that the goals may be more explicit and therapy may be time-limited. Shields takes an educational approach to recovering couples groups, and the following are some of the goals he establishes for the members.

1. To remember that they are a couple and to strive for conflict resolution, expression of feelings, and stress reduction.
2. To understand dysfunction in terms of patterns rather than as random events.
3. To identify realistic and unrealistic expectations of each other.
4. To become comfortable with self-disclosure and the disclosures of others.
5. To develop awareness of the post-acute withdrawal (PAW) syndrome—a set of symptoms that includes recurrence of mood disorders, memory loss, and fragmented thinking. Similar to posttraumatic stress disorder the PAW syndrome is apparently common enough following recovery that couples need to be aware of it as a threat. It can lead to relapse and can disrupt the relationship by causing emotional distance.
6. To identify power and control issues in the relationship and negotiate new agreements.
7. To squarely address the subject of relapse.
8. To identify "markers" for success. Each couple sets up unique goals, which can be observed in group.

9. To develop a "validation process" between partners—that is, to increase the compliments and "positive strokes."

Coping and Communication Skills Training

McCrady and Epstein (1995) described a behaviorally oriented treatment program for couples with alcohol problems that emphasizes coping and communication skills. The program is effective for when either one or both members are alcoholic. Besides setting goals concerning abstinence, the program addresses (1) developing coping skills for both partners to deal with alcohol-related situations, and (2) developing effective communication and problem-solving skills.

These skills are taught in the couple sessions about midway through a 20-week program, depending on the progress the couple is making. The emphasis in couples therapy is on helping each member develop personal management skills and to help them both work together on communication. For example, the alcoholic may need to improve assertiveness skills to refuse drinks, and the partner may need to learn to communicate his or her need to share household and family responsibilities.

Another approach is to teach these skills to family members and alcoholics separately. Family education programs are available from most alcohol treatment programs and may take place when the alcoholic is receiving aftercare services.

Relapse Prevention

Relapse prevention is an idea that has become prominent only in the last 15 years (Gorski & Miller, 1982). Previously, looking at high-risk situations and coping procedures following treatment took place through AA groups. No direct training was aimed at preventing relapse during treatment. Relapse prevention now focuses on identifying key triggers that create urges to drink and on developing assertiveness skills to refuse invitations or fulfill needs in more positive ways. Prevention may also include building in leisure activities and learning methods for better negotiation of conflicts.

Couples work can be important in relapse prevention. One way to address this directly is through the use of a "relapse contract" (Marlatt & Gordon, 1985). In essence, both members of the couple describe how each will handle "slips" and strong urges to return to drinking. Specifically, partners decide on the conditions under which the alcoholic agrees to increase AA attendance or return to treatment.

THE INTEGRATIVE MODEL AND COUPLES WITH ALCOHOL PROBLEMS

Assessment Issues

Before looking at an example of how the integrative model of couples therapy can be applied to alcohol problems, let us spend a little more time on the area of assessment and interactive definitions, the first two steps in the process. Because of the denial and defensiveness of both alcoholics and their partners, these are the trickiest steps.

When couples come for therapy, they may be willing to discuss problems in communication or disagreements over finances, but they have unspoken agreements not to publicly mention certain topics. Anything that would embarrass the other partner and disrupt the fragile agreement to seek therapy is usually avoided until much later in the therapy process. Among the issues avoided are sexual dissatisfactions, extended family problems, and substance abuse. When these areas are assessed in the initial sessions, couples may deny or hedge when asked directly about them. A couple may have to have some confidence in the therapy process and the therapist before getting to these highly charged issues.

Another factor to consider is that a high percentage of alcoholics also suffer from some other psychiatric disorder. Specifically, sobriety uncovers depression and anxiety disorders. According to some sources, even as much as 60% of male alcoholics can show major depression as a secondary diagnosis (Hasin, Grant, & Endicott, 1988).

Assessing the Alcoholic and the Relationship

Any screening questionnaire or interview should contain questions about alcohol and other substance abuse. Asking such questions in a structured way and as a matter of course takes away some of their sting. When substance abuse is suspected, a medical history should be taken, as well as a review of the immediate stressors in the couple's life and the availability of social support.

The Revised Marital Relationship Scale (RMRS) (Azrin, Naster, & Jones, 1973) can be used to gauge the strength of the cohesiveness in the relationship. As indicated previously, if the partner is to be involved in treating the alcoholic, this bond must be strong. The Spouse Hardship Scale (Orford & Edwards, 1977) can be used with the partner to determine the amount of support available to the alcoholic. When these two scales show little support or bonding in the relationship, the partner is asked to play a minimal role in treatment (Zweben & Barrett, 1993).

Further assessment of the alcoholic is available from standardized instruments. Among these are the well-known Michigan Alcohol Screening Test (MAST-A) (Selzer, Vinokur, & Van Rooijen, 1975), which contains only 13 items in a true/false format and measures lifetime patterns. The questions are administered via interview and take very little time. A score of 3 indicates alcoholism, and a score of 2 indicates possible alcoholism. In addition, therapists might use the Time-Line Follow-Back Alcohol Use Interview (Sobell, Maisto, & Sobell, 1979) and the Alcohol Dependence Scale (Skinner & Horn, 1984) to look at current consumption patterns and degree of dependence on alcohol.

In Chapter 5, we described the use of the genogram as an assessment tool, and it can be particularly effective in charting family histories of chemical dependency. It can also be a means for confronting a client or couple in denial. Recently we saw a client's genogram in which 60% of the people depicted were acknowledged to be chemically dependent. Whether one believes this trend is genetic transmission or a family or cultural tradition, one begins to see the pattern that shapes current behavior. Evidence is strong that the closer the contact with an "alcoholic family of origin," the more likely one is to experience alcohol problems (Bennett & Wolin, 1990).

The genogram, the MAST, and other screening devices serve the dual functions of heightening client awareness and giving information to the therapist. Another avenue is to require a medical examination in cases where alcoholism is suspected. Liver function is affected by excessive alcohol consumption and can be evaluated by blood test. Other physical signs and concern from a knowledgeable physician can help push a client toward treatment. Alternately, a general practitioner who is not well schooled in substance abuse can strengthen the client's denial process.

Developing the Interactive Definition

Earlier we discussed a three-stage model of alcohol interventions described by Arkin, Lewis, and Carlson (1990). At each stage, a different set of problems becomes focal for the couple, and each stage involves couple patterns, not just issues for the alcoholic. The integrative model is appropriate for helping couples identify inter-actionally defined problems at each of these stages of recovery. Couples who are struggling with alcohol issues may initially decide on an interactive definition, such as, "We will each seek our own treatment for alcohol and codependency issues." A holistic treatment approach will not stop once a couple has been convinced to enter a detoxification and treatment facility and codependency treatment. Later, when the alcoholic is sober, couples will develop interactive definitions based on issues in their new relationship. Finally, couples therapy can be aimed at helping couples deal with relapse prevention by (1) engaging in wellness behaviors that prevent relationship problems and enhance sobriety, and (2) identifying high-risk situations that endanger sobriety and how the partner can deal with these situations. For example, how will the partner react when the alcoholic, recently out of treatment, goes to a bar with co-workers and orders a Coke? The partner's view of this action as a high-risk behavior could be crucial information for the alcoholic; on the other hand, it might be considered interfer-ence. A couple can develop an "interactional definition" of these problems during the recovery process.

In short, the integrative model recommends a start-and-stop approach to couples therapy. The initial issue can require specific inpatient treatment, but couples therapy can be resumed immediately as part of the aftercare plan, first to deal with issues around supporting sobriety, and eventually to deal with relation-ship enhancement and relapse prevention.

Case Example: Luis and Marina

Luis and Marina had been married only 3 years when Luis's drinking became a problem. As his drinking increased, he worked less at his construction job and spent less time with his wife and infant daughter. Luis left home and moved in with another alcoholic co-worker, Andre, for about 3 months; then he returned and tried to convince his wife to take him back. His return was prompted by the fact that his place of employment had become a "drug-free work site" and had instituted random testing. Andre was fired when he hurt himself at work and the hospital reported marijuana and alcohol in his system.

While Luis was living with Andre, Marina had been in individual counseling with her priest. When Luis returned, Marina insisted that he enter alcohol treatment before discussing the future of their marriage. Luis went to a detoxification/treatment program sponsored by a local alcohol and drug treatment agency. Marina took part in the family education meetings while Luis was an inpatient, but she carried a lot of resentment and made no agreement to take him back when he was released. Luis went to live in a halfway house on his release because of Marina's ambivalence. After about 40 days in the halfway house, Marina and Luis had decided that they wanted to reunite and have Luis moved back home. Since his return, the couple has been having problems.

Application of the Integrative Model: Alcoholism

Stage 1: Assessing and Developing an Interactive Definition of the Problem

During the initial couples therapy session, a genogram was completed for each member of the couple and the history of the relationship was discussed. In many ways the couple had lived together more as roommates. Each kept a separate checking account, they shared the bills equally, and each had a scheduled night out each week with friends. The two were compatible sexually, but both admitted that there was little understanding of their differences. They were also concerned that every discussion turned into a fight. Apparently the relationship had changed after the birth of their daughter, when Luis complained that Marina took less interest in the relationship and their old "party friends." Marina indicated that Luis became involved with drinking to the exclusion of his family. Maria admitted that she withdrew, turning her attention to the child, and Luis grudgingly agreed that he ignored the relationship too. The couple speculated that Luis's drinking gave Marina all the responsibility for decision making and thus reduced conflict. Since he became sober, though, conflict has returned. The therapist reinforced the fact that both members of the couple should continue in aftercare through AA and Alanon.

When these two sides of the story had been brought to light, the couple was able, during the first session, to agree that one of the most important issues was dealing with conflict. They felt that if they could communicate and deal with the many problems by negotiating, they would be able to improve the relationship and reduce the overall level of stress. The interactive definition of the problem was framed as "We tend to withdraw when a conflict or crisis occurs."

Stage 2: Goal Setting

During the same session, the therapist explained that, rather than focus on the problems of the past, the couple should identify some specific goals regarding conflict. The therapist was surprised when the couple indicated that they would like to have an open disagreement. They felt that they would have a healthy relationship when they are able to directly face some issue.

Externalizing   In this session, the therapist picked up on the couple's goal statement about being able to handle conflict. The therapist continued to refer to the problem as "the conflict phobia." This actually helped the partners see the problem in a less pathological way. They were able to laugh about it when they realized they were avoiding conflict rather than blame each other as they had before. The therapist reinforced the fact that the couple was well on their way to conquering the "phobia" by getting together.

Stage 3: Adopting New Perceptions and Behaviors

Before the third session, each partner was instructed to think about the other partner's strengths. They were each to bring a list to the next session. When the couple arrived, neither partner had completed a list but both said they had thought about it. Rather than chastise the couple, the therapist proceeded to make a list of each person's strengths as identified by the other partner. Marina saw Luis as a hard worker and as determined, humorous, and creative. Luis said that Marina was sensitive to feelings, intelligent, and a good planner. When Luis started to list the down side of each trait, the therapist stopped him and focused him back on the goal of looking at strengths.

Next (externalizing) the therapist asked both partners to indicate how they might use their individual strengths to attack the "conflict phobia." Luis immediately chimed in that Marina was more sensitive to recognizing when the problem was happening and that she could be the one to signal when a discussion was needed. The therapist suggested that Luis's determination or perseverance would help the couple stay with the argument until a conclusion was reached. By the end of the third session, the couple had indicated that Marina would bring up an issue they were avoiding during the next week, and both would take turns expressing themselves uninterrupted for 5 minutes. Before beginning again, each member would have to correctly paraphrase the partner's statement. It was Luis's job to make certain that they stick to the argument and not "kitchen sink," or bring in outside issues. They were to engage in this conflict for no more than 15 minutes, but they were to continue these 15-minute sessions each day until the issue was resolved. If the issue was still not resolved by the next therapy session, the couple would discuss it with the therapist. The therapist indicated that because the two were not used to conflict, they should keep it to a minimum at first. The therapist went on to indicate that conflict was a normal part of relationships and the key to growth.

The next two sessions of couples therapy were spent in communication and conflict management training using homework assignments and role playing in the session. It turned out that both members of the couple had difficulty talking about sexual issues, and their first conflict had been over this issue. There had been immediate improvement in the relationship, however, because Marina finally admitted she did not like to have sex late at night when she was tired, something Luis never knew. The two changed their schedule and both partners felt more satisfied.

Stage 4: Maintaining New Perceptions and Behaviors

By the sixth session, the couple was ready to end couples therapy; however, the therapist believed that communication skills had not been fully learned. The couple seemed to be experiencing less stress and a better sexual relationship, so the therapist agreed to see the couple on a monthly basis for "booster sessions." During the booster sessions, both partners were asked to list those things they were doing to further the change process. Marina indicated that she was bringing up her concerns more frequently but that Luis seemed to be withdrawing. Luis eventually admitted that he was depressed and was having urges to drink. He said that he did not always feel like dealing with problems when he came home from work. His attendance at AA had slacked off, and Marina had not been attending Alanon at all. The therapist focused immediately on this issue and indicated that regular AA and Alanon attendance was necessary for couples therapy to continue. The therapist did not see any indication of major depression, but Luis's down moods appeared to be related to a letdown after the rosy period immediately following sobriety. The couple agreed to the stipulation of continued support group attendance.

During the session, the couple identified the fact that not having enough "fun time" was affecting the relationship and that simply dealing with difficulties was turning their interactions into a chore. The couple agreed to build in more time together doing inexpensive things for fun. They indicated that they must now find a balance between not avoiding important issues and spending all of their time hashing things out. The therapist congratulated the couple for addressing one of the obstacles to change that they had encountered and continued to schedule monthly sessions.

Stage 5: Validating New Perceptions and Behaviors

Three months after they had begun couples therapy, Luis's sobriety was of good quality and the couple was more stable than when therapy first began. Certainly a number of issues still needed to be dealt with. There were still extreme financial problems, issues about child care and household responsibilities, and issues about how to spend free time. During these final sessions, the therapist directed the partners to recognize their achievement in learning to deal more effectively with conflict and supporting each other's recovery. The therapist asked both members of the couple to indicate something each has appreciated in the other during the past 3 months. Luis said, "She never got discouraged and always fought back to make everything work." Marina said, "He felt like drinking but didn't. I hope he was thinking about me and the baby."

The therapist asked the two what sort of issues they thought might be the biggest threat to the kinds of changes that had been made. Both agreed that Luis's return to drinking was the biggest issue. The therapist again encouraged follow-up with support groups, also asking the partners to think about what they had learned in couples therapy or in their support group over the past weeks and how they might apply that learning to upcoming stressors in the future. Luis said, "This time, if we have a fight, I am going to hang in there until we get it resolved. If I am mad, I'll call my sponsor or someone else but eventually we will get it straightened out." Marina said, "I am not going to hide my feelings when something Luis does disappoints me. But I am not going to make him feel bad, just work it out." The therapist scheduled a follow-up session in 3 months.

CONCLUSION

This chapter addressed the treatment of a couple when alcohol affects one of the partners. We chose not to address other substances of abuse for brevity's sake and because alcohol is the most significant drug problem today. Alcohol is the cause of many couples problems, and many people drink to cope with problems in their relationships.

It is clear that couple patterns such as codependency can actually support alcoholism, but it is also the case that the relationship can be the medium for achieving sobriety. The traditional wisdom has been that each member of a couple must be treated separately before the two can work on the issues that confront them jointly. There is evidence to suggest that interventions aimed at improving the quality of the couple relationship will not embroil the couple in more conflict and may establish a good environment to support sobriety. Couples who improve their communication skills and who develop relapse prevention strategies together can create a higher level of sobriety in the alcoholic partner and eliminate maladaptive patterns in the relationship.

14

Blending Couples

KEY CONCEPTS

- The blending family is distinctly different from the biological nuclear family, and it has unique problems and concerns.
- There are many myths about stepfamilies that can limit growth and positive interactions in the family.
- There are predictable stages through which the blending family progresses.
- The nonresidential parent usually plays an important role in the blending family formation.
- The couple is the foundation of the blending family and requires special considerations in therapy.
- Family therapy and group therapy are the preferred methods of treatment for blending families.

Case Example: Corey and Corina

Corey and Corina have been married for 6 months. Corey was married previously for 9 years and has two children, ages 7 and 9. Both children currently reside with Corey's former wife, and his contact consists of every Wednesday evening and every other weekend. Corina was married for a brief 3 years and has a daughter, Alana, age 2. She maintains primary residence for her daughter with flexible contact for her former spouse. Because of her child's age, Corina has frequent contact with Alana's father. He is also very active in all decision making regarding the child's welfare.

Corey and Corina expected that they would jointly make parenting decisions for Alana. However, Alana's biological father calls or comes over on a daily basis to see her or to bring her special treats. He maintains that it is his right and that no one else is going to raise his daughter. Recently, Corey has become angry about the time Corina spends talking to her "ex" on the phone and about the frequent intrusions into their family life by his constant visits. When Corey and Corina try to talk about this problem, they argue and Corina cries. Corey slams the door and leaves the house to "cool off." The two spend less time together doing pleasant activities because they are angry and frustrated. Corina feels helpless and cannot disappoint her former spouse because of the guilt she feels for taking his daughter from his home. Corey says that the ex-husband might as well move in with them because he is present so often. Many times, when Corey's children come to visit, they are unable to do things as a family because Alana is with her father. Corey's children have little contact with Alana, so when she is at home they ignore her.

The couple comes to marriage therapy with the following concerns:

1. Corina is frustrated with the constant criticism she hears from Corey and feels very unsupported.
2. Corey wants to limit the time Alana's father spends with her so that they can be "a family."
3. Corey wants his children to have more contact with Alana.
4. Corey and Corina want to be able to communicate more effectively as a couple.
5. Corey wants more time alone with Corina and would like to hire a baby-sitter more often.

BLENDING COUPLES

Sociological Context

The remarried couple or the stepfamily is the fastest growing family form in the United States (Glick, 1989). A stepfamily is defined as one in which children live some, most, or all of the time with two married adults, one of whom is not a biological parent (Stanton, 1986). Although this family unit is becoming the norm, most of these families are modeling their relationships after the biological nuclear family (Mills, 1984; Kelley, 1992). However, remarried couples and their stepchildren are different from traditional families and exhibit stress when they attempt to replicate the structure of the nuclear family. Clearly, under these conditions, the stepfamily begins with a great handicap (Cissna, Cox, & Bochner, 1990; Satir, 1972).

Traditional couple intimacy is challenged by the formation of the "instant family," whose focus becomes the stepparent-stepchild relationship. Little attention is paid to the needs of the couple because the needs of the children receive priority. Often, this child-focused couple is affected by former spouses, who maintain influence on the new relationship through contact with their biological children. It is unfortunate that researchers of divorce and remarriage have evaded what the role of the stepparent means and how it affects one's marital life (Ambert, 1986).

Issues for Blending Couples

There is a vast array of complex pairings for remarried couples, such as:

1. Both previously married but have no children.
2. Both previously married and each has children.

3. Both previously married and only one has children.
4. One previously married and has children, and one has not been married before.
5. One has not been previously married but has a biological child, and the other has not been married before.
6. One has never been married and does not have children, and one has been previously married with no children.

Often, in addition to the various pairings, the new couple plays host to a cast of characters ranging from former spouses, children who were not expected to live with the couple or visit often, former in-laws, old friends, or even old bill collectors (Kaslow & Schwartz, 1987). Unfortunately, the couple does not have time to establish a separate identity before dealing with these other people. Thus, rarely is there time to build a strong foundation to support the remarriage before the couple is involved with the difficulties of stepparenting (Kaslow & Schwartz, 1987).

Differences between Blending Families and Biological Nuclear Families

Usually, in a blending family, each member has experienced significant loss. Dreams for the future have been shattered, and even if the dissolution was desired, sorrow and pain accompany the loss of the previous relationship. Couples merge with partners saddled with their own pain as they venture to develop a new, exciting relationship. Children may have lost contact with a biological parent, a grandparent, other relatives, friends, or schoolmates (Visher, 1985).

In stepfamilies, each person brings a set of expectations about how to parent, clean house, cook, socialize, or work. These individual beliefs may be in contradiction with other family member's beliefs and become a target for the unresolved pain in the family.

Alternatively, the stepfamily created from loss can provide a safe arena for intimacy. Restoration of the security of companionship, partnership, and a satisfying sexual relationship are examples of goals for remarried couples (Hobart, 1989). Economic gains and relief from single parenting can also generate growth and increased stability in the family (Hobart, 1989).

In blending families, the bond between the biological parent and the child proves stronger than the newly created relationship between the stepchild and the stepparent. There may be loyalty conflicts, as the biological parent-child relationship has had more longevity than the couple's relationship has. In some families, the nonresidential parent may continue to be actively involved with the child and, at times, can be viewed as interfering in the couple's life. In some cases, one child may be active in going back and forth to both parents' household, while another child may have little contact with the other biological parent. These schedules can create jealousy and logistical challenges for families.

As couples attempt to solve lifestyle variations while creating a new family unit, they must accept the lack of a legal relationship existing between the stepparent and stepchild. This places the stepparent in a position of assuming responsibilities without rights or privileges (Visher & Visher, 1990). Often, these tasks can be

SIGNE
WORKING WOMAN
New York
USA

1. Bride 2. Groom 3. Groom's daughter from first marriage 4. Bride's mother 5. Bride's mother's current lover 6. Bride's sperm donor father 7. & 8. Sperm donor's parents who sued for visitation rights to bride 9. Bride's mother's lover at time of bride's birth 10. Groom's mother 11. Groom's mother's boyfriend 12. Groom's father 13. Groom's stepmother 14. Groom's father's third wife 15. Groom's grandfather 16. Groom's grandfather's lover 17. Groom's first wife

overwhelming for partners who have not yet developed their own style of problem-solving and negotiating with each other. The most challenging task, however, is establishing the creditability of the stepparent regarding parental authority in the home (Cissna, Cos, & Bochner, 1990).

The Role of Stepmother

In addition to the complexities involved in stepfamily formation, stepmothers face their own unique challenges. The role of the biological mother, whether she is deceased, absent, or available, becomes idealized for the children. The negative stereotype of the "wicked" stepmother found in several traditional fairy tales continues to have an impact on contemporary imagination (Salwen, 1990). In fact, many stepmothers struggle with the internalized negative self-concept related to the connotations of evil, cruelty, jealousy, and selfishness derived from the stories of Hansel and Gretel, Snow White, and Cinderella (Salwen, 1990).

Bettelheim (1977) explained the persistent stereotype as related to the psychological needs the negative stepparent role meets for stepchildren. The fantasy of the wicked stepmother allows the child who is unable to integrate loving and hateful feelings toward a new and highly influential person in his or her life to cope, by focusing anger and rage on the mythical evil person. Thus, the relationship with the biological mother remains intact. Feelings of anger and disappointment the child may harbor about the biological parent's role in the divorce are unexpressed and instead are directed toward the "new" person in the child's life.

The role of stepmother may be most difficult in traditional family structures where the father is the primary breadwinner and the mother remains in the home, assuming responsibility for the household, the cooking, and child care. Stepmothers most often are thrust into roles of disciplinarians and rule setters more intensely than are traditional stepfathers. Additional responsibilities, a negative social definition of stepmother, and the lack of empirical research on stepmothers who reside with their stepchildren can create unique situations for stepmothers and stepchildren to resolve (Ambert, 1986; Coleman, Marshall, & Ganong, 1986).

The Role of Stepfather

Because mothers continue to be the primary custodians of their children after divorce, most stepfamilies are stepfather families. The stepfather is often viewed as the financial rescuer or supporter of the new family, but he may be minimally involved with the caretaking of the children. Stepfathers may view the mother-child bond as strong and exclusive and may not make attempts to integrate himself in the relationship.

Just as negative stereotypical myths pollute the ideal of stepmother, the stereotype of the "abusive" (both physically and sexually) stepfather is perpetuated by the media. The myths serve the same purpose of distancing the stepparent and stepchild, regardless of the gender of the stepparent (Claxton-Oldfield, 1992).

Some stepfathers feel guilty about the lack of time they spent with their biological children and so become extremely involved in the lives of their stepchildren. On the other hand, some perceive their roles as the one who should be in control in order to "shape up" the new family. Such stepfathers are viewed as overly restrictive and domineering and may be feared or disliked by the stepchild. This situation can be particularly destructive if the stepchild is an adolescent girl (Coleman & Ganong, 1991).

The following concerns about their role are most often cited by stepfathers.

1. Uncertainty over the degree of authority to exert in the new family.
2. The amount and type of expression of affection toward stepchildren.
3. The discipline of stepchildren and the enforcement of rules.
4. Financial conflicts.
5. Guilt over leaving children from a previous marriage.
6. Loyalty conflicts with the mother-child relationship.
7. Sexual conflicts between stepfather and stepchild, or sibling conflicts.
8. Conflict over surnames.

Although these issues may be prevalent to some extent in biological nuclear families, the stigma against stepfamilies continues to exist in our society (Robinson, 1984). In fact, clinical researchers cite evidence showing that some stepparents camouflage their step status or deny that they are in a stepfamily (Claxton-Oldfield, 1992).

Healthy Stepfamily Characteristics

Flexibility and Adaptability

The need for flexibility in stepfamilies is paramount. Holidays, birthdays, vacations, and other family events require the accommodation of two families' schedules. Sometimes plans and ideas must be changed at a moment's notice (Kelley, 1992).

Patience

Patience is crucial, as remarried couples do not have the time to develop cohesiveness before they become an instant family. Attempting to force the family to be a unit prematurely can lead to anger and resentment. Children must adjust at their own pace and learn respect for their stepparent. Love for a stepparent will not come automatically, and it may never occur. Stepparents can demonstrate respect for the stepchildren by being aware of the changes they are forced to make by the addition of an unfamiliar parent in the home.

Realistic Expectations

There must be a realization that the stepfamily will be different from a biological nuclear family. When family members do not mourn the loss of the old family structure and continue to idealize the former family, progress is unlikely to be made in the newly created family formation. The stepfamily cannot replicate the biological nuclear family, nor should it try. Roles within the family for each person must be renegotiated, thus establishing a unique relationship among family members. Unfortunately, appropriate models have not been available. In fact, research indicates that interpersonal stress is the major problem in stepfamily relationships and their extended families (Stanton, 1986).

Cooperation of Separate Households

For healthy stepfamily functioning, it is important for couples to develop a parenting coalition that includes adults from both households who are involved in raising the children. Sometimes there may be stepparents from two families involved in the coalition. In cases where all parents have remarried, six adults could be providing input to raise the children. With several conflicting ideas, needs, and agendas, it is easy to imagine how complicated this task might be (Visher & Visher, 1990).

Unified Couple

Strong, unified couples create healthy stepfamilies. With a parent-child bond preceding the new couple relationship, stepfamily couples must plan time to nourish each partner and the relationship. Lack of trust of intimate relationships resulting from the divorce and guilt from spending time away from the children can weaken the relationship. The security of a strong, stable, and happy couple is essential for the couple to provide guidance and direction for the stepfamily (Visher & Visher, 1990).

Establishment of Constructive Rituals

Solid relationships grow from positive shared memories, just as feelings of belonging develop from familiar ways of interacting (Visher & Visher, 1990). The establishment of rituals and traditions is important for healthy stepfamilies. When possible, positive former traditions should be retained, or at least be combined to form new traditions. For example, one family had always opened gifts on Christmas Eve, whereas the other had opened them on Christmas Day during a large family celebration. The stepfamily decided to open one special gift on Christmas Eve with caroling and a light dinner afterward. On Christmas Day, they would open the remainder of the gifts and celebrate with a family gathering at breakfast, because two of the children were leaving to celebrate the holiday with the other parent in the early afternoon. These accommodations include both families yet provide new experiences for the stepfamily.

Formation of Satisfactory Step-Relationships

Step-relations develop over a long period of time, and not necessarily at the same time that the couple is achieving a strong bond (Visher & Visher, 1990). Stepparents enter the family with little power. In fact, most experts recommend that stepparents form a friendly relationship with their stepchildren rather than an authoritative one, and then gradually assume more of the discipline.

The relationship between the stepparent and the stepchild is affected both by the messages the stepchild receives from the biological parent about the stepparent and by the stepchild's view of the stepparent relationship in the home. Couples should balance time spent on themselves and time spent on family needs so that jealousies and resentments do not emerge.

Strengths of Stepfamilies

Although much of the research focuses on problems in stepfamilies, members of such families have the potential for growth from the many positive experiences of living in a stepfamily. Coleman, Ganong, and Gingrich (1985) have identified the following ten most often mentioned strengths of stepfamilies.

1. Each family member is exposed to a broader range of people and experiences. Diverse traditions, careers, hobbies, foods, vacations, and family daily life can enrich the lives of all family members.
2. A positive model, rather than a bitter dysfunctional model, of adult intimacy and marriage is exhibited by the adult couple.
3. There are more adults available when children require assistance. A stepparent may compensate for a quality the biological parent lacks and can serve as a guide for the children.
4. Parents are typically happier and less strained in the stepfamily than in the biological nuclear family.

5. Stepparents can be more objective and can provide a more rational opinion than can the biological parent whose emotional bond is strong.

6. Adults may be more experienced, mature, and motivated to create a successful relationship and family after being embroiled in conflict and disappointment in the former marriage.

7. Parents exhibit more cooperation and sharing because the roles must be flexible and constantly in a state of change. The blending of two disparate family styles provides opportunity for negotiation and problem solving.

8. Stepchildren become more adaptable so that parents can focus on their own relationship and adult needs.

9. Stepfamilies are more stable emotionally and economically than are single-parent families. In fact, research indicates that stability for stepfamilies is very similar to that for biological nuclear families.

10. Sometimes there is a "change" in birth order, so that the oldest child gets a chance to be a middle child or the youngest now has a younger brother or sister. This new view of self in relation to the family can produce new perceptions and expectations of each family member.

In addition to the ten strengths listed above, Hobart (1989) reports that "if the trend of increasing numbers of remarried families and declining birth rates continues, there is a possibility that remarried families will have more available extended family resources than nuclear families."

Stepfamily Hurdles: Stressors in the Family

It is generally agreed that the most frequent problem area in stepfamilies is the stepparent-stepchild relationship. In many families, the biological parent remains very involved and continues to set limits and provide guidance to the children.

The stepparent's assumption of an immediate parental role is detrimental in these situations. In fact, a significant number of stepparents do not ever choose a parental role with stepchildren. The age of the children and the involvement of the nonresidential parent significantly influence this decision (Mills, 1984). Research indicates that stepfamilies with preadolescents and adolescents have the most difficulty adjusting (Coleman, Marshall, & Ganong, 1986; Visher & Visher, 1988).

Lack of time and energy for the couple to nurture their relationship is also cited as problematic for many remarried couples. Orchestrating many family member's activities and responding to their varied needs leaves many parents drained physically and emotionally, with little time to spare for their partner. Learning how to balance the adult and child needs and to prioritize the marital relationship requires commitment and flexibility from both partners.

STAGES OF STEPFAMILY DEVELOPMENT

Papernow (1984; 1995) describes seven stages of stepfamily development. In the three early stages, the family remains primarily divided along biological lines. Most nurturing, rules and limit setting, and rituals occur within the biological subsystems. During the middle stages, the family loosens biological boundaries and begins to restructure the family on the basis of the step-relations. The couple must be the first to begin making these changes, becoming the architects of the stepfamily systems (Mills, 1984). In the later stages, the stepfamily structure is in place and the role of the stepparent emerges. These seven stages typically require between 4 and 12 years to complete.

> *Stage 1: Fantasy.* Stepfamiles embrace many myths and have many unrealistic ideas about blending together. Some of these ideas include rescuing children from the ex-spouse, healing a "broken family," having a stepparent adoring their stepchildren, marrying a nurturing parent, and having someone with whom to share the load.

> *Stage 2: Assimilation.* The couple joins in an attempt to carry out the plan of the fantasy of the new family. As one stepmother described it, "I was trying so hard to put the two pieces of the broken plate back together again, but they didn't fit. They came from two different plates" (Papernow, 1984, p. 357). Stepparents who attempt to join the biological unit feel jealous, resentful, confused, and inadequate when they are unsuccessful in their attempt.

> *Stage 3: Awareness and Getting Clear.* Increasing clarity of the reality of the difficulties of blending helps the couple understand what is happening. Sometimes resolving the relationship with the previous spouse takes place in this stage. The step-relations open somewhat to the stepparent and include the stepparent in some decision making or family structuring. There is still much reservation though, as biological parents are low in trust yet do not want to fail in another relationship.

> *Stage 4: Mobilization and Airing Differences.* During this stage, stepfamilies begin to voice opinions about their thoughts, perceptions, and feelings. Arguments may be more prevalent as the stepparent makes more demands on the biological parent's time and parenting style. Dissatisfaction is usually high as the biological parent becomes more distressed.

> *Stage 5: Action or Going into Business Together.* The energy and expressiveness of the prior stage initiates an "unfreezing" of the old system and marks the beginning of a new phase of building a family unit with some integration of all family members. The couple is the driving force in this stage because the partners actually change the family structure by establishing stepcouple boundaries such as creating time to be alone together, closing the bedroom door, and consulting each other on childrearing and visitation issues. Decisions are also made about how the nonresidential parent is going to be involved in the stepfamily structure. Celebrations of holidays, rituals, and traditions are reestablished at this stage.

> *Stage 6: Contact and Intimacy in Step-Relationships.* In this stage, the partners previously polarized by stepfamily issues view each other as someone with whom they can express feelings and share issues, including painful or difficult ones. The role of stepparent is more solid, with clearer communi-

cation evident between the couple and the children. The couple experiences the relationship as separate from the children and from the stepfamily.

Stage 7: Resolution: Holding On and Letting Go. Step-relationships provide some sense of satisfaction as the family settles in a lifestyle more reliable for each person in the family. Members know what to expect from each other, and they communicate their needs more openly. Occasionally issues about how closely or distantly to interact with stepchildren emerge, although at times a distant relationship is established and maintained throughout the family cycle.

The resolution stage is also a time for grieving. The stepparent realizes that he or she must share the stepchild with the biological and more "entitled" parent. This realization is most acute at visitation and holiday times. The biological parent realizes that there will be interrupted parenting and significant influences on the children from someone outside of the home. Letting go becomes easier because it occurs on a regular basis as children move back and forth between parents. In this stage, however, the stepparent has become the "intimate outsider" and can be a confidante of children when biological parents may be too involved to be objective.

During all these stages, couples must continually evaluate and reevaluate their relationship and provide protective boundaries around the couple unit. Children will attempt to permeate the boundaries, as will such outsiders as former spouses, in-laws, or social institutions that are not sensitive to stepfamily issues.

The Impact of Blending Families at Various Stages of the Life Cycle

Spouses at Different Life Cycle Stages   In general, the wider the discrepancy in family life cycle experiences between the new partners, the greater the difficulty of transition and the longer it will take to integrate a functioning stepfamily (McGoldrick & Carter, 1980). A woman with two small children who marries a man with grown children is likely to have more difficulty adjusting than will a man and a woman of similar ages and life stages who both have young children or children who are grown and live on their own.

Children at Various Life Stages   The most complex remarried families are those in which one or both partners have children under the age of 18. There are some indications that preschool children, if they are able to mourn their losses successfully, are the most adaptable to the new stepfamily, while adjustment is most difficult for teenagers (Visher & Visher, 1979). Children of latency age seem to have the most difficulty resolving their feelings of divided loyalties and benefit from contact with both biological parents (Wallerstein & Kelley, 1980). It is clear that children in divorced families adapt best when they have parents who are cooperative and they have continuous contact with both parents (Landis, 1991; Luepnitz, 1986).

Stepfamilies with Adolescents   The nuclear family with adolescents is frequently at a turbulent stage, and the difficulties are usually exacerbated in stepfamilies. Conflict often occurs because the stepfamily is promoting cohesiveness at a time when the adolescent needs to separate from the family and form an independent identity. Boundaries must be renegotiated when adolescents want freedom and fewer restrictions and home responsibilities, even if the stepfamily is in an infant stage.

Minuchin (1974) believes that parents cannot protect and guide without being restrictive and controlling. Children cannot grow and become individuated without rebelling or rejecting their parents' protection. The process of socialization is inherently filled with conflict (Cissna, Cox, & Bochner, 1990), and adolescents are very aware of how to play the parents and stepparents against each other to get what they want (McGoldrick & Carter, 1980).

Blending in Later Life Stages   Remarriage at a postchildrearing phase of the family life cycle requires significant readjustment of relationships throughout both family systems, which may include in-laws or grandchildren (McGoldrick & Carter, 1980). Grown children sometimes complain when family traditions change and family events such as graduations, weddings, or birthdays are rearranged. Sometimes there are difficulties about how much financial assistance to provide for adult children and how legal wills are to be designed. There is evidence that when former spouses are cooperative and attend family functions at the same time, acceptance of the new marriage and blending of the families is optimum (McGoldrick & Carter, 1980).

THERAPY ISSUES FOR BLENDING FAMILIES

In addition to issues relevant to couples in general, there are some common therapeutic themes peculiar to stepfamily couples.

Economic Issues

Unresolved issues from prior marriages often haunt the stepfamily. Initially, there may be unfinished economic connections (Kaslow, 1992). Rarely does the economic marriage end at the same time that the legal marriage does. Sale of properties in common, child support, and in some cases, permanent alimony are issues in most stepfamilies. Sometimes one partner may feel resentful toward the ex-spouse because there is little money left available after child support payments are made. For example, in the case illustration of Corey and Corina, Corina admits feeling frustrated that she and her husband are inhibited financially and cannot enjoy the vacations she would like due to alimony and child support demands from Corey's first marriage. One stepparent may also feel deprived or may view the other children as deprived if more money is available for only one child because of incoming financial support from a biological, nonresidential parent.

Noxious Behaviors

Ineffective coping styles developed during difficult first marriages may continue into second marriages if issues are not resolved. Couples may be too tired or overwhelmed initially to resolve their own strains when much of the attention is paid to the children and the stepsibling relationships in the new household. Feelings of incompetence and powerlessness can lead to thwarted problem-solving skills at a time when they are necessary for a successful transition to a new family structure (Kaslow, 1992). For example, Corey and Corina reported a decrease in couple activities and an increase in frustration about their marriage that ultimately brought them to therapy.

Movement of Children between Households

Parents often feel a lack of autonomy over their family life when they must share decision making with the other biological parent. Vacations, holidays, activities for school and weekends are now subject to the approval of the nonresidential parent. When conflicts cannot be accommodated, hostility may develop between households and loyalty issues may arise for the children. This often results in the child's placing increased pressure on the stepfamily by refusing to be cooperative or by attempting to reunite the biological parents, thus sabotaging the new couple. In our case illustration, Corey expressed feelings of alienation and helplessness about the continued presence of Alana's father in their new family.

New Roles and Rules

One of the most common tasks in stepfamily development is the negotiation of new roles and rules in the family. The biological parent must adjust to another person in the household who takes on the role of parent, in addition to the role of partner (Nolan, Coleman, & Ganong, 1984). Partners need to be flexible and supportive of each other as they "try on" these new roles. Rules that worked in a previous relationship may no longer work because they were based on the prior family structure of the two adults. For example, a husband who had a very active role in caretaking and disciplining the children with his former wife may feel rejected or unimportant if he remains in the background while his new wife sets limits and cares for her children. If the discrepancy is not discussed and a plan made for parenting the children, resentment and hostility may develop.

Treatment Issues

Developmental versus Clinical

It is important to remember that couples enter into new partnerships with high hopes and much trepidation. Therapists must distinguish between normal step-family issues and clinical issues, such as personality disorders, addictions, sexual problems, or clinical depression and other diagnosable disorders (Kaslow, 1992). Clinical issues can exacerbate an already tenuous situation in blending families and can make decision making more difficult (Kaslow, 1992).

Normalization and the Development of Love

A basic therapeutic task is to normalize the stepfamily and help the members feel positive about their new family structure. This includes dispelling the notion that they must behave and be organized the way a biological nuclear family is. Ways that therapists can validate the family include focusing on the couple as the primary unit, empathizing with the feelings emerging from the stepfamily situation, and emphasizing the positive attributes and possibilities for stepfamilies (Visher & Visher, 1990).

Therapists can also assist the stepfamily with the formation of realistic expectations about the development of love between stepparents and their stepchildren and the acceptance of the new partner by extended family members. Time and patience are key elements in this process.

Negotiations

Therapists can facilitate negotiations about how the new family and couple will spend their time together and their time apart. Couples will decide how much influence the biological parents and extended family will have on their decisions and new way of life together. Interventions such as behavioral contracts, task assignments, and other problem-solving techniques can be helpful tools.

Boundaries for the Couple

With overwhelming issues involved in blending two families, couples frequently place their needs last in the hierarchy. Therapists can help couples arrange time for nurturing the relationship and supporting their adult goals. Often, difficulties in setting appropriate boundaries in prior relationships may have led to their dissolution. Therapists can guide couples in formulating, maintaining, and renegotiating healthy couple boundaries by focusing on specific behaviors that contribute to the problem and by helping the couple brainstorm about more viable interactions that would protect their relationship. For example, with Corey and Corina, the therapist might stress their need to include each other in planning family activities.

Cultural and Racial Differences

Other blending issues can be complicated when there are cultural or racial differences within the new family structure. Religious or cultural codes rather than preferences may be issues for negotiation and may have great emotional implications for family members. Sometimes strong influences from the nonresidential parent can sabotage the customs of the new partner. In extreme situations, the nonresidential parent may pursue these issues in court in an attempt to thwart any new cultural influences over the children. Therapists can help the couple clarify which customs are most important to maintain and which can be accommodated or changed for the new family.

Differences in Sexual Orientation

Increasing numbers of individuals are identifying themselves as gay or lesbian. Many have declared their sexual identities after years of living in a heterosexual relationship that produced children (Baptiste, 1987). The challenges of gay and lesbian stepfamilies are vast, ranging from the belief that homosexuality is psychologically unhealthy and that it is a choice made, not an inherent characteristic. The choice theory complicates issues because the other biological parent may be concerned that children raised with a gay or lesbian parental lifestyle will be taught to be gay or lesbian.

Therapists must educate themselves and their clients about these notions and help couples address these stereotypes. At the same time, they must also deal with complexities common to stepfamily living (Baptiste, 1987).

Types of Treatment

Family Therapy

Because there are many players in the drama of blending families, all parties involved must have access to therapy if they are to effect change in the family structure. The therapist can decide which dyads or family members should be at each session. Sometimes the session will include the whole family, and at other times it might include the couple, the stepparent and stepchild, or stepsiblings.

On some occasions, it may be necessary to include nonresidential parents or grandparents, depending on the presenting issues for therapy. Shifts in roles, rules, and loyalties can be addressed in a family format.

Group Work

The group process provides a psychoeducational forum for helping members of stepfamilies share their concerns and receive support from others who share similar circumstances. This arena can provide an air of normalcy and can provide information about typical developmental sequences that families may have in common. This may offer a more realistic picture of family life, allowing families to focus on a variety of possibilities, rather than on replication of the "old" structure from the original blueprint of the nuclear family.

Individual Therapy

Although individual therapy is not recommended often for blending families, it should not be discounted if one member suffers from a clinical disorder such as anxiety, panic, depression, addiction, or other personality disorders—apart from the reaction to the stepfamily transition. The therapist can then refer the individual to couples, group, or family therapy, depending on the needs of the individual family members.

THE INTEGRATIVE MODEL AND BLENDING COUPLES

Application of the Integrative Model: Blending Couple

Stage 1: Assessing and Obtaining an Interactive View of the Problem

Corey and Corina each have an individual concern about the problem. Corina wants Corey to stop criticizing her and to be more supportive; Corey wants to spend more time with Corina and to be more included in the decisions regarding Alana. After some discussion in therapy, the two agree that they need to learn how to set limits with Alana's father and how to implement a more structured schedule of contact. In addition, Corey and Corina express a desire to increase their time together as a couple while decreasing disputes pertaining to Alana.

Stage 2: Goal Setting

The couple agrees to work on the following goals:

1. To create a detailed contact schedule so they will both know exactly when Alana will be with them and when she will be with her father. This schedule will free them to plan family events and begin to feel more connected as a family.
2. Learn how to negotiate rules for the family and decide how they want to organize their time at home. Each wants to feel more equally included in making family plans.
3. Spend time alone at least once a week in order to feel more intimate with each other.

Stage 3: Adopting New Perceptions and Behaviors

Corey and Corina reflect on times when they were dating and were making specific arrangements to spend time together. Corina says she loves to plan creative activities for them, but she is less energetic about the details involved in implementing the plan. Corey admits that he can be very detailed if he knows exactly when they will have opportunities for time alone and assurance that Alana is cared for by either her father or a trusted caretaker.

They also discuss the need for both of them to be involved in their dating plans. It is agreed that each week they will alternate in planning and implementing their date. Corina agrees to discuss the plan with her ex-spouse if any variation of the contact schedule is involved.

Stage 4: Maintaining New Perceptions and Behaviors

Corey and Corina agree they will exercise caution to implement their plan while maintaining specific structure about their time schedule. Corina voices concern that she will have difficulty being assertive with Alana's father. In order to provide support, they agree that a schedule change will not occur until they have an opportunity as a couple to discuss the deviation and potential change of circumstances. Corina will inform her former spouse that she will consider his request and respond at a designated time. Corey and Corina emphasize their commitment to their dates together and agree to hold each other responsible for continued success.

Stage 5: Validating New Perceptions and Behaviors

Corey and Corina compliment each other on their abilities to problem-solve together and to remain firm in their plan to manage Alana's contact schedule. They report that they each feel more freedom and personal power over their daily lives and feel more supported in their relationship. Both vow to continue communication about these issues and agree to confront the other if either perceives that one of them is returning to "old ways."

Techniques for Working with Blending Couples

1. Basic communication and listening skills training
2. Problem-solving methods training
3. Role reversal
4. Contracting
5. Time management planning
6. Detriangulating the family (moving the ex-partner from the family, while being aware of his or her influence in their lives)
7. Creating couple time and a boundary around the couple dyad
8. Slowly creating a stepparent role that is different from a parent role

SCENARIOS FOR DISCUSSION AND ROLE PLAYING

Following are some sample scenarios that can be used to stimulate discussion and as topics for role-playing.

Who's the Fairest of Them All?

Jane has been married to Mark for 2 years. Her stepdaughter, Maxi, is openly hostile and refuses to respond to Jane's requests of her. Mark is out of town frequently and does not like to discipline his daughter when he is home. Maxi invites her father to attend her school functions but does not want Jane to attend because "she is not comfortable with the situation yet." Jane expresses to Mark that she does not agree with the idea, yet Mark sides with Maxi and informs Jane that she just needs to be patient.

The Great Escape

Malia and Derek have been married 4 years and reside with two of Malia's children from a previous marriage and one child of their own. Both work outside the home and are tired at night. Weekends are typically spent getting the house in order, running errands, and attending parenting events with the children. Derek is unhappy and complains to Malia that they do not seem to have any fun with each other. Malia says she is too tired and hopes that in a few years, when the children are older, she and Derek will have more time together as a couple.

The "Brady Bunch"

Sharla and Todd have been married for 1 year and have five children residing with them. Two are from Sharla's previous marriage, and three are from Todd's first two marriages. The house they live in is too small and requires that two of the male stepsiblings share a room. The teenagers are seeking more autonomy and want to spend less time at home, which requires the use of the family car. Sharla works outside the home but also transports the girls to ballet classes and softball practice on Tuesdays, Thursdays, and Saturdays. She also participates in a carpool for their youngest son's karate lessons. Often these activities conflict, but Todd is unable to assist her with the driving because another child has use of his car in the afternoons. There is insufficient money to purchase another automobile, and both parents agree that the activities are important for the children. Sharla and Todd once enjoyed going to the lake for fishing and boating, but they recently realized they had not done so in quite a while.

'Til Death Do Us Part

Pam and Paul married 6 months ago and have two children from Pam's prior marriage. Paul does not have any biological children, but he was close to his stepdaughter from his previous marriage. Paul's former wife will not allow any contact between Paul and her daughter because she believes that Pam would be a "bad influence" on her daughter. Paul has no legal recourse, but he misses the child a great deal. He had raised her from the time she was an infant. Paul feels guilty for the divorce and is withdrawn and depressed much of the time. Pam interprets his behavior as being regretful that he left his former wife. Paul resists talking to Pam about his guilt because she reacts angrily.

The Birds and the Bees Revisited

Robin and Justin have been married for 3 years, and each has a son and a daughter from previous marriages. Justin's son and Robin's daughter are in the same grade in school and have some of the same friends. Lately, Robin has noticed that her daughter is not dressing properly around the house and enters her stepbrother's room without knocking and when inappropriately dressed. One day Justin came home early from work and found the two stepsiblings in their underclothing on the family room sofa. They seemed embarrassed, but later when Robin confronted her daughter she was told that she was overreacting and being ridiculous.

CONCLUSION

The blending family is a unique family constellation that requires special considerations from therapists who work with them. Some of the issues these families face include the usage of joint monies, creating couple time together, parenting with two households, rule setting, grieving the previous family structure, and step-parent-stepchild relationships.

Sometimes, the manner in which these issues are addressed depends on the ages of the children and the life stages of the adults. However, there are predictable stages through which most stepfamilies progress, from the fantasy stage, through assimilation, awareness, airing differences, action, and intimacy to resolution. Stepfamilies need to be made aware that these are normal stages that require time and effort to negotiate successfully.

Once the family members can relinquish the myth that they should interact the way a biological nuclear family does, they can define their roles more realistically and can negotiate rules more appropriate for all family members. The partners must create clear boundaries and they must establish time for themselves as a couple. In healthy stepfamilies, the development of love between stepparent and stepchild is viewed as a gradual process that may never develop as the parents would like. However, a realistic, consistent relationship can be defined for each parent and child. Blending couples become aware that the challenge of creating a new family structure is a long, complicated one that can be very gratifying for all family members if they can be flexible and patient.

15

Dual-Career Couples

KEY CONCEPTS

- Changes in society, including the rising number of women in the workplace, have created new configurations in the roles of present-day couples.
- The two-career family has grown to become the most prevalent U.S. family configuration.
- Dual-career couples face special external stressors, such as role overload and role conflict associated with their pioneering lifestyle.
- Dual-career partners are often in conflict with each other because everything must be negotiated. Full agendas lead to lack of intimacy.
- Gender-role ideologies are key factors that influence the couple's ability to navigate the dual-career lifestyle successfully.
- The integrated model of couples therapy applies to dual-career couples. The assessment phase may involve career assessment, and at Stages 4 and 5, interventions are mostly aimed at greater intimacy.
- Implementing rituals and marriage enrichment programs are two specific methods that can aid dual-career couples by preventing communication and negotiation breakdown.

If I had known what it was like to have it all, I might have settled for less.
(Wagner, 1986, p.184)

SOCIOLOGICAL CONTEXT: UPHEAVAL IN THE FAMILY

The feminist movement in the 1960s began to broaden men's and women's ideas about the boundaries of the narrowly prescribed self-definitions of the 1950s. As changing ideas about the traditional roles of women and men grew stronger, the financial setbacks of the 1970s and 1980s made two incomes almost a necessity for survival for many families. Between 1970 and 1982, the number of career women jumped from 18.4 million to 25.8 million (40%) (Paddock & Schwartz, 1986), and that number has been rising 7% annually. The dominant lifestyle in America has shifted from the single breadwinner to the family with two jobs, so that dual-career (as opposed to dual-job) couples constitute 20% of all working couples (Stoltz-Loike, 1992).

In addition, the goal of self-fulfillment—to "be all that you can be"—has grown in prominence in the U.S. psyche over the past decades. Women work to enhance self-esteem and achieve self-actualization as well as for economic reasons. When considered with the skyrocketing divorce rate over this same period of time, the upheaval in the American family is unprecedented.

Dual-career couples at the turn of the 21st century are pioneers who are carving a new identity without much cultural support (Pleck, 1985). These members of a "Brave New Marriage" (Alger, 1991) cannot look to their parents' generation for successful role models. Their lifestyle is stressful, energetic, and demanding, and the pressures leave them isolated and lacking social support from friends. Institutions such as the workplace, the church, and the schools often do not support families with two working parents (Hoffman & Hoffman, 1985). Quality child care is hard to come by, and family-leave policies have yet to be implemented in most companies.

THE DUAL-CAREER COUPLE DEFINED

The dual-career couple was first described by Rapoport and Rapoport (1971) as an arrangement where both people pursue jobs that are personally fulfilling, have a developmental sequence or career ladder, and require a high degree of commitment. Both individuals are highly qualified and work in jobs that require responsibility (Yogev, 1983). The term *dual-career* also suggests that decisions are based on what is best for both careers (Hertz, 1991). For example, the family may no longer automatically move when Dad is offered a transfer. He may seek another job in the local area if his wife's job is more important to the couple's joint career.

Although this standard definition will guide our discussion in this chapter, it is well to remember that another group of "dual-job" couples exist. These couples are lower in socioeconomic status than the professional couples described as dual-career, but they also experience similar conflicts whether or not their jobs require a similar amount of commitment. Many of the same issues that trouble professional couples are also concerns for dual-job couples. For many counselors and therapists, dual-job clients are more common.

THE LIFESTYLE'S EFFECT ON THE COUPLE

As we have noted, the nature of the committed couple relationship has changed in the last three decades through a combination of economic forces and consciousness raising. There are both benefits and losses in the new arrangements between couples; as one corollary of Murphy's Law states, "Every solution creates new problems." Still, there is no foreseeable return to the old one-paycheck/one-stays-home arrangement. Couples who survive on one income are less likely to achieve financially, and having one member as a full-time homemaker is no longer the socially approved norm. Individuals who stay home to take care of children and attend to family maintenance are unlikely to obtain the same kind of support that they did in the past (Stoltz-Loike, 1992).

Early studies of dual-career couples (Axelson, 1963; Blood, 1963) found that changing the family structure by adding a working wife resulted in more conflict and less marital happiness. A blurring of the gender roles was thought to be the cause of conflict in shared tasks. Later studies (Burke & Weir, 1976; Poloma & Garland, 1971; St. John-Parsons, 1978) did not find a blurring of roles or increased conflict; they found more marital happiness and satisfaction as well as more sharing and enjoyment. But more recent findings (Thomas, Albrecht, & White, 1984; Yogev, 1983) have suggested that there are significant couples problems (both intrapersonal and interpersonal) associated with the division of child care and housework caused by this novel arrangement. Compared to the average divorce rate, divorce rates are significantly higher for professional women and women with higher salaries. With demanding schedules, multiple-role responsibilities, diverse goals, and strong needs for achievement, the two-profession marriage is now considered to be more conflict-ridden and unstable. Conflict is not unique to dual-career couples, of course; it is merely that the continuous nature of the conflict presents challenges to the quality of day-to-day interactions (Berman, Sacks, & Lief, 1975; Hertz, 1991).

SOURCES OF CONFLICT AND SUPPORT IN THE DUAL-CAREER LIFESTYLE

Stress affects both the happiness of each person in the dual-career couple and the content and number of conflicts (Guelzow, Bird, & Koball, 1991; Rice, 1979). Two general groups of stressors can be identified: internal and external. External stressors are the pressures coming from the environment, work, and the realities of life, such as child care arrangements. Internal stressors are individual dysfunctional beliefs and psychological needs that cause discomfort.

External Stressors

Role Overload
Role overload is a sociological term referring to the taking on of more work than one can manage in a specific role or roles. Dual-career couples must assume the roles of both workers and homemakers, requiring large responsibilities for each role, especially if children are present. Role overload creates stress and strain in a relationship because there is less emphasis on the rewarding aspects of interaction and more on maintenance and scheduling functions.

Because the dual-career arrangement allows less flexibility in scheduling, dual-career couples spend more time discussing and negotiating. This leads to a diminishing of intimacy because there is less time to discuss emotional or internal sources of conflict. External demands need to be discussed early enough in the therapy process so that time remains to discuss those more personal internal ones.

Role Conflict

Role conflict is usually divided into two categories for dual-career couples: professional/parent conflict and professional/spouse conflict (Burley, 1991). Conflict occurs when priorities and unexpected events arise. Meetings set up months in advance coincide with a child's illness and create a professional/parent role conflict. Similarly, the professional role and spouse role conflict when duties, important responsibilities, and family functions coincide with crucial work duties. Role conflict is a dilemma when it becomes difficult to decide where to spend one's time, energy, and resources. Can I afford to take a 3-day weekend for my wedding anniversary, or should I postpone it to next year after the merger goes through?

Work/Family Spillover

Job satisfaction and marital satisfaction are correlated in dual-career couples (Klein, 1988). In other words, happiness at work and at home seem to go together. It is also true that unhappiness at work can be brought home. *Work/family spillover* refers to the tendency to take work problems home at the end of the day, and frustration or anger is commonly displaced on family members.

Family/Work Spillover

Family/work spillover happens when problems at home are taken to work. Burley (1991) found that there is less tolerance for family spillover in the workplace for men than for women. The effect of family/work spillover on the couple may be increased conflict because of a perceived inequity when one person takes more time off for child-oriented activities. Women are often more willing to take time off work for family problems, and they expect their partners to do the same. Women typically attend more PTA meetings, make more doctor and dentist visits for the children, and even attend more Little League games. Birthday presents, letter writing, and other family obligations are an expected part of the woman's role. Later in the ordinary developmental cycle, an ailing parent who needs continuing care will often become the wife's responsibility, even if it is the husband's parent who needs caretaking.

Dividing Housework and Child Care

If the dual-career couple is described as two husbands and no wife (Rapoport & Rapoport, 1971, 1976), a big question becomes, "Who is going to do what has traditionally been the wife's work?" The issue of dividing what has been called "the second shift" (housework and child care) is a major stumbling block for many dual-career couples. The career of homemaking is no longer desired by either member of the dual-career couple (Hertz, 1991), but both members may still view the house as the woman's domain. It has been found that married women do more housework than do cohabiting women, which suggests that, once married, many women feel that they must assume their traditional gender-related behavior (Shelton & John, 1993). Although this might seem to be an easily solved problem, its roots reach deep into the upbringing of both men and women.

The issues of inequity and shared responsibility also surface in childrearing. Even if couples have hired child care such as a nanny or baby-sitter, the women normally oversee these arrangements. For equity to be achieved, women must be able to gently relinquish their control and not second-guess their partners, and men must initiate fathering and take a real interest in childrearing. When men do take a more active role, families are changed because children look to both parents for nurturance and support. This issue, which divides so many couples, can also be framed as an educational problem: Do couples need to be reeducated in order to deal with the housework-childcare problem? To this end, some attempts have been made to establish family life education programs aimed at resolving this knotty problem (see Hawkins, Roberts, Christiansen, & Marshall, 1994).

Children and the Dual-Career Couple

Research has shown that there is a life cycle stage associated with the problems of balancing work and family demands (see Higgins, Duxbury, & Lee, 1994; Keith & Schafer, 1991). This is the stage of the family life cycle that involves the conceiving, raising and launching of children. In the beginning, the dispute about whether or not to have children may be a major concern for couples. Many dual-career couples become DINCs—Double Income No Children. Although this choice may be agreed on, the loss they suffer may be a hidden and pervasive problem. Schlossberg (1993) has written about the impact on mental health of nonevents—things that one expects to happen as part of the normal development of life but that do not occur.

When a dual-career couple does decide to have children, it can send the family and the couple relationship into a tailspin (Sefton, 1990). In a crowded schedule, a child's needs can become a "wild card" that throws carefully crafted arrangements into disarray. Health maintenance, leisure and couple activities, and work responsibilities may all be reduced when a child enters the equation. Dual-career couples, who must plan so much of their lives, are astounded at the amount of flexibility that having a baby now requires of them.

As children grow beyond the day care and early childhood illness that wreak havoc with work commitments, parents start to take a breather. Now different demands arise. Parents must take time from work to deal with transportation conflicts, medical and dental work, soccer games, and school awards, not to mention the time required to be a listening ear for adolescent ups and downs. It is a hectic time for most families but even more so for the dual-career couple, because no one person is always present in the home to direct traffic.

Multicultural Issues

Evidence from other countries including Australia (Sefton, 1990) and India (Aleem & Khandelwal, 1988; Sekaran, 1985) suggests that the dilemmas facing dual-career couples in other cultures are rather similar to the issues discussed above. Still, there are special challenges based on cultural background, ethnicity, and race that make some dual-career couples special. One emerging group is the dual-career African American couple. Thomas (1990) studied 82 such couples and found that typical problems included difficulty finding affordable, high-quality child care; inequitable distribution of family chores; dealing with money issues; and "selfishness" of the partner. Most of these issues are expected to be problems for all dual-career couples, but several are specific because of racial, cultural, or socioeconomic differences:

1. Racial discrimination on the job can spill over to family life.
2. When financial crises arise, many African American couples cannot rely on extended family for support because they are more likely to have economically disadvantaged families.
3. The couple may feel conflicted about living an affluent lifestyle while relatives are struggling.
4. African American couples trying to expose their children to African American culture and values must compete with those predominant in the majority culture.
5. The professional African American on the job often feels isolated in a primarily white workplace. This may extend to the neighborhood as well, as one can feel isolated as an affluent African American in a primarily black lower-class neighborhood as well as in a primarily white area.

Internal Stressors

Early Gender-Role Socialization

Being a member of a dual-career couple forces one to adopt behaviors, if not attitudes, that are likely to be inconsistent with one's upbringing (Yogev, 1983). The man must learn to change diapers, cook dinner, and be an appropriate "ornament" to the woman's success. The woman must assert herself at work, take care of her own car, cut the grass, and coach the soccer team. The sex-role ideology of the couple is very important in determining how comfortable partners feel in making this transition. For many, resentment can grow when they are forced to give up deeply ingrained ideas about themselves. A man may feel that he is unmanly even if he agrees to do "woman's work," and a woman may resent the fact that her husband is not taking care of her in a protective role and that she must take on tasks that are not hers.

High Achievement Needs

Dual-career couples almost by definition are high achievers and tend to look on their family responsibilities and duties as tasks to be accomplished. As a result, the bills get paid and the pool gets cleaned, but the emotional life of the couple may suffer. In a related study, Rice (1979) found that members of dual-career couples are sometimes rigid and find it difficult to express their feelings. They have learned in their professional lives to treat problems rationally and so tend to be intellectualizers. Consequently, they tend to deny emotional problems. They may even view the relationship itself as an achievement, and so when the lifestyle fails, it may also be met with denial.

High achievement needs have other implications for the relationship between two people. Dual-career couples can become competitive with each other rather than supportive, creating "dueling careers" (McCook, Folzer, Charlesworth, & Scholl, 1991). Therapists working dealing with dual-career couples must ask their clients to look at subtle forms of competitiveness between them as well as competitiveness on the career front.

No Time for Intimacy

As a relationship progresses, couples learn that their partners cannot fulfill all of their social, intellectual, emotional, and recreational needs. Because the lives of dual-career couples are hectic, partners have less time to spend with each other and less time to spend with friends. Maintaining friendships may take away time from one's primary relationship. Some couples may seek to get many of their intimacy needs met with co-workers or other family members other than their partner. Taking one's partner for granted is an old story but is especially damaging in the highly regimented world of many dual-career couples, where time is at a premium.

Special Issues for Men

Rapoport and Rapoport (1971) talked about an "identity tension line," which refers to the amount of traditionally feminine activity a man could engage in before feeling he had lost a sense of masculine identity. Women also have such an identity tension line: How much traditionally masculine behavior can a well-socialized woman engage in before feeling she is less feminine? In other words, the identity tension line is how far someone is willing to go before reaching a point of discomfort that threatens self-esteem. Keith and Schafer (1980) found a linkage between involvement in "feminine" household jobs and depression in dual-career men. Our experience as couples therapists suggests that men generally have a lower threshold for such activities than women do, possibly because of the link between feminine behaviors and homosexuality. Homophobia is a subtle and deeply rooted fear held by most men.

Men have been expected to assume the role of provider in a male-female relationship. Obviously, a woman who is self-sufficient or who is more successful than her male partner represents a threat to this socialized gender role. Pleck (1978) found that husbands accept wives' employment as long as it does not compete with their own careers in terms of prestige, earnings, or commitment demands. According to Yogev (1983), men in the lower socioeconomic classes find their working wives to be a threat to their identity, and they express a sense of having failed.

There is evidence, though, that the gender gap is narrowing (Holden, 1991) and that men are taking a greater part in housework and child care (Coverman & Sheley, 1986). Men are learning to shift their priorities and better balance home and career. Ultimately this shift will change the traditional role of men and reduce role overload and conflict for their partners as well(Gilbert, 1985).

Special Issues for Women

Stoltz-Loike (1992) asserts that "dual-career issues largely remain women's issues" (p. xxi). Women are more likely than men are to base career decisions on family needs, and women continue to bear a disproportionate amount of the responsibility for home and child care, even when both partners work. Women are thus more likely to report role overload than men are. Women become resentful about this imbalance, and conflict between the partners may ensue.

As one might expect, women feel more role conflict when their career interferes with other responsibilities. For men, high career commitment is the norm. Although women may possess more flexible attitudes about engaging in "male behavior," they still face gender-role dilemmas. When a mother leaves her child at day care, she faces this issue. Feelings of guilt and fear about the child's well-being are constant pressures for a woman.

Corporate America has not yet caught up with the social innovation of the dual-career couple (Hatcher, 1991). Companies still hire individuals, not couples or families. Traditionally, children have been the purview of the corporate wife, not of the company. Women who work in these kinds of traditional companies face "a test of manhood"; the test is, "Can you have children without letting it affect your career?" (Hertz, 1991). The increased stress caused by this expectation that nothing must be allowed to "slide" affects women's feelings about work and for many becomes a self-esteem issue when faced with choices between mothering and career.

Career Counseling Issues

Career planning has always been seen as an individual enterprise in which one's interests, abilities, and values are assessed and fit to a potential work environment. Career planning in the next century will likely involve both members of the couple if the trend toward rapid job change, volatile hiring and layoffs, and geographic mobility of the culture continues. Following are some of the career problems that dual-career couples face.

1. Whose career should take precedence? Should one member take up the slack in child care and housework because the other's job is more promising to the couple?
2. When one member receives a promotion on the other side of the country or the other side of the world, should the other member be expected to start over in his or her career?
3. When two professionals decide to get married and both live in different locales, should one give up his or her job or should they develop a "commuter marriage," seeing each other on the weekends? (O'Neil, Fishman, & Kinsella-Shaw, 1987).

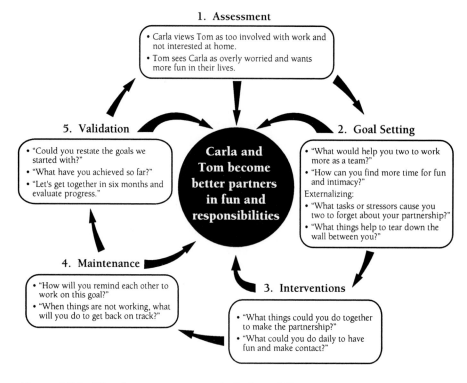

Figure 15.1   The therapy process with Carla and Tom

Benefits of the Dual-Career Lifestyle

Given all the problem issues we have outlined, it is important to remember that there are many positive aspects of a couple arrangement where both individuals lead stimulating and productive lives (Gilbert, 1988). A partner who has many interests is more exciting (Russo, 1987). The quality of conversations and personal support regarding career issues are likely to be factors that enhance the relationship (Paddock & Schwartz, 1986). A working partner is also better able to be supportive and give career guidance than is one who does not work (Shaevitz & Shaevitz, 1980).

An important benefit of the dual-career lifestyle is that the couple is better off financially. Couples who make the most money report a better quality of life (Hoseknecht & Spanier, 1980). Anxiety may be reduced because there is less worry about the fluctuations of a single salary. There is also the opportunity for one partner to develop a venture that does not immediately pay off and can be supported initially by the other's income (Hertz, 1991). Money can buffer many of the stressors that all couples face, including child care, transportation conflicts, and household maintenance.

THE INTEGRATIVE MODEL AND DUAL-CAREER COUPLES

Case Example: Carla and Tom

Carla is a 32-year-old, newly established real estate broker who has been married for 5 years to Tom, an insurance executive in the early stages of a promising career. The couple has a 2-year-old child who stays home with a baby-sitter most days but goes twice a week to a day care center near the wife's job. The couple had moved to Seattle, far from their families in the Northeast, because of Tom's job, and it took some time for Carla to find a position that she enjoyed and that seemed to have the possibility of increased earnings. Her career is now on the upswing, and, due to successes in the commercial area, she is earning more than her husband. Because of the couple's hectic schedules and 10- to 12-hour workdays, the couple has only weekends together and a little time in the evenings that they generally devote to playing with their daughter and getting her to bed. Over the past year, Tom has taken up playing golf during the summer months and a weekly card game at his boss's house during the winter. Carla spends most of her at-home time doing child care, and often works on her home computer when she is not otherwise engaged. Both members of the couple feel that they are estranged from one another. The frequency of sex has decreased, as has the amount of free time the couple spends together. They admit they are avoiding each other.

The couple comes to therapy with the following concerns:

1. Carla complains that Tom is never at home and does not share enough of the responsibilities in the raising of their child.
2. Tom complains that he and Carla can never get away by themselves for a weekend and that they never have any time together as a couple. When they are together, Carla worries about their child, her work, and home maintenance concerns. Tom says she is not "a fun person to be with."
3. Carla responds that she feels guilty when they spend time away from their daughter and that it is difficult for her to relax away from home. She admits that she is serious most of the time but feels that with work, home, and child care responsibilities, she is overwhelmed. Tom could help out by taking on more responsibilities.
4. Tom replies that he works hard and deserves some play time. He adds that Carla always corrects him when he is caring for their daughter and he feels shut out by the two of them.

Application of the Integrated Model: Dual-Career Couples

By this point, the process of the integrative model should be familiar. Rather than examine a lengthy case example, refer to Figure 15.1, which shows the therapy process for Tom and Carla. In the last four steps of the model, we have included some therapist questions that help the couple focus on the task at each stage.

At the assessment and interactive definition stage, Tom and Carla both have the opportunity to express concerns about their relationship; by the end of this phase, they have generated an interactive definition. In this case, they agree that "the relationship is not an equal partnership and there is little fun." Although they are not sure just what solving this might entail—nor are they are confident that this is achievable—it is clear that solving this would meet the needs of both individuals and would enhance their relationship.

In Figure 15.1, the box for goal setting (stage 2) contains some questions that help Carla and Tom both think about some potential outcomes and externalize the problem. In the intervening stage (stage 3), the two are asked to brainstorm some ways they might change the relationship to make it a more equal partnership and develop more fun and intimacy. In the maintenance phase (stage 4), the therapist indicates that relapse is always a possibility and urges the couple to consider some plans to deal with backsliding and to continue to work for change. Finally, in the validation stage (5), the therapist asks the couple to evaluate progress and plan a follow-up session.

Stage 1: Assessment and Obtaining an Interactive Definition of the Problem

Assessment with the dual-career couple can take several directions. Two important areas to look at are the couple's adherence to traditional family ideology and happiness or marital satisfaction. Some proprietary and nonproprietary tests have been developed for this purpose (Spanier, 1976; Stoltz-Loike, 1992). One paper-and-pencil test is the SRES, which measures egalitarian attitudes. It is available from Sigma Assessment Systems. Informal assessment devices such as the Gender Role Survey included in this chapter can help start the discussion toward obtaining an interactive definition of the problem. If a genogram has been completed, it can be referred to at this point and certainly male/female roles should be addressed even in the absence of assessment devices.

Listed below are several other thoughts to keep in mind in the initial assessment of dual-career couples (Kater, 1985; O'Neil et al., 1987):

1. Discuss the careers of each couple in the assessment phase of the integrated model. Also, address the issue of the "joint career" as a way of seeing the partners' commitment to this arena. The joint career encompasses the career, leisure, and lifestyle goals that the partners have in common.
2. Take a developmental history and assess career transitions and career problems.
3. Assess and treat gender-role dilemmas as couple problems, rather than blaming one member's attitude.
4. Help the partners identify lifestyle priorities and the role of children in their lives.
5. Determine whether the couple experiences inequity in decision making and in assuming responsibilities. Help them renegotiate answers to these problems.
6. Assess communication and negotiation skills.

SPECIFIC INTERVENTION METHODS

Addressing Sex-Role Ideologies Directly

For some couples, the first time both partners have different ideas about a major decision, such as the purchase of a car or house, is the first time that the sex-role ideologies of the couple become painfully obvious. One way this is expressed is in the question, "Who is (really) the boss?" From that vantage point, the partners in a dual-career relationship, who both have high control needs and advanced problem-solving skills, become two conductors in the same orchestra (Hertz, 1991). Therapists attempt to renegotiate this problem in interactive terms and like to propose a different question: "How can the couple negotiate a relationship that is perceived as equitable with shared decision making?" This takes a good deal of negotiation and implies that both members of the couple are willing to let go of their family of origin expectations about what a man does or what a woman does. When role problems have been negotiated in a way that satisfies both members of the couple, the general relationship quality is enhanced (Bird & Bird, 1986; Hosenecht & Spanier, 1980).

It seems imperative that both men and women be more flexible in their sex-role definitions for the relationships of the future to survive. It is now becoming clear that the acceptance of nontraditional gender-role orientations is highly related to marital satisfaction (Ray, 1990). In short, the couple's ability to negotiate an equitable division of labor and the partners' willingness to cross over traditional gender boundaries bode well for the couple's overall marital health (Vannoy-Hiller & Philliber, 1989).

With these findings in mind, the question is, "Should the therapist actively attempt to move couples toward equitable distribution of responsibilities, and should the therapist confront gender-role allegiance when it interferes with the relationship?" For many therapists, this question raises ethical and practical issues. There is something almost sacred about statements such as "A man's home is his castle" and "A woman's work is never done." Should one cast doubt on a client's upbringing, and is it practical to change something so basic and deeply ingrained? Are we as therapists biting off more than we can chew?

The therapist risks losing the client if these issues are confronted too early in therapy. Still, the data seem to be overwhelming that the couple's basic attitudes about division of labor and gender roles are crucial to problem resolution. It is our position that in many instances (not just the dual-career couple) the therapist is in the business of helping each member through gender-role transitions, expanding each person's notions about assigned responsibilities, and dealing with guilt, confusion, anxiety threat, and even shame (O'Neil, Fishman, & Kinsella-Shaw, 1987).

The therapist's best approach to this kind of issue may be in a group psychoeducational format, where these issues can be explored in a less threatening atmosphere and where subtle peer pressure can help shift attitudes. This modality is described in the next section. Another strategy in couples therapy is the use of surveys or exercises that the couple can complete on the spot or as homework. An example

Box 15.1
Gender-Role Survey
(Each member completes a separate copy.)

Please answer each of the following questions, which we will discuss together.

- As you were growing up, what jobs around the house did your father or the adult male member of the household routinely perform?
- What jobs did your mother or another female adult perform regularly?
- How were tasks divided among siblings? Who did what?
- Who performs each of the following tasks around your house now? Check the appropriate space.

	Mainly Man	Mainly Women	Together	Half/Half
Lawn and garden care	_____	_____	_____	_____
Planning vacations	_____	_____	_____	_____
Household repairs	_____	_____	_____	_____
Caring for cars	_____	_____	_____	_____
Paying bills	_____	_____	_____	_____
Cooking meals	_____	_____	_____	_____
Transporting children	_____	_____	_____	_____
Bathing and bedtime for children	_____	_____	_____	_____
Cleaning house	_____	_____	_____	_____
Doing laundry	_____	_____	_____	_____

- Does conflict over household responsibilities ever become a problem for you as a couple?
- As you look over the list, does there appear to be an equal distribution between the two of you?
- Which of these jobs were you responsible for when you were growing up?
- If friends or family came to see you, would you feel uncomfortable performing any of these jobs in their presence?
- Do you and your partner spend equal amounts of time in leisure activities during a typical week?
- Do you think your spouse spends too much or too little time on maintenance activities?
- Would you like to see any of these responsibilities reassigned? If so, what do you suggest?

of a gender-role survey is shown in Box 15.1. Following completion of the exercise, the partners discuss their findings with the therapist. The survey provides an assessment of attitudes for the therapist while at the same time bringing awareness to the participants. No matter how this issue is addressed, it can be negotiated as a shared problem in the integrated model.

Enrichment Programs

Enrichment programs are psychoeducational formats for couples who are not in crisis. The partners may be experiencing conflict, but the prevention of problems is ordinarily the aim rather than the resolution of specific difficulties. Many of these seminars are now specifically aimed at dual-career couples.

Typically, these sessions are conducted with 4 to 8 couples meeting anywhere from 4 to 12 times a week. The dual-career enrichment program helps couples by allowing them to interact with each other and with other couples. As a group, the couples can discuss mutual difficulties with the dual-career lifestyle, which tends to normalize problems and provide support and reinforcement. It is also a reevaluation opportunity, where one can examine values and priorities concerning work and family. The issues of gender-role socialization and division of work can be introduced by a neutral party (the workshop organizers). Usually, couples are also trained in better communication and are encouraged to develop more supportive relationships (Avis, 1986). Young couples seem to respond well to this approach.

Amatea and Cross (1983) developed a workshop format for dual-career couples involving five phases:

Phase I: Examining the Dual-Career Lifestyle. The couples take turns sharing the benefits and problems inherent in the lifestyle.

Phase II: Assessing Role Conflict and Coping Styles. This is a more in-depth look at how each member of the couple copes with stress.

Phase III: Clarifying and Prioritizing Personal Expectations. Here the major focus is on helping each individual examine and share personal expectations. Typically self-expectations and high achievement needs are identified as major stressors.

Phase IV: Joint Decision Making as a Dual-Career Couple. In this phase, the leaders introduce a model of joint decision making.

Phase V: Building the Collaborative Relationship. This final phase focuses on skills that lead to better communication, negotiation, and understanding. This provides an additional opportunity for the leaders and group members to identify common communication boondoggles such as mind reading, keeping score, and jumping to conclusions.

Problems and Precautions

The workshop format described above was held over a weekend: 3 hours on Friday night and 7 hours on Saturday. Another alternative is to make it a weekly event for 2 hours over a 5-week period. A weekly get-together even for a short period of time can be beneficial to the relationship, in addition to whatever is learned in the workshop.

There are several pitfalls when working with couples in a therapy group format, but many of them are avoided in a structured workshop such as this. In a workshop, couples are asked to interact on specific topics, and unhealthy alliances among members are minimized by the brevity of the workshop. Still, problem members who dominate discussions or who absent themselves by their silence are two major problems in these groups. In a longer-term group, the members might be able to confront these behaviors, but in a short-term educational format, the responsibility to deal immediately with antitherapeutic behaviors falls on the leaders. In such cases, the leader should be straightforward with monopolizers or silent members and should discuss their behavior with them privately after the meeting.

Rituals for Dual-Career Couples

As one becomes wrapped up in the demands of work, it is easy to let one's own accomplishments and those of one's partner slip by without much recognition. When you are on the fast track, there is always another mountain to climb. Sometimes even jealousy and competition prevent people from celebrating a partner's success. One way that families have learned to celebrate successes and make connections is through the use of rituals.

As we discussed in an earlier chapter, rituals are repetitive symbolic gestures or behaviors that help people feel more in control of their lives. Just as decorations for a religious holiday such as Christmas, Hannukah, or Diwali serve to bind people together, rituals can be established between couples for the same purpose: to confirm feelings, to reinforce commitment, and to provide a joint acknowledgment that the relationship exists (Paddock & Schwartz, 1986).

Encouraging Dual-Career Couples to Establish Rituals

The forces working against dual-career couples are strong, as is the tendency for couples to neglect their relationships under the pressures of work. Getting a couple to institute rituals as a therapeutic technique is one way to prevent serious fractures. However, it is better used as a long-term strategy to promote the health of a relationship or a family rather than for use in a crisis. Rituals are especially effective when the presenting problem involves feelings of estrangement, neglect, and competition. Instituting rituals is a couple's way of announcing that the two are a family, both to each other and to the world at large. In the past, dinner at 6:00 served this function, but for the dual-career couple this is not always possible. Instead, couples must be creative in formulating their own traditions that reinforce bonding. Here are a few suggestions.

Saying good-night to everyone in the household or giving a kiss before falling asleep.
Having a party following a promotion.
Establishing a once-a-month "date" for the couple.

SCENARIOS FOR DISCUSSION AND ROLE PLAYING

Following are some sample scenarios that can be used to stimulate discussion and as topics for role-playing.

Great Expectations

The woman thinks that the wedding vows have been violated. She never intended to work full-time outside of the home and feels forced by economics and that her husband has failed to provide for her. Alternatively, she wants to quit working because they now earn enough money to afford her return to being a full-time homemaker. He is angry because he is enjoying their comfortable economic status and worries that she wants to have another baby.

Walking the Walk

The husband is verbally supportive of his wife's returning to work but is now experiencing a lot of discomfort and time pressure. Now he is faced with spending additional time in maintenance tasks such as housework and child care. He resents the intrusion on his free time. She is confused because he says the right things but she doesn't feel supported. She feels guilty about asking him to do more and tends to back down and take over when he complains.

Who's in Charge?

Both partners are attorneys and they have two children. She is the managing partner in the firm and he is a partner. Although the husband is supportive of his wife's working and shares equally in housework and child care, he feels that he is subordinate to his wife at home as well as at work. The major decisions are always made or managed by her. He feels left out of the children's lives because they prefer their mother, and he thinks she overrules his discipline and undermines his authority with the children. She indicates that she does not often agree with his ideas about childrearing. She finds him too lenient and does not feel he is totally committed at work.

Shot Down

His career fizzles while hers takes off. She covers up her successes because it makes him feel worse. She allows him to make decisions she doesn't necessarily agree with to compensate. They do not discuss the fact that he is feeling unsuccessful and is jealous.

Ships Passing

The husband works every night until 7:00 P.M. He begins his day at 6:00 A.M. and is exhausted when he comes home. His wife's job is less demanding. She feels neglected because he often works weekends and is too tired during the week to do anything but watch TV following dinner. He is satisfied with the arrangement because he likes being alone. He is a morning person; she likes to stay up late.

Falling Asleep

The wife has a demanding job and the husband is tired of hearing about it all the time. The wife is an accountant; the husband is a respiratory therapist. Her job is technical and boring to him. She is under a lot of stress and needs a way to let off steam. Neither is feeling close to each other.

Mom Goes Back to Work (or School)

(See Houser, Konstam, & Ham, 1990.) The wife returns to school after being a mother and homemaker for 10 years. The couple's three children are all in school. Still, the mother's class schedule makes it impossible for her to take the two oldest children to soccer practice two days a week. Everyone appears resentful that dinner is often delayed. She develops headaches and chronic neck pain and says she feels "overwhelmed." She adds, "Maybe going back to school right now is not a very good idea." Her husband says he is supportive but also feels neglected.

Mr. Mom Meets Cinderella

He is egalitarian in his ideas about sex roles. He cooks, likes taking care of the children, and has never been ambitious at work. She no longer finds him attractive. Although she appreciates his "help" around the house, she secretly feels he is "not much of a man." He is satisfied with his life but feels unappreciated and angry at her rejection.

Can I Change Macho Man?

She is living with a man who was raised believing that men and women should have separate responsibilities in the home. Although they have no children, she is tired of doing all the cooking, laundry, and housework while he spends all of his free time with his friends, playing racquetball and softball. He does not understand why she is so upset by this minor issue. They are planning to get married, but she has decided to stand firm on the issue of dividing household responsibilities and is determined they will not get married if he does not change. He says things will change once they are married but feels she is blackmailing him.

CONCLUSION

The dual-career couple at the turn of the century is experimenting with a new lifestyle. Fueled by economic pressures and changing gender roles, the dual-career lifestyle has special stresses and rewards. It has been observed that for the lifestyle to work the traditional roles assigned to men and women *must* change, and the therapist must be part of this process. Because these sex roles are deeply ingrained, they are often not recognized, and yet they form the battleground for many of the conflicts between couples.

The therapist who works with dual-career couples is likely to find intelligent, achievement-oriented, cognitive clients who approach therapy as another task to be managed. They may be as committed to their careers as they are to their relationships, and so career issues should not be neglected, especially if there is competition for time away from home. Dual-career couples are striving to find a way to have two careers and a shared life together. If they succeed, they will have the best of both worlds.

16

Same-Sex Couples

KEY CONCEPTS

- Although there are similarities between the types of issues same-sex couples and other couples face, there are a number of differences that must be addressed in therapy.
- Role models for same-sex couples have been limited. This may cause couples to attempt to fit their relationships into traditional marriage models.
- Same-sex relationships have many of the same stressors that other couples relationships do, but they are also unique. Same-sex couples have special difficulties dealing with their families, work situations, and a legal system that does not recognize their relationship.
- Same-sex couples are as likely as other couples to experience domestic violence.
- Therapists must examine their personal values and beliefs about same-sex couples before they can be effective as clinicians.

SOCIOLOGICAL CONTEXT

It can be very traumatic to be gay or lesbian in a rejecting and hostile society (Berzon, 1988). Although there are larger numbers of Americans who identify themselves as gay or lesbian, homophobia continues to be an issue for many individuals and social institutions (Baptiste, 1987). In the past, just being present in a gay bar could be grounds for legal arrest. Today, homophobia is manifested by rampant discrimination within families with gay or lesbian members, in the workplace, in schools, in the church or synagogue, and in society at large. Discrimination is evident in the way gay men and lesbians are viewed by society and by the terms used to define a marriage.

Terms such as *husband* and *wife* assume that the husband is a man and the wife is a woman. *Lover, partner, significant other, roommate, friend,* or other vague descriptors do not adequately express the committed relationship that many same-sex couples experience. These terms appear to omit same-sex couples who are in a committed relationship (Ussher, 1991).

The media and advertising agencies depict couples as heterosexual and portray relationship satisfaction as achievable by a male and female together. The homosexual bias is also evident in the professional arena. In fact, it was not until 1980 that the American Psychiatric Association removed homosexuality from the list of mental disorders in the *Diagnostic and Statistical Manual.* But the picture is not as bleak as it may appear. There has been a proliferation of research and literature on same-sex therapy issues as society moves beyond the moralistic argument or the etiological debate over whether homosexuality has genetic or environmental roots (Modcrin & Wyers, 1990).

Although there is some debate over the terminology for homosexuality, most prefer the term *gay* for male homosexuals and *lesbian* for female homosexuals. Gay men are identified as those who view themselves as interested in sexual and love relationships with other men, and lesbians are interested in love and sexual relationships with women. It must be noted, however, that some might identify themselves as gay or lesbian without ever having a sexual relationship, either by choice or by circumstance. In fact, one lesbian client reported that "it is safer to be nonsexual and 'pass' in a straight society."

There are many faulty assumptions about being gay or lesbian in a heterosexual society. It is not true that a model for same-sex relationships can be the same as or be a parallel model for heterosexual couples. For example, it is not true that in a gay relationship one man must be the "effeminate" one, while one is more traditionally identified as the "macho male." Nor is it accurate to project an image of the lesbian couple as one where one woman bears masculine traits, while the other is more passive and "feminine." It is also inappropriate to assume that all lesbian women exhibit masculine physical characteristics. Some lesbian women appear very feminine by society's standard. It has also been said that gay men are afraid of women. There is no evidence of misogyny or fear of women as a major characteristic of gay men. Neither must lesbians be "manhaters."

THE GAY OR LESBIAN LIFESTYLE'S EFFECTS ON THE COUPLE

Heterosexual couples have a variety of role models, including families, friends, fictional couples, and famous couples in history. The incongruity between these traditional role models and the needs of same-sex couples is vast (Friedman, 1991). Consequently, applying models of couple development to gay and lesbian couples is likely to be a bad fit.

Stage Model of Relationship Development for Same-Sex Couples

One model that has emerged is a six-stage model developed by Mattison and McWhirter (1987). Although based primarily on gay male couples, the model may also be appropriate for lesbians. There are many similarities among primary relationships regardless of the biological sex or sexual orientation of the individuals, but same-sex couples have unique characteristics that must be identified in order to understand and treat them (Mattison & McWhirter, 1987).

There are two assumptions for understanding this model: (1) each relationship is unique with its own history and life, and (2) each relationship passes through a series of predictable developmental sequences. Each stage provides a typical time frame, but the characteristics may vary from couple to couple (Mattison & McWhirter, 1987).

Stage 1: Blending

During this stage, both partners lose some of the self in the other. This period encompasses the first year of the relationship and is characterized by merging, limerance (intrusive thinking about the partner), intense feelings and idealization of the partner, and frequent sexual activity (Kurdek, 1988). Blending provides relief from loneliness and provides a sense of security and acceptance by the partner. The partners act as a couple and identify themselves as such.

Stage 2: Nesting

Nesting occurs in the second and third years of the relationship and is evidenced by homemaking and compatibility. Homemaking is a symbol of a deeper level of commitment and portrayal of the partners as a couple to society.

Compatibility emerges as the couple becomes more realistic and begins to examine differences as well as similarities. The partners must find a way to get along with each other yet strengthen the growing intimacy of the relationship (Kurdek, 1988). Some lesbians assert, however, that in today's society women are more apt to merge households sooner and may or may not present to society as a lesbian couple, thus earning the appellation "the invisible minority."

Stage 3: Maintaining

This stage encompasses the fourth and fifth years and is characterized by the reemergence of the individual after the couple has learned to accept differences. Risk taking increases as the couple strengthens from the resolution of disagreements and conflict that increases the level of intimacy. The partners also establish couple traditions as they gain confidence in the safety and security of the relationship. Again, mutual traditions may begin much earlier for some couples.

Stage 4: Building

Years 6 through 10 are described as the building stage, highlighted by collaboration, increased productivity, individual independence, and interdependence and dependability of the partners. The partners have found a way to disagree and resolve differences so that they can jointly make couple decisions. They understand they can rely on each other and operate as a couple as they attend to each other's needs and desires.

Stage 5: Releasing

During the 11th through the 20th years, couples establish a deepening trust for each other and for the long-term continuance of the relationship. Couples typically merge their finances and possessions, and they may take each other for granted at times. Security is a consistent theme in this stage. As previously discussed, this merging of resources may occur more quickly for women than for men.

Stage 6: Renewing

The period beyond 20 years is described as achieving security, shifting perspectives, restoring the partnership, and remembering. By this stage, the partners have established a rich history as a couple and have weathered many difficult times. Reliance on each other may be exhibited something like the bonding of the initial stage, where they present themselves as "one" to others in their community. Memories are increasingly important, as is pride in what they have accomplished as a couple. McWhirter and Mattison (1984) described this relationship development as a general movement from limerance and passion toward trust and security.

SOURCES OF CONFLICT IN THE GAY OR LESBIAN LIFESTYLE

As with other couples, relationship stressors for same-sex couples can come from both external and internal sources.

External Factors

Legal System

An important issue facing same-sex couples is the absence of legal privileges granted to heterosexuals. Marriage is not recognized for gay men and lesbians in the United States. This simple fact has implications for automatic inheritance under probate, paid bereavement for family illness or death, the ability to file joint tax returns, reduced family insurance rates, immediate access to each other in an emergency, decision making for an incompetent partner, the right to claim the partner's body after death, or shared parental rights. Parental issues can be extremely problematic. The possibility for adoption for same-sex couples is rare and in some states is illegal. A major deterrent for same-sex couples to present themselves together is the problems they face in custody battles. If a gay or lesbian parent had children in a previous heterosexual marriage, his or her ability to gain custody may be in jeopardy if judged "unfit" because of sexual orientation.

Family of Origin

Frequently there is a lack of emotional and economic support from families when gay men and lesbians "come out" or make their sexual orientation known to their family. Often family members who are opposed to the lifestyle "cutoff" or deny that their relative is gay or lesbian. There can also be legal consequences for the couple when family members omit them from their wills so "someone outside the family will not inherit family money."

Social Pressure

There are many social pressures on same-sex couples that heterosexual couples do not experience (Ussher, 1991). Prejudice is apparent in most social settings, including schools, courts, businesses, housing, medical settings, and churches and synagogues.

There are also gender socialization issues that affect same-sex couples. Our culture has promoted the notion that males are predators in their pursuit of women. Women, on the other hand, are thought to be more passive and dependent on men for survival. Society views gay couples as consisting of two predators and views lesbian couples as consisting of two passive, dependent individuals.

Career

The choice of a suitable career has important considerations for gay and lesbian couples. A lesbian may realize at an early age that she will not ever depend on a man's salary (Hetherington & Orzek, 1989) and may, therefore, choose a traditionally male-dominated profession in order to maximize her earning potential (Browning, Reynolds, & Dworkin, 1991). Because women are still not widely accepted in male-dominated fields, lesbians who choose these occupations may be discriminated against. Similarly, gay men may choose careers that are not traditionally male in order to escape discrimination. Many gay men express the belief that heterosexual women are more supportive of their lifestyles than are heterosexual males.

Both gay men and lesbians must decide whether to work in a setting where sexual orientation must be hidden or to self-disclose and risk discrimination. For example, many gay men and lesbians remain "closeted" in such fields as teaching, child care, and child psychology because of the widespread belief that they recruit children to the same-sex lifestyle or that they are more prone to molest children (Browning, Reynolds, & Dworkin, 1991).

Same-sex couples face the same dual-career issues that heterosexual couples do, but because their relationship is not validated by society, they do not get the support or assistance they require (Hetherington & Orzek, 1989). Many same-sex couples choose to live in large metropolitan areas because of a wider variety of career opportunities and the ability to contact other same-sex couples for support.

Race, Ethnicity, and Socioeconomic Factors

For men and women in some cultures and social strata, gay and lesbian lifestyles violate the culture's role expectations (Chan, 1989; Loiacano, 1989). For example, a lesbian raised in an upper-income family may choose a predominantly male-populated career in order to maximize her earning potential. The chosen career may be considered inappropriate by her family, and she may feel denigrated by family members.

Same-sex, biracial couples who live within a gay or lesbian community report widespread racism (Chan, 1989; Espin, 1987) and anti-Semitism (Beck, 1982). Because coming out to families within some racial or ethnic communities often means rejection and loss of support, survival in a racist culture becomes more difficult. Larger urban areas may be more suitable for same-sex couples because of the availability of a wider variety of racial and ethnic gay and lesbian organizations (Browning, Reynolds, & Dworkin, 1991).

Internal Factors

Identity Development

By "coming out," one is adopting a nontraditional identity that involves restructuring one's self-concept, reorganizing one's personal sense of history, and altering one's relations with others and with society (DeMonteflores & Schultz, 1978). Three phases of self-definition have been identified for lesbians that may apply to gay men in reverse order: (1) critical evaluation of dominant social norms, (2) encounters with stigma and internalized homophobia, and (3) sexual experiences.

Because gay and lesbian couples see themselves as violating social norms, they may come to view themselves in a negative light. Internalized homophobia is the conscious or nonconscious self-hatred that results from growing up with this dilemma. The devaluing of the gay or lesbian self may also be influenced by the attitudes of family members and early care givers.

Marilyn French (1977), in her best-selling novel *The Women's Room*, illustrates this devaluing:

> I don't know when I first knew that I was different. . . . It is not the difference, but the significance placed on that difference that is important . . . and I discovered that my feeling, my difference, had a name, that it was a nasty name, that the way I was, was considered wicked, depraved, sick. . . . I started to withdraw, to watch myself carefully, to dress and act so as not to cause attention to myself, hoping my depraved deviation wouldn't show. (pp. 504–505)

It is certain that antihomosexual expressions by society adversely affect the self-perceptions of gay and lesbian people (Friedman, 1991). Among the consequences of unconscious homophobia include a feeling that one is not entitled to give and receive love. Internalized homophobia is organized around feelings of shame, guilt, anger, and anxiety (Friedman, 1991). These feelings may be manifested in the couple's sexual experiences as lack of commitment to one partner, lack of trust, fear of intimacy, and problems of sexual expression.

Identity Management

Identity management is an ongoing, ever-changing process through which one defines and redefines what it means to be gay or lesbian (Cass, 1979). It has been suggested that increased contact with the gay and lesbian community, as well as a broadening definition of the meaning of *gay* and *lesbian*, creates opportunity for a positive identity even within a homophobic culture (Browning, Reynolds, & Dworkin, 1991).

Coming out to friends and family is an important step toward claiming an integrated identity and is important for self-acceptance and self-esteem (Murphy, 1989). Gay men and lesbians may come out with family and friends in order to decrease feelings of isolation and to maintain a sense of personal integrity (Browning, Reynolds, & Dworkin, 1991). Keeping secrets can be detrimental to a person's self-image and can create feelings of shame and worthlessness. Families often do not respond favorably to admissions of being gay or lesbian. Many parents may feel their own identity is threatened if they accept that they have a gay or lesbian child. Parents may believe they contributed to the homosexuality and berate themselves as having failed. Nongay friends may have less difficulty accepting a friend's disclosure than family members do because they have less at stake in the person's identity and less involvement in his or her future life (Moses & Hawkins, 1982).

Age-Related Factors

The notion that same-sex couples can be happy and grow old together is a new concept in our society (Lee, 1991). One widely recognized difficulty for the aging same-sex couple is the lack of social and legal support. McWhirter and Mattison (1984) describe the stage of development as one of trust and security for the couple. However, the couple must have a strong commitment to address issues ranging from legal constraints to health and medical concerns. Older same-sex couples fear they will not receive adequate care in institutions and senior-services centers because of discrimination (Browning, Reynolds, & Dworkin, 1991). Older gay men and lesbians may have come out during an era when these couples were viewed as sick or sinful. Often, they have abandoned their religious values because of discrimination and may be fearful of death and the afterlife. Many gay men and lesbians do not feel welcome today in mainstream churches.

Fusion or Distance under Stress

Krestan and Bepko (1980) found that a major gender issue for lesbians that is different from gay men is their style of relating, which they call "lesbian fusion." This concept refers to women's socialization process that makes them more homebound, erodes boundaries between them, and fuses them in a dysfunctional way under stress. It has also been described as a "two against the world" posture. Men, on the other hand, tend to distance themselves when under stress, staying away from home, involving themselves in other activities, and experimenting with extra- relationship sexual activity (Carl, 1991).

This difference is not surprising given that traditionally women have been the ones to hold the family together and keep the home intact. In addition, women have been the main source of emotional support for the family. Men still work outside the home and avail themselves of a larger world experience more frequently than women do (Carl, 1991). Lesbians report that they must work outside the home because it takes two women's salaries to support the household.

THERAPY ISSUES FOR SAME-SEX COUPLES

The most common therapy issues for same-sex couples are feelings of anxiety and stress. They also report significant levels of anger, depression, and a sense of alienation from society and family. This sense of aloneness is evident by the lack of support from religious groups and heterosexual friends. A constant theme for many gay men and lesbians is that of grief and loss. Suicidal ideation is cited frequently, especially among adolescents. Family problems, however, are the most traumatic. Many same-sex couples do not seek therapy because of the fear and implications of disclosure of their sexual identity (Savin-Williams, 1994).

There are differences in the presenting issues reported by gay men and lesbians when they seek therapy. Roth (1985) identified the following five issues most often presented by lesbians at the beginning of therapy.

1. Problems of distance and boundary maintenance
2. Problems of sexual expression
3. Problems related to unequal access to resources
4. Problems about ending the relationship, even when one or both have decided to do so
5. Problems arising from stage differences in coming out and in the development and management of each partner's lesbian identity

Couples Issues

George and Behrendt (1987) offer four possibilities for *relationship conflict* in addition to the individual challenges faced by gay men and lesbians.

1. Stereotypic male roles
2. Stereotypic sexual roles
3. Homophobia
4. Sexual dysfunctions

The array of problems identified is substantial. Overall, communication, sexual problems, and problems associated with possible separation were most often identified as the reasons same-sex couples seek help (Modcrin & Wyers, 1990). Table 16.1 lists a number of presenting problems, in rank order.

Specific presenting issues addressed in therapy with these couples focus on relationship interactions and issues surrounding coming out, the lack of appropriate couple rituals, the lack of avenues for meeting partners in nonbar and nonalcoholic atmospheres, legal issues, relationships with children, stepfamily issues, alcohol and substance abuse, AIDS, domestic violence, sexual problems, sexual abuse, and spirituality.

Table 16.1   Types of Problems for Which Professional Help Would Be Sought by Gay and Lesbian Couples, in Rank Order

Problem	Number	Percentage
Communication	30	26%
Sexual	22	19%
Unspecified	17	15%
Impending separation	11	10%
Alcohol or drug	7	6%
Uncertain	6	5%
Problems with children	5	4%
Nonmonogamy	5	4%
Financial	4	4%
Spiritual	3	3%
Pressure	2	2%
AIDS	1	1%
Boredom	1	1%

Source: From "Lesbian and Gay Couples: Where They Turn When Help Is Needed," by M. Modcrin and N. Wyers, *Journal of Gay and Lesbian Psychotherapy, 1*, p. 99. Copyright 1990 by Haworth Press, Inc. Reprinted by permission.

Relationship Interactions

Many of the difficulties experienced in same-sex relationships are centered around role definitions for each partner. Because of the lack of understanding of roles and the associated stress, there is often an imbalance between intimacy and autonomy that can result in either emotional distance or enmeshment (Browning, Reynolds, & Dworkin, 1991). Sometimes couples find themselves merged when they perceive a threat to their relationship or to one member of the couple; and societal homophobia forces them to define and affirm relational boundaries (Browning, Reynolds, & Dworkin, 1991). For example, during a family anniversary, the parents of a gay male might ask their son to come home to celebrate the event. They may ignore his partner and refuse to invite him, thereby arousing anger in the son, who must choose between family and significant relationship.

Coming out can create the greatest amount of stress on the couple, depending on how each partner has addressed the issue with friends, family, and co-workers. For example, Jane may be out to her family and friends but not at work. Susan, her partner, is out to her friends and her co-workers but cannot find the courage to tell her parents. Jane is unable to take Susan with her to work-related social functions, and so she leaves Susan alone quite often. Susan, on the other hand, does not take Jane with her when she goes home for all major holidays, leaving Jane to celebrate without her significant other.

An even more painful experience is when a member of the same-sex couple selects a date of the opposite sex to attend a family outing or work-related activity to mask a homosexual identity. Both become resentful—one feeling that the other will not come out and solidify their relationship, and the other feeling misunderstood. Without accommodation, each can become anxious and angry with the other and perceive a split in the relationship.

Couple Rituals

There are no legal rituals equivalent to marriage for same-sex couples. Weddings can be arranged, but they take place without legal sanctions. Also, depending on "who is out to whom," many family celebrations may be stressful for the same-sex couple because the partners cannot be with each other to provide emotional support during these times, either by choice or exclusion.

Legal Issues

In addition to the issue of marriage, the legal rights of survivorship, and decisions on illness and death, an important legal issue is the effect of gay and lesbian identity on legal rights over children. Some people marry and have children long before they accept their homosexuality. Decisions about how openly homosexual one can be is also influenced by fear of losing children in court decisions. Attempting to retain custody, fighting for joint custody, and fighting for alimony are legal issues gay and lesbian parents must face. An increasing number of gay fathers are seeking, at a minimum, joint custody. These options will continue to bring gay and lesbian issues to the forefront in the legal system, but in doing so they will engender feelings of anger, depression, and resentment for those who find that legal decisions seemingly are made on the basis of sexual orientation.

Child Custody

When children are already present in a gay or lesbian relationship, the role of the nonbiological parent must be considered, as well as the role of the biological parent who may have an influence the child's development. Most children in same-sex households were conceived in the context of a heterosexual relationship. Today, many lesbian women are choosing to have children either within a relationship or as a single parent (Clunis & Green, 1988). Studies have not found any deleterious effects on children raised by lesbian mothers (Falk, 1989). Raising children in same-sex families requires that parents clearly define their parenting roles and identify their support systems outside their families. Lack of role models are frequently cited as problematic for these families (Browning, Reynolds,& Dworkin, 1991).

Alcohol and Substance Abuse

Research indicates that the rates of alcohol abuse are higher for lesbians than for heterosexual women and that lesbians are more apt to be children of alcoholic parents (Glaus, 1989). Internalized homophobia is thought to influence the use of drugs and alcohol, which may be an attempt to numb oneself to emotions and to avoid accepting being gay or lesbian (Browning, Reynolds, & Dworkin, 1991). Thus, chemically dependent gay men and lesbians may be reacting with denial to a hostile environment (Glaus, 1989). Twelve-step programs such as Alcoholics Anonymous (AA) and similar support groups can be helpful, but, again, the issue of coming out will influence the decision to participate in the groups. Fortunately, Alcoholics Anonymous has many established gay and lesbian support groups.

AIDS

Although AIDS is prevalent in many communities, it has popularly been associated with gay men. If a gay man or lesbian tests HIV-positive, not only are they devastated by knowledge of the disease, but they feel the need for renewed secrecy in the workplace or with extended family members. An initial response of depression, fear, and anger permeate the relationship. Fear that the other partner will contract the disease is also a factor. Although gay men may be limiting the number of partners with whom they have sex for fear of contracting the AIDS virus, previous relationships may resurface as topics of conversation between the members of the couple. It is noteworthy that lesbians are currently one of the lowest risk groups.

Domestic Violence

Same-sex couples may not receive the same attention from support groups when domestic violence is reported, but it is clear that violence transcends all socioeconomic classes, all ages, all ethnic groups, and all sexual orientations (Hart, 1986). There is a myth that lesbians, because of their socialization as women, do not perpetrate or encounter domestic violence. Gay men and lesbians have attitudes similar to those of their heterosexual counterparts. These include the belief that people exist for the abuser's well-being, feelings of possessiveness, and the need to dominate. Abuse of alcohol and drugs can also be a factor (Hart, 1986). Unfortunately, in the legal system, abuse of same-sex partners is not always considered to be domestic violence.

Sexual Abuse

A survey by Loulan (1987) found that 38% of lesbians had experienced sexual abuse from a family member or stranger before the age of 18 (Browning, Reynolds, & Dworkin, 1991). Statistics for gay males remain unclear. The high proportion of women who have experienced abuse suggests that one or both partners of a couple may be survivors of abuse. They may be at different stages of awareness or recovery and may have different needs.

Flashbacks can produce anger, frustration, or fear of sexual experiences. Some people believe that their own gay or lesbian identity is a result of the abuse. The abuse, if not addressed as a couple, can create relationship and individual stress similar to the stress that affects heterosexual couples in similar circumstances. However, support groups for gay men and lesbians may be limited in number, and support groups for partners of survivors are almost nonexistent.

Sexual Problems

Differences in and absence of sexual desire are the most frequently reported problems of lesbians (Hall, 1987). Lack of desire is related to lack of time, lack of energy, and lack of understanding of one's partner. Absence of desire may be related to mixed messages women receive in our culture about female sexuality, added to the negative messages about lesbian sexuality. As the negative messages are internalized, they can be evidenced by shame, anxiety, guilt, or avoidance of sex. Also the process of recovery influences lesbian sexuality, including recovery from drug or alcohol abuse, illness, eating disorders, or sexual abuse (Browning, Reynolds, & Dworkin, 1991).

Monogamy has been a controversial issue in gay couples (Berger, 1990). Until recently, many gay men began relationships with the expectation of sexual exclusivity but later moved to a more open relationship sexually (McWhirter & Mattison, 1984). With the fear of AIDS in the forefront, there has been a move to monogamous relationships. In the early stage of the relationship, gay men report a high frequency of sexual activity with high sexual exclusivity. Any interruption in sexual rapport, such as a late night at work or phone call from a former lover, can be experienced as a threat to the relationship and can create jealousy, anxiety, and hurt. As more gay couples continue to be sexually exclusive, there will be more emphasis on working at loving relationships.

Spirituality

Spirituality concerns one's direct relationship with some higher power; religion, on the other hand, refers to institutions and organizations. There has been much interest in spirituality in the gay and lesbian community (Rainone, 1987). Because of the discrimination still prevalent in many organized religions, gay men and lesbians have left the church in vast numbers and have attempted to express their spirituality through alternative communities and support groups. Extended family members can be critical of their relative who has left the church and no longer embraces family tradition at family events. In addition, as same-sex couples age or become physically ill, there are questions about death and dying that they wish to discuss. If communication is open, partners are able to explore their spirituality with each other and identify a deeper, more personal meaning of life.

Working with Same-Sex Couples

As gay and lesbian couples are more visible, they are more willing to seek therapy to ameliorate stress in their relationship and to strengthen it (Modcrin & Wyers, 1990). Starting with the initial session, clinicians must form conceptual models that focus on the uniqueness of the same-sex couple.

Many same-sex couples come to therapy with issues of loss and grief. Therapists should be aware of the stages-of-grief models and be willing to help the couple express the grief. If the therapist is uncomfortable with same-sex couples, it is the responsibility of the therapist to refer the couple to someone who is accepting and understanding. The couple has spent years learning to read prejudice and will not be fooled by a therapist who is uneasy about the sexual orientations of clients.

Key areas for clinical evaluation of the couple include:
1. Determine extent of self-disclosure to parents and to others.
2. Focus on decisions about secrecy and disclosure to parents.

3. Provide support to each partner when one partner desires to "come out" to parents or others.
4. Help the couple grieve over the loss of "heterosexual privilege" in the family of origin.
5. Encourage the couple to challenge the ways they tolerate or perpetuate parental homophobia.
6. Help the couple to affirm their couple boundaries with parents, co-workers, and friends.
7. Recognize the need for couples to build and validate their friendship networks.
8. Affirm the couple's past history and hopes for the future.
9. Help the couple address issues related to children.
10. Help the partners learn to affirm themselves and each other and form a bond of friendship.

With these principles in mind, it is possible to assist same-sex couples as they adjust to a world where they have been ridiculed and oppressed and create a community where they can live in peace.

THE INTEGRATIVE MODEL AND SAME-SEX COUPLES

Case Example: Barbara and Melissa

Barbara and Melissa have been in a committed relationship for 3 years. Recently they have been having conflict because Melissa believes Barbara does not really love her. This issue has come to a head recently because Barbara is unwilling to take Melissa back to her hometown to attend Barbara's parents' 25th wedding anniversary. Melissa's parents have known she is a lesbian for many years, and they accept their daughter and her partner, Barbara. The couple frequently visits Melissa's parents and spends some holidays there.

Barbara has not come out to her family, although she thinks her sister may know. Melissa says that if Barbara does not tell her parents soon, she will leave the relationship because she is unwilling to spend one more Christmas or Thanksgiving alone. Barbara is angry and accuses Melissa of pressuring her and not understanding her situation. Barbara is from a small town in Georgia and her father is mayor of the town. Barbara believes such a disclosure would devastate her parents and perhaps jeopardize her father's career. On the other hand, she loves Melissa and does not want to lose her.

Application of the Integrative Model: Same-Sex Couple

Stage 1: Assessing and Obtaining an Interactional View of the Problem

Barbara and Melissa each have different perspectives of the problem. Melissa feels unloved and interprets Barbara's lack of self-disclosure as a lack of commitment. Barbara feels pressured and does not feel supported by her partner. Because Barbara perceives her family as rejecting and rigid, she believes they will be critical and rejecting if they learn that she is a lesbian. Melissa has not had the same experience with her parents and does not believe Barbara's parents will reject her. A shared view of the problem on which they can both agree is that they have difficulty with their relationship boundaries and need to find a way to create their own holidays, even if they are independent from their families.

Stage 2: Goal Setting

Together Barbara and Melissa agree they will: (1) plan to create their own traditions for the upcoming holidays of Thanksgiving and Christmas that will promote intimacy, (2) spend time together doing couple activities so they feel connected and appreciated, and (3) talk about how they can handle Barbara's parents in a way that they can both support. The couple agrees to take control of their relationship and "act like a couple" and conquer fears of being rejected by each other and by parents.

Stage 3: Adopting New Perceptions and Behaviors

The partners explore how they have handled celebrations in the past and point out that they both are very creative in their jobs. They determine to use that creativity to adopt new possibilities for shared time together. They also agree to begin a weekly meeting at their favorite restaurant to discuss some couple issues but will spend only one hour of the time together discussing problems. Finally, they decide to enact a weekly date to do some of the fun things they used to do when they were first dating.

Stage 4: Maintaining New Perceptions and Behaviors

The couple agrees they will need to have a plan when Barbara's mother tries to use guilt to induce her to come home every holiday. They agree that Barbara will not make any concrete plans with her family until she has discussed them with Melissa. They also agree that it will be easy to get off track with their couple play time, so they will spend time at the beginning of each week with their calendars to discuss a time for togetherness.

Stage 5: Validating New Perceptions and Behaviors

Each compliments the other on the willingness to work on these issues and the commitment to the relationship. As a result, Melissa feels more loved and Barbara feels more supported. They also have more confidence in their problem-solving skills and are anxious to try the same approach on another issue they have been fearful of addressing—the possibility of buying a home together.

At the completion of therapy, the couple that had arrived with a problem leaves with a solution appropriate to the couple's unique situation.

Intervention Strategies Useful for Same-Sex Couple Therapy

Although many of the strategies may be appropriate for many populations and situations, we will discuss a ritual of a committed relationship, a genogram of the family of creation, and a role-reversal strategy.

Rituals of Commitment

Because same-sex relationships are not legally sanctioned, a ceremony of commitment is one way to memorialize their joining. The ceremony can be planned by the couple and may include spoken vows, traditional toasts, and good wishes, surrounded by friends and family (if appropriate). The affair can be quite lavish or simple depending on the couple's wishes.

Genogram of Family of Creation

This genogram is very similar to the traditional genogram but differs in the definitions of family and the chronology of significant love relationships, rather than legal or biological unions. To accomplish this task, it is necessary to create appropriate symbols for the genogram and determine what information is useful to obtain for examining family messages, patterns, and behaviors.

Role Reversals

The purpose of this intervention is to bring about change by reorganizing the system and help each partner be more empathic of the other's position in the relationship. The technique also reduces blame because it fosters support for both perspectives. Using our previous case example, the therapist asks each member of the couple to "reverse roles" and then asks questions of each person, who responds as the partner might. For example, Melissa might play the role of Barbara and discuss how difficult it is to think of the possibility of losing her parents. In so doing, Melissa be able to empathize with Barbara's dilemma. Barbara might then play the role of Melissa, experiencing some of Melissa's fear that the relationship is just "pretend" because Barbara does not want to make it public. Later, when both assume their own roles, Barbara is able to understand how desperate Melissa must feel when they cannot share and create holiday memories together.

SCENARIOS FOR DISCUSSION AND ROLE PLAYING

Following are some sample scenarios that can be used to stimulate discussion and as topics for role playing.

Guess Who's Coming to Dinner?

Angelina and her partner, Josie, are going to her parents' home for dinner with the intent to tell them that they are a couple and want to purchase a home together. Angelina is anxious, but Josie insists they must confront the situation together because they are a couple. As they are about to leave to go to dinner, an argument ensues and Angelina goes alone.

The Great Wall

Jim has been attending graduate classes at a local university and has become quite friendly with several of the students. One night, a student saw Jim and his partner, Alan, at a local theater sitting close together and obviously involved in intimate conversation. Two weeks later, Jim discovered that several students had been at a party on the weekend to which Jim was not invited. The students also did not ask him to work with them on a class project due the following week. Jim arrives home and tells Alan he has "blown it" and that they cannot be seen in public together anymore.

The Wicked Stepmother
Nathetta and Tanella have been together for 3 years. Nathetta's daughter, Leticia, resides with them and has recently found out that her mother is a lesbian. Leticia is embarrassed and blames her mother's sexual identity on Tanella. Leticia has become hostile toward Tanella and refuses to eat meals or be seen in public with the two of them.

Who's That Knocking at the Door—Oh! It Must Be Our Imagination
Bob recently came out to his family and co-workers because he didn't want to live with secrecy anymore. Although most of his friends said they were comfortable with the admission, they have not contacted Bob since that time. Bob's attempts to get the old group together have been unsuccessful. Bob tries to talk to his partner, Sam, about his feeling of isolation, but Sam tells him that all they need is each other.

Peggy and Sue Get Married
Peggy and Sue have been in a relationship for 2 years and have decided to have a commitment ceremony in the fall. They are concerned about whom to invite because one family is aware of their lesbian identities and one is not. Also, some of their friends and co-workers are aware and others are not. As the date draws near, both Peggy and Sue become anxious and they consider canceling the idea. Peggy is resentful, however, and blames Sue for not wanting to tell the world about her love for Peggy.

A Day in Court
Frank and Carlos are in court attempting to get visitation rights to see Frank's son on a weekly basis. Frank's former wife is opposed to the idea because she is concerned that her son might become gay by associating with his father. Carlos has offered to leave the home he and Frank share in hopes that it will give Frank the opportunity to retain visits with his son. Frank is angry and refuses to consider the possibility.

Is This All There Is?
Ana and Jean have been experiencing sexual difficulty since Jean began attending therapy to work on her issues of childhood sexual abuse. Jean does not appear to have much desire for a physical relationship with Ana. Ana interprets Jean's behavior as rejection of her and begins to make comments about Jean having someone else. Jean accuses her of being jealous and claims she does not trust her.

"I Do," "We Do," "Do We?"

Sims wants to be in an exclusive relationship with Mike, but Mike has met someone at work to whom he is attracted. Sims is fearful of disease and also fearful that Mike will leave him altogether. Mike feels restricted and would like to continue the relationship with Sims but does not want to limit his opportunities. After many arguments, Sims threatens Mike that he will not have any involvement with him if he is not faithful. Mike refuses to be controlled but does not want to lose the relationship with Sims.

CONCLUSION

Same-sex couples experience some similar and some unique problems as they attempt to live harmoniously in a society that continues to reject and discriminate against them. Same-sex couples follow predictable stages and experience sources of conflict over communication, finances, recreational time, and problem-solving. Compared to heterosexual couples, same-sex couples may have other, more complicated issues regarding role identification, children, family of origin, legal concerns, and self-identity.

Same-sex couples also come to therapy to address coming out, lack of appropriate rituals, legal dilemmas, blending family concerns, substance abuse, sexual abuse, domestic violence, and spiritual concerns. Often these issues are misunderstood in society, so same-sex couples feel alienated and unsupported by social institutions. The therapist's attitudes of acceptance and knowledge about the gay and lesbian lifestyle are important if the therapist wishes to work with these couples.

REFERENCES

ADAMS, J. S. (1965). Inequity in social exchange. In L. Berkowitz (Ed.), *Advances in experimental social psychology*, Vol. 2 (pp. 267–299). New York: Academic Press.

ALBEE, E. (1991). Who's afraid of Virginia Woolf? In E. Albee, *Edward Albee: The plays*. New York: Macmillan.

ALEEM, S., & Khandelwal, P. (1988). Job involvement, perceived outcome importance: A study of dual-career couples. *Indian Journal of Applied Psychology, 25*, 27–34.

ALGER, I. (1991). Marital therapy with dual-career couples. *Psychiatric Annals, 21*, 455–458.

AMATEA, E. S., & Cross, E. G. (1983). Coupling and careers: A workshop for dual-career couples at the launching stage. *The Personnel and Guidance Journal, 62*, 48–52.

AMBERT, A. (1986). Being a stepparent: Live-in and visiting stepchildren. *Journal of Marriage and the Family, 48*, 795–804.

AMERICAN Association for Marriage and Family Therapy. (1991). *AAMFT code of ethical principles for marriage and family therapists*. Washington, DC: Author.

AMERICAN Psychiatric Association. (1994). *Diagnostic and statistical manual of mental disorders* (4th ed.). Washington, DC: Author.

ANDERSON, C. M., & Malloy, E. S. (1976). Family photographs. *Family Process, 6*, 313–321.

ANDERSON, W. T. (1990). *Reality isn't what it used to be*. San Francisco, CA: Harper & Row.

ARGYLE, M., & Furnam, A. (1983). Sources of satisfaction and conflict in long-term relationships. *Journal of Marriage and the Family, 9*, 481–492.

ARKIN, S., Lewis, J. A., & Carlson, J. (1990). Marital therapy with alcohol-affected couples: Treatment strategies. *Individual Psychology, 46*, 125–132.

ATWATER, L. (1979). Getting involved: Women's transition to first extramarital sex. *Alternative Lifestyles, 1*, 33–68.

ATWOOD, J., & Dershowitz, S. (1992). Constructing a sex and marital therapy frame: Ways to help couples deconstruct sexual problems. *Journal of Sex and Marital Therapy, 18*, 196–218.

ATWOOD, J., & Weinstein, E. (1989). The couple relationship as the focus of sex therapy. *Journal of Family Therapy, 10*, 161–168.

AVIS, J. M. (1986). Working together: An enrichment program for dual-career couples. *Marriage and Family Enrichment, 12*, 29–45.

AXELSON, S. J. (1963). The marital adjustment of marital role definitions of husbands of working and nonworking wives. *Marriage and Family Living, 25*, 94–108.

AYLMER, R. C. (1986). Bowen family systems marital therapy. In N. S. Jacobson & A. S. Gurman (Eds.), *Clinical handbook of marital therapy* (pp. 107–148). New York: Guilford Press.

AZRIN, N. H., Naster, B. J., & Jones, R. (1973). Reciprocity counseling: A rapid learning based procedure for marital counseling. *Behavior Research and Therapy, 11*, 365–382.

BACH, G., & Wyden, P. (1969). *The intimate enemy*. New York: Morrow.

BAPTISTE, D. (1987). Psychotherapy with gay/lesbian couples and their children in "stepfamilies": A challenge for marriage and family therapists. *Journal of Homosexuality, 14*, 223–238.

BAGAROZI, D. A., & Anderson, S. A. (1989). *Personal, marital and family myths: Theoretical formulations and clinical strategies*. New York: Norton.

BAUGH, C. W., Avery, A. W., & Sheets-Haworth, K. L. (1982). Marital Problem-Solving Scale: A measure to assess relationship conflict negotiation ability. *Family Therapy, 9*, 43–51.

BAUCOM, D. H., & Adams, A. N. (1987). In K. D. O'Leary (Ed.), *Assessment of marital discord: An integration for research and clinical practice* (pp. 139–182). Hillsdale, NJ: Erlbaum.

BAUCOM, D. H., & Epstein, N. (1990). Attributions in marriage: Review and critique. *Psychological Bulletin, 107*, 3–33.

BEAVERS, W. R. (1985). *Successful marriage: A family systems approach to couples therapy*. New York: Norton.

BEAVERS, W. R., & Hampson, R. B. (1990). *Successful families assessment and intervention*. New York: Norton.

BECK, A. T. (1988). *Love is never enough*. New York: Harper & Row.

BECK, E. T. (Ed.). (1982). *Nice Jewish girls: A lesbian anthology*. Watertown, MA: Persephone.

BENNETT, L. A., & Wolin, S. J. (1990). Family culture and alcoholism transmission. In R. L. Collins, K. E. Leonard, & S. J. Searles (Eds.), *Alcohol and the family: Research and clinical perspectives* (pp. 194–219). New York: Guilford Press.

BERGER, R. (1990). Men together: Understanding the gay couple. *Journal of Homosexuality, 19*, 31–47.

BERMAN, E., Sacks, S., & Lief, H. (1975). The two-professional marriage: A new conflict syndrome. *Journal of Sex and Marital Therapy, 1*, 242–253.

BERNE, E. (1961). *Transactional analysis in psychotherapy*. New York: Grove Press.

BERNE, E. (1964). *Games people play*. New York: Grove Press.

BERNE, E. (1970). *Sex in human loving*. New York: Simon & Schuster.

BERZON, B. A. (1988). *Permanent partners*. New York: Dutton.

BETTELHEIM, B. (1977). *The uses of enchantment: The meaning and importance of fairy tales*. New York: Vintage Books.

BIRCHLER, G. R., Weiss, R. L., & Vincent, J. P. (1975).A multimethod analysis of social reinforcement exchange between maritally distressed and nondistressed spouse and stranger dyads. *Journal of Personality and Social Psychology, 31*, 349–360.

BIRD, G. W., & Bird, G. A. (1986). Strategies for reducing role strain among dual-career couples. *International Journal of the Sociology of the Family, 16*, 83–94.

BLOOD, R. O. (1963). The husband-wife relationship. In F. I. Nye & L. W. Hoffman (Eds.), *Employed mothers in America*. Chicago, IL: Rand McNally.

BOEN, D. L. (1988). A practitioner looks at assessment in marital counseling. *Journal of Counseling and Development, 66*, 484–486.

BOHANNON, P. (1973). The six stages of divorce. In M. E. Lasswell & T. E. Lasswell (Eds.), *Love, marriage and family: A developmental approach* (pp. 475–489). Glenview, IL: Scott Foresman.

BOLAND, J. P., & Follingstad, D. R. (1987). *Journal of Sex and Marital Therapy, 13*, 286–313.

BORNSTEIN, P. H., & Bornstein, M. T. (1986). *Marital therapy: A behavioral communications approach*. New York: Pergamon Press.

BOWEN, M. (1978). *Family therapy in clinical practice*. New York: Aronson.

BOWEN, M. (1980). *Key to the genogram*. Washington, DC: Georgetown University Hospital.

BOWLBY, J. (1973). *Separation*. New York: Basic Books.

BRATTER, T. (1974). Dynamics of role reversal. In I. A. Greenberg (Ed.), *Psychodrama, theory and therapy* (pp. 101–109). New York: Behavioral Publications.

BRIDDELL, D., & Wilson, G. (1976). The effects of alcohol and expectancy set on male sexual arousal. *Journal of Abnormal Psychology, 85*, 225–234.

BROWN, E. M. (1991). *Patterns of infidelity and their treatment*. New York: Brunner/Mazel.

BROWNING, C., Reynolds, A., & Dworkin, S. (1991). Affirmative psychotherapy for lesbian women. *The Counseling Psychologist, 19*, 177–196.

BUBENZER, D. L., & West, J. D. (1992). *Counseling couples*. London: Sage.

BUDMAN, S. H. (1992). *The first session in brief therapy*. New York: Guilford Press.

BURKE, R. J., & Weir, T. (1976). Relationship of wives' employment status to husband, wife and pair satisfaction and performance. *Journal of Marriage and the Family, 38*, 279–287.

BURLEY, K. A. (1991). Family-work spillover in dual-career couples: A comparison of two time perspectives. *Psychological Reports, 68*, 471–480.

BUUNK, B. (1980). Extramarital sex in the Netherlands: Motivation in social and marital context. *Alternative Lifestyles, 3*, 11–39.

CADE, B., & O'Hanlon, W. H. (1993). *A brief guide to brief therapy*. New York: Norton.

CAHN, D. (1992). *Conflict in intimate relationships*. New York: Guilford Press.

CARL, D. (1990). *Therapy with same-sex couples*. New York: Norton.

CARTER, E., & McGoldrick, M. (1980). *The family life cycle: A framework for family therapy*. New York: Gardner.

CASS, V. C. (1979). Homosexuality identity formation: A theoretical model. *Journal of Homosexuality, 4*, 219–235.

CHAN, C. S. (1989). Issues of identity development among Asian-American lesbian and gay men. *Journal of Counseling and Development, 68*, 16–20.

CHASEN, R., Grunebaum, H., & Herzig, M. (1990). *One couple, four realities: Multiple perspectives on couple therapy*. New York: Guilford Press.

CISSNA, K. N., Cox, D. F., & Bochner, A. P. (1990). The dialectic of marital and parental relationships within the stepfamily. *Communication Monographs, 57*, 44–61.

CLAXTON-OLDFIELD, S. C. (1992). Perceptions of stepfathers: Disciplinary and affectionate behaviors. *Journal of Family Issues, 13*, 378–389.

CLUNIS, D. M., & Green, G. D. (1988). *Lesbian couples*. Seattle: Seal Press.

COLAPINTO, J. (1991). Structural family therapy. In A. M. Horne & J. L. Passmore (Eds.), *Family counseling and therapy* (pp. 77-106). Itasca, IL: F. E. Peacock.

COLEMAN, M., & Ganong, L. (1991). Remarriage and stepfamilies: What about the children? *Family and Conciliation Courts Review, 29*, 405–412.

COLEMAN, M., Ganong, L., & Gringich, R. (1985). Stepfamily strengths: A review of popular literature. *Family Relations, 34*, 583–589.

COLEMAN, M., Marshall, S., & Ganong, L. (1986). Beyond Cinderella: Relevant reading for young adolescents about stepfamilies. *Adolescence, 11*, 553–560.

COREY, G. (1994). *Theory and practice of counseling and psychotherapy* (4th ed.). Pacific Grove, CA: Brooks/Cole.

CORSO, K. (1993). Testing options for use in family therapy. Unpublished manuscript.

COSER, L. A. (1956). *The functions of social conflict*. New York: Free Press.

COVERMAN, S., & Sheley, J. F. (1986). Changes in men's housework and childcare time, 1965-1975. *Journal of Marriage and the Family, 48*, 413–422.

CROSBY, J. F. (1991). Cybernetics of cybernetics in assessment of marital quality. *Contemporary Family Therapy, 13*, 3–15.

CROSBY, J. F., Gage, B. A., & Raymond, M. C. (1983). The grief resolution process in divorce. *Journal of Divorce, 7*, 3–18.

CROWE, M., & Ridley, J. (1990). *Therapy with couples: A behavioural-systems approach to marital and sexual problems*. Oxford, England: Blackwell Scientific Publications.

CUPACH, W. R., & Comstock, J. (1990). Satisfaction with sexual communication in marriage: Links to sexual satisfaction and dyadic adjustment. *Journal of Social and Personal Relationships, 7*, 179–186.

CUPACH, W., & Metts, S. (1991). Sexuality and communication in close relationships. In K. McKinney & S. Sprecher (Eds.), *Sexuality in close relationships* (pp. 93–110).

DATILLIO, F. M., & Padesky, C. A. (1990). *Cognitive therapy with couples.* Sarasota, FL: Professional Resources Exhange.

DEMONTEFLORES, C., & Schultz, S. (1978). Coming out: Similarities and differences for lesbians and gay men. *Journal of Social Issues, 34*, 59–72.

DENTON, W. H. (1991). The role of affect in marital therapy. *Journal of Marital and Family Therapy, 17*, 257–261.

DE SHAZER, S. (1985). *Keys to solution in brief therapy.* New York: Guilford Press.

DE SHAZER, S. (1988). *Clues: Investigations solutions in brief therapy.* New York: Norton.

DE SHAZER, S., Berg, I., Nunnally, E., et al. (1986). Brief therapy: Focused solution development. *Family Process, 25*, 201–221.

DEUTSCH, M. (1973). *The resolution of conflict: Constructive and destructive processes.* New Haven, CT: Yale University Press.

DIAMOND, G. (1988). Thought and action in the contextual interview. In E. Lipchik (Ed.), *Interviewing* (pp. 71–84). Rockville, MD: Aspen Publishers.

DICKS, H. V. (1967). *Marital tensions.* New York: Basic Books.

DUHL, F. (1981). The use of the chronological chart in general systems family therapy. *Journal of Marital and Family Therapy, 7*, 361–373.

DUHL, F. (1986, October). *A fisherman's guide to interviewing.* Symposium conducted at the meeting of the American Association for Marital and Family Therapy, Orlando, FL.

DYM, B. (1995). *Readiness and change in couple therapy.* New York: Basic Books.

DYM, B. & Glenn, M. (1993). *Exploring and understanding the cycles of intimate relationships.* New York: Harper Collins.

ELLIS, A. (1977). The nature of disturbed marital interactions. In A. Ellis & R. Greiger (Eds.), *Handbook of rational-emotive therapy* (pp. 170–276). New York: Springer.

ELLIS, A. (1985). Jealousy: Its etiology and treatment. In D. C. Goldberg (Ed.), *Contemporary marriage* (pp. 420–428). Homewood, IL: Dorsey.

EPSTEIN, N. (1986). Cognitive marital therapy: A multilevel assessment and intervention. *Journal of Rational Emotive Therapy, 4*, 68–81.

ERIKSON, E. H. (1950). *Childhood and society.* New York: Norton.

ESPIN, O. (1987). Latina lesbian women. In Boston Lesbian Psychologies Collective (Ed.), *Lesbian psychologies* (pp. 35–55). Chicago: University of Illinois Press.

EVANS, P. (1992). *The verbally abusive relationship.* Holbrook, MA: Bob Adams Publishers.

FAIRBAIRN, W. R. D. (1952). *An object-relations theory of the personality.* New York: Basic Books.

FALICOV, C., & Karrer, B. (1980). Cultural variations in the family life cycle: The Mexican-American family. In E. Carter & M. McGoldrick (Eds.), *The family life cycle: A framework for family therapy* (pp. 383–425). New York: Gardner.

FALK, P. (1989). Lesbian mothers: Psychosocial assumptions in family law. *American Psychologist, 44*, 941–947.

FINKELSTEIN, L. (1987). Toward an object-relations approach in psychoanalytic marital therapy. *Journal of Marital and Family Therapy, 13*, 287–298.

FINNEY, J., Moos, R., & Mewborn, C. (1980). Post-treatment experiences and treatment outcome of alcoholic patients six months and two years after hospitalization. *Journal of Consulting and Clinical Psychology, 48*, 17–29.

FISH, L. S., & Piercy, F. P. (1987). The theory and practice of structural and strategic family therapies: A Delphi study. *Journal of Marital and Family Therapy, 13*, 113–125.

FISHER, H. (1992). *Anatomy of love: The mysteries of mating, marriage and why we stray.* New York: Fawcett Columbine.

FITZPATRICK, M. A. (1988). Approaches to marital interaction. In P. Noller & M. A. Fitzpatrick (Eds.), *Perspectives on marital interaction* (pp. 998–120). Philadelphia: Multilingual Matters.

FLOYD, F. J., Markman, H. J., Kelly, S., Blunberg, S. L., & Stanley, S. M. (1995). Preventive intervention and relationship enhancement. In N. S. Jacobson & A. S. Gurman (Eds.), *Clinical handbook of couple therapy* (pp. 212–226). New York: Guilford Press.

FRAMO, J. L. (1970). Symptoms from a family transactional viewpoint. In N. W. Ackerman (Ed.), *Family therapy in transition.* Boston: Little, Brown.

FRAMO, J. L. (1976). Family of origin as a therapeutic resource for adults in marital and family therapy: You can and should go home again. *Family Process, 15,* 193–201.

FRAMO, J. L. (1990). Integrating families of origin into couples therapy. In R. Chasin, H. Grunebaum, & M. Herzig (Eds.), *One couple, four realities: Multiple perspectives on couple therapy* (pp. 49–82). New York: Guilford Press.

FRAMO, J. L. (1993). *Demonstrations with couples in counseling: Dealing with family of origin problems* [Videotape]. (Available from American Counseling Association, 5999 Stevenson Avenue, Alexandria, VA 22304)

FRANK, J. D., & Frank, J. P. (1991). *Persuasion and healing: A comparative study of psychotherapy.* Baltimore: Johns Hopkins University Press.

FREDMAN, N., & Sherman, R. (1987). *Handbook of measurements for marriage and family therapy.* New York: Brunner/Mazel.

FRENCH, M. (1977). *The women's room.* New York: Jove Publications.

FREUD, S. (1963). *Introductory lectures on psychoanalysis. Part 3* (Standard ed.) (Vol. 16). London: Hogarth. (Originally published in 1917)

FRIEDMAN, E. H. (1990). *Friedman's fables.* New York: Guilford Press.

FRIEDMAN, R. (1991). Couple therapy with gay couples. *Psychiatric Annals, 21,* 485–490.

FRIEDMAN, S. (1992). Constructing solutions: Stories in brief family therapy. In S. H. Budman (Ed.), *The first session in brief therapy* (pp. 282–305). New York: Guilford Press.

FRIESEN, J. D. (1985). *Structural-strategic marriage and family therapy.* New York: Gardner.

GEORGE, K., & Behrendt, A. (1987). Therapy for male couples experiencing relationship problems and sexual problems. *Journal of Homosexuality, 14,* 77–88.

GILBERT, L. (1985). *Men in dual-career families: Current realities and future prospects.* Hillsdale, NJ: Erlbaum.

GILBERT, L. (1988). *Sharing it all: The rewards and struggles of two-career families.* New York: Plenum.

GILBERT, R. M. (1992). *Extraordinary relationships: A new way of thinking about human interactions.* Minneapolis, MN: Chronomed Publishing.

GILLIGAN, C. (1982). *In a different voice: Psychological theory and women's development.* Cambridge, MA: Harvard University Press.

GLASS, S. P., & Wright, T. L. (1992). Justifications for extramarital relationships: The association between attitudes, behaviors, and gender. *Journal of Sex Research, 29,* 361–387.

GLAUS, K. O. (1989). Alcoholism, chemical dependency, and the lesbian client. *Women and Therapy, 8,* 131–144.

GLICK, P. C. (1984). How American families are changing. *American Demographics, 38,* 9–11.

GLICK, P. C. (1989). Remarried families, stepfamilies, and stepchildren: A brief demographic analysis. *Family Relations, 38,* 24–27.

GLICK, P. C., & Lin, S. L. (1986). Recent changes in divorce and remarriage. *Jour-*

nal of Marriage and the Family, 48, 737–741.

GOLDENBERG, I., & Goldenberg, H. (1985). *Family therapy: An overview* (2nd ed.). Pacific Grove, CA: Brooks/Cole.

GOLOMBOK, S., Rust, J., & Pickard, C. (1984). Sexual problems encountered in general practice. *British Journal of Sexual Medicine, 11*, 65–72.

GORDON, D. (1978). *Therapeutic metaphors.* Cupertino, CA: Meta Publications.

GORDON, L. H. (1986). Assessment as an option in divorce mediation. In *Divorce and Family Mediation* (pp. 66–70). Washington, DC: American Bar Association.

GORDON, L. (1990). *Love knots.* New York: Bantam.

GORDON, T. (1970). *Parent effectiveness training.* New York: Wyden.

GORSKI, T., & Miller, M. (1982). *Counseling for relapse prevention.* Independence, MO: Independence Press.

GOTTMAN, J. M. (1991). Predicting the longitudinal course of marriages. *Journal of Marital and Family Therapy, 17*, 3–7.

GOTTMAN, J. M. (1994). *Why marriages succeed or fail . . . and how you can make yours last.* New York: Simon & Schuster.

GOTTMAN, J. M, & Krokoff, L. J. (1989). Marital interaction and satisfaction: A longitudinal view. *Journal of Consulting and Clinical Psychology, 57*, 47–52.

GOTTMAN, J. M., Notarius, C. I., Gonso, J., & Markman, H. J. (1976). *A couples guide to communication.* Champaign, IL: Research Press.

GRAY, J. (1993). *Men are from Mars, women are from Venus.* New York: Bantam.

GREENBERG, S. M., & Johnson, L. S. (1994). *The heart of the matter: Perspectives on emotion in marital therapy.* New York: Brunner/Mazel.

GROTEVANT, H. D., & Carlson, C. I. (1989). *Family assessment: A guide to methods and measures.* New York: Guilford Press.

GUELZOW, M. G., Bird, G. W., & Koball, E. H. (1991). An exploratory path analysis of the stress process for dual-career men and women. *Journal of Marriage and the Family, 53*, 151–164.

GUERIN, P., Fay, L., Burden, S., & Kautto, J. (1987). *The evaluation and treatment of marital conflict.* New York: Basic Books.

GUERNEY, G., Jr., Brock, G., & Coufal, J. (1986). Integrating marital therapy and enrichment: The relationship enhancement approach. In N. S. Jacobson & A. S. Gurman (Eds.), *Clinical handbook of marital therapy* (pp. 151–172). New York: Guilford Press.

HALEY, J. (1963a). Marriage therapy. *Archives of General Psychiatry, 8*, 213–234.

HALEY, J. (1963b). *Strategies of psychotherapy.* New York: Grune & Stratton.

HALEY, J. (1976). *Problem-solving therapy.* Harper Colophon Books.

HALEY, J. (1989, May). *Strategic family therapy.* Symposium presented at Stetson University, DeLand, FL.

HALFORD, W. K., & Osgarby, S. M. (1993). Alcohol abuse in clients presenting with marital problems. *Journal of Family Psychology, 6*, 245–254.

HALL, M. (1987). Sex therapy with lesbian couples: A four stage approach. *Journal of Homosexuality, 14*, 137–156.

HART, B. (1986). Lesbian battering: An examination. In K. Loebel (Ed.), *Naming the violence: Speaking out about lesbian battering* (pp. 173–189). Seattle: Seal Press.

HARVEY, J. (1995). *Odyssey of the heart: The search for closeness, intimacy, and love.* New York: Freeman.

HASIN, D. S., Grant, B. F., & Endicott, J. (1988). Lifetime psychiatric comorbidity in hospitalized alcoholics: Subject and family correlates. *International Journal of Addictions, 23*, 827–850.

HATCHER, M. A. (1991). The corporate woman in the 1990's: Maverick or innovator? *Psychology of Women Quarterly, 15*, 251–259.

HAWKINS, A. J., Roberts, T., Christiansen, S. L., & Marshall, C. M. (1994). An evaluation of a program to help dual-earner couples share the second shift. *Family Relations, 43*, 213–220.

HEIMAN, J., LoPiccolo, L., & LoPiccolo, J. (1981). The treatment of sexual dysfunction. In A. Gurman & D. Kniskern (Eds.), *Handbook of family therapy* (pp. 592–627). New York: Brunner/Mazel.

HENDRICK, S. (1988). A generic measure of relationship satisfaction. *Journal of Marriage and the Family, 50,* 93–98.

HENDRICK, S. S. (1995). *Close relationships: What couple therapists can learn.* Pacific Grove, CA: Brooks/Cole.

HERTZ, R. (1991). Dual-career couples and the American dream. *Journal of Comparative Family Studies, 22,* 247–253.

HETHERINGTON, C., & Orzek, A. (1989). Career therapy and life planning for lesbian women. *Journal of Counseling and Development, 68,* 52–57.

HIEBERT, W. J., Gillespie, J. P., & Stahman, R. F. (1993). *Dynamic assessment in couple therapy.* New York: Lexington Books.

HIGGINS, C., Duxbury, L., & Lee, C. (1994). Impact of life-cycle stage and gender on the ability to balance work and family responsibilities. *Family Relations, 43,* 144–150.

HILL, D. (1992). Ethical issues in marital and sexual therapy. *British Journal of Guidance and Therapy, 20,* 75–89.

HOBART, C. (1989). Experiences of remarried families. *Journal of Divorce, 13,* 121–144.

HOF, L., & Berman, E. (1986). The sexual genogram. *Journal of Marital and Family Therapy, 12,* 39–47.

HOFFMAN, L. (1981). *Foundations of family therapy: A conceptual framework.* New York: Basic Books.

HOFMAN, L. W., & Hoffman, H. J. (1985). The lives and adventures of dual-career couples. *Family Therapy, 12,* 123–149.

HOLDEN, C. (1991). Is "gender gap" narrowing? *Science, 253,* 959–960.

HOLT, M. L. (1977). *Intimacy inventory.* Unpublished doctoral dissertation.

HORNE, A. M. (1991). Social learning family therapy. In A. M. Horne & J. L. Passmore (Eds.), *Family counseling and therapy* (pp. 464–496). Itasca, IL: F. E. Peacock.

HORNE, A. M., & Passmore, J. L. (1991). *Family counseling and therapy.* Itasca, IL: F. E. Peacock.

HOSEKNECHT, S. K., & Spanier, G. B. (1980). Marital disruption and higher education among women in the United States. *Sociological Quarterly, 21,* 373–389.

HOUSER, R., Kinstam, V., & Ham, M. (1990). Coping and marital satisfaction in dual-career couples: Early stage dual-career couples—wives as college students. *Journal of College Student Development, 31,* 325–329.

HOVESTADT, A., Anderson, W., Piercy, F., Cochran, S., & Fine, M. (1985). A family of origin scale. *Journal of Marriage and Family Therapy, 11,* 287–298.

HOYT, M. F., Rosenbaum, R., & Talmon, M. (1992). Planned single session psychotherapy. In S. H. Budman (Ed.), *The first session in brief therapy* (pp. 59–86). New York: Guilford Press.

INSTITUTE FOR PERSONALITY ASSESSMENT AND TESTING. (1967). *The Cattell 16-PF Manual.* Champaign, IL: Author.

IVEY, A. E. (1994). *Intentional interviewing and counseling.* Pacific Grove, CA: Brooks/Cole.

IVEY, A. E., & Mathews, J. W. (1986). A metamodel for structuring the clinical interview. In W. P. Anderson (Ed.), *Innovative counseling: A handbook of readings* (pp. 77–83). Alexandria, VA: American Association for Counseling and Development.

JACOBSON, N. S. (1981). Marital problems. In J. L. Shelton & R. L. Levy (Eds.), *Behavioral assignments and treatment compliance* (pp. 147–166). Champaign, IL: Research Press.

JACOBSON, N. S., & Holtzworth-Munroe, A. (1986). Marital therapy: A social learning-cognitive perspective. In N. S. Jacobson & A. S. Gurman (Eds.), *Clinical handbook of marital therapy* (pp. 27–70). New York: Guilford Press.

JACOBSON, N. S., & Margolin, G. (1979). *Marital therapy: Strategies based on social learning and behavior exchange principles.* New York: Brunner/Mazel.

JACOBSON, N. S., Waldron, H., & Moore, D. (1980). Toward a behavioral profile of marital distress. *Journal of Consulting and Clinical Psychology, 49*, 269–277.

JANKOWIAK, W. R., & Fisher, E. F. (1992). A cross-cultural perspective on romantic love. *Ethnology, 31*, 149–155.

JOHNSON, L. S., & Greenberg, S. M. (1988). *Emotionally focused therapy for couples.* New York: Guilford Press.

JOHNSON, L. S., & Greenberg, S. M. (1994). *The heart of the matter: Perspectives on emotion in marital therapy.* New York: Brunner/Mazel.

JOHNSTON, J., & Campbell, L. (1988). *Impasses of divorce.* New York: Free Press.

JORDON, K., & Quinn, W. H. (1994). Session two outcome of the formula first session task in problem and solution focused approaches. *The American Journal of Family Therapy, 22*, 3–16.

JOURARD, S. M. (1964). *The transparent self: Self-disclosure and well-being.* Princeton, NJ: Van Nostrand.

KAMINER, W. (1990, February 11). Chances are you're codependent too. *New York Times Book Review*, pp. 26–29.

KAPLAN, H. (1979). *Disorders of sexual desire.* New York: Brunner/Mazel.

KAPLAN, H. (Ed.). (1983). *The evaluation of sexual disorders.* New York: Brunner/Mazel.

KARPEL, M. A. (1994). *Evaluating couples.* New York: Norton.

KARPEL, M. A. (1993, October). *Wounded hearts: Restoring trust in couples therapy.* Workshop presented at the 51st Annual Conference of the American Association for Marriage and Family Therapy, Anaheim, CA.

KASLOW, F. W. (1984). Divorce: An evolutionary process of change in the family system. *Journal of Divorce, 7*, 21–39.

KASLOW, F. W. (1992). Remarried couples: The architects of stepfamilies. In *Couples therapy in a family context.*

KASLOW, F. W. (1996). *Handbook of relational diagnoses and dysfunctional family patterns.* New York: Wiley.

KASLOW, F. W., & Friedman, J. (1977). Utilization of family photos in family therapy. *Journal of Marriage and Family Counseling, 3*, 19–25.

KASLOW, F. W., & Schwartz, L. (1987). *Dynamics of divorce: A life cycle perspective.* New York: Brunner/Mazel.

KATER, V. D. (1985). Management strategies for dual-career couples. *Journal of Career Development, 12*, 75–80.

KEENEY, B. P. (1985). *Mind in therapy.* New York: Basic Books.

KEITH, M. P., & Schafer, B. R. (1980). Role strain and depression in two-job families. *Family Relations, 28*, 485–488.

KEITH, M. P., & Schafer, B. R. (1991). *Relationships and well-being over the life stages.* New York: Praeger.

KELL, C. (1992). The internal dynamics of the extramarital relationship: A counselling perspective. *Sexual and Marital Therapy, 7*, 157–172.

KELLEY, P. (1992). Healthy stepfamily functioning. *Families in Society: The Journal of Contemporary Human Services, 73*, 579–587.

KILPATRICK, A. C., & Kilpatrick, E. G., Jr. (1991). Object relations family therapy. In A. M. Horne & J. L. Passmore (Eds.), *Family counseling and therapy* (pp. 207–234). Itasca, IL: F. E. Peacock.

KLEIN, H. (1988). Job satisfaction in professional dual-career couples: Psychological and socioeconomic variables. *Journal of Vocational Behavior, 32*, 255–268.

KOSCH, S. (1982). Sexual dysfunction. In E. Medley (Ed.), *Common health problems in medical practice.* Baltimore: Williams & Wilkins.

KOTTLER, J. (1994). *Beyond blame.* New York: Jossey-Bass.

KRESTAN, J., & Bepko, C. (1980). The problem of fusion in the lesbian relationship. *Family Process, 19*, 277–289.

KURDEK, L. (1988). Relationship quality of gay and lesbian cohabiting couples. *Journal of Homosexuality, 15*, 93–118.

L'ABATE, L., & Bagarozzi, D. A. (1993). *Sourcebook of marriage and family evaluation* (pp. 77–94). New York: Brunner/Mazel.

L'ABATE, L., & Weinstein, S. E. (1997). *Structured enrichment programs for couples and families.* New York: Brunner/Mazel.

LAIRD, W., & Hartmen, A. (1988). *Women, rituals, and family therapy.* New York: Haworth Press.

LAMINNA, M. A., & Riedmann, A. (1991). *Marriages and families: Making choices and facing change.* Pacific Grove, CA: Brooks/Cole.

LANDIS, L. (1991). *Interparental conflict and postdivorce adjustment.* Unpublished doctoral dissertation.

LANDIS, L., & Young, M. (1994). The reflecting team in counselor education. *Journal of Counselor Education and Supervision, 23,* 112–118.

LANGER, E., & Rodin, J. (1976). The effects of choice and enhanced personal responsibility for the aged: A field experiment in an institutional setting. *Journal of Personality and Social Psychology, 33,* 563–573.

LAWSON, A. (1990). *Adultery.* Oxford: Oxford University Press.

LAZARUS, A. A. (1985). *Marital myths.* San Luis Obispo, CA: Impact Publishers.

LEE, J. (1991). Can we talk? Can we really talk? Communication as a key factor in the maturing homosexual couple. *Journal of Homosexuality, 14,* 143–168.

LEFRANCOIS, G. (1993). *All about sex therapy.* New York: Plenum.

LEIBLUM, S. & Pervin, L. (1980). Introduction: The development of sex therapy from a sociocultural perspective. In S. Leiblum & L. Pervin (Eds.), *Principles and practices of sex therapy.* New York: Guilford Press.

LEIBLUM, S., & Rosen, R. (1984). *Alcohol and human sexual response.* New York: Haworth Press.

LERNER, H. G. (1985). *The dance of anger: A woman's guide to changing patterns in intimate relationships.* New York: Harper & Row.

LEVI-STRAUS, C. (1969). *The elementary structures of kinship.* Boston: Beacon.

LEVINGER, G., & Senn, D. J. (1967). Disclosure of feeling in marriage. *Merrill-Palmer Quarterly, 13,* 237–249.

LIDDLE, H. A. (1983). Diagnosis and assessment in family therapy: A comparative study of six schools of thought. In J. C. Hansen & B. P. Keeney (Eds.), *Diagnosis and assessment in family therapy.* Rockville, MD: Aspen Publishers.

LIPCHIK, E. (1988a). Preface. In E. Lipchik (Ed.), *Interviewing* (p. xi). Rockville, MD: Aspen Publishers.

LIPCHIK, E. (1988b). Purposeful sequences for beginning the solution-focused interview. In E. Lipchik (Ed.), *Interviewing* (pp. 105–118). Rockville, MD: Aspen Publishers.

LIPCHIK, E. (1994). The rush to be brief. *Networker, 14,* 35–39.

LIPCHIK, E., & de Shazer, S. (1985). The purposeful interview. *Journal of Strategic and Systemic Therapies, 5,* 88–99.

LIPPITT, G. L. (1982). Managing conflict in today's organizations. *Training and Developmental Journal, 36,* 67–75.

LOCKE, H. J., & Wallace, K. M. (1959). Short marital adjustment and prediction tests: Their reliability and validity. *Marriage and Family Living, 2,* 251–255.

LOIACANO, D. K. (1989). Gay identity issues among Black Americans: Racism, homophobia, and the need for validation. *Journal of Counseling and Development, 68,* 21–25.

LONG, E. C. J. (1993). Perspective-taking differences between high- and low-adjustment marriages: Implications for those in intervention. *The American Journal of Family Therapy, 21,* 248–259.

LOPICCOLO, J. (1985). Diagnosis and treatment of male sexual dysfunction. *Journal of Sex and Marital Therapy, 11,* 215–233.

LOPICCOLO, J., & LoPiccolo, L. (1978). *Handbook of sex therapy.* New York: Plenum.

LOPICCOLO, J., & Steger, J. C. (1974). The Sexual Interaction Inventory: A new instrument for assessment of sexual dysfunction. *Archives of Sexual Behavior, 3,* 585–595.

LOULAN, J. (1987). *Lesbian passion: Loving ourselves and each other.* San Francisco: Spinster/Aunt Lute.

LUEPNITZ, D. (1986). A comparison of maternal, paternal, and joint custody: Understanding the varieties in post-divorce life. *Journal of Divorce, 9,* 1–13.

LUKAS, S. (1993). *Where to start and what to ask.* New York: Norton.

MAISTO, S. A., O'Farrell, T. J., Connors, G. J., McKay, J. R., & Pelcovits, M. (1988). Alcoholics' attributions of factors affecting their relapse to drinking and reasons for terminating relapse episodes. *Addictive Behaviors, 13,* 79–82.

MARINO, T. (1994). O. J. aftermath: The battering of American women. *Guidepost, 27,* 12, 23.

MARKMAN, H. J. (1991). Backwards into the future of couples therapy and couples therapy research: A comment on Jacobson. *Journal of Family Psychology, 4,* 416–425.

MARKMAN, H. J., & Notarius, C. I. (1987). Coding marital and family interactions: Current status. In T. Jacob (Ed.), *Family interactions and psychopathology* (pp. 329–390). New York: Plenum.

MARKMAN, H. J., Renick, M. J., Floyd, F. J., Stanley, S. M., & Clements, M. (1993). Preventing marital distress through communication and conflict management training: A 4–and 5-year follow-up. *Journal of Consulting and Clinical Psychology, 61,* 70–77.

MARKMAN, H. J., Stanle, S., & Blumberg, S. L. (1994). *Fighting for your marriage: Positive steps for preventing divorce and preserving a lasting love.* San Francisco: Jossey-Bass.

MARLATT, G. A., & Gordon, J. R. (Eds.). (1985). *Relapse prevention.* New York: Guilford Press.

MARTIN, P. A., & Bird, H. W. (1959). The "love sick" wife and the "cold sick" husband. *Psychiatry, 22,* 246.

MASTERS, W., & Johnson, V. (1970). *Human sexual inadequacy.* London: Churchill.

MATTISON, A., & McWhirter, D. (1987). Male couples: The beginning years. *Journal of Homosexuality, 14,* 67–78.

MAYER, J. E. (1989). Strategies and techniques for the initial clinical interview. *The Clinical Supervisor, 7,* 89–99.

MCCOOK. L. I., Folzer, S. M., Charlesworth, D., & Scholl, J. N. (1991). Dueling careers. *Training and Development, 45,* 40–44.

MCCRADY, B. S., & Epstein, E. E. (1995). Marital therapy in the treatment of alcohol problems. In N. S. Jacobson & A. S. Gurman (Eds.), *Clinical handbook of couple therapy* (pp. 369–393). New York: Guilford Press.

MCCRADY, B. S., Paolino, T. J., Longabaugh, R., & Rossi, J. (1979). Effects of joint hospital admission and couples treatment for hospitalized alcoholics: A pilot study. *Addictive Behavior, 4,* 155–165.

MCGOLDRICK, M., & Carter, E. (Eds.). (1980). *The family life cycle.* New York: Gardner Press.

MCGOLDRICK, M., & Gerson, R. (1985). *Genograms in family assessment.* London/New York: Norton.

MCKAY, M., Fanning, P., & Paleg, K. (1994). *Couple skills: Making your relationship work.* Oakland, CA: New Harbinger.

MCWHIRTER, D., & Mattison, A. (1984). *The male couple.* Englewood Cliffs, NJ: Prentice-Hall.

MCWHIRTER, D., & Mattison, A. (1988). Psychotherapy for gay male couples. In J. P. DeCecco (Ed.), *Gay relationships* (pp. 247–256). New York: Haworth Press.

MEHRABIAN, A. (1972). *Nonverbal communication.* Chicago: Aldine.

MILLER, S., Wackman, D. B., & Nunnally, E. W. (1982). Couple communication: Equipping couples to be their own best problem solvers. *The Counseling Psychologist, 11,* 73–77.

MILLS, D. (1984). A model for stepfamily development. *Family Relations, 33,* 365–372.

MINUCHIN, S. (1974). *Families and family therapy.* Cambridge, MA: Harvard University Press.

MINUCHIN, S. (1984). *Family kaleidoscope.* Cambridge, MA: Harvard University Press.

MODCRIN, M., & Wyers, N. (1990). Lesbians and gay couples: Where they turn when help is needed. *Journal of Gay and Lesbian Psychotherapy, 1,* 89–104.

MOLNAR, A., & de Shazer, S. (1987). Solution-focused therapy: Toward the identification of therapeutic tasks. *Journal of Marriage and Family Therapy, 13,* 349–358.

MOOS, R. H., Finney, J. W., & Gamble, W. (1982). The process of recovery from alcoholism. II. Comparing spouses of alcoholic patients and matched community controls. *Journal of Studies on Alcohol, 43,* 888–909.

MOSES, A., & Hawkins, R. (1982). *Counseling lesbian women and gay men: A life issues approach.* St. Louis: C. V. Mosby.

MOULTRUP, D. J. (1990). *Husbands, wives, and lovers.* New York: Guilford Press.

MURPHY, B. C. (1989). Lesbian couples and their parents: The effects of perceived parental attitudes on the couple. *Journal of Counseling and Development, 68,* 50–51.

MURSTEIN, B., Wadlin, R., & Bond, C., Jr. (1987). The revised exchange-orientation scale. *Small Group Behavior, 18,* 212–223.

MYERHOFF, B. (1983, November). *Rites of passage.* Symposium presented by the National Association of Social Workers, Washington, DC.

NACE, E. P. (1982). Therapeutic approaches to the alcoholic marriage. *Psychiatric Clinics of North America, 5,* 543–545.

NATIONAL CENTER FOR HEALTH STATISTICS. (1984, January). Advance report of final divorce statistics, 1981. *Monthly Vital Statistics Report, 32* (Supp. 2) (DHSS Publication No. PHS 84–1120). Hyattsville, MD: Public Health Servces.

NAVRAN, L. (1967). Communication and adjustment in marriage. *Family Process, 6,* 173–184.

NELSON, T., Fleuridas, C., & Rosenthal, D. (1986). The evolution of circular questioning: Training family therapists. *Journal of Marital and Family Therapy, 12,* 113–127.

NICHOLS, W. (1987). *Marital therapy: An integrative approach.* New York: Guilford Press.

NOEL, N. E., McCrady, B. S., Sout, R. L., & Fisher-Nelson, H. (1987). Predictors of attrition from an outpatient alcoholism treatment program for couples. *Journal of Studies on Alcohol, 48,* 229–235.

NOLAN, J., Coleman, M., & Ganong, L. (1984). The presentation of stepfamilies in marriage and family textbooks. *Family Relations, 33,* 559–566.

NOLLER, P., Vernardos, C. (1986). Communication awareness in married couples. *Journal of Social and Personal Relationships, 3,* 31–42.

NORCROSS, J. C., & Newman, C. F. (1992). Psychotherapy integration: Setting the context. In J. C. Norcross & M. R. Goldfried (Eds.), *Handbook of psychotherapy integration* (pp. 3–45). New York: Basic Books.

NORTON, A. J., & Moorman, J. E. (1987). Current trends in marriage and divorce among American women. *Journal of Marriage and the Family, 49,* 3–14.

NOTARIUS, C. I., & Vanzetti, N. A. (1983). The marital agendas protocol. In E. Filsinger (Ed.), *Marriage and family assessment: A sourcebook for family therapy.*

O'FARRELL, T. J. (1987). Marital and family therapy for alcohol problems. In W. M. Cox (Ed.), *Treatment and prevention of alcohol problems: A resource manual.* New York: Academic Press.

O'FARRELL, T. J., & Birchler, G. R. (1987). Marital relationships of alcoholic conflicted and non-conflicted couples. *Journal of Marital and Family Therapy, 13,* 259–274.

O'FARRELL, T. J., Cutter, H. S. G., Choquette, K. A., Brown, E., McCourt, W., & Worobec, T. (1990, July). *Couples group behavioral marital therapy with and without addictive relapse prevention sessions for alcoholics and their wives.* Paper presented at the International Conference on Treatment of Addicted Behaviors, Sydney, New South Wales, Australia.

O'HANLON, W., & Weiner-Davis, M. (1989). *In search of solutions.* New York: Norton.

O'LEARY, K. D., & Turkewitz, H. (1978). The treatment of marital disorders from a behavioral perspective. In T. J. Paolino & B. S. McCrady (Eds.), *Marriage and marital therapy: Psychoanalytic, behavioral and systems theory perspective.* New York: Brunner/Mazel.

O'NEIL, J. M., Fishman, D. M., & Kinsella-Shaw, M. (1987). Dual-career couples' career transitions and normative dilemmas: A preliminary assessment model. *The Counseling Psychologist, 15,* 50–96.

OLSON, D. H., Fournier, D. G., & Druckman, J. M. (1982). *PREPARE-ENRICH: Counselor's manual.* Minneapolis, MN: Prepare-Enrich Inc.

OLSON, D. H., & Schaefer, M. T. (undated). *PAIR: Personal Assessment of Intimacy in Relationships, procedure manual.* St. Paul, MN: Family Social Science, University of Minnesota Press.

ORFORD, J., & Edwards, G. (1977). Alcoholism: A comparison of treatment and advice, with a study of the influence of marriage. *Institute of Psychiatry Maudsley Monographs* (Whole No. 26). New York: Oxford University Press.

PADDOCK, J. R., & Schwartz, K. M. (1986). Rituals for dual-career couples. *Psychotherapy, 3,* 453–459.

PALAZZOLI SELVINI, M., Boscolo, L., Cecchin, G., & Prate, G. (1980). Hypothesizing-circularity-neutrality: Three guidelines for the conductor of the session. *Family Process, 19,* 3–12.

PALMER, N. (1993, May). *Notes on mediation.* Symposium presented at Stetson University, DeLand, FL.

PALMER, N., & Landis, L. (1989). Child custody arrangements: Application of the "Best Interest" standard. *Florida Family Law Reporter, 4*(9), 283–923.

PAOLINO, T., & McGrady, B. (Eds.). (1978). *Marriage and marital therapy.* New York: Brunner/Mazel.

PAPERNOW, P. (1984). The stepfamily cycle: An experimental model of stepfamily development. *Family Relations, 33,* 355–363.

PAPERNOW, P. (1995). What's going on here? Separating (and weaving together) step and clinical issues in remarried families. In D. Huntley (Ed.), *Understanding stepfamilies: Implications for assessment and treatment.* Alexandria, VA: American Counseling Association.

PAPP, P. (1983). The process of change. New York: Guilford Press.

PATTERSON, G., Hops, H., & Weiss, R. (1975). Interpersonal skills training for couples in early stages of conflict. *Journal of Marriage and the Family, 39,* 295–303.

PENN, P. (1982). Circular questioning. *Family Process, 21,* 267–280.

PENNEBAKER, J. W. (1990). *Opening up: The healing power of confiding in others.* New York: William Morrow.

PHILLIPS, E. (1973). Some useful tests in marriage counseling. *The Family Coordinator, 12,* 43–53.

PIERCE, R. A. (1994). Helping couples make authentic emotional contact. In S. Johnson & L. Greenberg (Eds.), *The heart of the matter: Perspectives on emotion in marital therapy* (pp. 75–107). New York: Brunner/Mazel.

PITTMAN, F. S. (1989). *Private lies: Infidelity and the betrayal of intimacy.* New York: Norton.

PITTMAN, F. S., & Wagers, T. P. (1995). Crises of infidelity. In N. Jacobson & A. Gurman (Eds.), *Clinical handbook of couple therapy* (pp. 295–316). New York: Guilford Press.

PLECK, J. (1978). The work family role system. *Social Problems, 24,* 417–427.

PLECK, J. (1985). *Working wives/working husbands.* Newbury Park, CA: Sage.

POLOMA, M., & Garland, T. (1971). The myth of the egalitarian family: Familial roles and the professionally employed wife. In A. Theodore (Ed.), *The professional woman* (pp. 741–761).

PROCHASKA, J. O., Norcross, J. C., & Di-Clemente, C. C. (1994). *Changing for good*. New York: Morrow.

PROSKY, P. (1991). Marital life. *Family Therapy, 18*, 129–143.

RAINONE, F. L. (1987). Beyond community: Politics and spirituality. In Boston Lesbian Psychologies Collective (Ed.), *Lesbian psychologies* (pp. 344–363). Chicago: University of Illinois Press.

RANDS, M., Levinger, G., & Mellinger, G. D. (1981). Patterns of conflict resolution and marital satisfaction. *Journal of Family Issues, 2*, 297–321.

RAPOPORT, A. (1974). *Conflict in man-made environments*. Baltimore: Penguin Books.

RAPOPORT, R., & Rapoport, R. (1971). *Dual-career families*. Middlesex, England: Penguin Books.

RAPOPORT, R., & Rapoport, R. (1976). *Dual-career families reexamined*. London, England: Martin Robertson.

RAY, J. (1990). Interactional patterns and marital satisfaction among dual-career couples. *Journal of Independent Social Work, 4*, 61–72.

REICH, J., & Thompson, W. D. (1985). Marital status of schizophrenic and alcoholic patients. *Journal of Nervous and Mental Disease, 173*, 499–502.

RICE, D. G. (1979). *Dual-career marriage: Conflicts and treatment*. New York: Free Press.

ROBINSON, B. (1984). The contemporary American stepfather. *Family Relations, 33*, 381–388.

ROSENBAUM, J. (1992). *The use of metaphor*. Unpublished manuscript. Available from Counseling Department, Stetson University, DeLand, FL.

ROSENBAUM, A., & O'Leary, K. D. (1986). The treatment of marital violence. In N. S. Jacobson & A. S. Gurman (Eds.), *Clinical handbook of marital therapy* (pp. 385–405). New York: Guilford Press.

ROSSI, E. (1980a). *Collected papers of Milton Erickson on hypnosis* (Vol. 1). New York: Irvington.

ROSSI, E. (1980b). *Collected papers of Milton Erickson on hypnosis* (Vol. 2). New York: Irvington.

ROTH, A. (1985). Psychotherapy with lesbian couples: Individual issues, female socialization, and the social context. *Journal of Marital and Family Therapy, 121*, 273–286.

ROUGHAN, P., & Jenkins, A. (1990). A systems-developmental approach to counselling couples with sexual problems. *A.N.Z. Journal of Family Therapy, 2*, 129–139.

RUBIN, J., & Brown, B. (1975). *The social psychology of bargaining and negotiation*. New York: Academic Press.

RUSSO, N. F. (1987). Dual-career couples: Research, assessment, and public policy issues. *The Counseling Psychologist, 15*, 140–145.

RUST, J., Bennun, I., Crowe, M., & Golombok, S. (1988). *The Golombok Rust Inventory of Marital State (GRIMS) (Test and handbook)*. Windsor, Ontario: NFER-Nelson.

SAGER, C. (1976). *Marriage contracts and couple therapy*. New York: Brunner/Mazel.

SALWEN, L. (1990). *The myth of the wicked stepmother*. Haworth Press.

SATIR, V. (1964). *Conjoint family therapy*. Palo Alto, CA: Science and Behavioral Books.

SATIR, V. (1972). *Peoplemaking*. Palo Alto, CA: Science and Behavioral Books.

SATIR, V., Banmen, J., Gerber, J., & Gomori, M. (1991). *The Satir model: Family therapy and beyond*. Palo Alto, CA: Science and Behavior Books.

SAVIN-WILLIAMS, R. C. (1994). Verbal and physical abuse as stressors in the lives of lesbian, gay male, and bisexual youths: Associations with school problems, running away, substance abuse, prostitution, and suicide. *Journal of Consulting and Clinical Psychology, 62*, 266–267.

SCANZONI, J. (1978). *Sex roles, women's work, and marital conflict: A study of fam-*

ily change. Lexington, MA: D. C. Heath/Lexington Books.

SCANZONI, J., & Polonko, K. (1981). A conceptual approach to explicit marital negotiation. *Journal of Marriage and the Family, 42*, 31–44.

SCARF, M. (1987). *Intimate partners*. New York: Random House.

SCHARFF, D. E., & Scharff, J. S. (1991). *Object relations couple therapy*. Northvale, NJ: Aronson.

SCHILSON, E. A. (1991). Strategic therapy. In A. M. Horne & J. L. Passmore (Eds.), *Family counseling and therapy* (pp. 142–178). Itasca, IL: F. E. Peacock.

SCLOSSBERG, N. K. (1993). Non-events and mental health. *American Counselor, 2*, 28–33.

SCHULZ, W. (1976). The individual and the others. *Praxis-der-Psychotherapie, 21*, 149–157.

SEFTON, M. S. (1990). Dual-career families and the family life cycle. *Australian Journal of Sex, Marriage and Family, 8*, 118–123.

SEGAL, L. (1991). Brief family therapy. In A. M. Horne & J. L. Passmore (Eds.), *Family counseling and therapy* (pp. 180–205). Itasca, IL: F. E. Peacock.

SEINFELD, J. (1993). *Interpreting and holding: The maternal and paternal functions of the psychotherapist*. Northvale, NJ: Aronson.

SEKARAN, U. (1985). Enhancing the mental health of Indian dual-career family couples. *Indian Journal of Applied Psychology, 22*, 57–62.

SELZER, M. L., Vinokur, A., & Van Rooijen, L. (1975). A self-administered short Michigan Alcoholism Screening Text (MAST). *Journal of Studies on Alcohol, 36*, 117–126.

SHAEVITZ, M., & Shaevitz, M. (1980). *Making it together as a two-career couple*. Boston: Houghton Mifflin.

SHELTON, B. A. (1993). Does marital status make a difference? *Journal of Family Issues, 14*, 401–420.

SHERMAN, R., & Fredman, N. (1986). *Handbook of structured techniques in marriage and family therapy*. New York: Brunner/Mazel.

SHERMAN, R., Oresky, P., & Rountree, Y. (1991). *Solving problems in couples and family therapy*. New York: Brunner/Mazel.

SHIELDS, P. (1989). The recovering couples group: A viable treatment alternative. *Alcoholism Treatment Quarterly, 6*, pp. 135–149.

SIEGEL, J. (1991). Analysis of projective identification: An object relations approach to marital treatment. *Clinical Social Work Journal, 19*, 71–81.

SIMMEL, G. (1950). Fundamental problems in sociology. In *The sociology of George Simmel* (K. Wolff, Trans.) (pp. 3–84). New York: Free Press.

SKINNER, H. A., & Horn, J. (1984). *Alcohol dependence scale user's guide*. Toronto: Addiction Research Foundation.

SLIPP, S. (1988). *The technique and practice of object relations family therapy*. Northvale, NJ: Aronson.

SMITH, C. G. (Ed.). (1971). *Conflict resolution: Contributions of the behavioral sciences*. Notre Dame, IN: University of Notre Dame Press.

SOBELL, L. C., Maisto, S. A., & Sobell, M. B. (1979). Reliability of alcohol abusers' self-reports of drinking behavior. *Behavior Research and Therapy, 17*, 157–160.

SPANIER, G. (1976). Measuring dyadic adjustment: New scales for assessing the quality of marriage and similar dyads. *Journal of Marriage and the Family, 38*, 15–28.

SPANIER, G., & Filsinger, E. (1983). The Dyadic Adjustment Scale. In E. Filsinger (Ed.), *Marriage and family assessment*. Newbury Park, CA: Sage.

SPANIER, G., & Lewis, R. A. (1980). Marital quality: A review of the seventies. *Journal of Marriage and the Family, 42*, 825–839.

SPECTOR, I., & Carey, M. (1990). Incidence and prevalence of the sexual dysfunctions: A critical review of the empirical literature. *Archives of Sexual Behavior, 19*, 389–403.

SPERRY, L. (1989). Assessment in marital therapy: A couples-centered biopsychosocial approach. *Individual Psychology, 45*, 546–551.

SPERRY, L., & Carlson, J. (1991). *Marital therapy: Integrating theory and technique.* Denver, CO: Love Publishing.

SPIEGLER, M. D., & Guevremont, D. C. (1993). *Contemporary behavior therapy.* Pacific Grove, CA: Brooks/Cole.

SPRECHER, S., & McKinney, K. (1993). *Sexuality.* Thousand Oaks, CA: Sage.

SPRENKLE, D. H., & Storm, C. L. (1983). Divorce therapy and outcome research: A substantive and methodological review. *Journal of Marriage and the Family, 9,* 239–258.

SPREY, J. (1971). On the management of conflict in families. *Journal of Marriage and the Family, 33,* 722–731.

STANTON, G. W. (1986). Preventive intervention with stepfamilies. *Social Work, 31,* 201–206.

STANTON, M. D. (1980). Marital therapy from a structural/strategic viewpoint. In P. Sholevar (Ed.), *Marriage is a family affair.* New York: Spectrum Press.

STANTON, M. D., Todd, T. C., & Associates. (1982). *The family therapy of drug abuse and addiction.* New York: Guilford Press.

STAUFFER, J. (1987). Marital intimacy: Roadblocks and therapeutic interventions. *Family Therapy, 14,* 179–185.

ST. CLAIR, M. (1986). *Object relations and self-psychology: An introduction.* Pacific Grove, CA: Brooks/Cole.

STEINGLASS, P., Bennett, L. A., Wolin, S. J., & Reiss, D. (1987). *The alcoholic family.* New York: Basic Books.

STEINGLASS, P., Davis, D. I., & Berenson, D. (1977). Observations of conjointly hospitalized "alcoholic couples" during sobriety and intoxication: Implications for theory and therapy. *Family Process, 16,* 1.

STEINGLASS, P., Weiner, S., & Mendelson, J. H. (1971). A systems approach to alcoholism: A model and its clinical application. *Archives of General Psychiatry, 24,* 401–408.

ST. JOHN-PARSONS, D. (1978). Continuous dual-career families: A case study. *Psychology of Women Quarterly, 3,* 30–42.

STOLTZ-LOIKE, M. (1992). *Dual-career couples: New perspectives in counseling.* Alexandria, VA: American Association for Counseling and Development.

STRAUS, M. A. (1979). Measuring intrafamily conflict and violence: The conflict tactics (CT) scale. *Journal of Marriage and the Family, 41,* 75–88.

STREAN, H. S. (1985). *Resolving marital conflicts: A psychodynamic perspective.* New York: Wiley.

STRUPP, H. H., & Binder, J. L. (1984). *Psychotherapy in a new key.* New York: Basic Books.

STUART, R. B. (1969). Operant-interpersonal treatment for marital discord. *Journal of Consulting and Clinical Psychology, 33,* 675–682.

SULLAWAY, M., & Christensen, A. (1983). Assessment of dysfunctional interaction patterns in couples. *Journal of Marriage and the Family, 45,* 653–659.

SWENSON, C. H., & Fiore, A. (1982). A scale of marriage problems. In P. A. Keller & L. G. Ritt (Eds.), *Innovations in clinical practice: A source book* (pp. 240–256). Sarasota, FL: Professional Resource Exchange.

TANNEN, D. (1986). *That's not what I meant: How conversational style makes or breaks relationships.* New York: Ballantine Books.

TANNEN, D. (1990). *You just don't understand: Women and men in conversation.* New York: Morrow.

TANNEN, D. (1994). *Gender and discourse.* Oxford: Oxford University Press.

TENNOV, D. (1979). *Love and limerence: The experience of being in love.* New York: Stein & Day.

THIBAUT, J. W., & Kelley, H. H. (1959). *The social psychology of groups.* New York: Wiley.

THOMAS, S., Albrecht, K., & White, P. (1984). Determinants of marital quality in dual-career couples. *Family Relations, 33,* 513–521.

THOMAS, V. G. (1990). Problems of dual-career black couples: Identification and implications for family interventions. *Journal of Multicultural Counseling and Development, 18,* 58–67.

TING-TOOMEY, S. (1983). An analysis of verbal communication patterns in high and low marital adjustment groups. *Human Communication Research, 9,* 306–319.

TODD, T. C. (1986). Structural strategic marital therapy, In N. S. Jacobson & A. S. Gurman (Eds.), *Clinical handbook of marital therapy* (pp. 71–106). New York: Guilford Press.

TOMM, K. (1984a). One perspective on the Milan systemic approach: Part I. Overview of development, theory, and practice. *Journal of Marital and Family Therapy, 10,* 13–123.

TOMM, K. (1984b). One perspective on the Milan systemic approach: Part II. Description of session format, interviewing style, and interventions. *Journal of Marital and Family Therapy, 10,* 253–271.

TOMM, K. (1987a). Interventive interviewing: Part I. Strategizing as a fourth guideline for the therapist. *Family Process, 26,* 3–13.

TOMM, K. (1987b). Interventive interviewing: Part II. Reflexive questioning as a means to enable self-healing. *Family Process, 26,* 167–183.

TOMM, K. (1991, October). *Therapeutic conversation.* Presentation at Marriage and Family Therapy Fall Conference, Stetson University, DeLand, FL.

TOULIATOS, J., Perlmutter, F. F., & Straus, M. E. (Eds.). (1990). *Handbook of family measurement techniques.* Newbury Park, CA: Sage.

TRZEPACZ, P. T., & Baker, R. W. (1993). *The psychiatric mental status examination.* Oxford, England: Oxford University Press.

TURNER, R. (1970). *Family interaction.* New York: Wiley.

U.S. BUREAU OF THE CENSUS. (1990). *Marital status and living arrangements:*

March, 1989 (Report No. 445). Washington, DC: U.S. Government Printing Office.

USSHER, J. (1991). Couples therapy with gay clients: Issues facing counselors. *Consulting Psychologist Quarterly, 3,* 109–116.

VANNOY-HILLER, D., & Philliber, W. W. (1989). *Equal partners: Successful women in marriage.* Newbury Park, CA: Sage.

VAUGHAN, P. (1989). *The monogamy myth.* London: Grafton.

VIANO, E. (1992). *Intimate violence: Interdisciplinary perspectives.* Washington: Hemisphere Publishing.

VILLARD, K., & Whipple, L. (1976). *Beginnings in relational communication.* New York: Wiley.

VISHER, E. & Visher, J. (1979). *Stepfamilies: A guide to working with stepparents and stepchildren.* New York: Brunner/Mazel.

VISHER, E. & Visher, J. (1988). *Old loyalties, new ties: Therapeutic strategies with stepfamilies.* New York: Brunner/Mazel.

VISHER, J. (1985). Therapy for stepfamilies. *Medical Aspects of Human Sexuality, 19,* 69–72.

VISHER, J. & Visher, E. (1990). Therapy with stepfamily couples. *Psychiatric Annals, 21,* 462–465.

VUCHINICH, S. (1984). Sequencing and social structure in family conflict. *Social Psychology Quarterly, 47,* 217–234.

WAGNER, J. (1986). *The search for signs of intelligent life in the universe.* New York: Harper & Row.

WALKER, B. G. (1985). *The crone: Woman of age, wisdom, and power.* San Francisco: Harper & Row.

WALKER, L. (1991). Post-traumatic stress disorder in women: Diagnosis and treatment of battered woman syndrome. *Psychotherapy, 28,* 21–29.

WALL, V., & Nolan, L. (1987). Small group conflict: A look at equity, satisfaction, and styles of conflict management. *Small Group Behavior, 18,* 188–211.

WALLERSTEIN, J. (1993, October). *The psychological tasks of marriage.* Paper presented at Harvard Medical School Couples Workshop, Boston, MA.

WALLERSTEIN, J., & Kelly, J. (1980). *Surviving the breakup: How children and parents cope with divorce.* New York: Basic Books.

WARING, E. (1980). Marital intimacy, psychosomatic symptoms, and cognitive therapy. *Psychosomatics, 21,* 595–601.

WARING, E. M. (1988). *Enhancing marital intimacy through facilitating cognitive self-disclosure.* New York: Brunner/Mazel.

WATERS, D., & Lawrence, E. (1993, November/December). Creating a therapeutic vision. *Networker,* pp. 53–58.

WATZLAWICK, P., Weakland, J., & Fisch, R. (1974). *Change: Problem formation and problem resolution.* New York: Norton.

WEBER, T., McKeever, J., & McDaniel, S. (1985). A beginner's guide to problem-oriented first family interview. *Family Process, 32,* 357–364.

WEEKS, G., & Treat, S. (1992). *Couples in treatment.* New York: Brunner/Mazel.

WEINER-DAVIS, M. (1992). *Divorce busting.* New York: Summit Books.

WEINSTEIN, E., & Rosen, R. (1988). *Sexuality counseling: Issues and implications.* Pacific Grove, CA: Brooks/Cole.

WEISS, R. L. (1975). Contracts, cognition and change: A behavioral approach to marital therapy. *The Counseling Psychologist, 5,* 15–26.

WEISS, R. L., & Cerreto, M. (1980). The Marital Status Inventory: Development of a measure of dissolution potential. *American Journal of Family Therapy, 8,* 80–85.

WEISS, R. L., Hops, H., & Patterson, G. R. (1973). A framework for conceptualizing marital conflict: A technology for altering it, some data for evaluating it. In L. A. Hammerlynck, L. C. Handy, & E. J. Marsh (Eds.), *Behavior change: Methodology, concepts and practice* (pp. 309–342). Champaign, IL: Research Press.

WESTHEIMER, R., & Lieberman, L. (1988). *Sex and morality: Who is teaching our sex standards?* Boston, MA: Harcourt Brace Jovanovich.

WHITE, M. (1989). *The externalizing of the problem and the re-authoring of lives and relationships.* Adelaide, Australia: Dulwich Centre Publishers.

WHITE, M., & Epston, D. (1990). *Narrative means to therapeutic ends.* New York: Norton.

WILE, D. (1993). *Couples therapy: A nontraditional approach.* New York: Wiley.

WILK, D. M., & Storm, C. L. (1991). Structural marital therapy: Assessment of pas de deux families. *The American Journal of Family Therapy, 19,* 257–265.

WILLI, J. (1982). *Couples in collusion.* New York: Aronson.

WILLS, T. A., Weiss, R. L., & Patterson, G. R. (1974). A behavioral analysis of the determinants of marital satisfaction. *Journal of Consulting and Clinical Psychology, 42,* 802–811.

WILSON, G. T. (1981). The effects of alcohol on human sexual behavior. *Advances in Substance Abuse, 2,* 1–40.

WILSON, K., & James, A. (1992). Child sexual abuse and couples therapy. *Journal of Sexual and Marital Therapy, 7,* 197–212.

WING, D. M. (1992). A field study of couples recovering from alcoholism. *Issues in Mental Health Nursing, 13,* 333–348.

YALOM, I. D. (1995). *The theory and practice of group psychotherapy.* New York: Basic Books.

YOGEV, S. (1983). Dual-career couples: Conflicts and treatment. *The American Journal of Family Therapy, 11,* 38–44.

YOUNG, M. E. (1992). *Counseling methods and techniques: An eclectic approach.* New York: Macmillan.

YOUNG, M. E. (1998). *Learning the art of helping.* New York: Prentice-Hall.

YOUNG, M. E., & Bemak, F. (1996). The role of emotional arousal and expression in mental health counseling. *Journal of Mental Health Counseling, 18,* 316–332.

ZIMMER, D. (1987). Does marital therapy enhance the effectiveness of treatment of sexual dysfunction? *Journal of Sex and Marital Therapy, 12,* 193–207.

ZWEBEN, A. (1991). Motivational counseling with alcoholic couples. In W. R. Miller & S. Rollnick (Eds.), *Motivational interviewing: Preparing people to change addictive behavior* (pp. 225–235). New York: Guilford Press.

ZWEBEN, A., & Barrett, D. (1983). Brief couple treatment for alcohol problems. In T. J. O'Farrell (Ed.), *Treating alcohol problems: Marital and family interventions* (pp. 353–380). New York: Guilford Press.

NAME INDEX

SUBJECT INDEX

A-B-C theory of emotional disturbance, 27
Abreaction, 131
Abstinence, 247
Abuse. *See also* Alcoholism; Drug abuse
  child sexual abuse, 175, 310
  domestic violence as, 187–191
  verbal, 183
Accidental infidelity, 224, 226
Action-centered orientations, 179
Action level of change, 124
Adjustment disorder diagnoses, 115, 117
Adolescents. *See also* Children
  stepfamily life stages and, 273–274
Adult Children of Alcoholics, 246
Affairs
  constructively dealing with, 230–234
  cultural differences and, 229–230
  gender differences and, 227–228
  guidelines for revealing, 232, 233–234
  integrative therapy model and, 234–240
  prevalence of, 223–224
  reasons for, 226–230
  romance and, 228–229
  societal factors and, 229
  types of, 224–226
Affection, 161
Affective goals, 70, 74–75, 132, 134
A-frame relationships, 118
African American couples, 287
Age-related factors for same-sex couples, 306
Aggression
  domestic violence and, 187–191
  nonverbal communication and, 141–142
  verbal abuse and, 183
AIDS (acquired immune deficiency syndrome), 174, 310
Alanon, 87, 246, 248–249
Alcohol abuse, 247
Alcohol dependence, 247
Alcohol Dependence Scale, 258

Alcoholics Anonymous, 250–251, 309–310
Alcoholic system, 250
Alcoholism
  assessment of, 86–87, 257–259, 260
  brief couples treatment for, 252
  couple patterns supporting, 248
  family history of, 103
  integrative therapy model and, 257–262
  marital problems and, 245–246
  problem drinking vs., 251–253
  referrals for treatment of, 247–248
  relapse prevention for, 257
  same-sex couples and, 309–310
  sexuality and, 174
  spousal help in treating, 248–249, 253–257
  synchrony in recovery for, 249–250
  systems approach to, 250–251
  terminology of, 246–247
  therapy techniques for, 253–257
Alignment, 47
Alliances, 47
American Association for Marriage and Family Therapy, 231
American Counseling Association, 35
American Psychiatric Association, 115, 301
Anger. *See also* Aggression
  conflict and, 181–182
Antabuse, 255
Arbitrary inference, 28
Area of Change Questionnaire, 90
Assessment. *See also* Initial interview
  of alcohol problems, 86–87, 257–260
  biases and assumptions in, 83–85
  client knowledge of data from, 91
  of communication problems and strengths, 149–150
  of conflictual issues, 197
  diagnosis compared to, 114–115

TO THE OWNER OF THIS BOOK:

We hope that you have found *Counseling and Therapy for Couples* useful. So that this book can be improved in a future edition, would you take the time to complete this sheet and return it? Thank you.

School and address: ——————————————————————————

Department: ———————————————————————————————

Instructor's name: —————————————————————————————

1. What I like most about this book is: ————————————————

——

——

2. What I like least about this book is: ————————————————

——

——

3. My general reaction to this book is: —————————————————

——

4. The name of the course in which I used this book is: ——————————

——

5. Were all of the chapters of the book assigned for you to read? ——————

   If not, which ones weren't? ———————————————————————

6. In the space below, or on a separate sheet of paper, please write specific suggestions for improving this book and anything else you'd care to share about your experience in using the book.

——

——

——

——

——

Optional:

Your name: _____ Date: _____

May Brooks/Cole quote you, either in promotion for *Counseling and Therapy for Couples* or in future publishing ventures?

Yes: _____ No: _____

Sincerely,

Mark E. Young
Lynn L. Long

Brooks/Cole is dedicated to publishing quality books for the helping professions. If you would like to learn more about our publications, please use the mailer to request our catalog.

Name: _____

Street Address: _____

City, State, and Zip: _____

FOLD HERE

- -

NO POSTAGE
NECESSARY
IF MAILED
IN THE
UNITED STATES

BUSINESS REPLY MAIL

FIRST CLASS   PERMIT NO. 358   PACIFIC GROVE, CA

POSTAGE WILL BE PAID BY ADDRESSEE

ATT: *Human Services Catalogue*

Brooks/Cole Publishing Company
511 Forest Lodge Road
Pacific Grove, California 93950-9968

FOLD HERE